Eastern Hemisphere

HAMMOND'S

Complete

WORLD ATLAS

C. S. HAMMOND & CO., *New York*, U.S.A.

Preface

This new Hammond's Complete World Atlas provides the most thorough, accurate and complete global coverage in any popular atlas . . . it presents it in a volume that is both convenient to use and to keep with other books. Both the state and foreign maps have been planned to render it of utmost value as a geographical reference work. To attain this end, as much accurate, up-to-the-minute, useful information as possible has been included on each map.

Special attention is called to the attractive new series of state maps. Land relief has been incorporated into the maps in such a way that a three-dimensional effect is produced and the layman can determine the land formation at a glance. This feature is in addition to other characteristics, such as complete coverage of all possible existing cities, towns and communities, physical features, Indian reservations, National parks and monuments, historical sites, and Army, Air Force and Naval establishments. Further, the railroads are shown in a separate color for legibility and are keyed by number to an accompanying list to make possible quick and accurate identification of each railroad line.

In examining the foreign maps, it will be noted that nowhere can be found a more thorough presentation of the world in maps. The quality of a foreign map collection is directly proportionate to the effort and care of gathering and interpreting editorial data. The maps in this atlas were prepared and revised up to press time by a highly trained staff—guided by the company's fifty years of experience in cartographic research and by a wealth of source material painstakingly assembled. From no other collection of maps can be obtained a better geographic knowledge of the world. This is important in evaluating the news of today as it will affect the world of tomorrow.

In addition to the maps, there is a wealth of other information covered by this atlas. The value of the indexes, Gazetteers of the United States and the World, the World Statistics, Orientation and Products Maps, and many other features can be appreciated only through constant use. This atlas is material evidence of the fifty years of constant striving by C. S. Hammond & Company to give to the public the best in maps.

It is believed you will find this fine volume as interesting as it is useful.

Caleb D. Hammond, Jr., President,

C. S. HAMMOND & COMPANY

Contents

GAZETTEER-INDEX OF THE WORLD

This alphabetical list of grand divisions, countries, states, colonial possessions, etc., gives area, population, capital, seat of government or chief town, and index references and numbers of plates on which they are shown on the largest scale. The mother country of colonial possessions is indicated by italic abbreviations enclosed in paren - theses. The index reference shows the square on the respective map in which the name of the country, state or co - lonial possession is located.

ABBREVIATIONS

Aust. = Australian.	I. = Island.	Pak. = Pakistan.	Trust. = Trust Territory.	
Belg. = Belgian or Belgium.	Is. = Islands.	pen. = peninsula.	U. S. A. = United States of America.	
Br. = British Commonwealth of Nations.	It. = Italian or Italy.	Port. = Portugal or Portuguese.	U. S. Occ. = U. S. Occupied.	
	Jap. = Japan or Japanese.	Rep. = Republic.	U. S. S. R. = Union of Soviet Socialist Republics.	
Dan. = Danish or Denmark.	Mand. = Mandate.	So. = South.		
E. = East.	N. = North.	Sp. = Spain or Spanish.	U. of So. Africa = Union of South Africa.	
Fr. = France or French.	Neth. = Netherlands.	sq. mi. = square miles.		
Gr. = Greece or Greek.	N. Z. = New Zealand.	S. S. R. = Soviet Socialist Republic.	W. = West.	

Country	Area (Sq. Miles)	Population	Index Ref.	Plate No.
A den (incl. Protectorate) (Br.)	112,000	600,000	C 5	81
Aden Colony	75	50,000	C 6	81
Admiralty Is. (Aust. Tr.)	820	13,000	E 6	104
Afghanistan	250,000	12,000,000	K 6	74
Africa	11,500,000	171,000,000		94-97
Alabama, U.S.A.	51,078	3,061,743		156,157
Alaska (U.S.A.)	571,065	128,643		155
Albania	11,096	1,120,000	E 5	67
Alberta, Canada	248,800	796,169		148,149
Aleutian Islands (U.S.A.)	6,800	1,298	E 4	155
Algeria (Fr.)	851,284	7,234,684	G 5	94
Andaman Is. (India)	2,508	21,316	F 6	83
Andorra	191	5,265	G 1	59
Anglo-Egyptian Sudan	967,500	6,590,996	M 8	95
Angola (Port.)	481,351	3,788,010	K 14	96
Annam, Indochina	56,988	7,183,500	E 3	86
Antarctica	....	....		39
Antigua (Br.) (incl. Barbuda and Redonda)	171	41,757	E 11	139
Antilles, Greater, Lesser	....	....		136,137
Arabia	1,000,000	10,000,000		81
Arctic Ocean	....	....		38
Argentina	1,078,266	16,108,573		122,123
Arizona, U.S.A.	113,580	749,587		158,159
Arkansas, U.S.A.	52,725	1,909,511		160,161
Armenian S.S.R. (U.S.S.R.)	11,544	1,281,600	F 6	69
Ascension Island (Br.)	34	169	D 13	96
Asia (Less U.S.S.R.)	10,300,000	1,173,000,000		74,75
Australia, Commonwealth of (Br.)	2,974,581	7,580,820		102,103
Australian Capital Territory.	939	16,905	J 7	103
Austria	32,369	6,818,600	C 3	65
Azerbaidzhan S.S.R. (U.S.S.R.)	33,011	3,209,730	G 6	69
Azores Islands (Port.)	890	287,091	B 4	94
B ahama Islands (Br.)	4,375	68,846	C 1	136
Bahrein Islands (Br.)	213	120,000	D 3	81
Balearic Islands (Sp.)	1,936	411,273	H 3	59
Baluchistan (Pak.)	134,002	857,835	A 3	82
Barbados (Br.)	166	192,841	B 8	139
Barbuda and Redonda Is. (Br.)	63	980	G 3	137
Basutoland (Br.)	11,716	673,584	D 2	99
Bechuanaland Prot. (Br.)	275,000	294,232	L 16	97
Belgian Congo	902,274	10,422,942	L 12	97
Belgium	11,775	8,344,534	E 7	55
Bermuda (Br.)	21	33,925	G 3	137
Bhutan	18,000	300,000	F 3	82
Bismarck Archipelago (Aust. Trust.)	19,660	140,759	E 6	104
Bolivia	412,777	3,722,700		118,119
Borneo, Indonesia	208,286	2,168,661	E 5	88
Brazil	3,286,170	46,200,000		116,117
British Columbia, Canada	359,279	817,861		152,153
British Honduras	8,867	59,220	C 2	134
Brunei (Br.)	2,226	40,786	E 5	88
Bulgaria	42,796	7,022,206	G 4	66
Burma	261,610	16,823,798	C 2	86
Byelorussian S.S.R. (White Russian S.S.R., U.S.S.R.)	83,012	9,400,000	C 4	69
C alifornia, U.S.A.	156,803	10,586,223		162,163
Cambodia, Indochina	69,884	3,227,000	E 4	86
Cameroons (Br. Trust.)	34,081	991,100	J 10	94
Cameroun (Fr. Trust.)	161,787	2,779,819	J 10	94
Canada, Dominion of (Br.)	3,621,616	11,811,655		128,129
Canal Zone (U.S.A.)	362	52,822	G 6	135
Canary Islands (Sp.)	2,894	687,937	B 4	58
Cape of Good Hope, U. of So. Africa	277,169	4,045,805	C 3	99
Cape Verde Islands (Port.)	1,557	181,286	N 5	37
Caroline Islands (U.S. Trust.)	525	35,301	E 5	104
Cayman Is., Jamaica (Br.)	104	6,670	B 3	136
Celebes	72,986	4,231,906	G 6	89
Central America	217,813	9,031,455		134,135
Ceylon	25,332	6,695,605	D 7	83
Chandernagor, India	4	38,284	E 4	82
Channel Islands (Br.)	75	93,205	E 8	45
Chatham Islands (N.Z.)	372	702	J 9	105
Chile	286,396	5,023,539		120,121
China	3,759,181	461,006,285		84,85
Cochin China, Indochina	24,980	5,579,000	E 5	86
Colombia	439,828	10,100,000		112,113
Colorado, U.S.A.	103,967	1,325,089		164,165
Comoro Is. (Is. Comores, Fr.)	849	128,608	P 14	97
Connecticut, U.S.A.	4,899	2,007,280		166,167
Cook Islands (N.Z.)	99	14,519	K 7	105
Corsica (Corse, Fr.)	3,367	267,971	G 6	57
Costa Rica	19,238	771,503	E 5	134
Cuba	42,857	4,778,583	H 1	138
Curaçao (Neth.)	403	127,866	G 8	139

GAZETTEER-INDEX OF THE WORLD

Country	Area (Sq. Miles)	Population	Index Ref.	Plate No.
Cyprus (Br.)............	3,572	449,490	E 5	76
Czechoslovakia.........	49,356	12,164,631	D 2	65
Cyrenaica, Libya........	......	......	L 5	95
Dahomey (Fr.).........	42,471	1,458,000	G 10	94
Damão (Port.)...........	213	63,521	B 4	83
Delaware, U.S.A.........	1,978	318,085	....	189
Denmark...............	16,556	4,045,232	F 9	51
District of Columbia, U.S.A..	61	802,178	B 5	188
Diu (Port.).............	12	19,731	B 4	83
Dominica (Br.)..........	305	53,900	E 7	139
Dominican Republic.......	19,129	2,182,109	D 6	138
Ecuador........approx.	115,000	3,089,078	C 3	114
Egypt.................	386,000	17,423,000	....	98
Eire (Ireland)..........	26,601	2,953,452	....	49
England and Wales......	58,340	39,952,377	....	44,45
Eritrea	15,754	600,573	O 8	95
Estonia (Estonian S.S.R., U.S.S.R.).............	17,838	968,680	C 3	68
Ethiopia...............	350,000	10,000,000	O 9	95
Europe (excluding U.S.S.R.)	1,920,000	380,000,000	....	40,41
Faeröe Islands (Dan.)....	540	25,744	D 2	40
Falkland Islands (Br.) (incl. S. Georgia)..........	5,618	2,721	E 7	123
Fernando Póo (island, Sp. Guinea)..............	800	17,249	H 11	94
Fezzan, Libya...........	......	......	J 6	94
Fiji (Br.)..............	7,083	259,638	H 7	104
Finland...............	130,500	3,887,217	P 4	50
Florida, U.S.A..........	54,262	2,771,305	..	168,169
Formosa (Taiwan, China)..	13,885	6,126,006	K 7	85
France................	212,736	40,502,513	....	56,57
Franz Josef Land (Zemlya Frantsa Iosifa)........	......	......	B 12	38
French Equatorial Africa...	961,392	4,168,910	K 10	95
French Indochina (Indochina)	285,867	27,030,000	E 4	86
French Sudan...........	584,942	3,797,000	F 8	94
French West Africa.......	1,814,852	15,786,000	F 8	94
Gabon (Fr.)...........	90,733	423,904	J 12	96
Galápagos Islands, Ecuador	3,042	2,192	B 9	115
Gambia (Br.)..........	3,999	216,107	C 9	94
Georgia, U.S.A.........	58,518	3,444,578	..	170,171
Georgian S.S.R. (U.S.S.R.).	28,687	3,577,290	F 6	69
Germany...............	142,200	65,910,999	....	52,53
Gibraltar (Br.)..........	2	22,532	D 4	58
Gilbert, Ellice and Phoenix Islands..............	196	35,000	H 6	104
Gôa (Port.)............	1,313	540,925	B 5	83
Gold Coast (Br.).........	88,802	4,095,276	F 10	94
Great Britain and Northern Ireland...............	94,279	48,182,000	....	42,43
Greece...............	51,182	7,466,906	E 6	67
Greenland (Dan.)........	839,999	21,412	D 22	38
Grenada (Br.)..........	133	90,085	D 9	139
Guadeloupe and Dependencies (Fr.)............	688	278,864	A 6	139
Guam (U.S.A.)..........	203	59,498	E 4	104
Guatemala.............	45,452	3,283,209	B 3	134
Guiana, British..........	89,480	364,694	E 2	108
Guiana, French..........	35,135	25,499	E 2	108
Guiana, Netherlands (Surinam)................	54,300	195,602	E 2	108
Guinea, French..........	96,525	2,125,000	D 9	94
Guinea, Portuguese......	13,948	351,089	C 9	94
Guinea, Spanish........	10,830	161,032	J 11	96

Country	Area (Sq. Miles)	Population	Index Ref.	Plate No.
Haiti.................	10,714	3,000,000	C 5	138
Hawaii (U.S.A.).........	6,420	499,794	....	248
Holland (Netherlands). land	12,883	9,124,871	F 4	54
Honduras..............	45,000	1,200,542	D 3	134
Honduras, British.........	8,867	59,220	C 2	134
Hong Kong (Br.).........	391	1,071,893	J 7	85
Hungary...............	35,875	9,106,252	E 3	65
Iceland...............	39,709	130,356	F 20	38
Idaho, U.S.A............	82,808	588,637	..	172,173
Ilfni (Sp.)..............	676	45,852	D 6	94
Illinois, U.S.A...........	55,947	8,712,176	..	174,175
India.................	1,059,342	299,490,000	..	82,83
Indiana, U.S.A...........	36,205	3,934,224	..	176,177
Indochina (Fr.)..........	285,867	27,030,000	E 4	86
Indonesia (Neth. Indies)...	735,286	71,534,000	..	88,89
Iowa, U.S.A.............	55,986	2,621,073	..	178,179
Iran (Persia)............	628,000	15,000,000	....	79
Iraq (Mesopotamia)......	116,600	3,700,000	....	78
Ireland (Eire)...........	26,601	2,953,452	....	49
Ireland, Northern........	5,238	1,279,745	....	48
Isle of Man (Br.).........	221	49,308	C 3	44
Israel................	7,100	850,000	B 3	80
Italy..................	116,000	45,600,000	..	62,63
Ivory Coast (Fr.).........	183,397	4,021,000	E 10	94
Jamaica (Br.).........	4,450	1,237,391	H 7	138
Japan.................	144,550	81,191,604	....	92
Java and Madoera......	51,032	49,144,000	K 2	89
Jordan (Trans-Jordan)....	34,740	400,000	D 4	80
Kansas, U.S.A.........	82,113	1,905,299	....	180
Karelo-Finnish S.S.R. (U.S.S.R.)...........	72,780	500,000	D 2	68
Karikal, India (Fr.).......	52	60,555	D 6	83
Kentucky, U.S.A..........	40,109	2,944,806	..	182,183
Kenya (Br.)............	219,730	4,046,968	O 11	97
Kerguelen Arch. (Fr.).....	......	......	T 8	37
Korea................	85,228	25,900,142	C 4	92
Krêtê (Crete), Greece.....	3,232	441,687	G 8	67
Kuria Muria Is. (Br.)......	......	......	E 5	81
Kuril Is. (Chishima, U.S.S.R.).	3,944	......	P 5	71
Kuwait................	......	50,000	C 3	81
Labrador, Nfld., Canada..	112,000	5,000	K 5	129
Laccadive Islands (India)..	746	18,393	B 6	83
Laos, Indochina.........	89,343	1,189,000	E 3	86
Latvia (Latvian S.S.R., U.S.S.R.).............	24,954	1,765,320	B 3	68
Lebanon..............	3,475	1,157,142	F 6	77
Leeward Islands (Br.)....	423	100,500	G 3	137
Liberia...............	43,000	2,000,000	E 10	94
Libya.................	679,358	888,400	K 6	95
Liechtenstein............	65	11,218	J 2	61
Lithuania (Lithuanian S.S.R., U.S.S.R.)...........	24,151	3,032,000	B 3	68
Louisiana, U.S.A.........	45,177	2,683,516	..	184,185
Loyalty Islands (Fr.)......	800	11,100	G 8	104
Luxembourg............	999	290,992	J 9	55
Macao (Port.).........	6	374,735	H 7	85
Madagascar (Fr.)........	241,094	3,900,000	R 16	97
Madeira Islands (Port.)...	308	249,540	A 2	58
Madoera...............	1,725	11,585	K 2	89
Mahé, India (Fr.)........	23	14,092	C 6	83
Maine, U.S.A............	31,040	913,774	..	186,187
Malayan Federation (Br.)	50,680	4,877,678	E 6	87
Malta (Br.).............	122	306,996	E 7	62

GAZETTEER-INDEX OF THE WORLD

Country	Area (Sq. Miles)	Population	Index Ref.	Plate No.
Manchuria (China)	412,801	35,704,958	K 2	85
Manitoba, Canada	219,723	729,744	..	146,147
Mariana Islands (U.S. Trust.)	247	31,284	E 4	104
Marquesas Is. (Fr.)	480	2,988	N 6	105
Marshall Islands (U.S. Trust.)	74	9,998	H 4	104
Martinique (Fr.)	425	244,233	D 5	139
Maryland, U.S.A.	9,887	2,343,001	..	188,189
Massachusetts, U.S.A.	7,907	4,690,514	..	190,191
Mauritania (Fr.)	328,185	497,000	D 8	94
Mauritius (Br.)	720	424,453	S 19	97
Mesopotamia (See Iraq)	....	....	....	78
Mexico	760,373	19,653,552	..	132,133
Michigan, U.S.A.	57,022	6,371,766	..	192,193
Midway Islands (U.S.A.)	2	437	J 3	105
Minnesota, U.S.A.	80,009	2,982,483	..	194,195
Mississippi, U.S.A.	47,420	2,178,914	..	196,197
Missouri, U.S.A.	69,270	3,954,653	..	198,199
Moldavian S.S.R. (U.S.S.R.)	13,012	2,400,000	C 5	69
Molucca Islands (Neth.)	30,168	544,302	C 6	104
Monaco	370 Acres	19,242	G 6	57
Mongolian Republic	625,946	1,000,000	F 2	84
Montana, U.S.A.	146,316	591,024	..	200,201
Montserrat (Br.)	32	14,329	G 3	137
Morocco, French Zone	153,870	8,617,387	E 5	94
Morocco, Sp., Northern Zone	7,674	1,100,000	F 4	94
Morocco, Sp., Southern Zone	10,039	10,000	D 6	94
Moyen Congo (Fr.)	175,676	624,137	J 12	96
Mozambique (Port.)	297,731	5,685,630	O15	97
Natal, Union of So. Africa	35,284	2,197,879	E 2	99
Nauru (Austr.-N.Z.—Br. Tr. Terr.)	8	2,794	G 6	104
Nebraska, U.S.A.	76,653	1,325,510	..	202,203
Nepal	54,000	6,283,649	D 3	82
Netherlands (Holland) land	12,883	9,124,871	F 4	54
Netherlands Indies (Indonesia)	735,268	71,534,000	....	88,89
Nevada, U.S.A.	109,802	160,083	..	204,205
New Britain (island, Aust. Trust.)	14,600	90,349	F 6	104
New Brunswick, Canada	27,473	457,401	C 3	140
New Caledonia (Fr.)	7,201	60,015	G 8	104
Newfoundland, Canada	42,734	300,000	K 4	141
New Guinea, N.E. (Aust. Trust.)	93,000	670,000	B 7	88
New Guinea, Netherlands	161,514	331,467	K 6	89
New Hampshire, U.S.A.	9,024	533,242	..	206,207
New Hebrides Islands (Br. & Fr.)	5,700	45,000	G 7	104
New Ireland (island, Aust. Trust.)	3,800	36,960	F 6	104
New Jersey, U.S.A.	7,522	4,835,329	..	208,209
New Mexico, U.S.A.	121,511	681,187	..	210,211
New South Wales, Australia	309,432	2,985,464	H 6	103
New York, U.S.A.	47,929	14,830,192	..	212,213
New Zealand, Dominion of (Br.)	103,934	1,702,298	....	100
Nicaragua	57,143	1,095,488	E 4	134
Nicobar Islands (India)	635	12,452	F 7	83
Nigeria (Br.)	372,674	21,826,389	H 10	94
Niger Colony (Fr.)	501,930	2,168,000	H 8	94
Niue I. (Br.)	100	4,242	K 7	105
North America	8,500,000	187,000,000	..	126,127
North Borneo (Br.)	29,347	331,361	F 5	88
North Carolina, U.S.A.	49,142	4,061,929	..	214,215
North Dakota, U.S.A.	70,054	619,636	..	216,217
Northern Ireland (Br.)	5,238	1,279,745	..	48
Northern Rhodesia (Br.)	290,320	1,386,081	M14	97
Northern Territory, Algeria	80,117	6,592,033	H 4	94
Northern Territory, Australia	523,620	10,866	E 3	102
Northwest Territories, Canada	1,258,217	12,028	F 2	128
Norway	124,560	3,123,338	F 6	50,51
Nova Scotia, Canada	20,743	577,962	E 5	140
Nyasaland Prot. (Br.)	36,829	2,050,051	N 14	97
Ohio, U.S.A.	41,122	7,946,627	..	218,219
Oklahoma, U.S.A.	69,283	2,233,351	..	220,221
Oman, Sultanate of	82,000	500,000	E 4	81
Ontario, Canada	363,282	3,787,655	..	144,145
Orange Free State, U. of So. Africa	49,647	876,634	D 2	99
Oregon, U.S.A.	96,350	1,521,341	..	222,223
Orkney Islands, Scotland	376	21,700	K 1	46
Oubangui Chari (Fr.)	239,382	1,068,400	K 10	95
Pacific Ocean	....	....	..	104,105
Pakistan	361,007	70,103,000	A3&F4	82
Palau Islands (U.S.Trust.)	175	13,609	D 5	104
Palestine	....	....	..	80
Panama (excluding Canal Zone)	28,575	622,576	G 6	135
Papua Territory (Aust.)	90,540	338,820	B 7	88
Paraguay	150,518	1,160,000	..	124
Pennsylvania, U.S.A.	45,045	10,498,012	..	224,225
Persia (Iran)	628,000	15,000,000	..	79
Peru	513,000	7,023,111 approx.	..	114,115
Philippines, Republic of the.	*115,600	19,234,182	..	90,91
Phoenix Is. (U.S. & Br.)	16	850	J 6	105
Pitcairn Island (Br.)	2	220	O 8	105
Poland	119,734	23,929,757	..	64
Pondichéry, India (Fr.)	112	204,653	D 6	83
Portugal	35,413	7,755,423	B 3	58
Prince Edward Island, Canada	2,184	95,047	F 3	141
Principe and S. Tomé (Port.)	372	60,490	H 11	96
Puerto Rico (U.S.A.)	3,423	2,210,703	G 2	139
Québec, Canada	523,860	3,331,882	..	142,143
Queensland, Australia	670,500	1,106,269	G 4	103
Réunion (Fr.)	970	242,067	P 20	97
Rhode Island, U.S.A.	1,058	791,896	..	191
Rio de Oro (Sp.)	71,583	24,000	D 7	94
Rio Muni (continental Sp. Guinea)	10,040	142,237	J 11	96
Ruanda-Urundi (Belg. Tr.)	20,309	3,756,705	N 12	97
Rumania	91,671	16,409,367	G 3	66
Russian S.F.S.R. (U.S.S.R.)	6,532,939	109,922,580	F 3	68
Ryukyu Islands (U.S. Occ.)	921	574,579	L 6	92
Saguia el Hamra (Sp.)	31,660	13,116	D 6	94
St. Croix, Virgin Is. (U.S.A.)	80	12,096	G 4	139
St. Helena I. (Br.)	47	3,995	E 15	96
St. John, Virgin Is. (U.S.A.)	20	747	C 4	139
St. Lucia (Br.)	233	69,091	G 6	139
St. Pierre and Miquelon Is. (Fr.)	93	4,354	L 6	129
St. Thomas, Virgin Is. (U.S.A.)	32	13,811	B 4	139
St. Vincent (Br.)	150	61,593	A 8	139
Sakhalin (U.S.S.R.)	29,000	....	P 4	71
Salvador, El	13,176	2,072,506	C 4	134
Samoa, Western (N.Z. Tr.)	1,133	68,197	J 7	105
Samoa (U.S.A.)	*76	18,937	J 7	105
San Marino	38	12,100	D 3	62
Sarawak (Br.)	50,000	490,585	E 5	88
Sardinia (Sardegna, It.)	9,301	1,034,206	B 4	63

* Includes both land and water.

GAZETTEER-INDEX OF THE WORLD

Country	Area (Sq. Miles)	Population	Index Ref.	Plate No.
Saskatchewan, Canada...	237,975	895,992	..	150,151
Saudi Arabia, Kingdom of.	350,000	5,000,000	B 3	81
Scotland..............	30,405	4,842,980	....	46,47
Senegal (Fr.)............	77,401	1,720,000	D 9	94
Seychelles (Br.).........	156	34,637	T 6	37
Shetland Islands, Scotland.	550	19,700	M 3	46
Siam (Thailand)..........	200,148	15,718,000	D 4	86
Sicily (It.)..............	9,926	4,000,078	D 6	63
Sierra Leone (Br.).......	27,925	2,000,000	D 10	94
Singapore (Br.).........	220	940,756	J 4	89
Sinkiang, China.........	660,977	4,012,330	C 3	84
Society Islands (Fr.).....	650	23,486	L 7	105
Socotra (Br.)...........	1,400	12,000	D 6	81
Solomon Islands (Aust. Tr.).	4,070	49,067	F 6	104
Solomon Islands Prot. (Br.).	11,000	95,400	F 6	104
Somaliland, French.......	8,492	44,240	P 9	95
Somaliland, Italian (Tr. Terr.)	194,000	1,021,572	R 10	95
Somaliland Prot. (Br.)....	68,000	700,000	R 10	95
South America..........	6,814,000	99,000,000	..	108,109
South Australia, Australia..	380,070	646,216	E 5	102
South Carolina, U.S.A....	30,594	2,117,027	..	226,227
South Dakota, U.S.A.....	76,536	652,740	..	228,229
Southern Rhodesia (Br.)..	150,354	1,916,000	M 15	97
Southern Territories, Algeria	767,435	642,651	G 6	94
South West Africa (U. of South Africa Mand.)....	312,194	416,602	K 16	96
Spain.................	195,258	25,877,971	....	58,59
Spanish Sahara..........	103,243	37,116	D 7	94
Spitsbergen (Svalbard, Nor.)	24,294	2,210	C 2	30
Sumatra	164,148	10,500,000	C 6	88
Surinam (Netherlands Guiana)..............	54,300	195,602	E 2	108
Swaziland (Br.)..........	6,704	187,265	E 2	99
Sweden...............	173,394	6,371,432	J 6	51
Switzerland............	15,944	4,265,703	....	60,61
Syria.................	72,587	2,901,316	H 5	77
Tahiti (island, Fr.)......	600	17,256	M 7	105
Tanganyika Territory (Br. Trust.)	340,000	5,545,450	N 13	97
Tangier, International Zone.	225	102,306	E 4	94
Tasmania, Australia......	26,215	257,117	H 8	103
Tchad (Fr.)............	455,598	2,052,469	K 8	94
Tennessee, U.S.A........	41,961	3,291,718	..	230,231
Texas, U.S.A.............	263,644	7,711,194	..	232,233
Tibet, China...........	469,413	1,000,000	C 5	84
Timor (Port.)...........	7,332	463,996	H 7	89
Timor Archipelago (Indon.)	24,450	1,657,376	G 8	89
Togo (Fr. Trust.)........	20,733	763,000	G 10	94
Togoland (Br. Trust.).....	13,041	378,660	G 10	94
Tokelau (Union Group) (N.Z. and U.S.)............	4	1,388	J 6	105
Tonga (Friendly) Is. (Br.)...	250	40,668	J 7	105
Tonkin, Indochina........	44,672	9,851,200	E 2	86
Trans-Jordan (Jordan)....	34,740	400,000	D 4	80
Transvaal, Union of So. Africa..............	110,450	4,271,631	D 1	99

Country	Area (Sq. Miles)	Population	Index Ref.	Plate No.
Trieste, Free Territory of...	276	299,104	A 2	66
Trinidad and Tobago (Br.).	1,980	557,970	A 10	139
Tripolitania, Libya........	......	......	J 5	94
Tristan da Cunha (Br.)....	28	167	N 7	37
Trucial Oman...........	......	95,000	D 4	81
Tuamotu (Low) Arch. (Fr.)..	332	5,127	M 7	105
Tunisia (Fr.).............	48,300	2,991,403	H 5	94
Turkey................	296,185	18,860,222	....	76,77
Turks and Caicos Is., Jamaica (Br.)..............	166	6,148	D 2	136
Uganda Protectorate (Br.)	80,292	3,997,690	N 11	97
Ukrainian S.S.R. (U.S.S.R.)..	226,687	40,548,310	C 5	69
Union of South Africa.....	472,494	11,391,949	..	99
Union of Soviet Socialist Republics..............	8,548,478	193,227,889	....	68–71
United Kingdom.........	94,279	48,182,000	..	42,43
United States of America land	2,977,128	150,697,361	..	130,131
land and water	3,022,387			
Upper Volta (Fr.)........	......	......	F 9	94
Uruguay...............	72,172	2,218,968	..	125
Utah, U.S.A.............	82,346	688,862	..	234,235
Vatican City...........	109 Acres	1,025	B 6	63
Venezuela.............	352,143	3,850,771	..	110,111
Vermont, U.S.A..........	9,278	377,747	..	236,237
Victoria, Australia.......	87,884	2,055,252	G 7	103
Viet Nam (includes Tonkin Annam and Cochin China	......	......	E2,3	86
Virgin Islands (Br.).......	58	6,508	A 4	139
Virgin Islands (U.S.A.).....	132	26,665	A 4	139
Virginia, U.S.A..........	39,899	3,318,680	..	238,239
Wake Island (U.S.A.)....	3	......	G 4	104
Wales (excluding Monmouthshire)...........	7,466	2,158,374	D 5	45
Walvis Bay (Br.).........	430	......	A 1	99
Washington, U.S.A........	66,977	2,378,963	..	240,241
Western Australia, Australia	975,920	502,731	C 4	102
West Indies.............	......	......	..	136,137
West Virginia, U.S.A.......	24,090	2,005,552	..	242,243
White Russian S.S.R. (Byelorussian S.S.R., U.S.S.R.)..	83,012	9,400,000	C 4	69
Windward Islands........	821	298,985	G 4	137
Wisconsin, U.S.A........	54,715	3,434,575	..	244,245
World................	57,510,000	2,200,000,000	..	36,37
Wyoming, U.S.A.........	97,506	290,529	..	246,247
Yanaon, India (Fr.)......	6½	5,711	D 5	83
Yap (U.S. Trust.)..........	87	6,650	D 5	104
Yemen................	75,000	3,500,000	B 6	81
Yugoslavia.............	99,079	15,751,935	C 3	66
Yukon Territory, Canada..	205,346	4,914	C 2	128
Zanzibar Prot (Br.)......	1,020	250,000	P 13	97

GLOSSARY OF GEOGRAPHICAL TERMS

A. = Arabic   Ch. = Chinese   Dan. = Danish   Du. = Dutch   Finn. = Finnish   Fr. = French   Ger. = German
It. = Italian   Jap. = Japanese   Mo. = Mongol   Nor. = Norwegian   Per. = Persian   Port. = Portuguese
Russ. = Russian   Sp. = Spanish   Sw. = Swedish   Turk. = Turkish

Å............Nor., Sw......Stream
Aas...........Dan., Nor.........Hill
Abajo...........Sp...........Lower
Ada, Adasi......Turk..........Island
Altipiano........It.........Plateau
Altiplano........Sp.........Plateau
Älv, Älf, Elf.....Sw.........River
Ås..............Nor., Sw......Hill
Asaga...........Turk.........Lower
Austral.........Sp.........Southern

Baai............Du...........Bay
Bab.............A......Gate or Strait
Bahia...........Sp...........Bay
Bahr............A.......Sea, River
Baie............Fr.......Gulf, Bay
Baixo...........Port.........Low
Bakke...........Dan..........Hill
Bana...........Jap...........Cape
Bänd...........Per....Mt. Range
Bel............Turk..........Pass
Berg...........Ger., Du....Mountain
Bir............A...........Well
Bogaz, Boghaz...Turk.........Strait
Bolshoi, Bolshaya..Russ.........Big
Boreal..........Sp........Northern
Bro...........Dan., Nor., Sw..Bridge
Bucht..........Ger........Bight
Bukt..........Nor., Sw....Bay, Gulf
Burnu, Burun....Turk.........Cape
By............Dan., Nor., Sw..Town

Cabo...........Sp., Port.......Cape
Campos.........Port.........Plains
Cap, Capo......Fr., It.........Cape
Catena.........It.....Mt. Range
Catingas.........Port..Open Woodlands
Central, Centrale..Fr., It.........Middle
Cerro...........Sp.........Hill
Chow..........Ch......Town of the second rank
Ciudad.........Sp.........Town
Col............Fr.........Pass
Cordillera......Sp....Mt. Range
Côte...........Fr.........Coast
Coxilha, Cuchilla..Sp....Mt. Range

Dag, Dagh......Turk......Mountain
Daglari........Turk......Mt. Range
Dal...........Nor., Sw......Valley
Dar...........A...........Land
Darya.........Per...........River
Dasht.........Per...Desert, Plain
Deniz, Dengiz....Turk.......Lake, Sea
Désert, Deserto,
    Desierto....Fr., It., Sp.....Desert
Détroit.........Fr.........Strait
Djebel.........A.........Mountain
Djeziret........A., Turk.....Island

Eiland..........Du.........Island
Elv...........Dan., Nor......River
Erg...........A...........Dune
Eski..........Turk..........Old
Est, Este.......Fr., Port........East
Estrecho, Estreito..Sp., Port.....Strait
Étang.........Fr.....Lagoon, Lake

Fedja, Feij......A...........Pass
Fiume..........It.........River
Fjäll.........Sw.....Mountain
Fjeld, Fjell....Nor.....Mountain
Fjord..........Dan., Nor., Sw..Fiord
    (narrow inlet or sea)
Fleuve.........Fr.........River
Fluss.........Ger...........River

Fokani, Fukani....A...........Upper
Fors.........Sw......Waterfall
Fos, Foss.......Dan., Nor....Waterfall
Fu.............Ch.........Town of
    Importance

Gamla.........Nor.........Old
Gamle.........Dan.........Old
Gawa..........Jap.........River
Gebel.........A.........Mountain
Gebergte.......Du....Mt. Range
Gebirge........Ger....Mt. Range
Ghubbet........A.........Bay
Gobi..........Mo.........Desert
Goe...........Jap.........Pass
Golf..........Ger., Du.........Gulf
Golfe.........Fr.........Gulf
Golfo.........Sp., It., Port....Gulf
Göla..........Turk.........Lake
Gora..........Russ.....Mountain
Grand, Grande....Fr., Sp.........Big
Groot.........Du.........Big
Gross.........Ger.........Big
Grosso........It., Port.........Big
Guba..........Russ......Bay, Gulf
Gunto.........Jap.....Archipelago

Hai...........Ch.........Sea
Halbinsel......Ger.....Peninsula
Halvöy........Nor.....Peninsula
Hamáda,
    Hammada.....A....Rocky Plateau
Hamn.........Sw......Harbour
Hamún........Per.....Desert,
    Swampy lake
Hantō........Jap.....Peninsula
Has, Hassi.....A.........Well
Hav..........Dan., Nor., Sw...Sea,
    Ocean
Havn.........Dan., Nor....Harbour
Higashi, Higasi...Jap.........East
Ho...........Ch.........Land
Hochebene......Ger.........Plateau
Hoek.........Du.........Cape
Hoku.........Jap.........North
Holm.........Dan., Nor., Sw..Island
Hoved........Dan., Nor.....Cape
Hsien........Ch......Town of the
    third class
Hu...........Ch.........Lake
Huk..........Dan., Nor., Sw .Point
Hus, Huus.....Dan., Nor., Sw..House
Hwang........Ch.........Yellow

Ile.............Fr............Island
Ilha...........Port.........Island
Indre.........Dan., Nor....Inner
Inferieur, Inferiore..Fr., It........Lower
Inner, Inre....Sw.........Inner
Insel.........Ger..........Island
Irmak........Turk........River
Isla..........Sp.........Island
Isola.........It.........Island

Järvi.........Finn.........Lake
Jebel.........A.........Mountain
Jezira, Jeziret....A.........Island
Jima..........Jap.........Island
Joki..........Finn.........River

Kaap.........Du.........Cape
Kabir, Kebir....A.........Big
Kai...........Jap.........Sea
Kaikyō........Jap.........Strait
Kami.........Turk.........Upper
Kap, Kapp......Nor., Sw.....Cape

Kaupunki.......Finn.........Town
Kawa.........Jap.........River
Khrebet.......Russ......Mt. Range
Kiang.........Ch.........River
Kiao..........Ch.........Point
Kita..........Jap.........North
Klein.........Du., Ger.....Small
Kô...........Jap.........Lake
Kong.........Ch.........River
Köping.........Sw...Market, Borough
Körfez, Körfezi...Turk.........Gulf
Kosui.........Jap.........Lake
Kraal.........Du....Native Village
Kuchuk.......Turk.........Small
Kum..........Turk.........Desert
Kuro.........Jap.........Black

Laag.........Du.........Low
Lac...........Fr.........Lake
Lago.........Sp., Port., It....Lake
Lahti.........Finn.....Bay, Bight
Län..........Sw.........County
Lilla.........Sw........Small
Lille.........Dan., Nor....Small
Ling..........Ch.....Mountain
Llanos........Sp.........Plains

Mali, Malaya....Russ.........Small
Mar..........Sp., Port.........Sea
Mare.........It.........Sea
Medio........Sp.........Middle
Meer.........Du.........Lake
Meer.........Ger.........Sea
Mer..........Fr.........Sea
Meridionale....It.........Southern
Middelst, Midden..Du.........Middle
Minami........Jap.......Southern
Mis..........Russ.........Cape
Misaki........Jap.........Cape
Mittel........Ger.........Middle
Mont.........Fr.....Mountain
Montagnes......Fr.....Mt. Range
Monte........Sp., It., Port.Mountain
More.........Russ.........Sea
Morro........Port.....Mountain
Moyen........Fr.........Middle
Muong........Siamese.......Town

Nada.........Jap.........Sea
Naka.........Jap.........Middle
Nan..........Ch., Jap......South
Nes..........Nor......Cape, Point
Nieder........Ger.........Lower
Nishi, Nisi.....Jap.........West
Nizhni, Nizhnyaya.Russ........Lower
Njarga........Finn.....Peninsula,
    Promontory
Noord........Du...North, Northern
Nord.........Fr., Ger.......North
Norte.........Sp., It., Port.....North
Nos..........Russ.........Cape
Novi, Novaya....Russ.........New
Ny, Nya.......Nor., Sw......New

O............Jap.........Big
Ö............Nor., Sw......Island
Ober.........Ger.........Upper
Occidental,
    Occidentale....Sp., It........Western
Oeste.........Port.........West
Ooster........Du.........Eastern
Opper, Over....Du.........Upper
Oriental.......Sp., Fr.......Eastern
Orientale......It.........Eastern
Orta.........Turk.........Middle
Ost..........Ger.........East

GLOSSARY OF GEOGRAPHICAL TERMS *continued*

Ostrov..........Russ..........Island	Serra..........Port......Mt. Range	Tao..........Ch..........Island
Ouest..........Fr..........West	Serranía..........Sp......Mt. Ridge	Tell..........A..........Hill
Öy..........Nor..........Island	Seto..........Jap......Strait	Tind..........Nor..........Peak
Ozero..........Russ..........Lake	Settentrionale......It..........Northern	Tô..........Jap..........East
	Severni, Severnaya. Russ..........North	To..........Jap..........Island
Pampas..........Sp......Grass Plains	Shan..........Ch., Jap...Hill,	Toge..........Jap..........Pass
Pas..........Fr....Channel, Strait	Mt. Range	Trask..........Finn..........Lake
Paso..........Sp..........Pass	Shang..........Ch..........Upper	Tung..........Ch..........Eastern
Passo..........It., Port......Pass	Shat, Shatt......A.....River or Coast	
Peh, Pei..........Ch..........North	Shima..........Jap..........Island	Unter..........Ger..........Lower
Penisola..........It..........Peninsula	Shimo..........Jap..........Lower	Ura..........Jap..........Bay
Pequeño..........Sp..........Small	Shin..........Jap..........Land	
Pereval..........Russ..........Pass	Shiro..........Jap..........White	Vatn..........Nor..........Lake
Petit..........Fr..........Small	Si..........Ch..........West	Vecchio..........It..........Old
Piccolo..........It..........Small	Siao..........Ch..........Small	Velho..........Port..........Old
Planalto..........Port..........Plateau	Sierra..........Sp......Mt. Range	Verkhni..........Russ..........Upper
Pointe..........Fr..........Point	Sjö..........Nor., Sw.......Lake	Vieho..........Sp..........Old
Poluostrov..........Russ..........Peninsula	Sok, Suk, Souk...A., Ar. Fr.....Market	Vik..........Nor., Sw..........Bay
Ponta..........Port..........Point	Sredni, Srednyaya..Russ..........Middle	Vishni, Vishnyaya..Russ..........High
Presqu'île..........Fr..........Peninsula	Stad..........Dan., Nor., Sw...City	Vostochni,
Proliv..........Russ..........Strait	Stari, Staraya......Russ..........Old	Vostochnaya....Russ....East, Eastern
Pulo, Poulo......Malay..........Island	Step..........Russ....Treeless Plain	
Punta..........It., Sp..........Point	Straat..........Du..........Strait	Wad, Wadi......A.......Watercourse,
	Strasse..........Ger..........Strait	dry in summer
Qum..........Turk..........Desert	Stretto..........It..........Strait	Wan..........Jap., Ch...Bay, Gulf
	Ström..........Dan., Nor., Sw..River	Westersch..........Du..........Western
Ras..........A..........Cape	Su..........Turk..........River	Wüste..........Ger..........Desert
Reka..........Russ..........River	Sud, Süd..........Fr., Ger......South	
Retto..........Jap....Archipelago	Suido..........Jap..........Strait	Yama..........Jap..........Mountain
Rio..........Sp., Port., It....River	Sul..........Port..........South	Yarim Ada......Turk..........Peninsula
Rivier, Rivière..Du., Fr......River	Sund..........Dan., Nor., Sw..Sound	Yokara..........Turk..........Upper
	Supérieur..........Fr..........Upper	Yug, Yuzhni,
	Superior, Superiore. Sp., It........Upper	Yuzhnaya......Russ..South, Southern
Saghir..........A..........Small	Sur..........Sp..........South	
Sai..........Jap..........West	Suyu..........Turk..........River	Zaki..........Jap..........Cape
Saki..........Jap..........Cape		Zaliv..........Russ..........Bay, Gulf
San..........Jap., Ch...Hill,	Ta..........Ch..........Big	Zapadni,
Mountain	Tafelland..........Du..........Plateau	Zapadnaya......Russ..........Western
Schiereiland......Du..........Peninsula	Take..........Jap......Peak, Ridge	Zee..........Du..........Sea
See..........Ger......Sea, Lake	Takht..........A..........Lower	Zemlya..........Russ..........Land
Selvas..........Sp., Port......Woods,	Tanjong,	Zuid..........Du..........South
Forests	Tandjoeng......Malay..........Cape	

This map of an imaginary area defines graphically many common geographic terms.

EARTH AND SOLAR SYSTEM

Elements of the Solar System

Planets	Distance from Sun in Miles Maximum	Minimum	Period of Revolution Around Sun in Days	Diameter in Miles	Density (Earth = 1)
Sun	—	—	—	864,392	0.26
Mercury	43,355,000	28,566,000	87.97	3,008	0.68
Venus	67,653,000	66,738,000	224.70	7,576	0.94
Earth	94,452,000	91,342,000	365.26	7,918	1.00
Mars	154,760,000	128,330,000	686.98	4,216	0.71
Jupiter	506,710,000	459,940,000	4,332.59	86,682	0.24
Saturn	935,570,000	836,700,000	10,759.20	72,332	0.12
Uranus	1,866,800,000	1,698,800,000	30,685.93	30,878	0.25
Neptune	2,817,400,000	2,769,600,000	60,187.64	32,932	0.24
Pluto	4,580,000,000	2,750,000,000	90,470.23	6,500 *approx.*	0.91

Dimensions of the Earth

Superficial area	196,950,000	sq. miles
Land surface	57,510,000	"
North America	8,500,000	"
South America	6,814,000	"
Europe	3,872,000	"
Asia	16,990,000	"
Africa	11,500,000	"
Australia	2,974,581	"
Water surface	139,440,000	"
Atlantic Ocean	31,830,000	"
Pacific Ocean	63,801,000	"
Indian Ocean	28,356,000	"
Arctic Ocean	5,440,000	"
Equatorial circumference	24,902	miles
Meridianal circumference	24,860	"
Equatorial diameter	7,926.677	"
Polar diameter	7,899.988	"
Equatorial radius	3,963.34	"
Polar radius	3,949.99	"
Volume of the Earth	260,000,000,000	cubic miles
Mass, or weight	6,592,000,000,000,000,000,000	tons
Mean distance from the Sun	92,897,416	miles

The Moon, the only satellite of the Earth, from which her mean distance is 238,857 miles, occupies an average period in her revolution round the earth, of 29 days, 12 hours, 44 minutes, 3 seconds; her diameter is 2,160 miles, and her mean density 0.60.

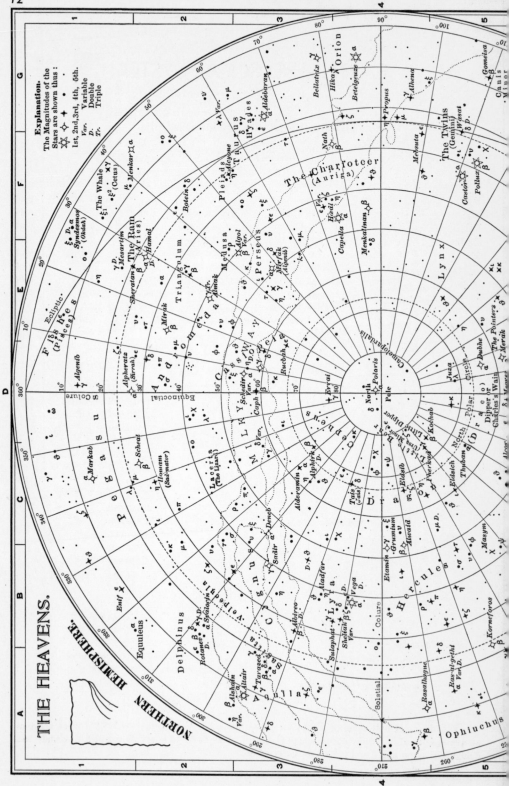

THE HEAVENS.

NORTHERN HEMISPHERE.

Explanation.
The Magnitudes of the Stars are shown thus:
1st, 2nd, 3rd, 4th, 5th.
Var. Variable
D. Double
Tr. Triple

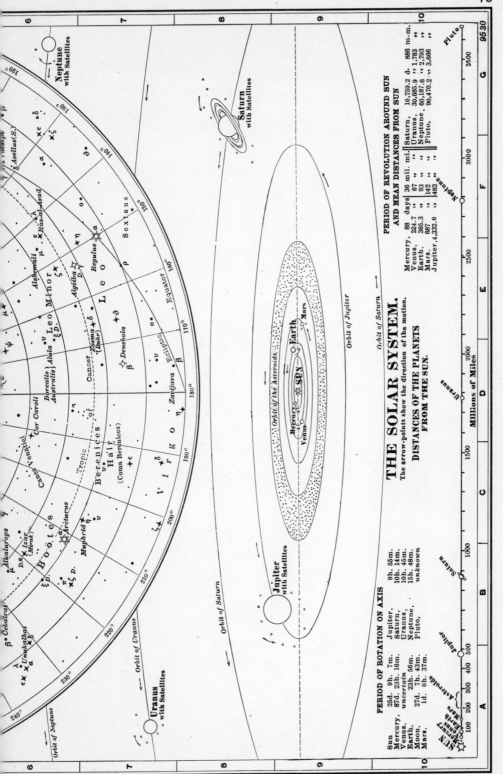

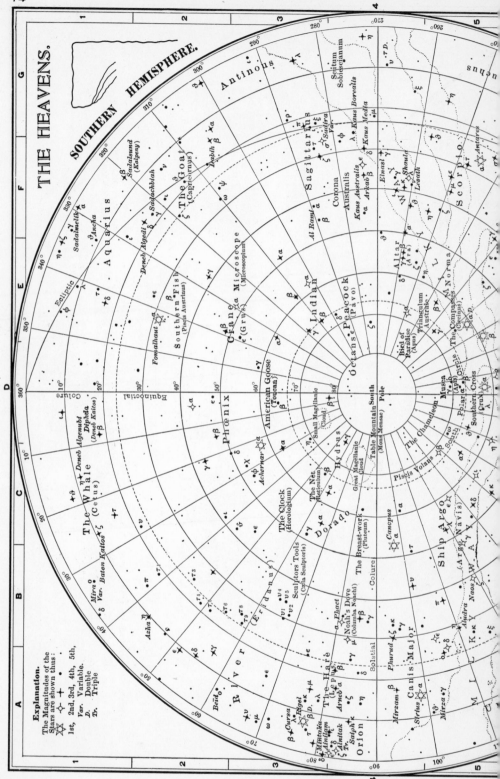

14

THE HEAVENS.

SOUTHERN HEMISPHERE.

Explanation.
The Magnitudes of the
Stars are shown thus :
1st, 2nd, 3rd, 4th, 5th,
Var. Variable.
D. Double
Tr. Triple

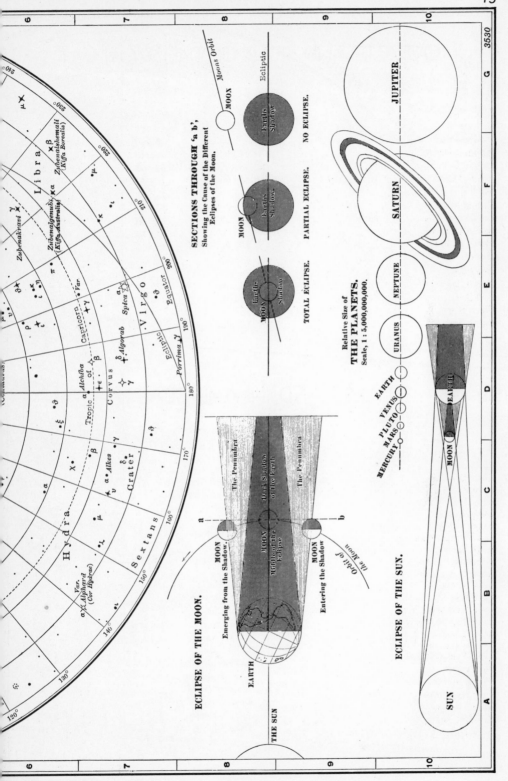

15

3530

ECLIPSE OF THE MOON.

MOON
Emerging from the Shadow.

The Penumbra

Dark Shadow
of the Earth

MOON
Middle of the
Eclipse

a

b

The Penumbra

MOON
Entering the Shadow.

Orbit of
the Moon

EARTH

THE SUN

SECTIONS THROUGH 'a b',
Showing the Cause of the Different
Eclipses of the Moon.

MOON Orbit

MOON

Ecliptic

MOON

Earth's
Shadow

NO ECLIPSE.

Earth's
Shadow

MOON

Earth's
Shadow

PARTIAL ECLIPSE.

Earth's
Shadow

MOON

TOTAL ECLIPSE.

Relative Size of
THE PLANETS.
Scale, 1 : 5,000,000,000.

MERCURY
MARS
PLUTO
VENUS
EARTH

URANUS

NEPTUNE

SATURN

JUPITER

ECLIPSE OF THE SUN.

SUN

EARTH

MOON

Libra

Zubenelgenubi
(Kiffa Australis)

Zubenalschemali
(Kiffa Borealis)

Zubenakrani

Porrima

Equator

Ecliptic

Virgo

Spica

Algorab

Corvus

γ

β

of

Capricorn

Alchiba

Tropic

Crater

Alkes

Hydra

Sextans

Var.
Alphard
(Cor Hydrae)

OCEANS AND SEAS OF THE WORLD

	Area in Sq. Miles	Greatest Depth Feet	Volume in Cubic Miles
Pacific Ocean	63,801,000	35,400	162,870,600
Atlantic Ocean	31,830,000	30,246	75,533,900
Indian Ocean	28,356,000	22,968	69,225,200
Arctic Ocean	5,440,000	17,850	4,029,400
Mediterranean Sea	1,145,000	15,197	1,019,400
Bering Sea	876,000	13,422	788,500
Caribbean Sea	750,000	23,748	2,298,400
Sea of Okhotsk	590,000	11,070	454,700
East China Sea	482,000	10,500	52,700
Hudson Bay	475,000	1,500	37,590
Japan Sea	389,000	13,242	383,200
North Sea	222,000	2,654	12,890
Red Sea	169,000	7,254	53,700
Black Sea	165,000	7,200	—
Baltic Sea	163,000	1,506	5,360

LAKES AND INLAND SEAS

	Area in Sq. Miles		Area in Sq. Miles
Caspian Sea	163,800	Vänern	2,149
Lake Superior	31,820	Lake Urmia	1,795
Lake Victoria	26,828	Great Salt Lake	1,700
Lake Aral	24,900	Lake Albert	1,640
Lake Huron	23,010	Lake Van	1,453
Lake Michigan	22,400	Lake Peipus	1,400
Lake Tanganyika	12,700	Lake Tana	1,219
Lake Baikal	12,150	Lake Bangweulu...Approx..	1,000
Great Bear Lake	12,000	Vättern	733
Great Slave Lake	11,170	Dead Sea	405
Lake Nyasa	11,000	Lake Balaton	266
Lake Erie	9,940	Lake Geneva	225
Lake Winnipeg	9,398	Lake Constance	208
Lake Ontario	7,540	Lough Neagh	153
Lake Ladoga	7,100	Lake Garda	143
Lake Balkhash	6,700	Lake Neuchâtel	83
Lake Tchad (Chad)	6,500	Lake Maggiore	82
Lake Onega	3,765	Lough Corrib	71
Lake Titicaca	3,200	Lake Como	56
Lake Nicaragua	3,100	Lake Lucerne	44½
Lake Athabaska	3,058	Lake Zürich	34
Reindeer Lake	2,444		
Issyk-kul	2,276		

Longest Rivers

River	Length in Miles	River	Length in Miles
Nile, *Africa*	4,159	Japurá, *S. A.*	1,500
Amazon, *S. A.*	4,000	Arkansas, *U. S. A.*	1,450
Mississippi-Missouri, *U. S. A.*	3,892	Dneiper, *U. S. S. R.*	1,418
Ob-Irtish, *U. S. S. R.*	3,200	Rio Negro, *S. A.*	1,400
Yangtze, *China*	3,100	Colorado, *Ariz, U. S. A.*	1,360
Congo, *Africa*	2,900	Kolyma, *U. S. S. R.*	1,335
Amur, *Asia*	2,704	Ohio, *U. S. A.*	1,306
Hwang (Yellow), *China*	2,700	Orange, *Africa*	1,300
Lena, *U. S. S. R.*	2,648	Red, *Texas, U. S. A.*	1,300
Mekong, *Asia*	2,600	Kama, *U. S. S. R.*	1,262
Niger, *Africa*	2,600	Irrawaddy, *Burma*	1,250
Mackenzie, *Canada*	2,514	Don, *U. S. S. R.*	1,222
Paraná, *S. A.*	2,450	Columbia, *U. S.-Canada*	1,214
Yenisei, *U. S. S. R.*	2,364	Saskatchewan, *Canada*	1,205
Murray, *Australia*	2,310	Darling, *Australia*	1,160
Volga, *U. S. S. R.*	2,290	Angara, *U. S. S. R.*	1,151
Madeira, *S. A.*	2,000	Tigris, *Iraq*	1,150
Yukon, *Alaska*	1,979	Sungari, *Asia*	1,130
St. Lawrence, *Canada*	1,900	Pechora, *U. S. S. R.*	1,111
Purus, *S. A.*	1,850	Peace, *Canada*	1,054
Rio Grande, *U. S. A.*	1,800	Snake, *U. S. A.*	1,038
São Francisco, *S. A.*	1,800	Churchill, *Canada*	1,000
Salween, *Burma*	1,750	Pilcomayo, *S. A.*	1,000
Danube, *Europe*	1,725	Uruguay, *S. A.*	1,000
Euphrates, *Iraq*	1,700	Magdalena, *S. A.*	950
Indus, *Pakistan*	1,700	Platte, *U. S. A.*	928
Orinoco, *S. A.*	1,700	Oka, *U. S. S. R.*	918
Tocantins, *S. A.*	1,700	Canadian, *U. S. A.*	906
Brahmaputra, *India*	1,680	Tennessee, *U. S. A.*	900
Syr Darya, *U. S. S. R.*	1,680	Brazos, *U. S. A.*	870
Si, *China*	1,650	Dneister, *U. S. S. R.*	852
Nelson, *Canada*	1,600	Fraser, *Canada*	850
Zambezi, *Africa*	1,600	Colorado, *Tex., U. S. A.*	840
Ural, *U. S. S. R.*	1,574	Northern Dvina, *U. S. S. R.*	803
Amu Darya, *U. S. S. R.*	1,550	Tisza, *Europe*	800
Ganges, *India*	1,540	Athabaska, *Canada*	765
Olenek, *U. S. S. R.*	1,500	North Canadian, *U. S. A.*	760
Paraguay, *S. A.*	1,500	North Saskatchewan, *Canada*	760

Great Ship Canals

	Opened	Length in Statute Miles	Depth in Feet (minimum)	Width in Feet (minimum)
Amsterdam-North Sea, *Netherlands*	1876	16.5	41	164
Houston, *U.S.A.; reconstructed*	1914	50	33	200
Kiel, *Germany; reconstructed*	1895	61	37	144
Manchester, *England*	1894	35.5	28	120
Panama, *Canal Zone, U.S.A.*	1914	50.72	40	110
Sault Ste. Marie, *U.S.A.*	1919	1.6	24.5	80
Suez, *Egypt*	1869	100.76	34	196
Welland, *Canada*	1932	27.6	25	80

Mountains of the World

	Feet		Feet
Mt. Everest, *Nepal-Tibet*	29,002	Mt. Ararat, *Turkey*	16,916
Mt. Godwin Austen, *India*	28,250	Ruwenzori, *Uganda*	16,787
Kanchenjunga, *Nepal-India*	28,146	Klyuchevskaya Volcano,	
Mt. Makalu, *Tibet-Nepal*	27,790	*U.S.S.R.*	15,912
Dhaulagiri, *Nepal*	26,795	Mont Blanc, *France*	15,781
Nanga Parbat, *India*	26,620	Carstensz Toppen, *New Guinea*	15,709
Nanda Devi, *India*	25,645	Mt. Kazbek, *U.S.S.R.*	15,545
Mt. Kamet, *India*	25,447	Monte Rosa, *Switzerland*	15,217
Tirich-Mir, *Pakistan*	25,263	Mt. Belukha, *U.S.S.R.*	15,154
Anne Machin, *China*	25,000	Mt. Markham, *Antarctica*	15,102
Minya Konka, *China*	24,900	Matterhorn, *Switzerland*	14,780
Stalin Peak, *U.S.S.R.*	24,589	Ras Dashan, *Ethiopia*	14,760
Pobedy Peak, *U.S.S.R.*	24,403	Mt. Morrison, *Formosa*	14,720
Mt. Chomo Lhari, *Bhutan*	23,997	Mt. Whitney, *California*	14,495
Muztagh, *Sinkiang*	23,885	Mt. Elbert, *Colorado*	14,431
Tengri Khan, *U.S.S.R.*	23,600	Mt. Rainier, *Washington*	14,408
Aconcagua Volcano, *Argentina*	23,080	Mt. Shasta, *California*	14,162
Cerro Ojas del Salado, *Argentina*	22,402	Pikes Peak, *Colorado*	14,110
Cerro Huascarán, *Peru*	22,180	Finsteraarhorn, *Switzerland*	14,026
Llullaillaco Volcano, *Chile*	22,145	Mauna Loa, *Hawaii*	13,680
Cerro Mercedario, *Argentina*	21,870	Jungfrau, *Switzerland*	13,667
Tupungato, *Chile*	21,810	Jebel Toubkal, *Morocco*	13,665
Mt. Illampú, *Bolivia*	21,489	Mt. Kinabalu, *North Borneo*	13,451
Sajama Volcano, *Bolivia*	21,320	Cameroon Mt., *Cameroon*	13,349
Mt. Illimani, *Bolivia*	21,151	Gran Paradiso, *Italy*	13,323
Chimborazo, *Ecuador*	20,702	Mt. Robson, *British Columbia*	12,972
Mt. McKinley, *Alaska*	20,300	Gross Glockner, *Austria*	12,461
Mt. Logan, *Yukon*	19,850	Fujisan, *Japan*	12,395
Cotopaxi Volcano, *Ecuador*	19,498	Mt. Cook, *New Zealand*	12,349
Kilimanjaro, *Tanganyika Terr.*	19,319	Pico de Teyde, *Tenerife*	12,200
Misti Volcano, *Peru*	19,200	Mt. Semeroe, *Java*	12,057
Citlaltepetl, *Mexico*	18,696	Mulhacén, *Spain*	11,417
Mt. Demavend, *Iran*	18,550	Mt. Löser, *Sumatra*	11,093
Mt. Elbrus, *U.S.S.R.*	18,468	Mt. Etna, *Sicily*	10,741
Mt. Tolima, *Colombia*	18,438	Volcano Irazu, *Costa Rica*	10,525
Mt. St. Elias, *Alaska*	18,008	Lassen Peak, *California*	10,453
Mt. Popocatepetl, *Mexico*	17,888	Mt. Tina, *Dominican Rep.*	10,301
Dikh-Tau, *U.S.S.R.*	17,085	Mt. Kosciusco, *Australia*	7,352
Mt. Kenya, *Kenya*	17,040	Mt. Mitchell, *North Carolina*	6,684

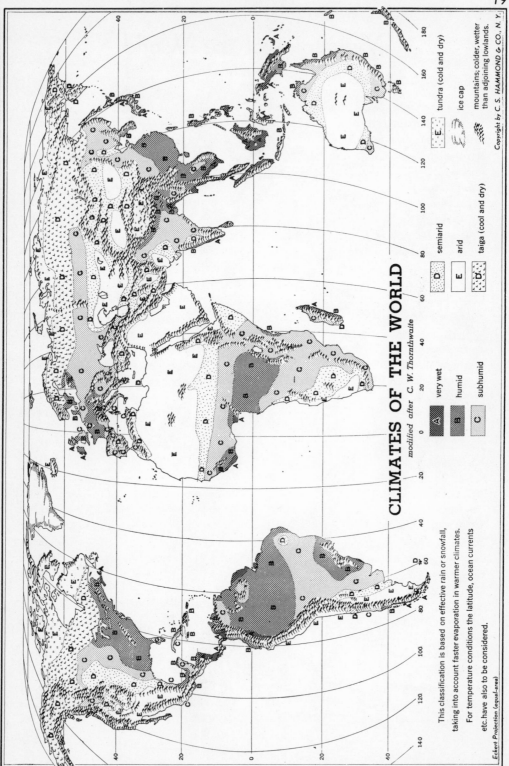

CLIMATES OF THE WORLD

modified after C. W. Thornthwaite

A	very wet	D	semiarid
B	humid	E	arid
C	subhumid	D	taiga (cool and dry)

E tundra (cold and dry)

ice cap

mountains; colder, wetter than adjoining lowlands.

This classification is based on effective rain or snowfall, taking into account faster evaporation in warmer climates.

For temperature conditions the latitude, ocean currents etc. have also to be considered.

Eckert Projection (equal-area)

Copyright by C. S. HAMMOND & CO., N. Y.

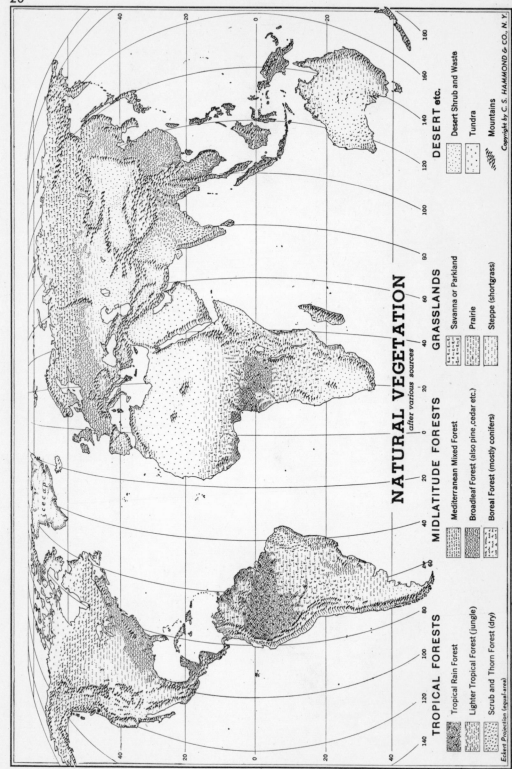

NATURAL VEGETATION
(after various sources)

TROPICAL FORESTS
- Tropical Rain Forest
- Lighter Tropical Forest (jungle)
- Scrub and Thorn Forest (dry)

MIDLATITUDE FORESTS
- Mediterranean Mixed Forest
- Broadleaf Forest (also pine, cedar etc.)
- Boreal Forest (mostly conifers)

GRASSLANDS
- Savanna or Parkland
- Prairie
- Steppe (shortgrass)

DESERT etc.
- Desert Shrub and Waste
- Tundra
- Mountains

Eckert Projection (equal-area)

Copyright by C. S. HAMMOND & CO., N. Y.

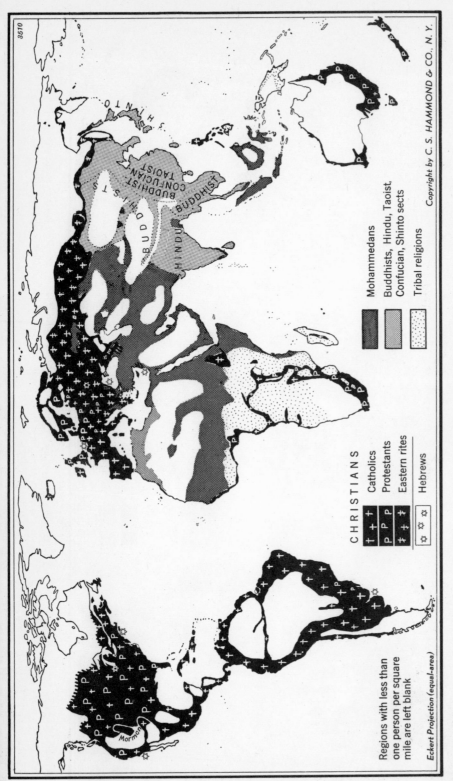

Eckert Projection (equal-area)

CHRISTIANS

Catholics	† †
Protestants	P P
Eastern rites	† †
Hebrews	✡ ✡

Regions with less than one person per square mile are left blank

Mohammedans

Buddhists, Hindu, Taoist, Confucian, Shinto sects

Tribal religions

Copyright by C. S. HAMMOND & CO., N. Y.

RELIGIONS. Most people of the Earth belong to four major religions: Christians, Mohammedans, Brahmans, Buddhists and derivatives. The Eastern rites of the Christians include the Greek Orthodox, Greek Catholic, Armenian, Syrian, Coptic and more minor churches. The lamaism of Tibet and Mongolia differs a great deal from Buddhism in Burma and Thailand. In the religion of China the teachings of Buddha, Confucius and Tao are mixed, while in Shinto a great deal of ancestor and emperor worship is added. About 11 million Hebrews live scattered over the globe, chiefly in cities and in the state of Israel.

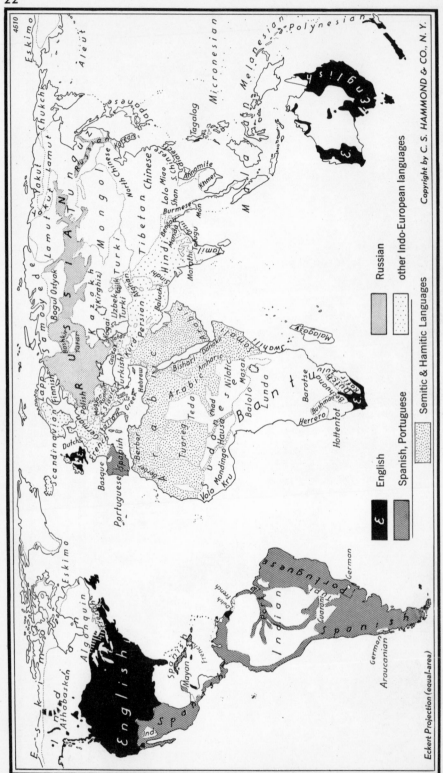

LANGUAGES. Several hundred different languages are spoken in the World, and in many places two or more languages are spoken, sometimes by the same people. The map above shows the dominant languages in each locality. English, French, Spanish, Russian, Arabic and Swahili are spoken by many people as a second language for commerce or travel.

Copyright by C. S. HAMMOND & CO., N. Y.

English

Spanish, Portuguese

Russian

other Indo-European languages

Semitic & Hamitic Languages

Eckert Projection (equal-area)

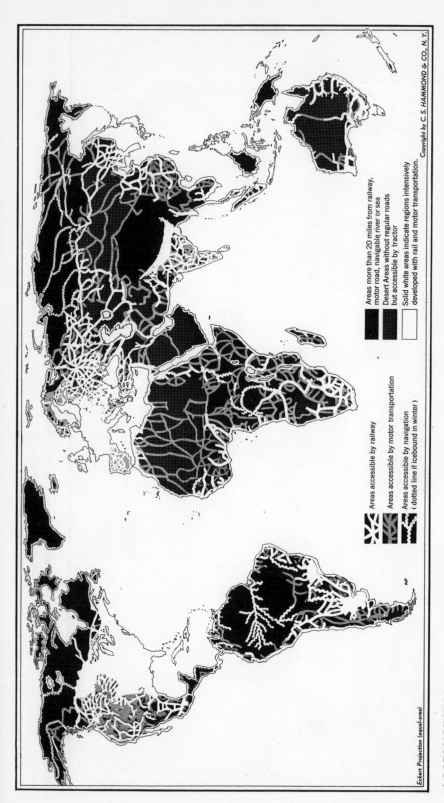

Eckert Projection (equal-area)

ACCESSIBILITY. Many regions in the world are far from railways, roads, navigable rivers or the seas. Their economic development is retarded because their products can be brought to the world's markets only at great expense. Such areas are in the tundra (alpine), the boreal forest and in the equatorial rain forest regions. Desert areas, if not too mountainous, can be crossed by tractors. The largest inaccessible area is in Tibet, on account of high mountains, the alpine climate and isolationist attitude of the people. Airplane transportation will help to bring inaccessible areas into the orbit of civilization.

Areas accessible by railway

Areas accessible by motor transportation

Areas accessible by navigation (dotted line if icebound in winter)

Areas more than 20 miles from railway, motor road, navigable river or sea

Desert Areas without regular roads but accessible by tractor

Solid white areas indicate regions intensively developed with rail and motor transportation.

Copyright by C. S. HAMMOND & CO., N. Y.

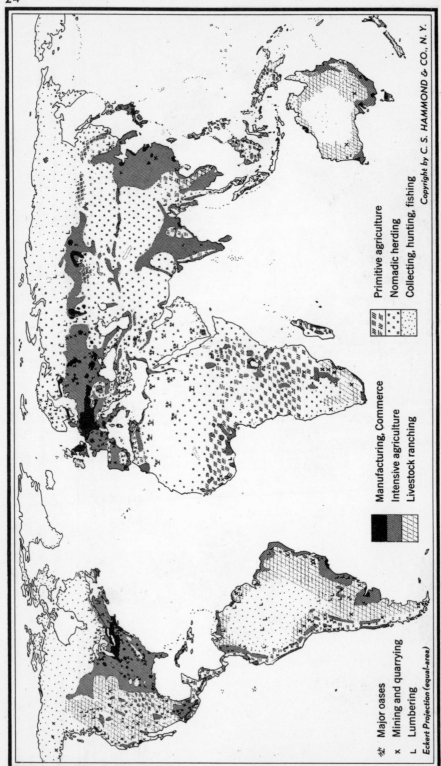

Major oases
x   Mining and quarrying
L   Lumbering

Eckert Projection (equal-area)

Manufacturing, Commerce

Intensive agriculture

Livestock ranching

Primitive agriculture

Nomadic herding

Collecting, hunting, fishing

Copyright by C. S. HAMMOND & CO., N. Y.

OCCUPATIONS. Correlation with the density of population shows that the most densely populated areas fall into the regions of manufacturing and intensive farming. All other economies require considerable space. The most sparsely inhabited areas are those of collecting, hunting and fishing. Areas with practically no habitation are left blank

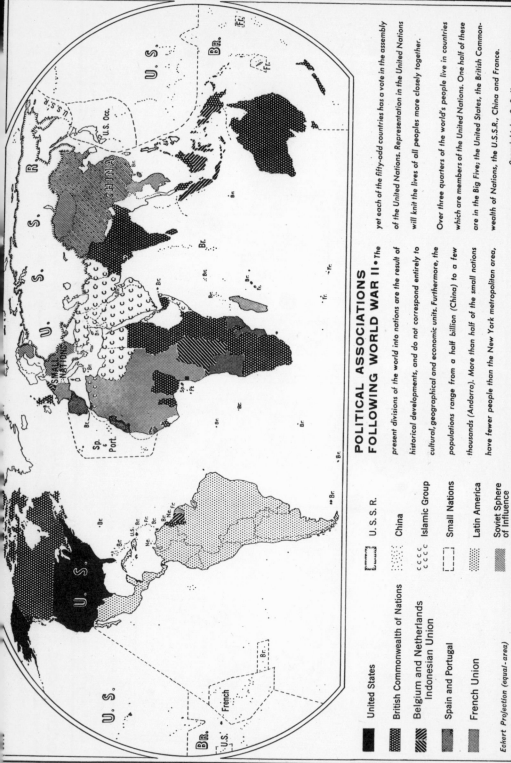

POLITICAL ASSOCIATIONS FOLLOWING WORLD WAR II ● The

present divisions of the world into nations are the result of historical developments, and do not correspond entirely to cultural, geographical and economic units. Furthermore, the populations range from a half billion (China) to a few thousands (Andorra). More than half of the small nations have fewer people than the New York metropolitan area, yet each of the fifty-odd countries has a vote in the assembly of the United Nations. Representation in the United Nations will knit the lives of all peoples more closely together.

Over three quarters of the world's people live in countries which are members of the United Nations. One half of these are in the Big Five; the United States, the British Commonwealth of Nations, the U.S.S.R., China and France.

Copyright by C. S. Hammond & Co., N. Y.

United States

British Commonwealth of Nations

Belgium and Netherlands Indonesian Union

Spain and Portugal

French Union

Eckert Projection (equal-area)

U. S. S. R.

China

Islamic Group

Small Nations

Latin America

Soviet Sphere of Influence

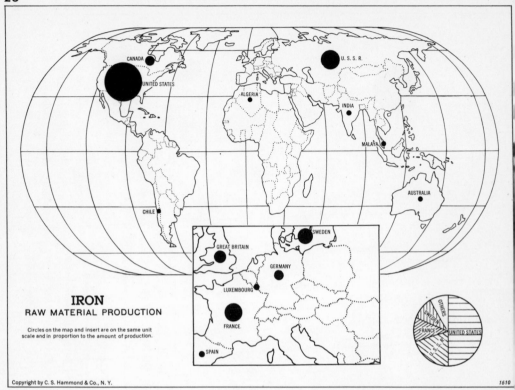

IRON
RAW MATERIAL PRODUCTION

Circles on the map and insert are on the same unit
scale and in proportion to the amount of production.

1610

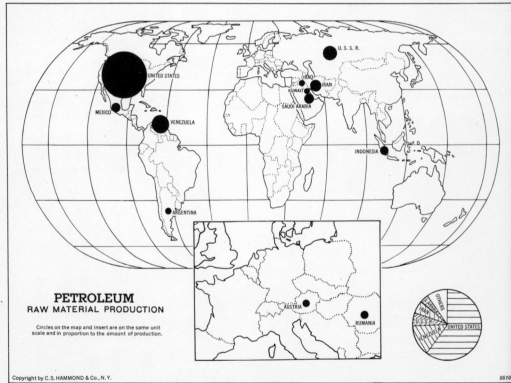

PETROLEUM
RAW MATERIAL PRODUCTION

Circles on the map and insert are on the same unit
scale and in proportion to the amount of production.

9510

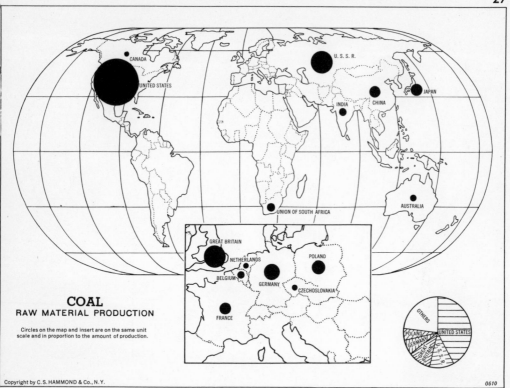

COAL
RAW MATERIAL PRODUCTION

Circles on the map and insert are on the same unit
scale and in proportion to the amount of production.

0510

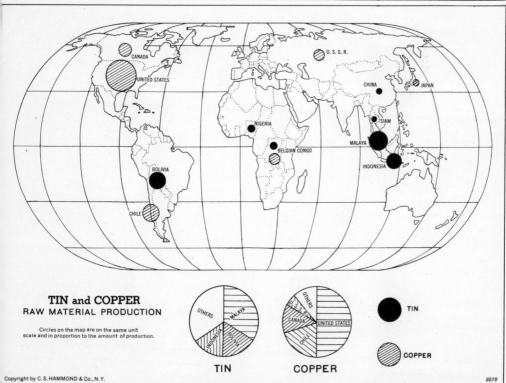

TIN and COPPER
RAW MATERIAL PRODUCTION

Circles on the map are on the same unit
scale and in proportion to the amount of production.

8510

Production data based on Monthly Bulletin of Statistics,
Statistical Office of the United Nations.

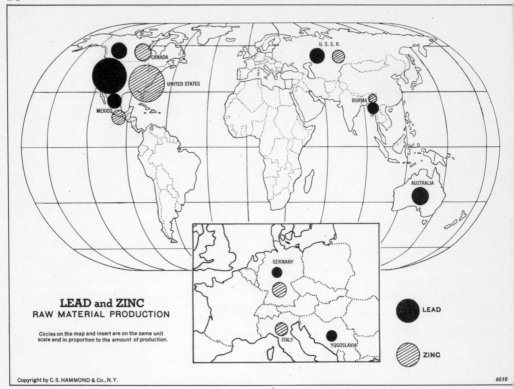

LEAD and ZINC
RAW MATERIAL PRODUCTION

Circles on the map and insert are on the same unit
scale and in proportion to the amount of production.

LEAD

ZINC

6510

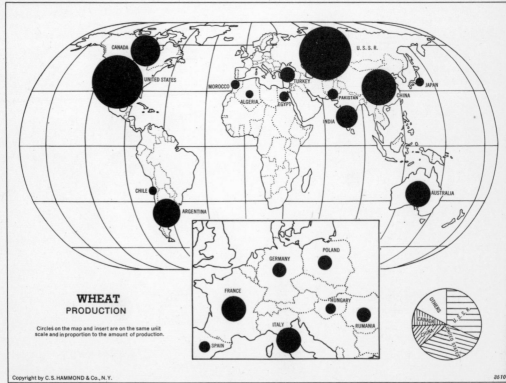

WHEAT
PRODUCTION

Circles on the map and insert are on the same unit
scale and in proportion to the amount of production.

3510

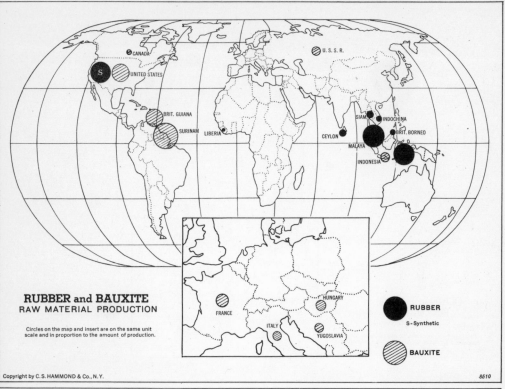

RUBBER and BAUXITE
RAW MATERIAL PRODUCTION

Circles on the map and insert are on the same unit scale and in proportion to the amount of production.

Copyright by C.S. HAMMOND & Co., N.Y.

RUBBER
S-Synthetic

BAUXITE

8510

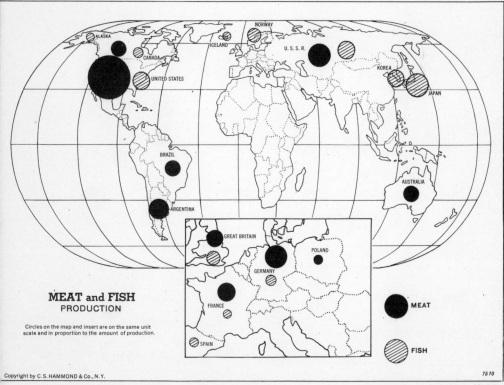

MEAT and FISH
PRODUCTION

Circles on the map and insert are on the same unit scale and in proportion to the amount of production.

Copyright by C.S. HAMMOND & Co., N.Y.

MEAT

FISH

7510

Production data based on Monthly Bulletin of Statistics, Statistical Office of the United Nations.

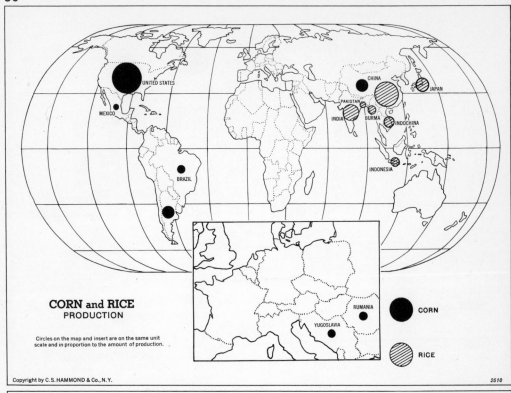

CORN and RICE
PRODUCTION

Circles on the map and insert are on the same unit
scale and in proportion to the amount of production.

● CORN

▨ RICE

2510

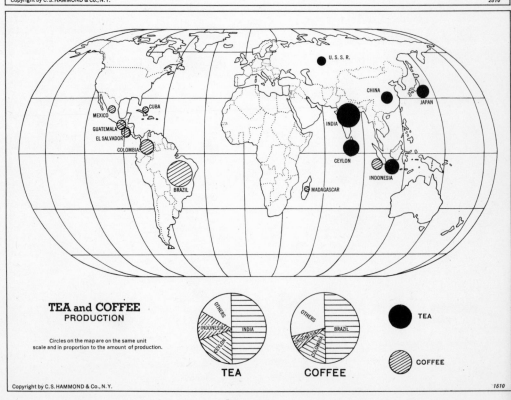

TEA and COFFEE
PRODUCTION

Circles on the map are on the same unit
scale and in proportion to the amount of production.

● TEA

▨ COFFEE

TEA

COFFEE

1510

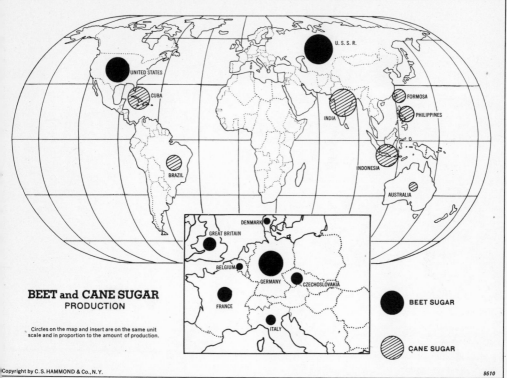

BEET and CANE SUGAR
PRODUCTION

Circles on the map and insert are on the same unit
scale and in proportion to the amount of production.

BEET SUGAR

CANE SUGAR

9510

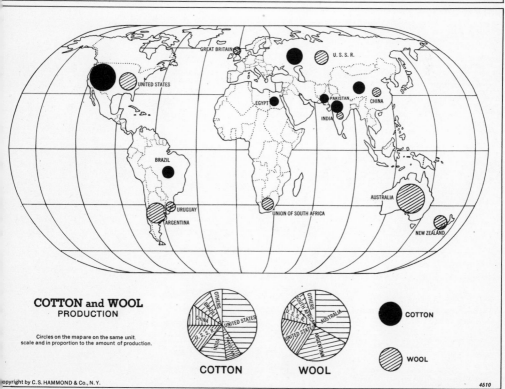

COTTON and WOOL
PRODUCTION

Circles on the map are on the same unit
scale and in proportion to the amount of production.

COTTON

WOOL

COTTON

WOOL

4510

Production data based on Monthly Bulletin of Statistics,
Statistical Office of the United Nations.

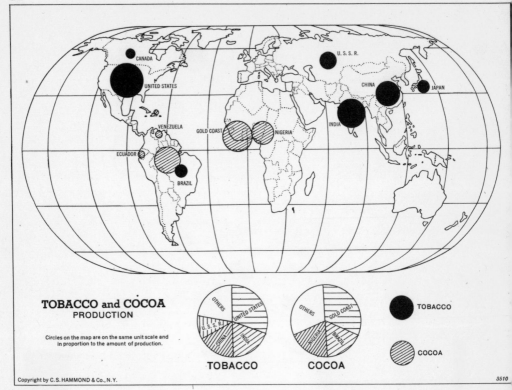

TOBACCO and COCOA
PRODUCTION

Circles on the map are on the same unit scale and
in proportion to the amount of production.

TOBACCO

COCOA

● TOBACCO

▨ COCOA

3510

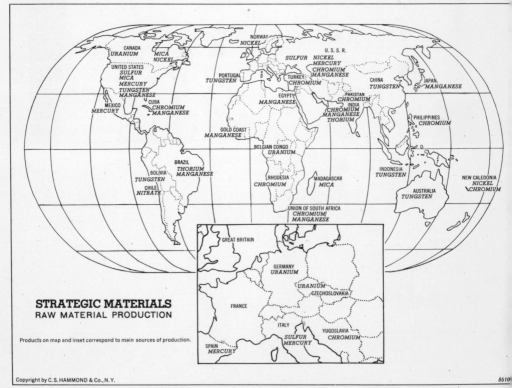

STRATEGIC MATERIALS
RAW MATERIAL PRODUCTION

Products on map and inset correspond to main sources of production.

8510

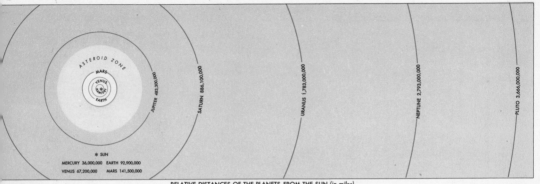

RELATIVE DISTANCES OF THE PLANETS FROM THE SUN *(in miles)*

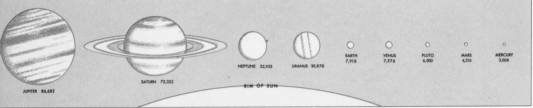

RELATIVE DIAMETERS OF THE PLANETS *(in miles)*

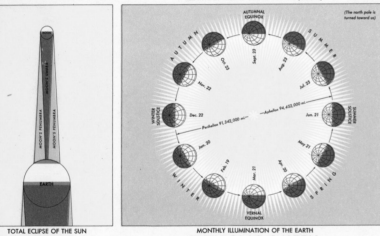

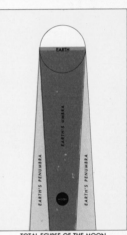

TOTAL ECLIPSE OF THE SUN

MONTHLY ILLUMINATION OF THE EARTH

TOTAL ECLIPSE OF THE MOON

THE SOLAR SYSTEM

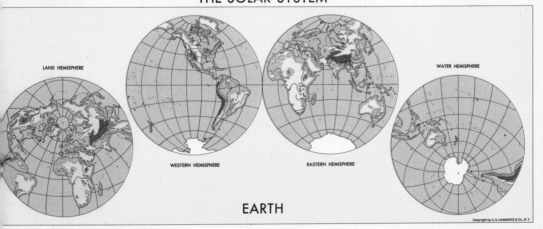

LAND HEMISPHERE

WESTERN HEMISPHERE

EASTERN HEMISPHERE

WATER HEMISPHERE

EARTH

34

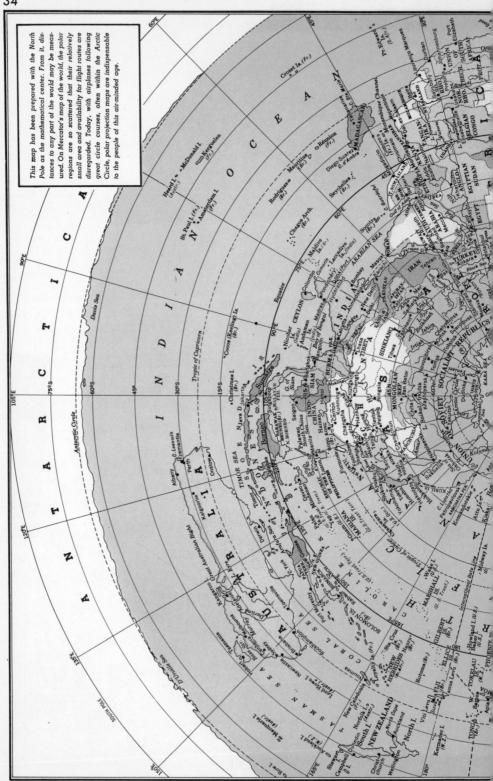

This map has been prepared with the North Pole as the mathematical center. From it, distances to any part of the world may be measured. On Mercator's map of the world, the polar regions are so scattered that their relatively small area and availability for flight routes are disregarded. Today, with airplanes following great circle courses, often within the Arctic Circle, polar projection maps are indispensable to the people of this air-minded age.

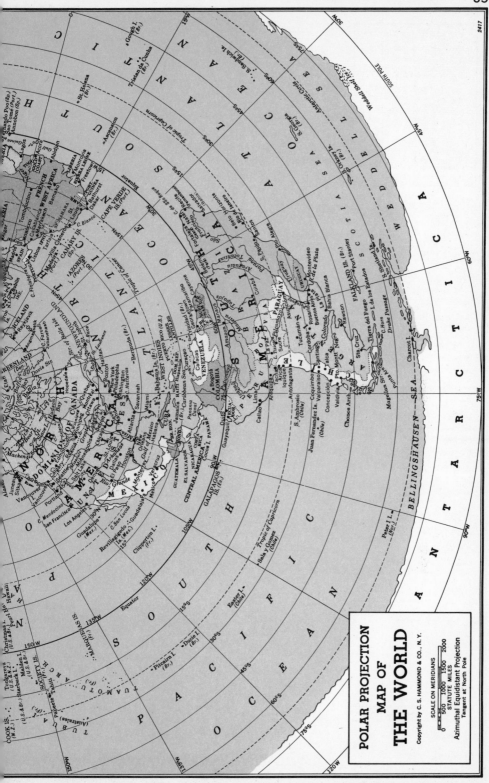

POLAR PROJECTION
MAP OF
THE WORLD

Copyright by C. S. HAMMOND & CO., N. Y.

SCALE ON MERIDIANS

0   500 1000 1500 2000
STATUTE MILES
Azimuthal Equidistant Projection
Tangent at North Pole

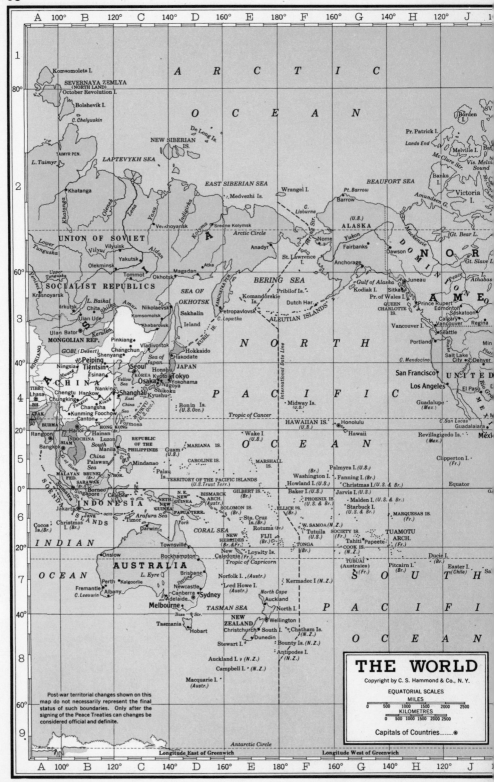

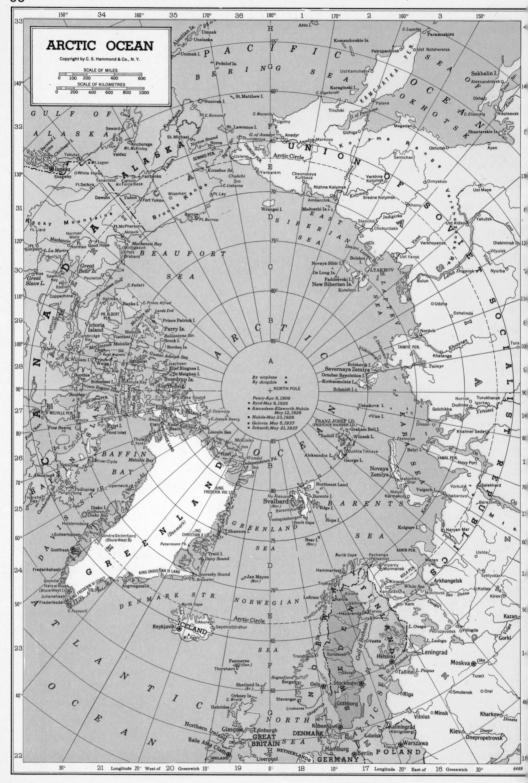

ARCTIC OCEAN

Copyright by C. S. Hammond & Co., N. Y.

SCALE OF MILES

0 100 200 400 600

SCALE OF KILOMETRES

0 200 400 600 800 1000

NORTH POLE

By airplane ■
By dirigible ●

- Peary—Apr. 6, 1909
- Byrd—May 9, 1926
- Amundsen-Ellsworth-Nobile May 12, 1926
- Nobile—May 23, 1928
- Golovin—May 5, 1937
- Schmidt, May 21, 1937

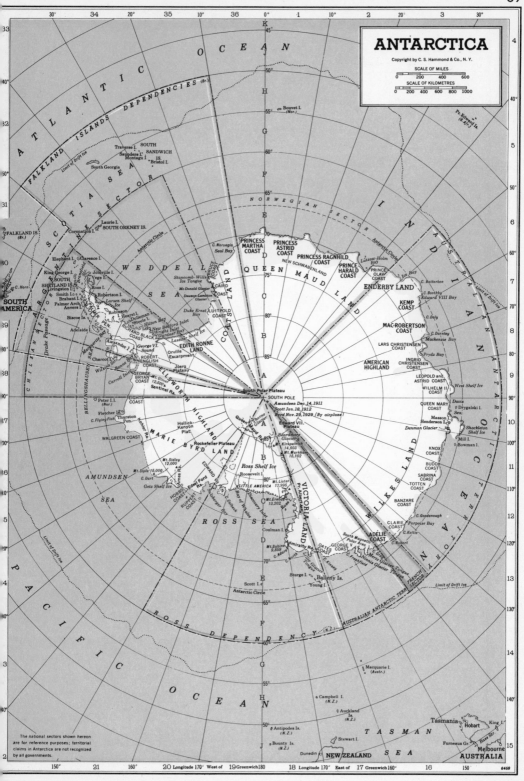

Post-war territorial changes shown on this map do not necessarily represent the final status of such boundaries. Only after the signing of the Peace Treaties can changes be considered official and definite.

ATLANTIC OCEAN

ICELAND
Reykjavík
Akureyri
Breidha Fjördhur
Húnaflói
Langanes
Seydhisfjördhur
Hornafjördhur

Arctic Circle

Jan Mayen
(Nor.)

Nord Kap

Vesterålen
Lofoten
Vestfjorden
Mosjøen

NORWAY

Trondheimsfjord
Namsos
Kristiansund
Trondheim
Ålesund
Sognefjord Lillehammer
Bergen
Hardangerfjord
Haugesund
Stavanger

Faeroe Is.
(Dan.)
Thorshavn

Shetland Is.
Lerwick

Orkney Is.
Kirkwall
Pentland Firth

Hebrides
The Minch

SCOTLAND
Inverness
Moray Firth
Aberdeen
Glasgow
Dundee
Edinburgh

BRITISH ISLES

GREAT BRITAIN

Drammen
Oslo
Fredrikstad
Larvik
Halden
Lindesnes
Kristiansand
Skagerrak

SWEDEN

Östersund
Sundsvall
Falun
Uppsala
Västerås
Örebro
Karlstad
Vänern

Göteborg
Borås Jönköping
Vättern

NORTH SEA

DENMARK
Aalborg
Århus
Esbjerg
Odense
København
Malmö
Helsingborg
Lund

Kattegat
Halsingborg
Bornholm

BALTIC

Kiel
Lübeck
Rostock
Hamburg
Stralsund
Szczecin
(Stettin)

Donegal Bay
IRELAND
Galway
Baile Átha Cliath
(Dublin)
Limerick
Waterford
Cork
Cobh
C. Clear

NO. IRELAND
Belfast
Dundalk

IRISH SEA

Carlisle
Newcastle
Leeds
Hull

Manchester
Liverpool
Sheffield

WALES
Swansea Cardiff
St. George's Chan.

ENGLAND
Birmingham
Bristol
LONDON
The Wash
Gravesend
Amsterdam
The Hague
Frisian Is.
Helgoland
Bremen
Hannover
Magdeburg
BERLIN

NETHERLANDS
Rotterdam
Gent
Antwerp
BELGIUM
Bruxelles
Aachen Köln
Bonn
Essen Dortmund
Düsseldorf

GERMANY
Leipzig
Dresden
Erfurt
Chemnitz

CZECHOSLOVAKIA
Praha
(Prague)
Plzeň
Olomouc

Plymouth
Southampton Portsmouth
Lands End
English Channel
Cherbourg
Le Havre
Amiens

Lille
Calais
Boulogne

LUX.
Mainz
Frankfurt
Mannheim
Wiesbaden
Karlsruhe
Stuttgart
Nürnberg
Regensburg
Augsburg
München
Linz
WIEN
(Vienna)
Salzburg
AUSTRIA
Graz

Channel Is.
(Br.)
Brest
Rennes
St. Nazaire
Nantes
Belle Isle

FRANCE

Versailles
PARIS
Reims
Nancy
Saarbrücken
Strasbourg
Mulhouse
Basel
Zürich
Bern
Freiburg
Bodensee
Innsbruck
Bolzano
Trento

SWITZERLAND

Bay of Biscay

La Rochelle
Île d'Oléron
Limoges
Tours
Orléans
Angers
Loire
Dijon
Vichy
Lyon
Grenoble
Mt. Blanc
Genève
Torino
Milano
Verona
Venezia
(Venice)
Trieste
Ljubljana

El Ferrol
La Coruña
C. Finisterre
Vigo
Porto
(Oporto)
Coimbra

Gijón
Oviedo
Santander
San Sebastián
Biarritz
Bayonne
Bordeaux
Garonne
Dordogne
Bilbao
León
Burgos
Zaragoza

Clermont-Ferrand
St. Étienne
Montauban
Toulouse
Pyrenees
ANDORRA
Nîmes
Montpellier
G. du Lion
Marseille
Toulon
Nice
MONACO
Genova
La Spezia
Parma
Bologna
Ferrara
Firenze
(Florence)
Livorno
(Leghorn)
Siena
SAN MARINO
Ancona
Zadar
Zagreb
Rijeka
(Fiume)

YUGOSLAVIA
Banja Luka
Split

PORTUGAL

Lisboa
(Lisbon)
Setúbal
Évora
Guadiana
Badajoz

Duero
Valladolid
Salamanca
Sa. de Guadarrama
MADRID
Toledo
SPAIN
Tagus

Barcelona
Tarragona

Corse
(Corsica)
Elba
Ajaccio

ROMA

VATICAN
CITY

ITALY

C. São Vicente

Córdoba
Sierra Morena
Albacete
Valencia
Balearic Is.
Menorca
Palma
Mallorca
(Majorca)
Ibiza

Sassari
Terranova
Sardegna
(Sardinia)

Foggia
Napoli
(Naples)
Vesuvio
Taranto

G. of Cadiz
Sevilla
Jerez
Guadalquivir
Lorca
Cádiz
Málaga
Sa. Nevada
Granada
Murcia
Alicante
Cartagena
Almería

MEDITERRANEAN

Iglesias
Cagliari

TYRRHENIAN SEA

Palermo
Messina
Reggio
Sicilia
(Sicily)
Catania
Siracusa

Str. of Gibraltar
GIBRALTAR
(Br.)
TANGIER
(Internat. Zone)
Tetuán
MOROCCO

Alger
(Algiers)
Philippeville
Bizerte
Bône
C. Bon
Pantelleria

Malta (Br.)
Valletta

Port Lyautey
Casablanca
Rabat
Meknes
Fez
Melilla
Oran
Marrakech
(Morocco)
Biskra

MOROCCO
(Fr.)

ALGERIA
Constantine
Sousse
Tunis
TUNISIA

Longitude West D of Greenwich   0°   Longitude East E of Greenwich   10°

EUROPE

Copyright by C. S. HAMMOND & CO., N. Y.

SCALE OF MILES

SCALE OF KILOMETRES

Capitals of Countries	☆	Towns over 1,000,000	◉
International Boundaries	---	Towns of 500,000 - 1,000,000	●
Canals	·····	Towns of 100,000 - 500,000	●
		Towns of less than 100,000	○

7426

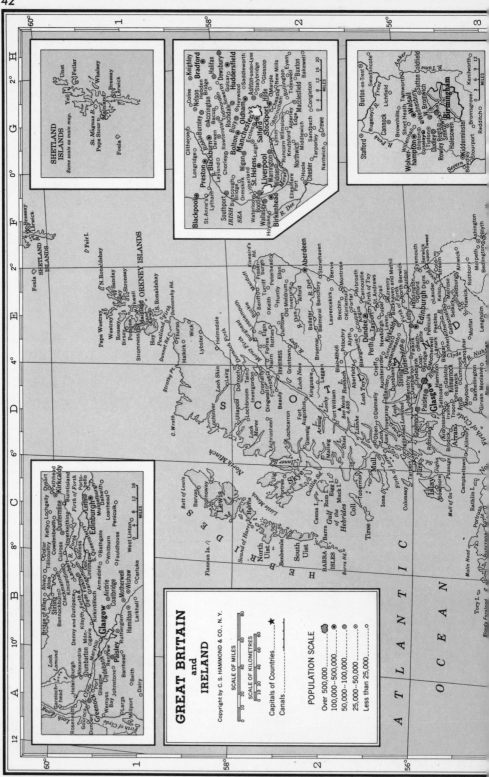

GREAT BRITAIN and IRELAND

Copyright by C. S. HAMMOND & CO., N. Y.

SCALE OF MILES

SCALE OF KILOMETRES

Capitals of Countries ·········· ★

Canals ··········

POPULATION SCALE

Over 500,000 ············
100,000–500,000 ············
50,000–100,000 ············
25,000–50,000 ············
Less than 25,000 ············

SHETLAND ISLANDS

Same scale as main map.

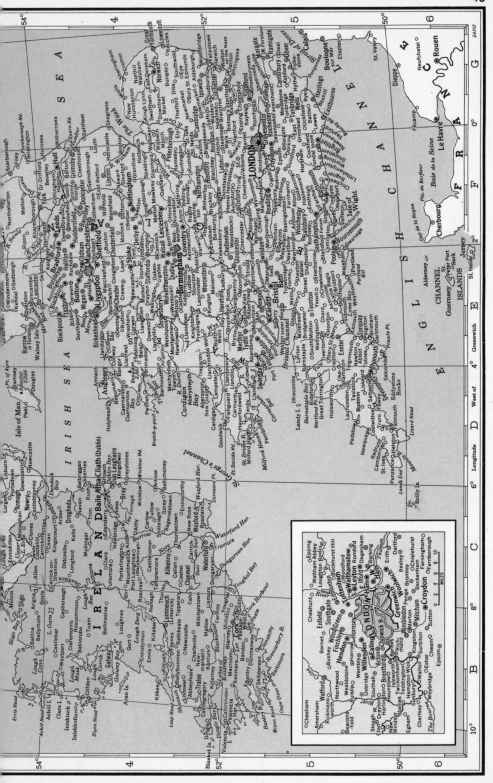

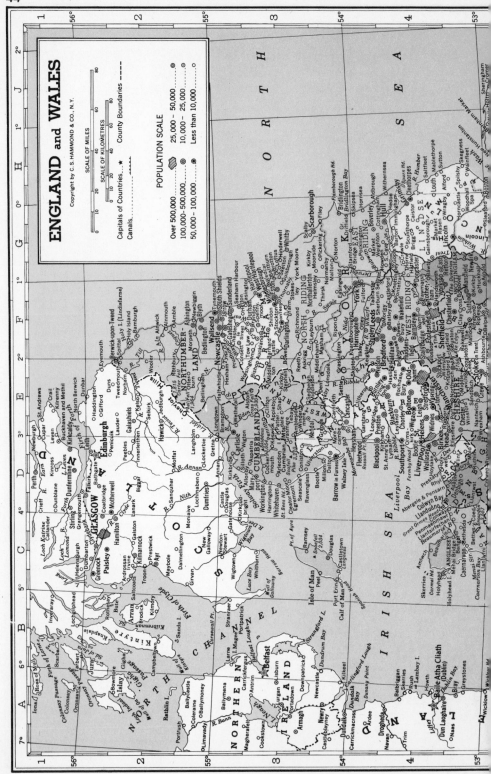

ENGLAND and WALES

Copyright by C. S. HAMMOND & CO., N.Y.

SCALE OF MILES

SCALE OF KILOMETRES

Capitals of Countries... ★
Canals.................. ----

County Boundaries ----

POPULATION SCALE

Over 500,000
100,000–500,000
50,000–100,000
25,000–50,000
10,000–25,000
Less than 10,000

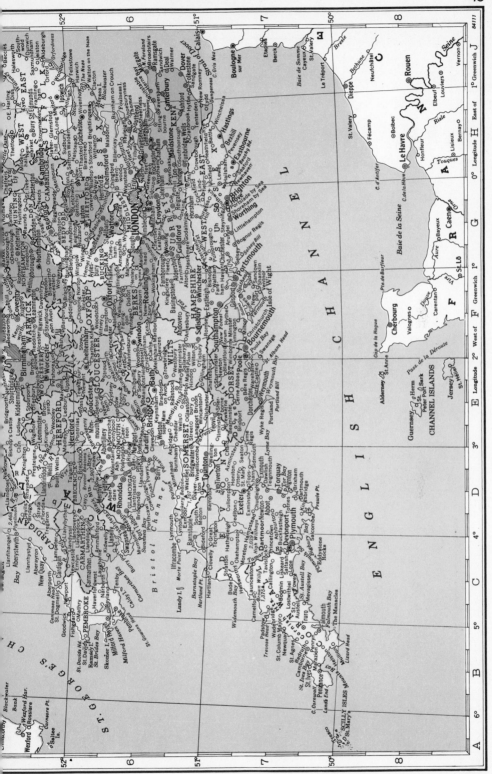

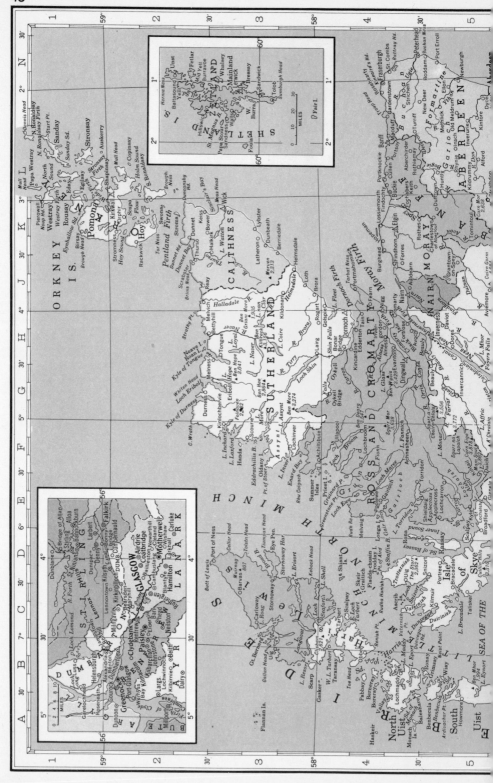

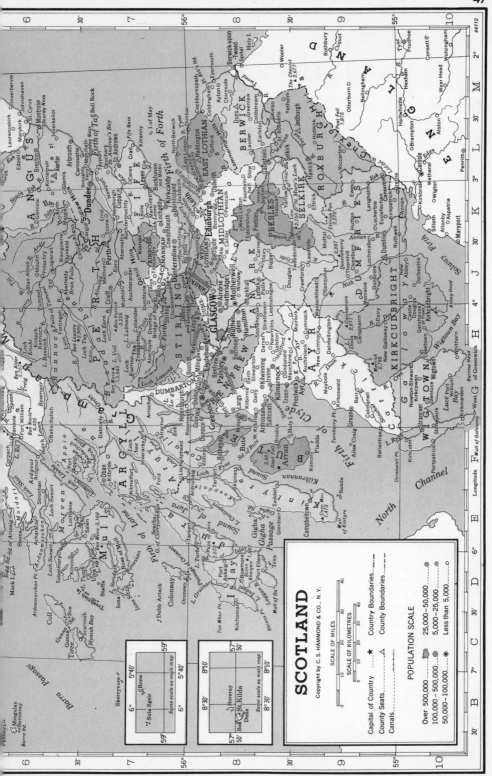

SCOTLAND

Copyright by C. S. HAMMOND & CO., N.Y.

SCALE OF MILES

SCALE OF KILOMETRES

POPULATION SCALE

Capital of Country

County Seats

Canals

Over 500,000

100,000 – 500,000

50,000 – 100,000

25,000 – 50,000

5,000 – 25,000

Less than 5,000

Country Boundaries

County Boundaries

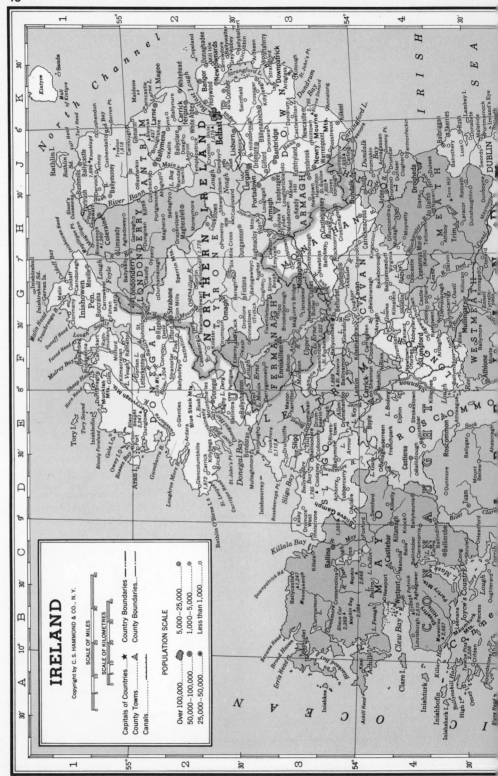

IRELAND

Copyright by C. S. HAMMOND & CO., N. Y.

SCALE OF MILES

SCALE OF KILOMETRES

Capitals of Countries....★
County Towns............▲
Canals.................

Country Boundaries.....
County Boundaries......

POPULATION SCALE

Over 100,000.......◉
50,000-100,000.....◉
25,000-50,000......◉

5,000-25,000.......◉
1,000-5,000........◉
Less than 1,000....○

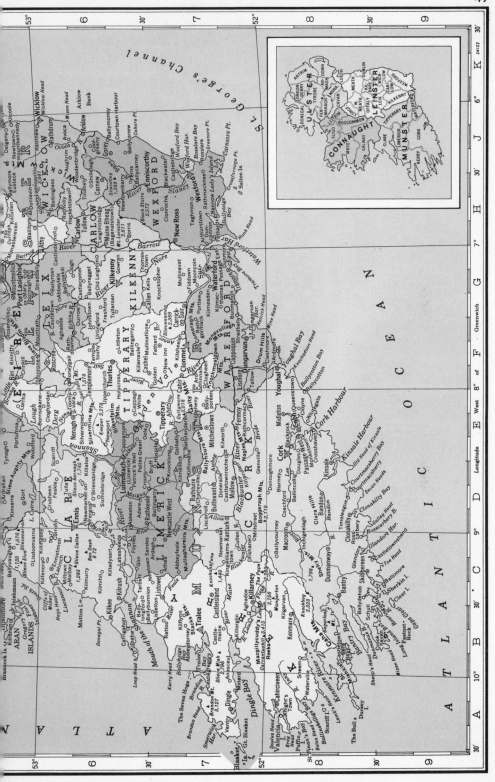

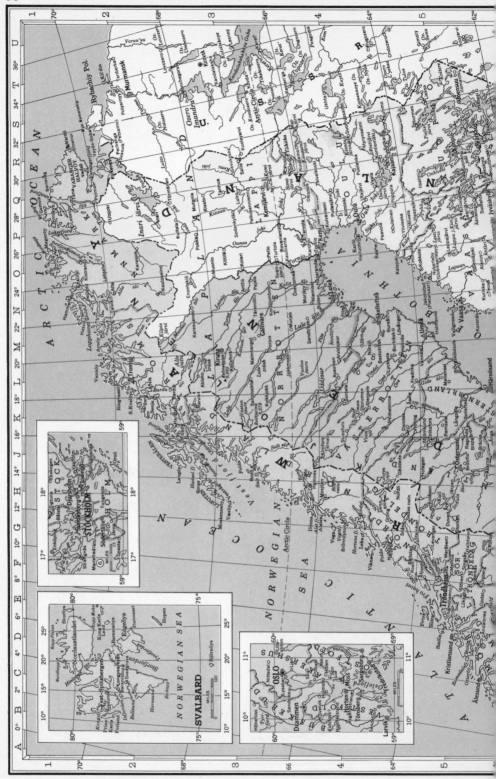

NORWAY, SWEDEN, FINLAND and DENMARK

Copyright by C. S. HAMMOND & CO., N.Y.

SCALE OF MILES

SCALE OF KILOMETRES

Capitals of Countries .... ★
Administrative Centers .... ▲
International Boundaries .... —·—·—
Internal Boundaries .... —··—··—
Canals ....
Railroads ....

POPULATION SCALE

Over 100,000
50,000-100,000
25,000-50,000
10,000-25,000
5,000-10,000
Less than 5,000

SUBDIVISIONS
Indicated by Numbers:
Fylker in NORWAY
1 Akershus G6
2 Vestfold G7
3 Östfold G7
Län in SWEDEN
4 Göteborg och G7
  Bohus
5 Västmanland K7
6 Södermanland K7
7 Östergötland J7
8 Malmöhus H9
9 Kristianstad J8

GERMANY

Copyright by C. S. HAMMOND & CO., N.Y.

Scale

KILOMETERS

MILES

Capitals of Countries....✪   International Boundaries....------

Land Capitals............△   Land Boundaries............-----

Canals..................

ZONES OF OCCUPATION

American   French

British   Soviet

Joint Administration

THE RUHR BASIN

GREATER BERLIN

BALTIC SEA

Bornholm
(To Denmark)

POLAND

WARSZAWA

Wrocław
(Breslau)

Poznań

Łódź

Katowice

CZECHOSLOVAKIA

Düsseldorf

484107

East of F Greenwich 16° G 18° H 20° J

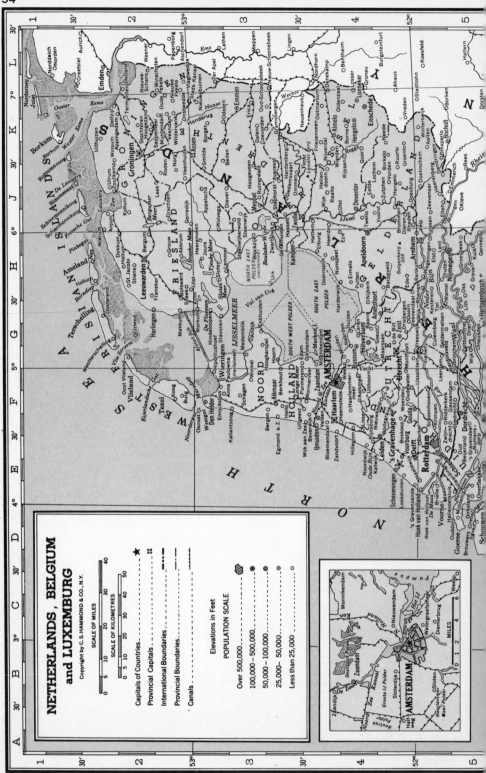

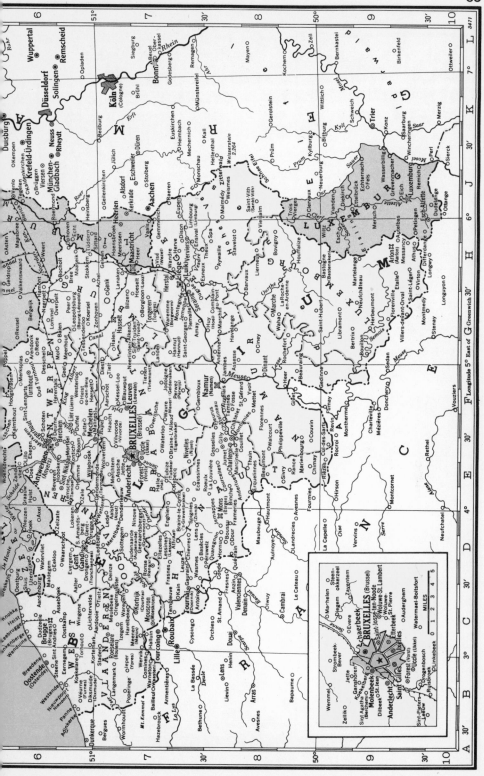

56

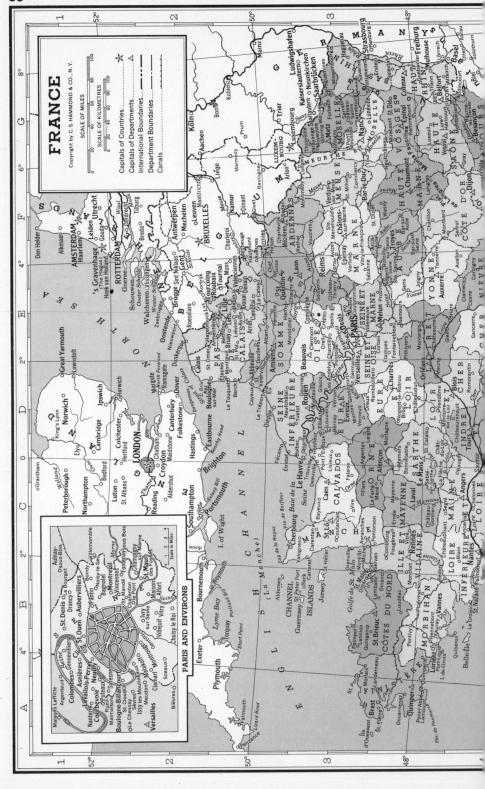

PARIS AND ENVIRONS

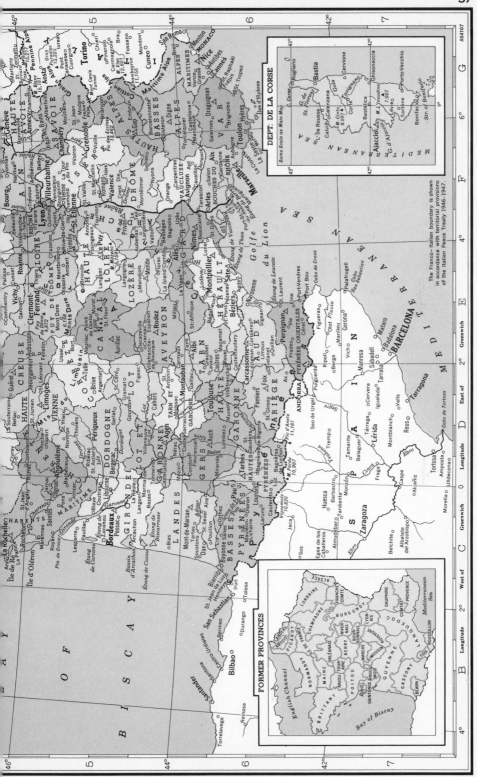

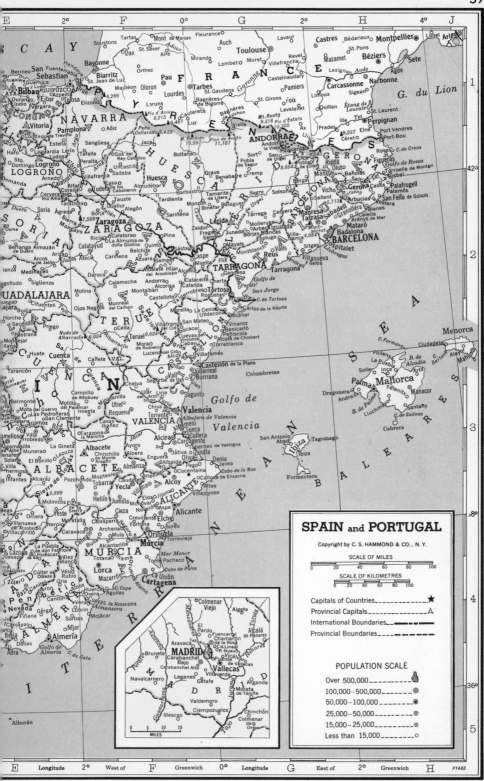

SPAIN and PORTUGAL

Copyright by C. S. HAMMOND & CO., N.Y.

SCALE OF MILES

0   20   40   60   80   100

SCALE OF KILOMETRES

0   20   40   60   80   100

Capitals of Countries _____ ★
Provincial Capitals _____ △
International Boundaries _____
Provincial Boundaries _____

POPULATION SCALE

Over 500,000 _____
100,000--500,000 _____
50,000--100,000 _____
25,000--50,000 _____
15,000--25,000 _____
Less than 15,000 _____

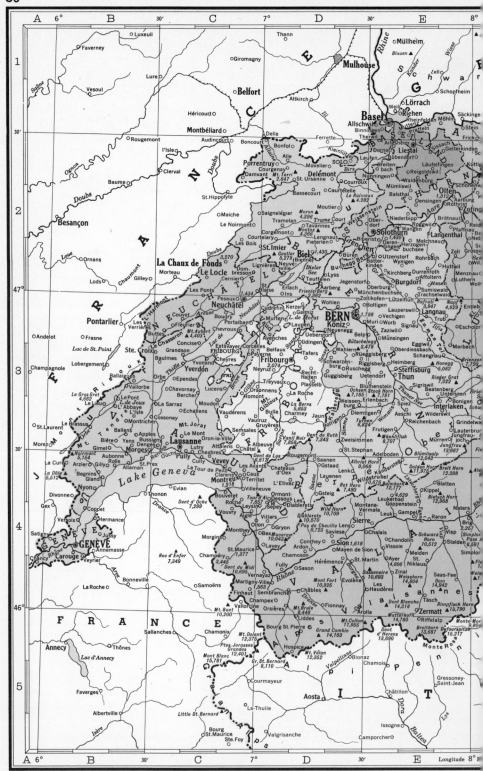

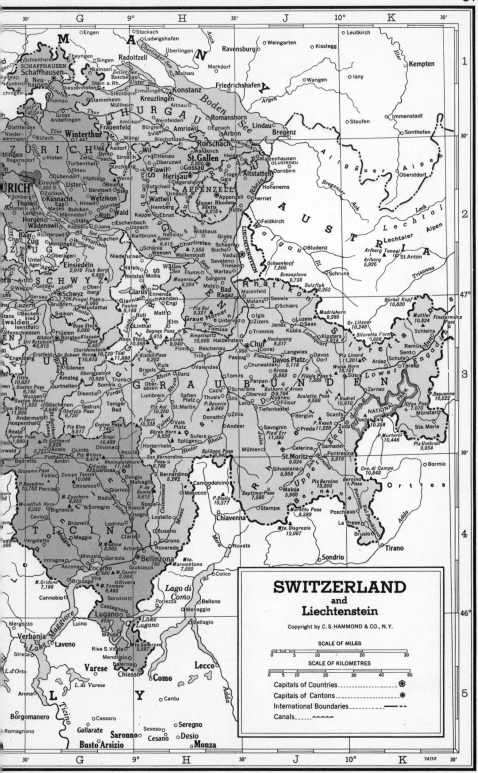

SWITZERLAND
and
Liechtenstein

Copyright by C.S. HAMMOND & CO., N.Y.

SCALE OF MILES

SCALE OF KILOMETRES

Capitals of Countries	⊛
Capitals of Cantons	◉
International Boundaries	------
Canals	

74110

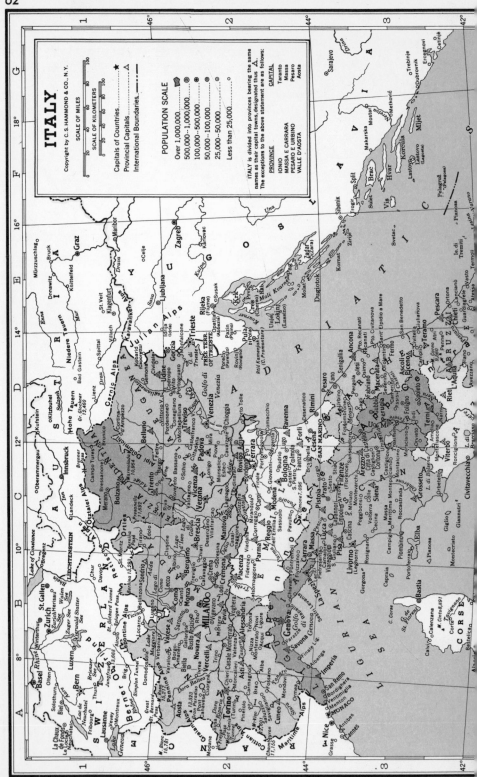

ITALY

Copyright by C. S. HAMMOND & CO., N. Y.

SCALE OF MILES

SCALE OF KILOMETERS

Capitals of Countries................ ★
Provincial Capitals................ △
International Boundaries............. ——————

POPULATION SCALE

Over 1,000,000.............
500,000–1,000,000.........
100,000–500,000...........
50,000–100,000............
25,000–50,000.............
Less than 25,000..........

ITALY is divided into provinces bearing the same
names as their capital towns, designated thus △.
The exceptions to the above statement are as follows:

PROVINCE	CAPITAL
IONIO	Taranto
MASSA E CARRARA	Massa
PESARO E URBINO	Pesaro
VALLE D'AOSTA	Aosta

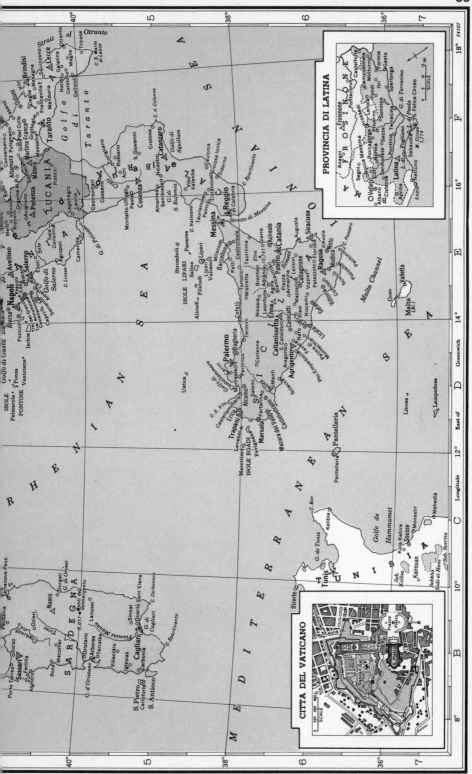

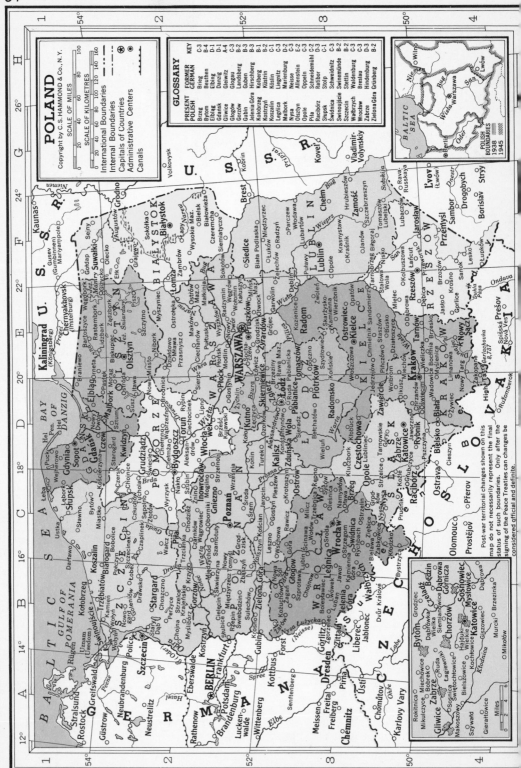

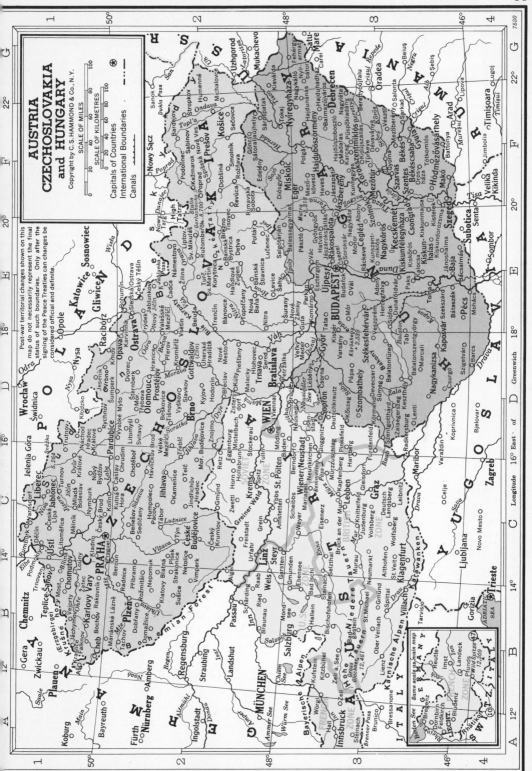

AUSTRIA
CZECHOSLOVAKIA
and HUNGARY

Copyright by C. S. HAMMOND & Co., N.Y.

SCALE OF MILES

SCALE OF KILOMETRES

Capitals of Countries ⊕
International Boundaries ___.___
Canals

Post-war territorial changes shown on this map do not necessarily represent the final status of such boundaries. Only after the signing of the Peace Treaties can changes be considered official and definite.

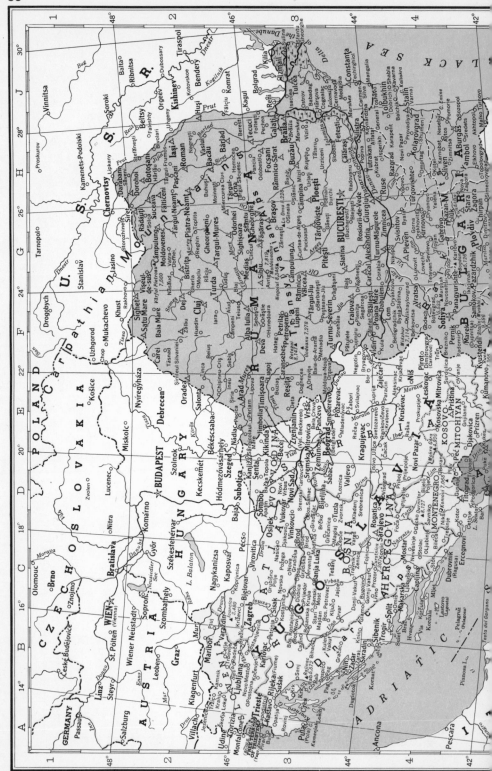

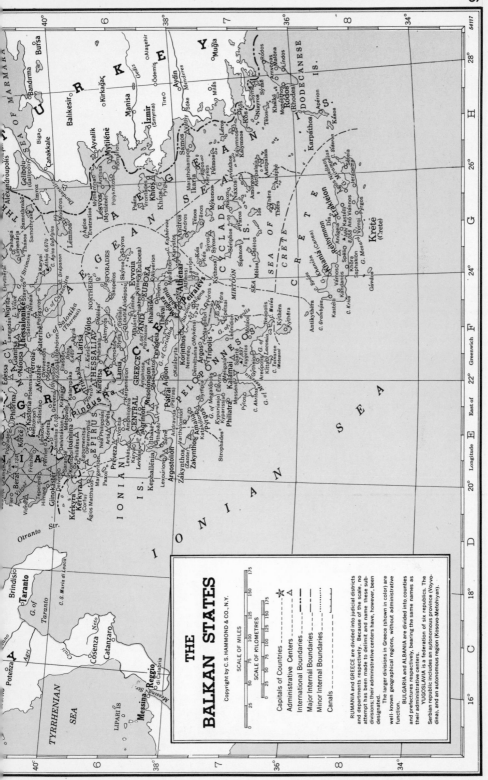

THE
BALKAN STATES

Copyright by C. S. HAMMOND & CO., N.Y.

SCALE OF MILES

SCALE OF KILOMETRES

Capitals of Countries	
Administrative Centers	
International Boundaries	
Major Internal Boundaries	
Minor Internal Boundaries	
Canals	

RUMANIA and GREECE are divided into judicial districts and departments respectively. Because of the scale, no attempt has been made to delimit and name these subdivisions; their administrative centers have, however, been designated. The larger divisions in Greece (shown in color) are well-known geographical regions, without administrative function.

BULGARIA and ALBANIA are divided into counties and prefectures respectively, bearing the same names as their administrative centers.

YUGOSLAVIA is a federation of six republics. The Serbian republic includes an autonomous province (Voyvodina), and an autonomous region (Kosovo-Metohiyan).

54117

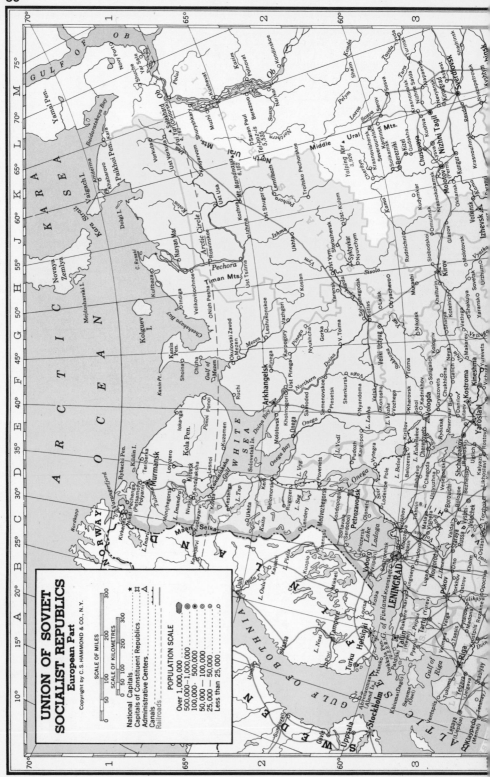

UNION OF SOVIET SOCIALIST REPUBLICS
European Part
Copyright by C.S. HAMMOND & CO., N.Y.

SCALE OF MILES

SCALE OF KILOMETRES

National Capitals .... ★
Capitals of Constituent Republics .... ◬
Administrative Centers ....
Canals ....
Railroads ....

POPULATION SCALE

Over 1,000,000
500,000—1,000,000
100,000— 500,000
50,000— 100,000
25,000— 50,000
Less than 25,000

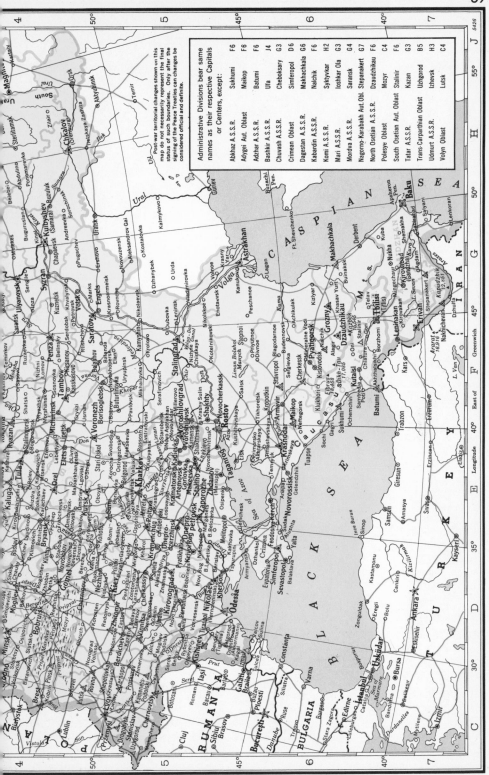

Post-war territorial changes shown on this map do not necessarily represent the final status of such boundaries. Only after the signing of the Peace Treaties can changes be considered official and definite.

Administrative Divisions bear same names as their respective Capitals or Centers, except:

Abkhaz A.S.S.R.	Sukhumi	F6
Adygei Aut. Oblast	Maikop	F6
Adzhar A.S.S.R.	Batumi	F6
Bashkir A.S.S.R.	Ufa	J4
Chuvash Oblast	Cheboksary	G3
Crimean Oblast	Simferopol	D6
Dagestan A.S.S.R.	Makhachkala	G6
Kabardin A.S.S.R.	Nalchik	F6
Komi A.S.S.R.	Syktyvkar	H2
Mari A.S.S.R.	Ioshkar Ola	G3
Mordva A.S.S.R.	Saransk	G4
Nagorno-Karabakh Aut. Obl.	Stepanakert	G7
North Osetian A.S.S.R.	Dzaudzhikau	G4
Polesye Oblast	Mozyr	C4
South Osetian Aut. Oblast	Stalinir	F6
Tatar A.S.S.R.	Kazan	G3
Trans-Carpathian Oblast	Uzhgorod	B5
Udmurt A.S.S.R.	Izhevsk	H3
Volyn Oblast	Lutsk	C4

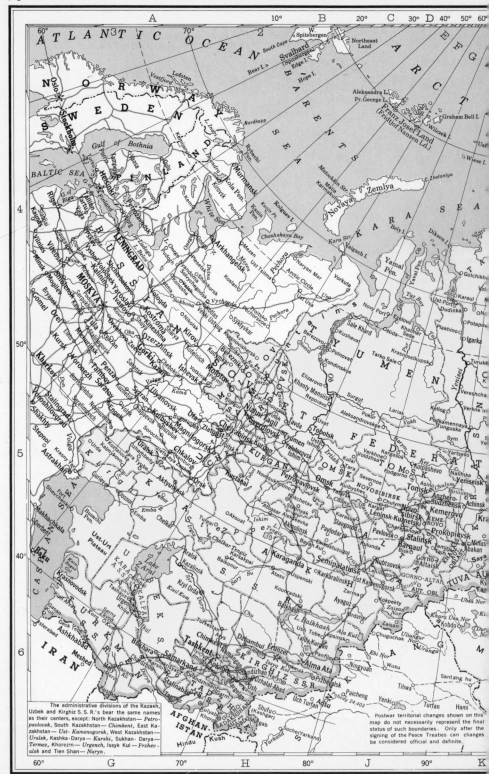

The administrative divisions of the Kazakh, Uzbek and Kirghiz S. S. R.'s bear the same names as their centers, except: North Kazakhstan— *Petropavlovsk*, South Kazakhstan— *Chimkent*, East Kazakhstan— *Ust-Kamenogorsk*, West Kazakhstan— *Uralsk*, Kashka-Darya— *Karshi*, Sukhan-Darya— *Termez*, Khorezm— *Urgench*, Issyk Kul— *Przhevalsk* and Tien Shan— *Naryn*.

Postwar territorial changes shown on this map do not necessarily represent the final status of such boundaries. Only after the signing of the Peace Treaties can changes be considered official and definite.

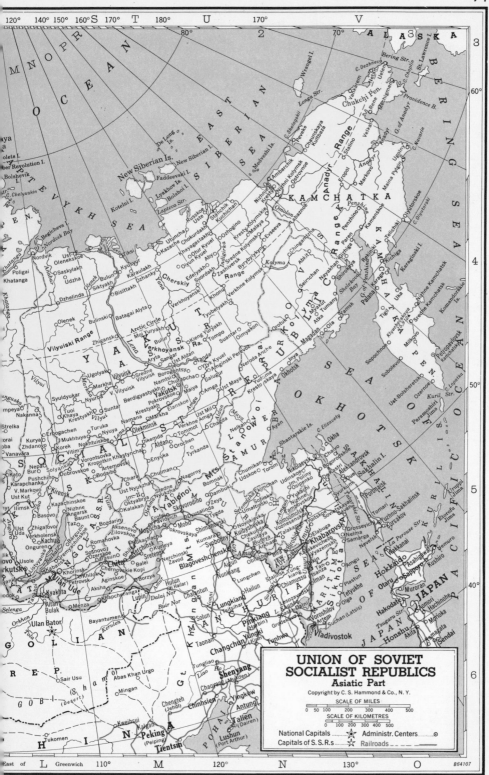

UNION OF SOVIET
SOCIALIST REPUBLICS
Asiatic Part

Copyright by C. S. Hammond & Co., N. Y.

SCALE OF MILES
0 50 100   200   300   400   500

SCALE OF KILOMETRES
0 100 200 300 400 500

National Capitals .... ☆   Administr. Centers .... ⊚
Capitals of S.S.R.s .... ★   Railroads .... ——

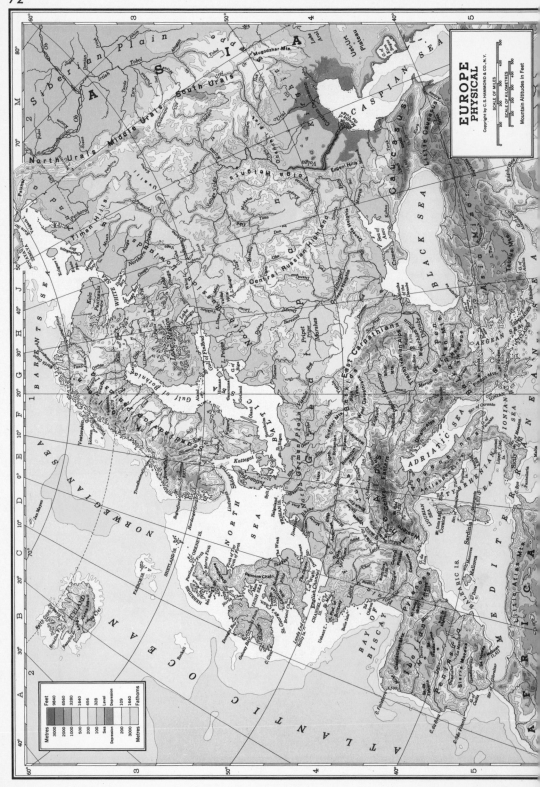

EUROPE
PHYSICAL

Copyright by C. S. HAMMOND & CO., N.Y.

SCALE OF MILES

SCALE OF KILOMETRES

Mountain Altitudes in Feet

Metres	Feet	Fathoms
3000	9840	
2000	6560	
1000	3280	
500	1640	
200	656	
100	328	
Sea	Level	
Depression	Depression	
200	109	
3000	1640	
Metres		Fathoms

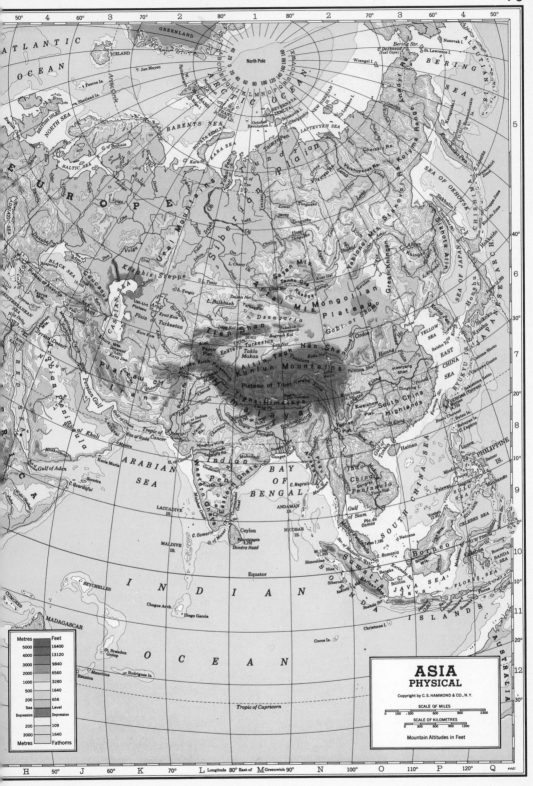

ASIA
PHYSICAL

Copyright by C. S. HAMMOND & CO., N.Y.

SCALE OF MILES
0   150   300   600   900   1200

SCALE OF KILOMETRES
0   300   600   900   1200

Mountain Altitudes in Feet

Metres	Feet
5000	16400
4000	13120
3000	9840
2000	6560
1000	3280
500	1640
200	656
Sea	Level
Depression	Depression
200	109
3000	1640
Metres	Fathoms

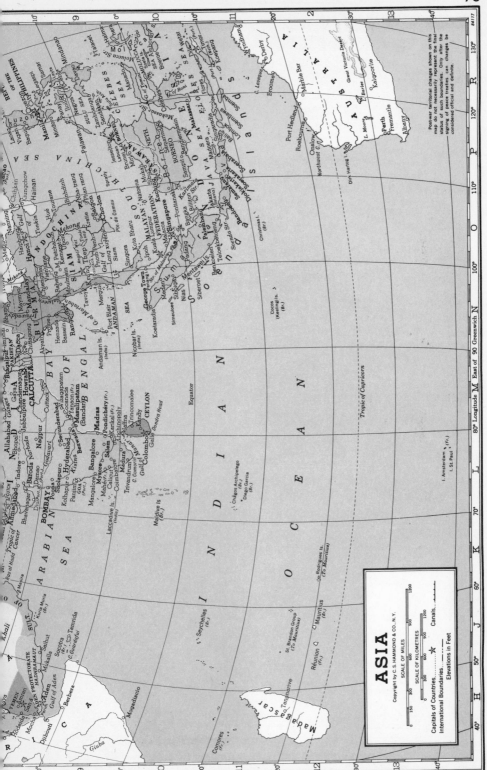

ASIA

Copyright by C. S. HAMMOND & CO., N.Y.

SCALE OF MILES

SCALE OF KILOMETRES

Capitals of Countries............... Canals.............
International Boundaries...........
Elevations in Feet

Postwar territorial changes shown on this map do not necessarily represent the final status of such boundaries. Only after the signing of peace treaties can changes be considered official and definite.

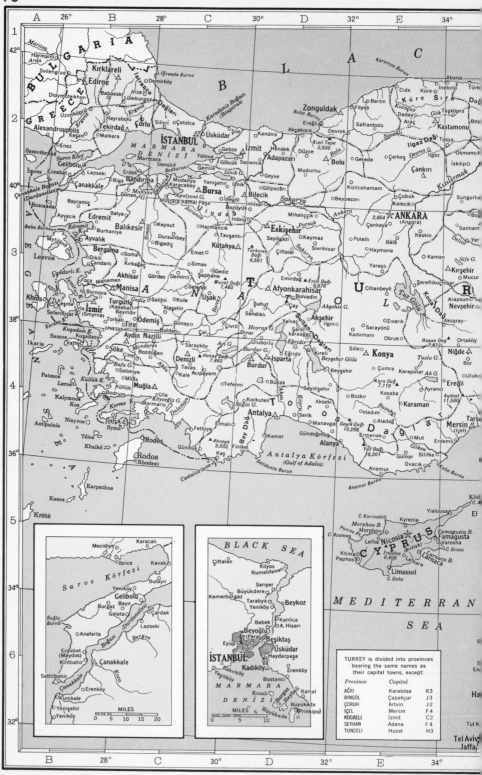

| A | 26° | B | 28° | C | 30° | D | 32° | E | 34° |

B L A C K

BULGARIA

Kırklareli
İğneada Burnu
Edirne
Harmanlık
Svilengrad
Arda
Maritsa
Didymoteikhon
Demirköy

GREECE

Uzunköprü
Hayrabolu
Tekirdağ
Çorlu
Silivri
Çatalca
Keşan
Makara
Alexandroupolis
Enez

Zonguldak
Filyos
Ereğli
Bartın
Safranbolu
Akçakoca
Devrek
Düzce
Bolu

Küre Sıra Dağı
Cide
Küre
İnebolu
Kastamonu
Daday
Araç
Taşköprü
Gök
Boy
Tosya
İğaz Dağı

Saros Körf.
Samothráke
İmroz
Gelibolu
Lapseki
Erdek
Çanakkale
Bozcaada

MARMARA DENİZİ
İSTANBUL
Üsküdar
Şile
Kandıra
İzmit
Hendek
Adapazarı
Sapanca
Geyve
Mudurnu
Gerede
Çerkeş
Çankırı
İskilip
Osmancık

Ankara
2,854
Çankaya
ANKARA (Angora)
Kalecik
Beypazarı
Kızılcahamam
Çubuk

MEDITERRANEAN SEA

Inset (lower left):
Saros Körfezi
Mecidiye
Karacalı
İbrice
Kavak
Yeniköy
Bulayır
Gelibolu
Bayır
Burgaz
Galata
Çardak
Lapseki
Anafarta
Bergos
Eceabat (Maydos)
Kilitbahir
Settilbahir
Çanakkale
Kumkale
Yenişehir
Yeniköy
MILES 0 5 10 15 20

Inset (center):
BLACK SEA
Çiftalan
Kilyos
Rumelifeneri
Kemerburgaz
Sarıyer
Büyükdere
Tarabya
Yeniköy
Beykoz
Bebek
Kanlıca
A. Hisarı
Beyoğlu (Pera)
Beşiktaş
Eyüp
Üsküdar
İSTANBUL
Haydarpaşa
Kadıköy
Erenköy
Bostancı
MARMARA DENİZİ
Kınalı
Burgaz
Heybeli
Büyükada (Prinkipo)
MILES 0 5 10

Inset (lower right box):
TURKEY is divided into provinces bearing the same names as their capital towns, except:

Province	Capital	
AĞRI	Karaköse	K3
BİNGÖL	Çapakçur	J3
ÇORUH	Artvin	J2
İÇEL	Mersin	F4
KOCAELİ	İzmit	C2
SEYHAN	Adana	F4
TUNCELİ	Hozat	H3

| B | 28° | C | 30° | D | 32° | E | 34° |

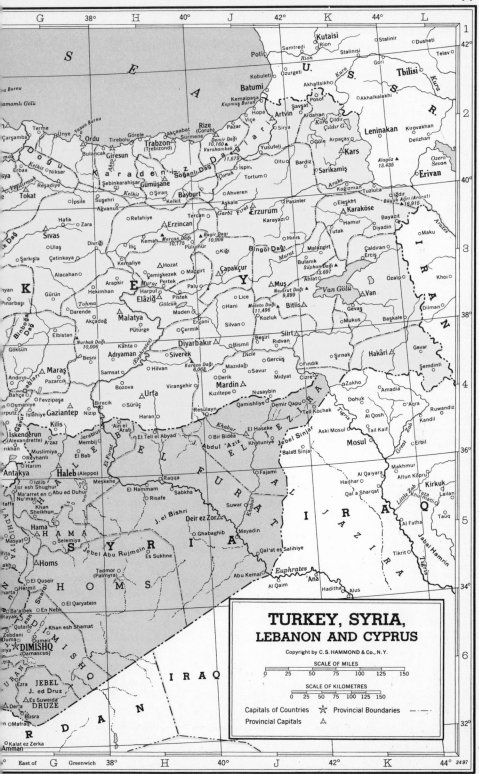

**TURKEY, SYRIA,
LEBANON AND CYPRUS**

Copyright by C.S. HAMMOND & Co., N.Y.

SCALE OF MILES

0   25   50   75   100   125   150

SCALE OF KILOMETRES

0   25   50   75   100   125   150

Capitals of Countries   ★   Provincial Boundaries — ·— ·—

Provincial Capitals   △

East of   G   Greenwich   38°   H   40°   J   42°   K   44°   3497

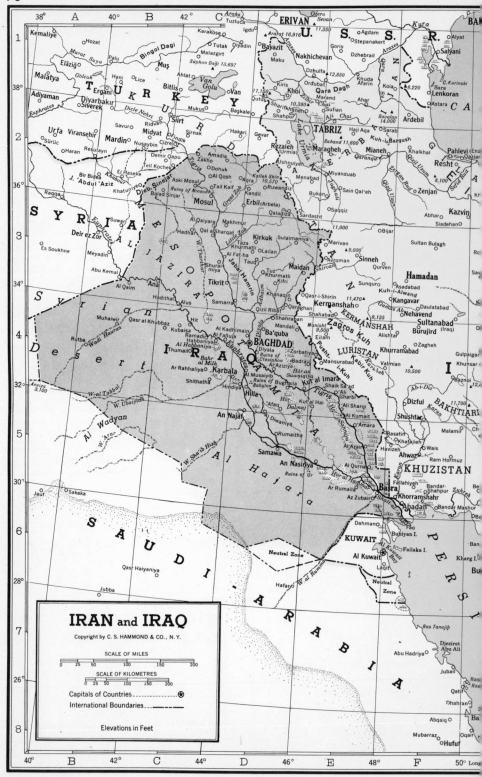

IRAN and IRAQ

Copyright by C. S. HAMMOND & CO., N. Y.

SCALE OF MILES

0 25 50   100   150   200

SCALE OF KILOMETRES

0 25 50   100   150   200

Capitals of Countries .... ⊛

International Boundaries ...... — · — · —

Elevations in Feet

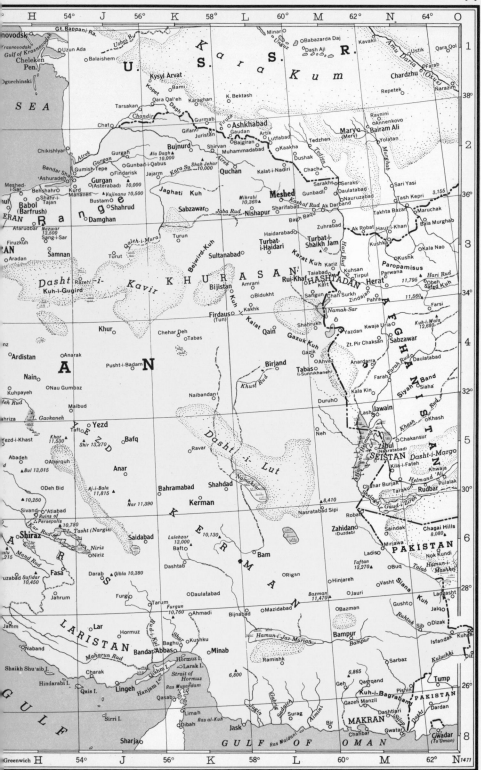

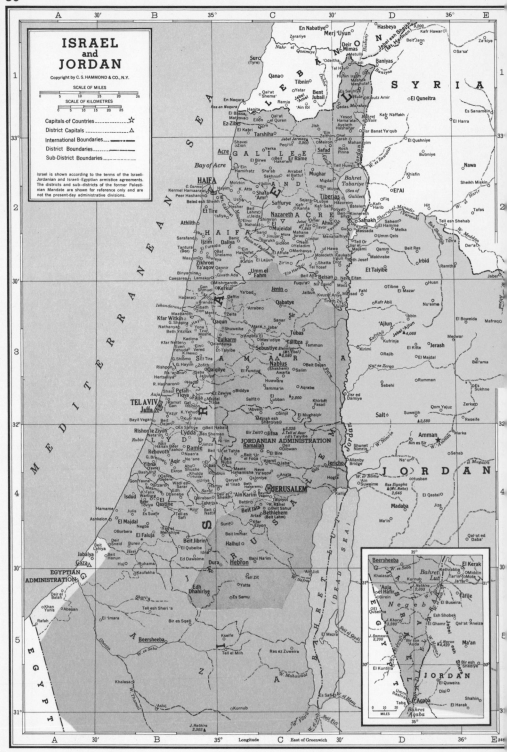

ISRAEL and JORDAN

Copyright by C. S. HAMMOND & CO., N.Y.

SCALE OF MILES

0 5 10 15 20 25

SCALE OF KILOMETRES

0 5 10 15 20 25

Capitals of Countries .... ☆
District Capitals .... △
International Boundaries ....
District Boundaries ....
Sub-District Boundaries ....

Israel is shown according to the terms of the Israeli-
Jordanian and Israeli-Egyptian armistice agreements.
The districts and sub-districts of the former Pales-
tinian Mandate are shown for reference only and are
not the present-day administrative divisions.

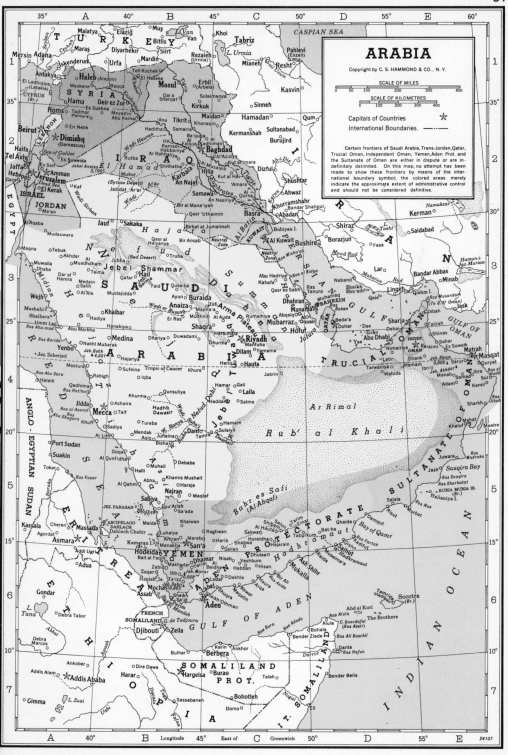

ARABIA

Copyright by C. S. HAMMOND & CO., N. Y.

SCALE OF MILES

SCALE OF KILOMETRES

Capitals of Countries .... ☆
International Boundaries. .... — · — · —

Certain frontiers of Saudi Arabia, Trans-Jordan, Qatar, Trucial Oman, Independent Oman, Yemen, Aden Prot. and the Sultanate of Oman are either in dispute or are in-definitely delimited. On this map, no attempt has been made to show these frontiers by means of the inter-national boundary symbol; the colored areas merely indicate the approximate extent of administrative control and should not be considered definitive.

CASPIAN SEA

24107

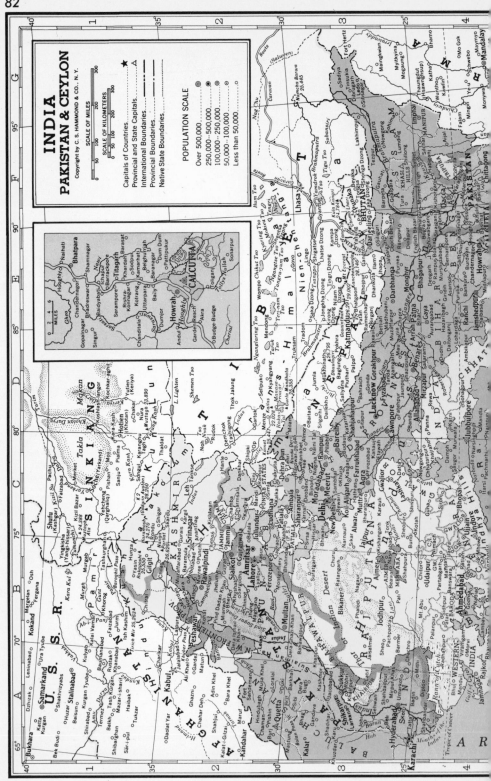

INDIA PAKISTAN & CEYLON

Copyright by C. S. HAMMOND & CO., N.Y.

SCALE OF MILES

SCALE OF KILOMETERS

Capitals of Countries.................. ★
Provincial and State Capitals......... ⊛
International Boundaries...............
Provincial Boundaries.................
Native State Boundaries...............

POPULATION SCALE

Over 500,000.................... ◉
250,000–500,000................ ◉
100,000–250,000................ ◉
50,000–100,000................. ◉
Less than 50,000............... ○

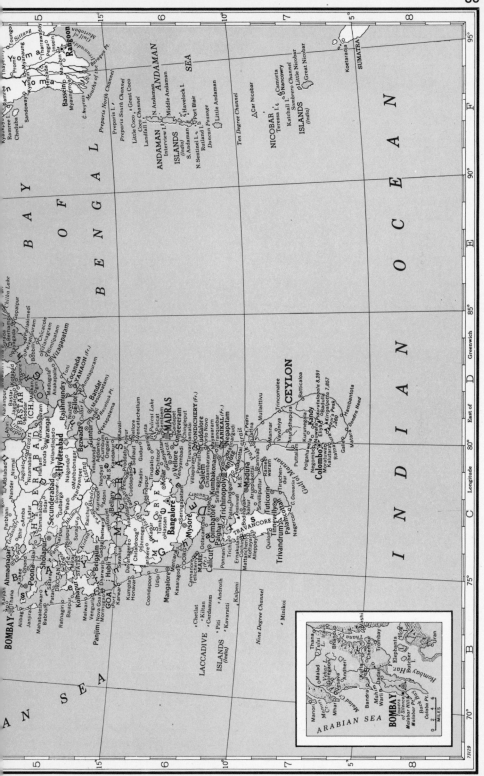

ARABIAN SEA

BOMBAY

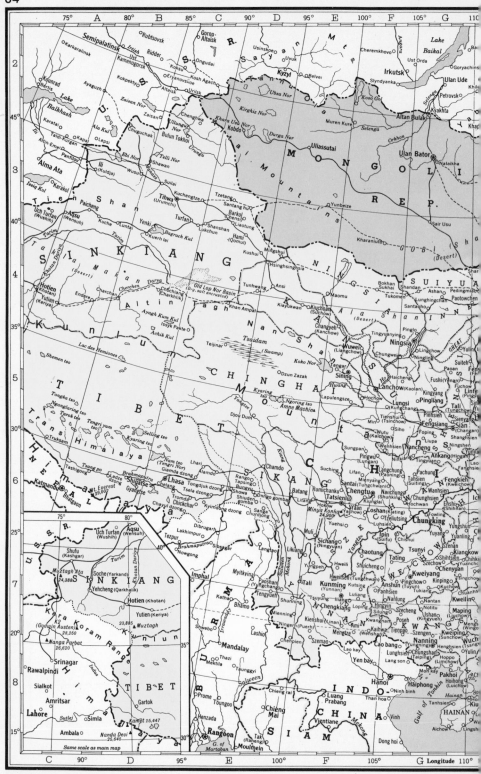

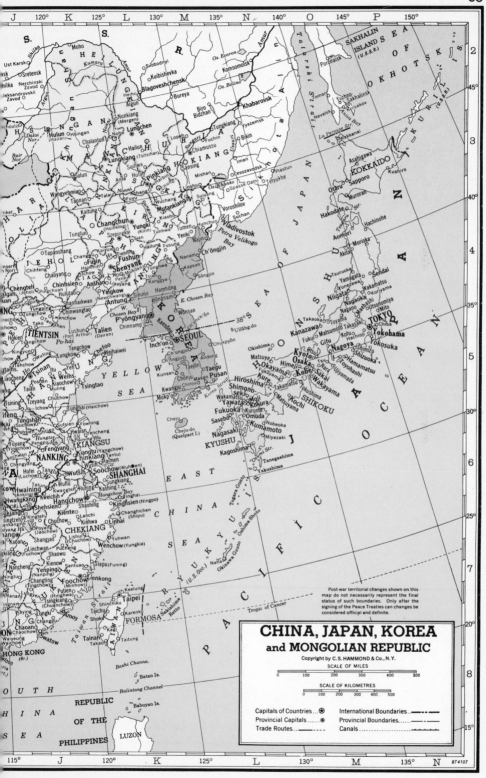

CHINA, JAPAN, KOREA
and MONGOLIAN REPUBLIC

Copyright by C. S. HAMMOND & Co., N.Y.

SCALE OF MILES

0   100   200   300   400   500

SCALE OF KILOMETRES

0   100   200   300   400   500

Post-war territorial changes shown on this map do not necessarily represent the final status of such boundaries. Only after the signing of the Peace Treaties can changes be considered official and definite.

Capitals of Countries ....⊛   International Boundaries ......____
Provincial Capitals ......⊚   Provincial Boundaries ......___
Trade Routes ......_____   Canals ......_____

B7 4107

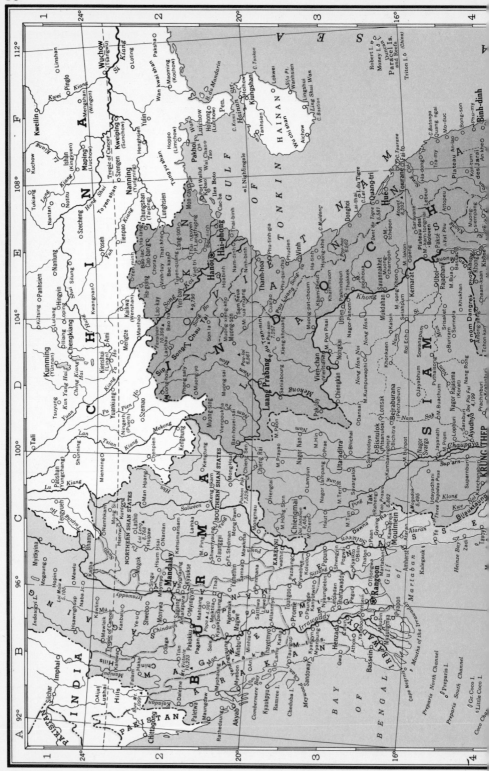

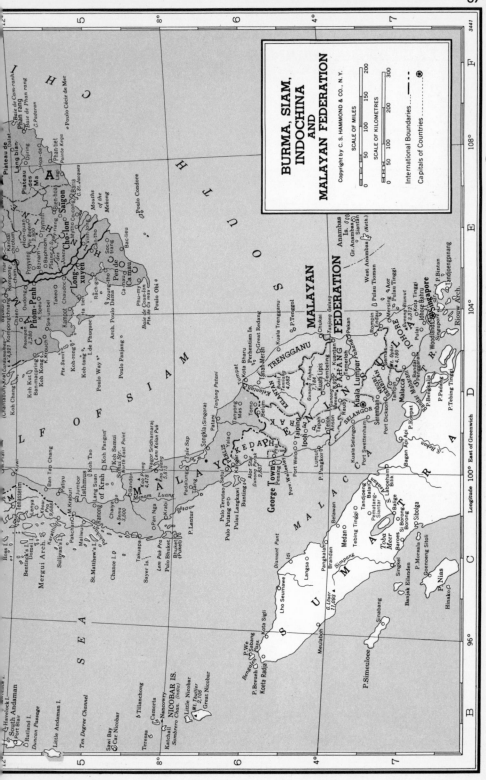

BURMA, SIAM,
AND
INDOCHINA
AND
MALAYAN FEDERATION

Copyright by C. S. HAMMOND & CO. N.Y.

SCALE OF MILES

SCALE OF KILOMETRES

International Boundaries
Capitals of Countries

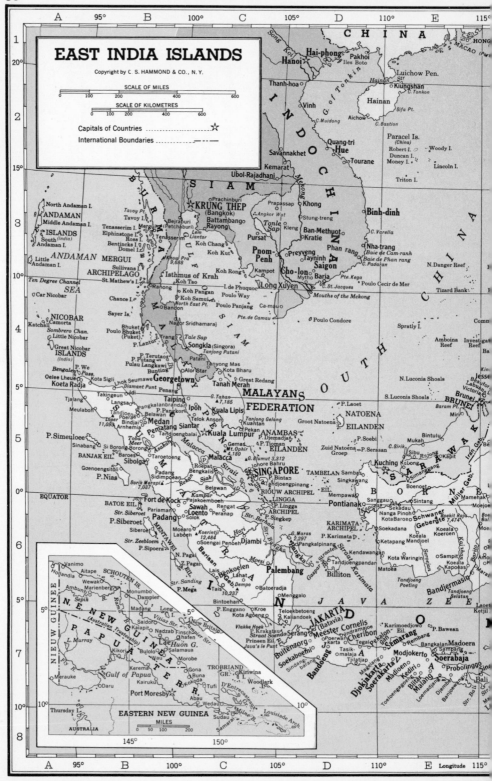

EAST INDIA ISLANDS

Copyright by C. S. HAMMOND & CO., N. Y.

SCALE OF MILES

SCALE OF KILOMETRES

Capitals of Countries .... ☆
International Boundaries .... — ·· —

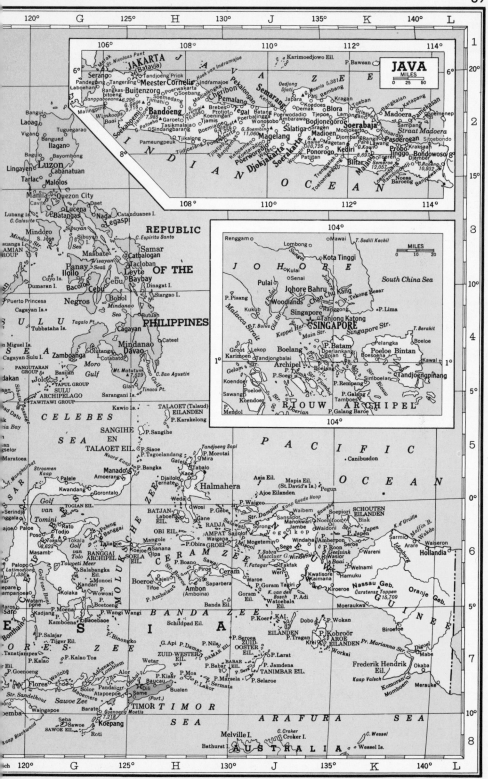

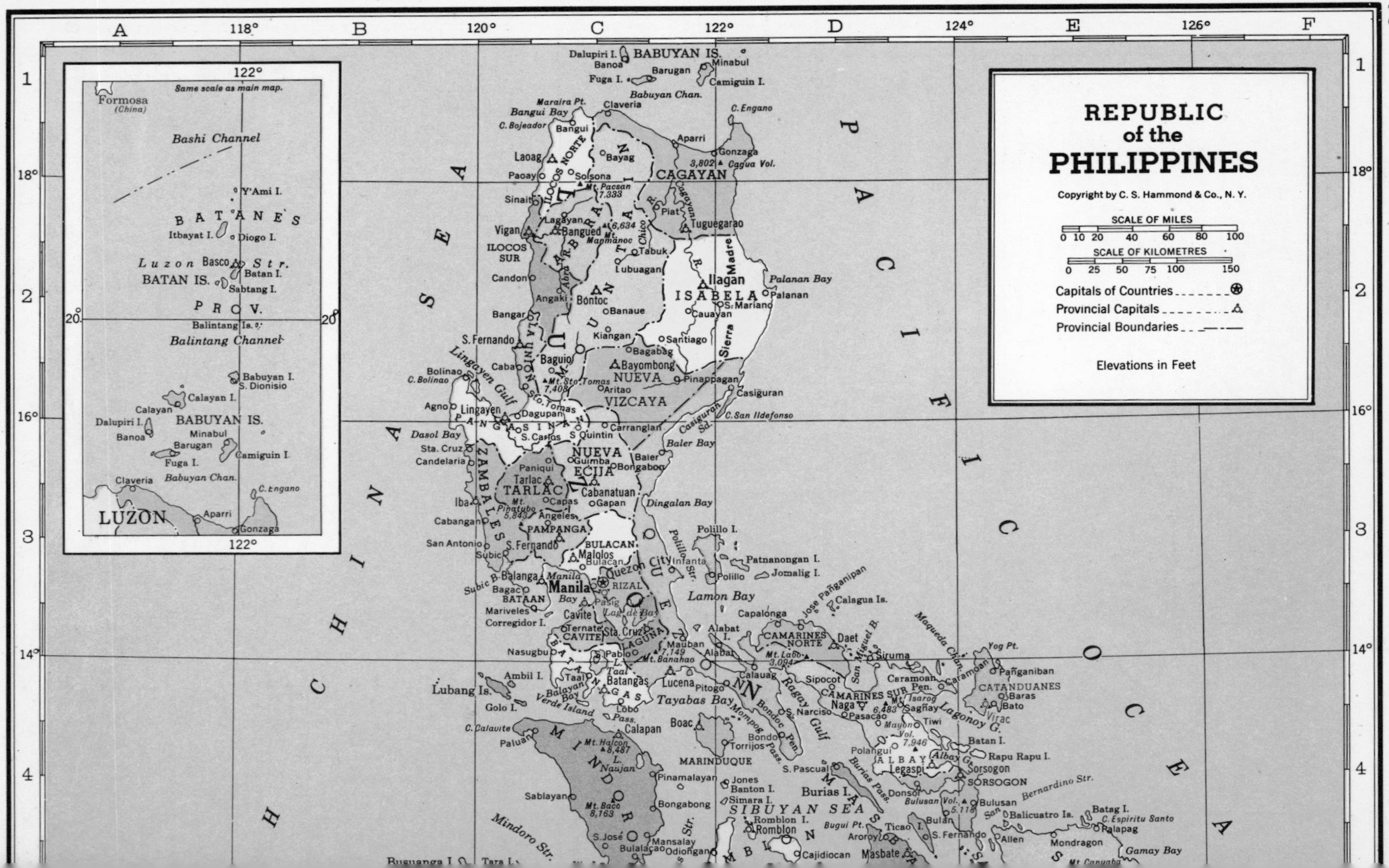
REPUBLIC
of the
PHILIPPINES
Copyright by C. S. Hammond & Co., N. Y.
SCALE OF MILES
0 10 20 40 60 80 100
SCALE OF KILOMETRES
0 25 50 75 100 150
Capitals of Countries
Provincial Capitals
Provincial Boundaries
Elevations in Feet
Same scale as main map.
Formosa (China)
Bashi Channel
BATANES PROV.
Y'Ami I.
Itbayat I.
Diogo I.
Luzon Str.
Basco
BATAN IS.
Batan I.
Sabtang I.
Balintang Is.
Balintang Channel
Babuyan I.
S. Dionisio
Calayan I.
Calayan
BABUYAN IS.
Dalupiri I.
Banoa
Minabul
Barugan
Camiguin I.
Fuga I.
Claveria
Babuyan Chan.
C. Engano
LUZON
Aparri
Gonzaga
SEA
PACIFIC OCEAN
CHINA SEA
Babuyan Chan.
Maraira Pt.
Bangui Bay
C. Bojeador
Bangui
Laoag
Paoay
Sinait
Vigan
ILOCOS NORTE
ILOCOS SUR
CAGAYAN
3,802 Cagua Vol.
Tuguegarao
Piat
Bayag
Solsona
Mt. Pacsan 7,333
ABRA
Bangued
Lagayan
Candon
Tabuk
Lubuagan
Ilagan
ISABELA
Palanan Bay
Palanan
Sierra Madre
S. Mariano
Cauayan
Angaki
Bontoc
Banaue
Bangar
Kiangan
Santiago
S. Fernando
LA UNION
Baguio
Bagabag
Bayombong
NUEVA VIZCAYA
Pinappagan
Casiguran
C. San Ildefonso
Lingayen Gulf
Bolinao
C. Bolinao
Caba
Mt. Sto. Tomas 7,408
Aritao
Agno
Lingayen
Dagupan
PANGASINAN
Dasol Bay
Sta. Cruz
Candelaria
S. Carlos
Quintin
Carranglan
Casiguran Sd.
Baler Bay
Baler
NUEVA ECIJA
Guimba
Bongabon
ZAMBALES
Paniqui
Tarlac
TARLAC
Cabanatuan
Gapan
Dingalan Bay
Iba
Mt. Pinatubo 5,843
Capas
Angeles
Cabangan
PAMPANGA
San Antonio
S. Fernando
BULACAN
Malolos
Bulacan
Subic
Subic B.
Balanga
Manila
Manila Bay
Quezon City
Infanta
RIZAL
Pasig
Polillo I.
Polillo Str.
Polillo
Patnanongan I.
Jomalig I.
Lamon Bay
Bagac
BATAAN
Mariveles
Corregidor I.
Cavite
Laguna de Bay
Ternate
CAVITE
Sta. Cruz
LAGUNA
Mauban
Mt. Banahao 7,149
Alabat I.
Alabat
Capalonga
Jose Panganiban
Calagua Is.
CAMARINES NORTE
Daet
San Miguel B.
Maqueda Chan.
Nasugbu
BATANGAS
Taal L.
Taal
Batangas
Lucena
Pitogo
Tayabas Bay
QUEZON
Calauag
Mt. Labo 3,094
Siruma
Yog Pt.
Panganiban
CATANDUANES
Baras
Bato
Virac
Caramoan Pen.
Caramoan
Lubang Is.
Ambil I.
Golo I.
Balayan Bay
Verde Island Pass.
Lobo
Calapan
Boac
MARINDUQUE
Mompog Pass.
Bondoc Pen.
Bondoc
Torrijos
Ragay Gulf
Sipocot
CAMARINES SUR
Naga
Mt. Isarog 6,483
Sagñay
Narciso
Pasacao
Tiwi
Lagonoy G.
Mayon Vol. 7,946
Polangui
ALBAY
Legaspi
Albay G.
Batan I.
Rapu Rapu I.
Sorsogon
SORSOGON
C. Calavite
Paluan
MINDORO
Mt. Halcon 8,487
L. Naujan
Pinamalayan
Jones
Banton I.
Simara I.
Romblon I.
Romblon
S. Pascual
Burias I.
Burias Pass.
MASBATE
SIBUYAN SEA
Donsol
Bulusan Vol. 5,118
Bulusan
San Bernardino Str.
Balicuatro Is.
Batag I.
C. Espiritu Santo
Palapag
Sablayan
Mt. Baco 8,163
Bongabong
S. José
Bulalacao
Mansalay
Odiongan
Mindoro Str.
Busuanga I.
Bugui Pt.
Aroroy
Ticao I.
Bulan
S. Fernando
Allen
Mondragon
Gamay Bay
Cajidiocan
Masbate
Tara I.
118° 120° 122° 124° 126°
14° 16° 18° 20°
A B C D E F
1 2 3 4

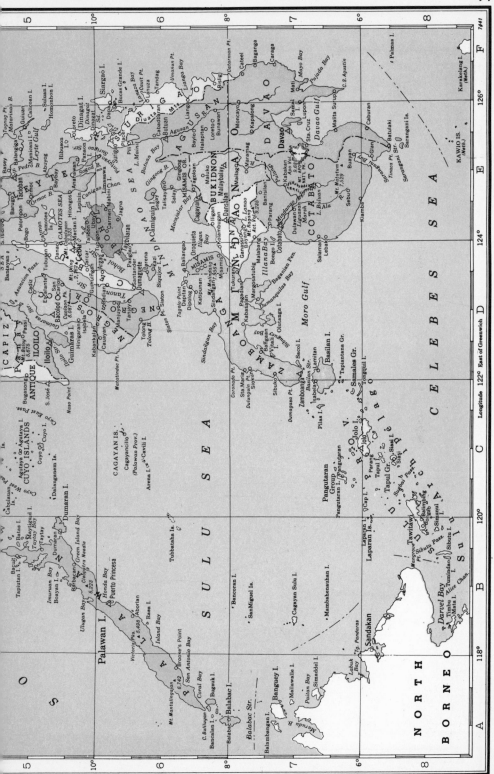

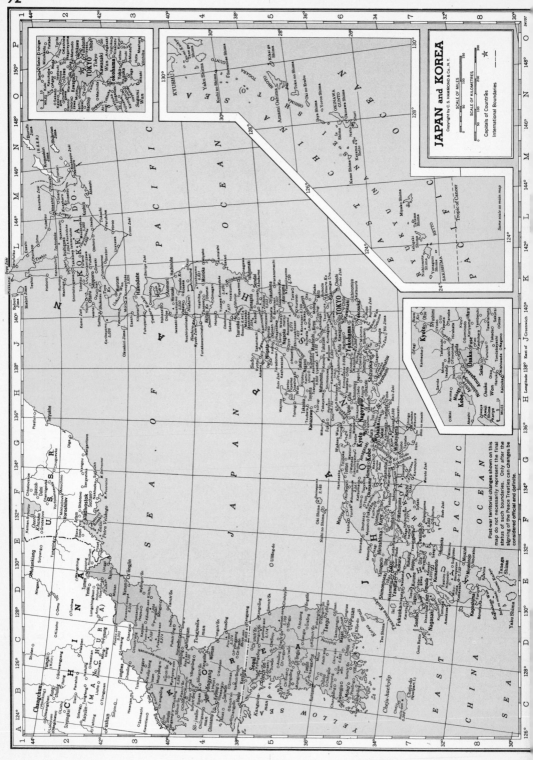

JAPAN and KOREA

Copyright by C. S. HAMMOND & Co., N. Y.

SCALE OF MILES

SCALE OF KILOMETRES

Capitals of Countries

International Boundaries

Post-war territorial changes shown on this map do not necessarily represent the final status of such boundaries. Only after the signing of the Peace Treaties can changes be considered official and definite.

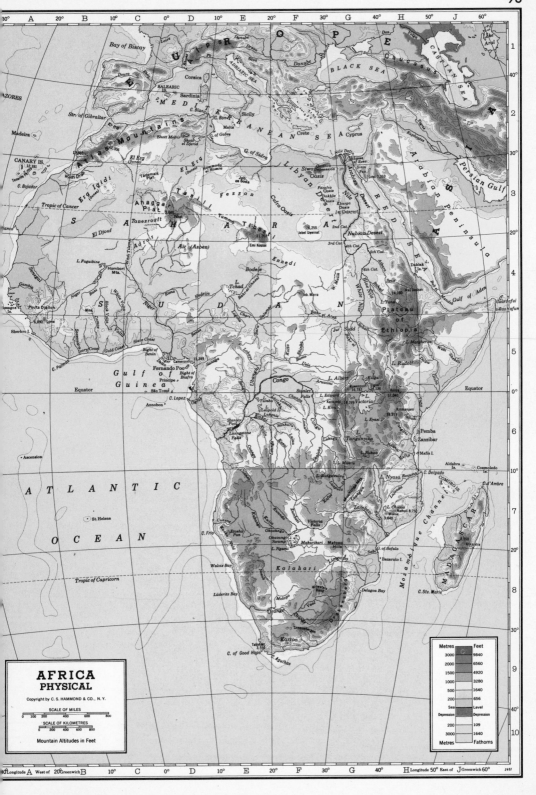

AFRICA
PHYSICAL

Copyright by C. S. HAMMOND & CO., N.Y.

SCALE OF MILES
0   100   200   400   600   800

SCALE OF KILOMETRES
0   200   400   600   800

Mountain Altitudes in Feet

Metres		Feet
3000		9840
2000		6560
1500		4920
1000		3280
500		1640
200		656
Sea		Level
Depression		Depression
200		109
3000		1640
Metres		Fathoms

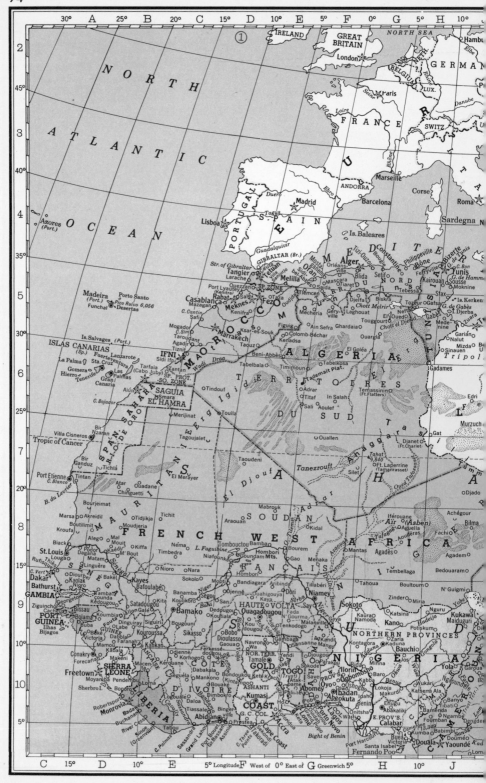

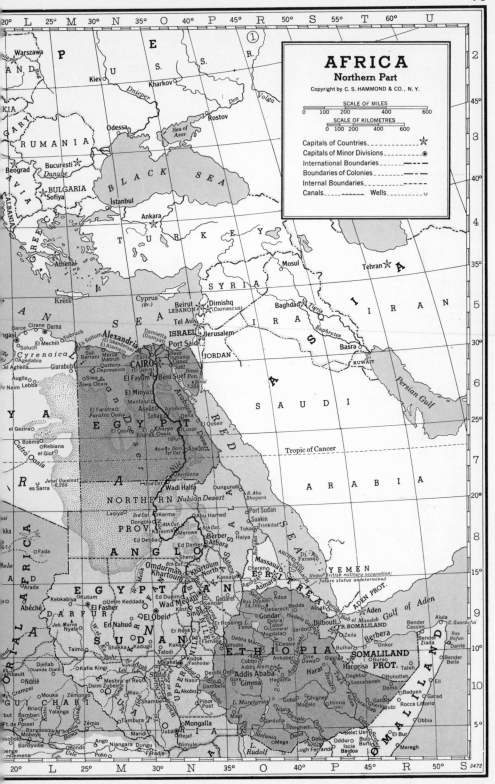

AFRICA
Northern Part
Copyright by C. S. HAMMOND & CO., N. Y.

SCALE OF MILES
0 100 200 400 600

SCALE OF KILOMETRES
0 100 200 400 600

Capitals of Countries .... ☆
Capitals of Minor Divisions .... ◉
International Boundaries _____
Boundaries of Colonies _ _ _ _ _
Internal Boundaries ....
Canals _____ Wells .... ○

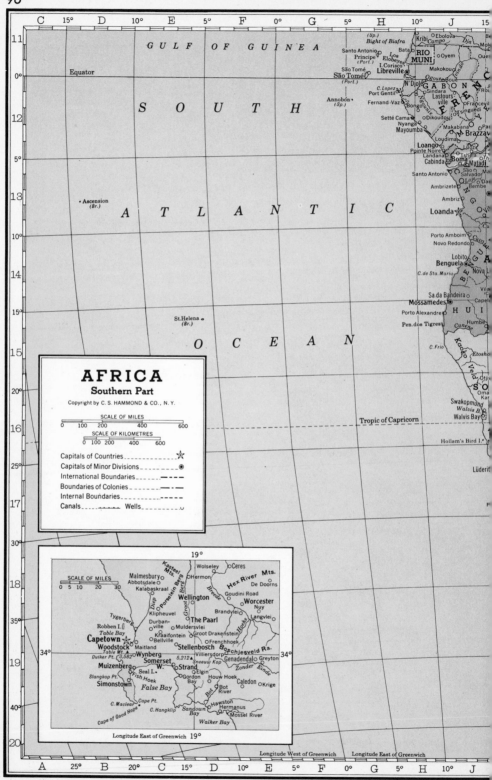

GULF OF GUINEA

SOUTH

ATLANTIC

Equator

Ascension
(Br.)

St.Helena
(Br.)

OCEAN

Tropic of Capricorn

AFRICA
Southern Part
Copyright by C. S. HAMMOND & CO., N. Y.

SCALE OF MILES
0   100   200   400   600

SCALE OF KILOMETRES
0   100   200   400   600

Capitals of Countries _____ ☆
Capitals of Minor Divisions _____ ◉
International Boundaries _____ —---—
Boundaries of Colonies _____ —-—
Internal Boundaries _____ -----
Canals _____ Wells _____ ○

Bight of Biafra
Santo Antonio
Principe
(Port.)
São Tomé
(Port.)
Annobón
(Sp.)

Kribi
Campo
Bata
Los
Elobeye
I. Corisco
Libreville
N'Djole
Port Gentil
Fernand-Vaz
Setté Cama
Nyanga
Mayoumba
Loango
Pointe Noire
Landana
Cabinda
Santo Antonio
Ambrizete
Ambriz
Loanda

Ebolova
Oyem
Makokou
GABON
Lastours-
ville
Brazzav
Boma
Matadi
São
Salvador
Bembe

Porto Amboim
Novo Redondo
Lobito
Benguela
C. de Sta. Maria
Nova L
Sa da Bandeira
Mossamedes
Porto Alexandre
Pen. dos Tigres
C. Frio
Etosha

Swakopmund
Walvis B.
Walvis Bay

Hollam's Bird I.

Lüderit

Capetown inset

19°

SCALE OF MILES
0 5 10   20   30

Malmesbury
Abbotsdale
Kalabaskraal
Wolseley
Hermon
Ceres
Hex River Mts.
De Doorns
Goudini Road
Wellington
Worcester
Nuy
Langvlei
Brandvlei
Tygerberg
Klipheuvel
Durban-
ville
The Paarl
Muldersvlei
Groot Drakenstein
Robben I.
Table Bay
Kraaifontein
Bellville
Frenchhoek
Capetown
Woodstock
Maitland
Stellenbosch
Villiersdorp
Genadendal
Greyton
Table Mt. (3,582)
Wynberg
Somerset
Sneuw Kop
Zonder Einde
Muizenberg
W.
Strand
Elgin
Seal I.
Fish Hoek
Houw Hoek
Caledon
Krige
Slangkop Pt.
Gordon
Bay
Bot
River
Simonstown
False Bay
C. Maclear
Cape Pt.
Hawston
Hermanus
C. Hangklip
Sandown
Bay
Mossel River
Cape of Good Hope
Walker Bay
34°
34°
Longitude East of Greenwich 19°

Longitude West of Greenwich   Longitude East of Greenwich

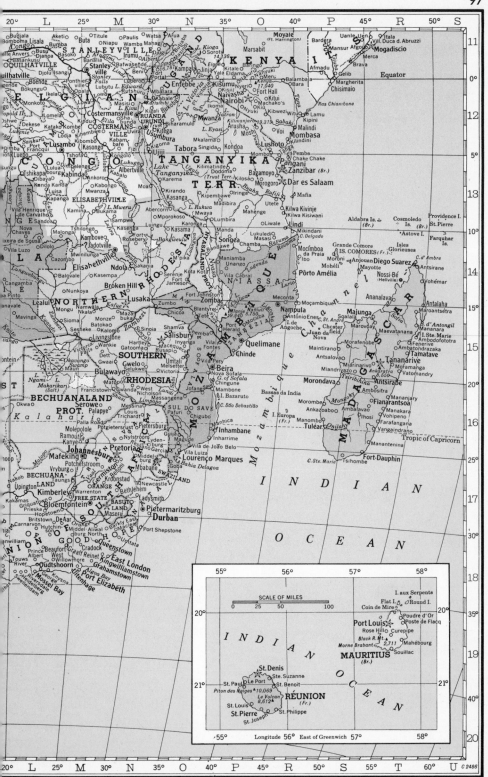

Map labels (selected):

Top region (Uganda / Kenya / Congo):
Budjala, Bomboma, Lisala, Akeito, Titule, Afua, Moyale (Ft. Harrington), Marsabit, Bordera, Uanle Uen, Itala, Vill. Duca d. Abruzzi
OQUILHATVILLE, Anvers, Busu, Djanga, Basoko, STANLEYVILLE, Irumu, Jinja, Wamba, Mahagi, L. Kioga, Sorotu, Marsabit, Merca, Mogadiscio
Boende, Bokungu, Ikela, Monkoto, Stanley Falls, Kampala, Entebbe, Kisumu, Kitale, Eldama, Nanyuki, Afmadu, Gelib, Brava
F E L G I A N, Costermansville, URUNDI, RUANDA, Nairobi, Fort Hall, Chisimaio, Margherita, Equator
Dekese, Lodja, Katako Kombe, COSTERMANS-VILLE, Kigali, Kitega, Mwanza, Arusha, Voi, Mombasa, Ras Chiambone
C U A N G O, Lusambo, Kasongo, Ujiji, Tabora, Singida, Kondoa, Tanga, Pemba, Chake Chake, Zanzibar (Br.)
T A N G A N Y I K A, Albertville, Kabinda, Lake Tanganyika, Dodoma, Bagamoyo, Dar es Salaam
ELISABETHVILLE, TERR., Kilosa, Morogoro, Rufiji, Mafia
RHODESIA, NIASSA, Kilwa Kivinje, Kilwa Kisiwani, Lindi
Aldabra Is. (Br.), Cosmoledo Is. (Br.), Providence I., St. Pierre, Astove I., Farquhar Is.
Grande Comore, IS. COMORES (Fr.), Anjouan, Mayotte, Diego Suarez, Antsirane, C. d'Ambre
Pôrto Amélia, Nossi-Bé (Helliville), Vohémar
NORTHERN RHODESIA, Broken Hill, Lusaka, Zomba, Blantyre, Nampula, Majunga, Antalaha
ELISABETHVILLE, Ndola, Fort Jameson, Quelimane, Tamatave, Tananarive
SOUTHERN RHODESIA, Salisbury, Chinde, Beira, Morondava, Antsirabe, Fianarantsoa
Bulawayo, Gwelo, Umtali, G. of Sofala, MADAGASCAR, Tuléar, Fort-Dauphin
BECHUANALAND PROT., Serowe, Palapye, Pietersburg, Inhambane, Tropic of Capricorn
Johannesburg, Pretoria, Lourenço Marques, SWAZILAND
BECHUANA-LAND, Kimberley, Bloemfontein, BASUTO-LAND, Pietermaritzburg, Durban
UNION OF SOUTH AFRICA, GOOD HOPE, Queenstown, East London, Port Elizabeth
ORANGE FREE STATE, Oudtshoorn, Mossel Bay

I N D I A N   O C E A N

Inset map (lower right):
SCALE OF MILES 0 25 50 100
I N D I A N   O C E A N
I. aux Serpents, Flat I., Round I., Coin de Mire, Poudre d'Or
Port Louis, Poste de Flacq, Rose Hill, Curepipe, Black R. Mt., Mahébourg
Morne Brabant 2,711, Souillac, MAURITIUS (Br.)
St. Denis, Ste. Suzanne, St. Paul, Le Port, St. Benoit
Piton des Neiges 10,069, Le Volcan 8,612, RÉUNION (Fr.)
St. Louis, St. Pierre, St. Joseph, St. Philippe
Longitude 56° East of Greenwich 57°

C 2488

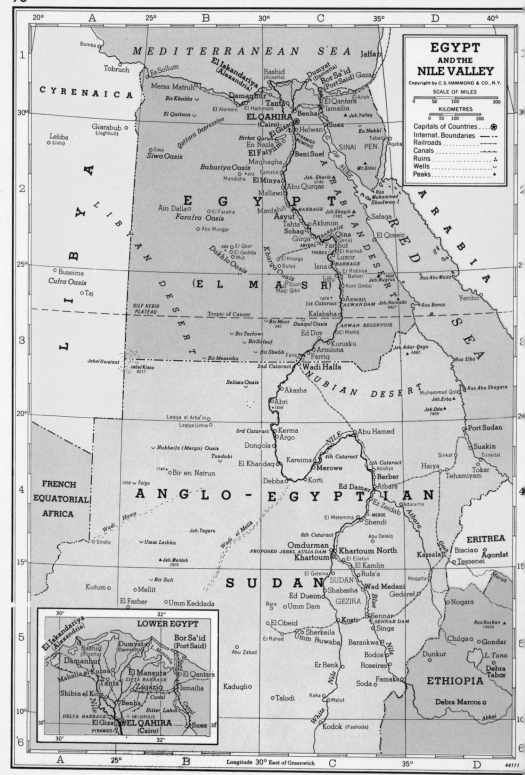

EGYPT
AND THE
NILE VALLEY

Copyright by C.S. HAMMOND & CO., N.Y.

SCALE OF MILES

0   50   100   200

KILOMETRES

0   50   100   200

Capitals of Countries .... ⊛
Internat. Boundaries ....
Railroads ....
Canals ....
Ruins ....
Wells ....
Peaks ....

LOWER EGYPT

Longitude 30° East of Greenwich

44111

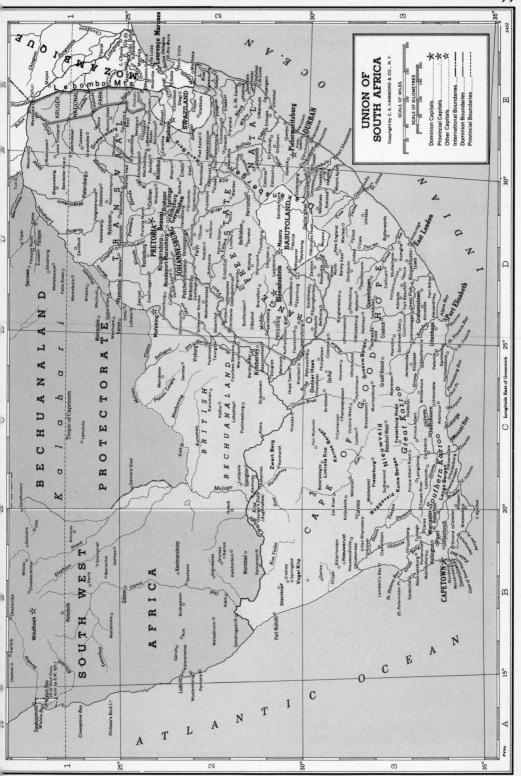

UNION OF
SOUTH AFRICA

Copyright by C. S. HAMMOND & CO., N.Y.

SCALE OF MILES

SCALE OF KILOMETERS

Dominion Capitals..........................★
Provincial Capitals.........................☆
Other Capitals.............................✪
International Boundaries.................———
Dominion Boundaries....................———
Provincial Boundaries...................———

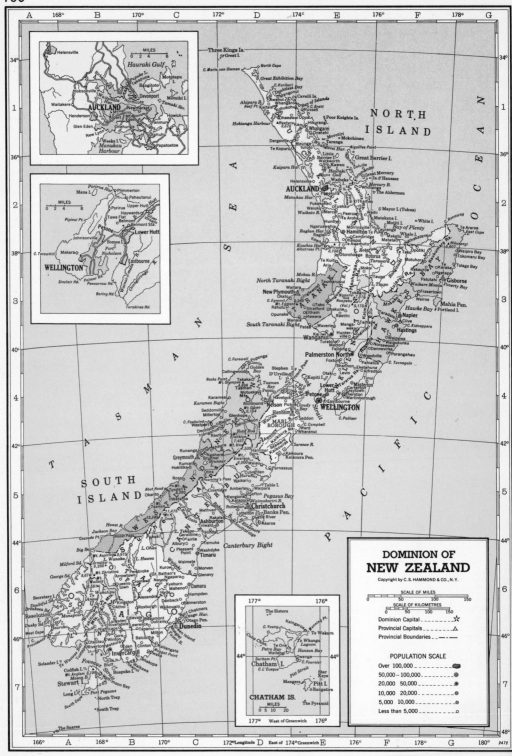

DOMINION OF
NEW ZEALAND

Copyright by C. S. HAMMOND & CO., N.Y.

SCALE OF MILES

SCALE OF KILOMETRES

Dominion Capital .... ☆
Provincial Capitals .... △
Provincial Boundaries .—.—.—

POPULATION SCALE

Over 100,000 ....
50,000 -- 100,000 ....
20,000   50,000 ....
10,000   20,000 ....
5,000   10,000 ....
Less than 5,000 ....

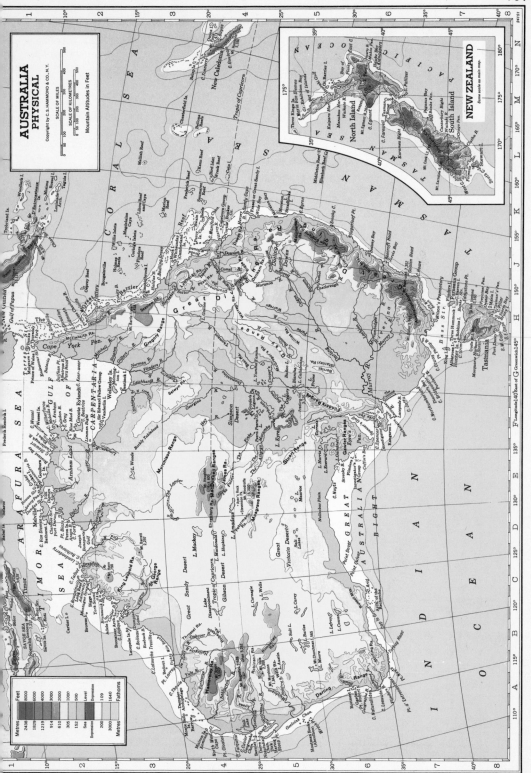

AUSTRALIA
PHYSICAL

Copyright by C. S. HAMMOND & CO., N.Y.

SCALE OF MILES

SCALE OF KILOMETRES

Mountain Altitudes in Feet

NEW ZEALAND

Same scale as main map.

Metres	Feet		Fathoms
2438	8000		
1829	6000		
1219	4000		
914	3000		
610	2000		
305	1000		
152	500		
Sea Level			
Depression		109	
2000			
3000	1640		Metres

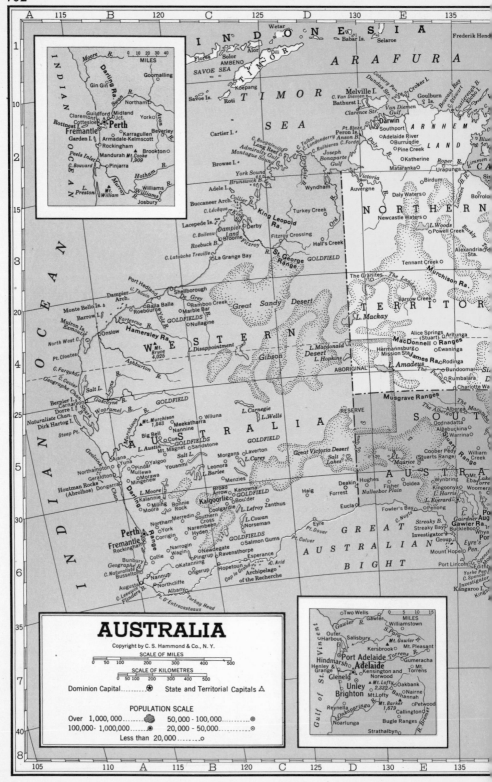

AUSTRALIA

Copyright by C. S. Hammond & Co., N.Y.

SCALE OF MILES

0   50   100   200   300   400   500

SCALE OF KILOMETRES

0 50 100   200   300   400   500

Dominion Capital.......... ✸   State and Territorial Capitals △

POPULATION SCALE

Over 1,000,000..........   50,000 - 100,000............ ◎
100,000 - 1,000,000......●   20,000 - 50,000............. ◉
Less than 20,000.........○

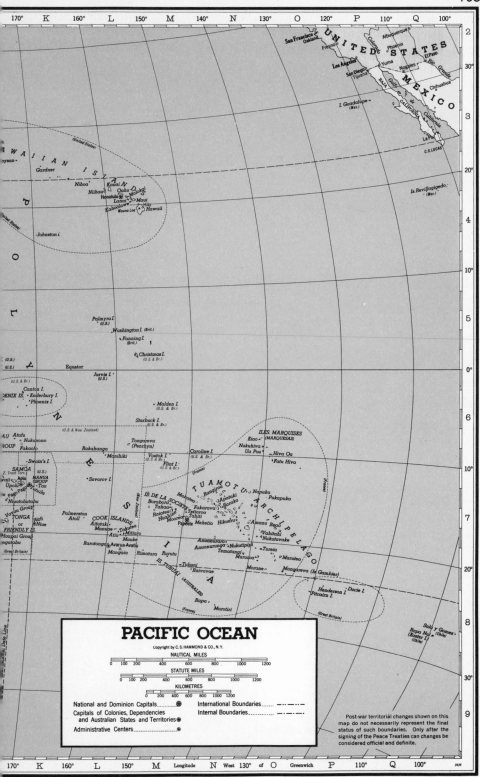

PACIFIC OCEAN

Copyright by C. S. HAMMOND & CO., N.Y.

NAUTICAL MILES

| 0 | 100 | 200 | 400 | 600 | 800 | 1000 | 1200 |

STATUTE MILES

| 0 | 100 | 200 | 400 | 600 | 800 | 1000 | 1200 |

KILOMETRES

| 0 | 200 | 400 | 600 | 800 | 1000 |

National and Dominion Capitals............⊛

Capitals of Colonies, Dependencies and Australian States and Territories⊛

Administrative Centers.......................⊛

International Boundaries.......– ∙– ∙–

Internal Boundaries.............– ∙∙– ∙∙–

Post-war territorial changes shown on this map do not necessarily represent the final status of such boundaries. Only after the signing of the Peace Treaties can changes be considered official and definite.

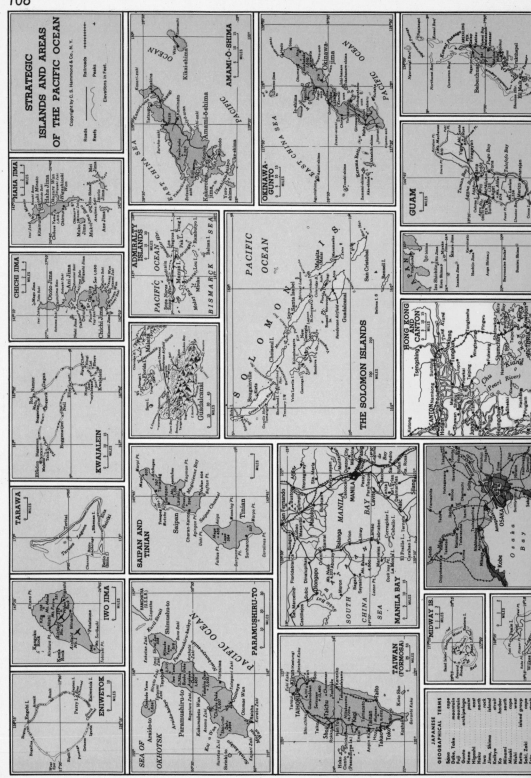

STRATEGIC ISLANDS AND AREAS OF THE PACIFIC OCEAN

Copyright by C. S. Hammond & Co., N. Y.

Roads
Railroads
Peaks
Reefs
Elevations in Feet.

HAHA JIMA

CHICHI JIMA

KWAJALEIN

TARAWA

IWO JIMA

ENIWETOK

PARAMUSHIRU-TO

SEA OF OKHOTSK

PACIFIC OCEAN

ADMIRALTY ISLANDS

BISMARCK SEA

SAIPAN AND TINIAN

Saipan

Tinian

Guadalcanal

TAIWAN (FORMOSA)

AMAMI-O-SHIMA

EAST CHINA SEA

OCEAN

PACIFIC

OKINAWA-GUNTO

Okinawa-jima

EAST CHINA SEA

PACIFIC OCEAN

SOLOMON IS.

THE SOLOMON ISLANDS

MANILA BAY

SOUTH CHINA SEA

GUAM

HONG KONG AND CANTON

CANTON

Chu (Pearl River)

OSAKA

Osaka Bay

Kobe

MIDWAY IS.

JAPANESE GEOGRAPHICAL TERMS

Saki .... cape
Dake, Take ...... mountain
Fuji .... mountain
Gunto .... archipelago
Hana .... point
Higashi .... east
Hoku .... north
Iwa .... rock
Jima, Shima ..... island
Kaikyo .... strait
Ko .... harbor
Minami .... south
Nishi .... west
Retto .... island group
Saki, Zaki ...... cape

SOUTH AMERICA
PHYSICAL

Copyright by C. S. HAMMOND & CO., N. Y.

SCALE OF MILES

SCALE OF KILOMETRES

Mountain Altitudes in Feet

Metres		Feet
5000		16400
4000		13120
3000		9840
2000		6560
1000		3280
500		1640
200		656
Sea		Level
200		109
3000		1640
Metres		Fathoms

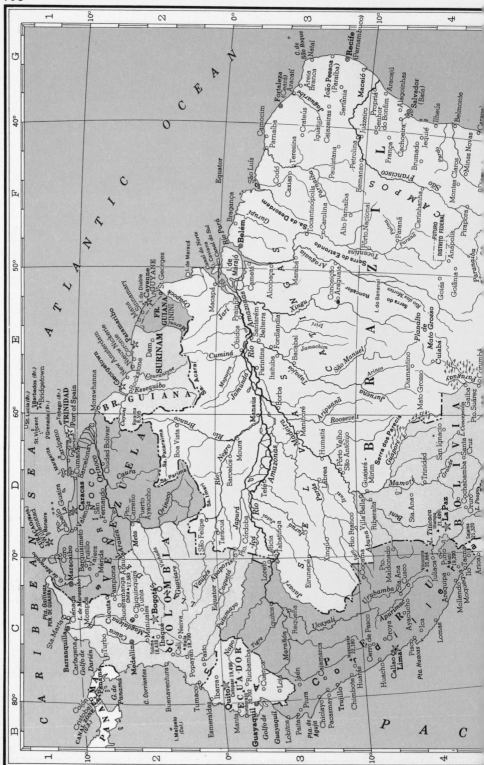

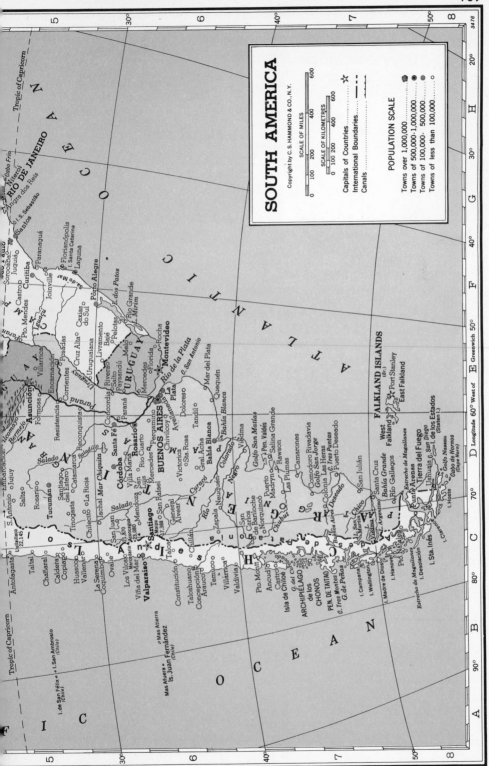

SOUTH AMERICA

Copyright by C. S. HAMMOND & CO., N. Y.

SCALE OF MILES
0   100   200   400   600

SCALE OF KILOMETRES
0   100 200   400   600

Capitals of Countries .... ☆
International Boundaries .... –·–·–·
Canals ....

POPULATION SCALE

Towns over 1,000,000 ....
Towns of 500,000-1,000,000 .... ◉
Towns of 100,000- 500,000 .... ◎
Towns of less than 100,000 .... ○

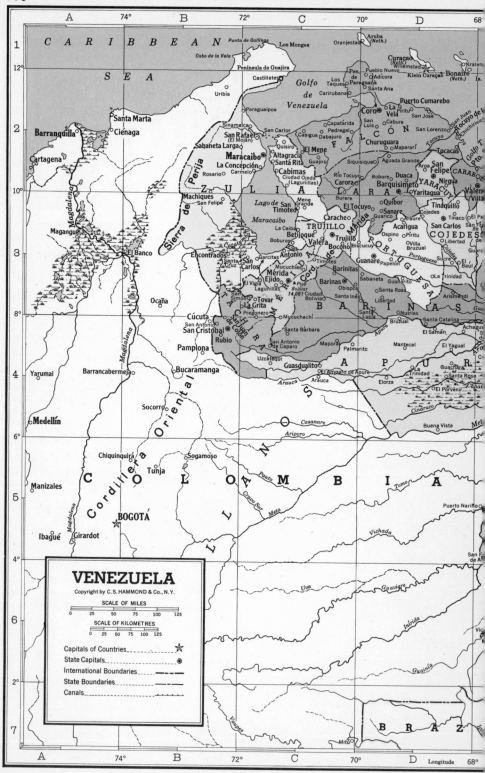

VENEZUELA

Copyright by C. S. HAMMOND & Co., N.Y.

SCALE OF MILES

0   25   50   75   100   125

SCALE OF KILOMETRES

0   25   50   75   100   125

Capitals of Countries .... ⭐
State Capitals .... ◎
International Boundaries .... — — —
State Boundaries .... — · — ·
Canals .... —

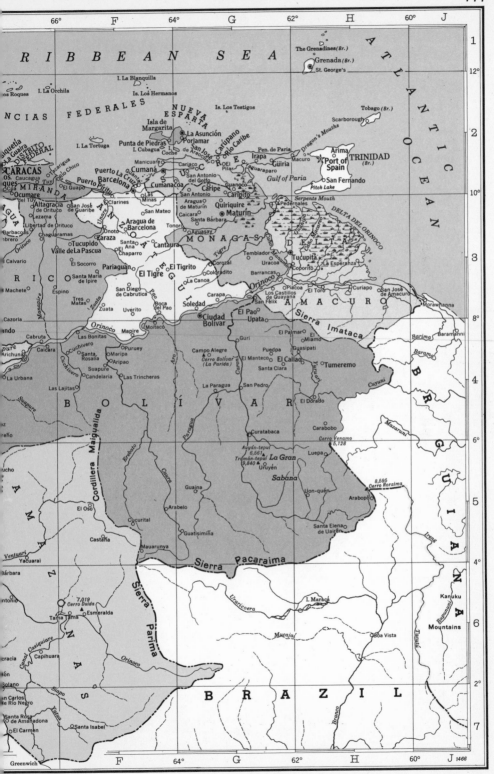

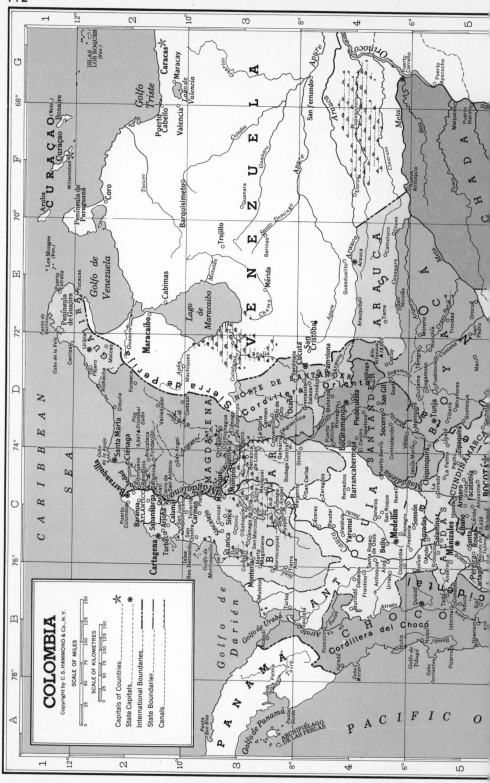

COLOMBIA

Copyright by C. S. HAMMOND & Co., N.Y.

SCALE OF MILES

0   25   50   75   100   125   150

SCALE OF KILOMETRES

0   25   50   75   100   125   150

Capitals of Countries .... ☆

State Capitals .... ◉

International Boundaries ....

State Boundaries ....

Canals ....

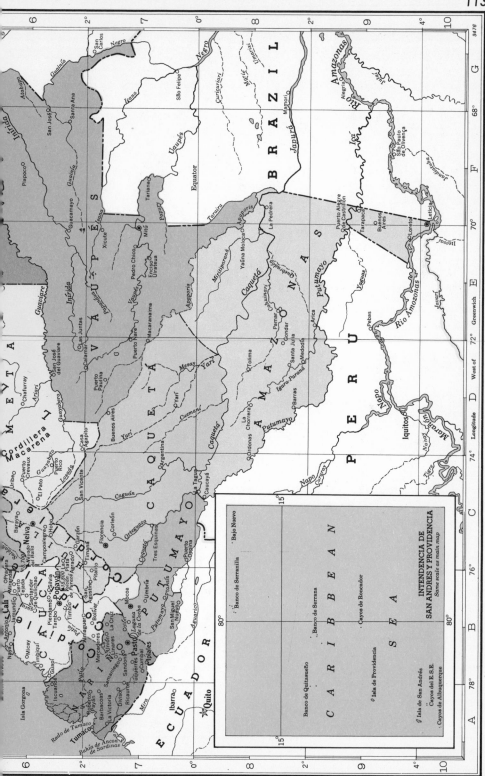

INTENDENCIA DE
SAN ANDRES Y PROVIDENCIA
Same scale as main map

Banco de Serranilla

Bajo Nuevo

Banco de Serrana

Cayos de Roncador

Isla de Providencia

C A R I B B E A N

S E A

Isla de San Andrés
Cayos del E.S.E.

Cayos de Albuquerque

Banco de Quitasueño

B R A Z I L

Río Amazonas

P E R U

A M A Z O N A S

C A Q U E T Á

P U T U M A Y O

V A U P É S

M E T A

ECUADOR

Quito

Iquitos

Leticia

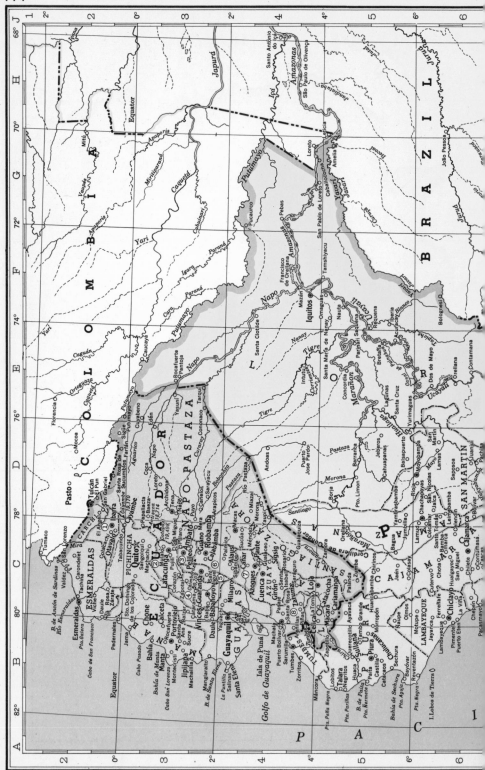

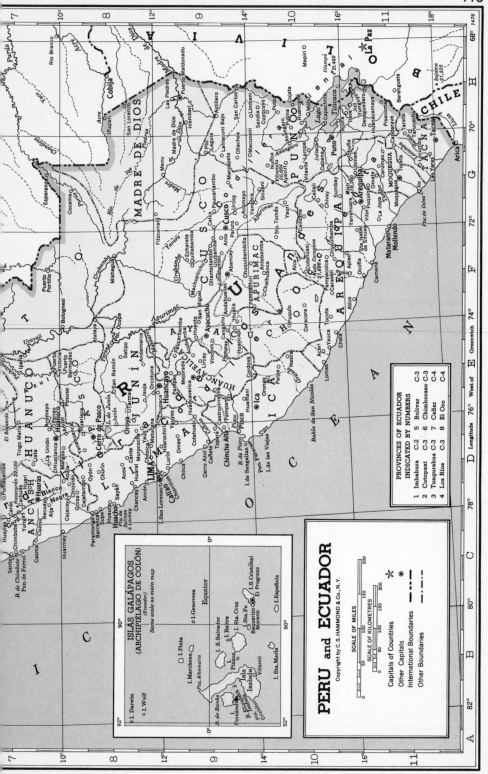

PERU and ECUADOR

Copyright by C. S. HAMMOND & Co., N.Y.

115

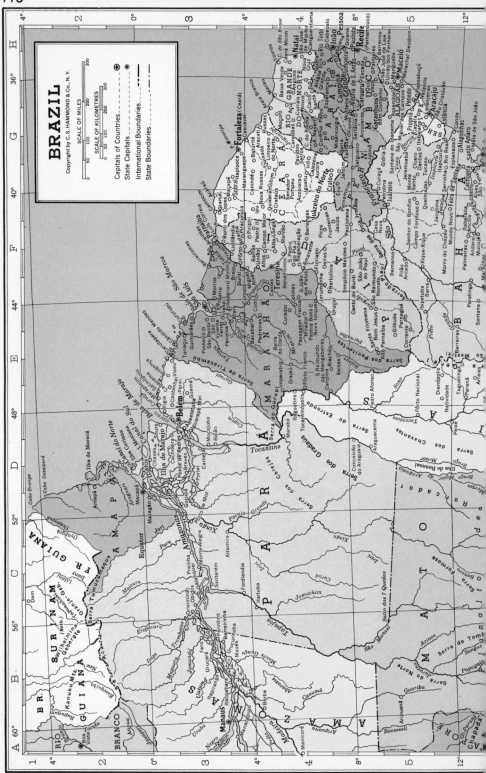

BRAZIL

Copyright by C.S. HAMMOND & Co., N.Y.

SCALE OF MILES

SCALE OF KILOMETRES

Capitals of Countries
State Capitals
International Boundaries
State Boundaries

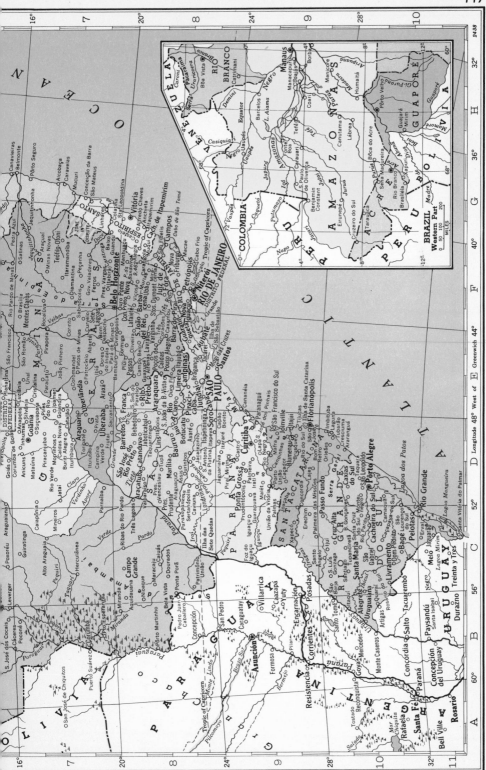

BRAZIL
Western Part
0 50 100 200
MILES

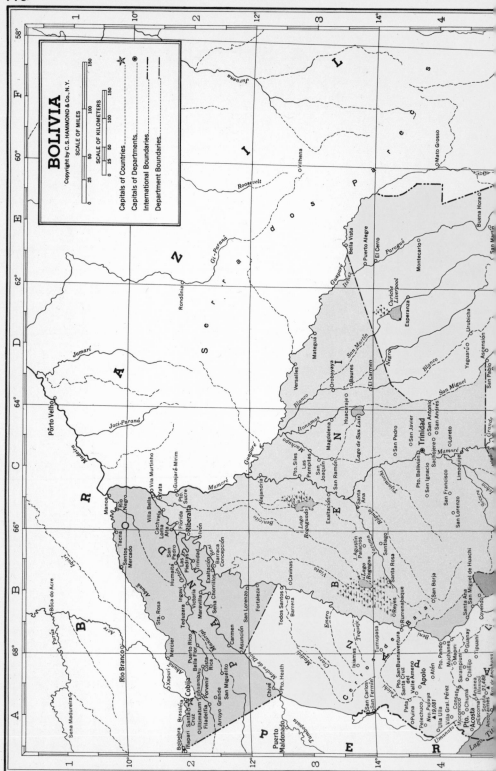

BOLIVIA

Copyright by C.S. HAMMOND & Co., N.Y.

SCALE OF MILES

SCALE OF KILOMETERS

Capitals of Countries........ ✪
Capitals of Departments...... ⊚
International Boundaries....... —··—··—
Department Boundaries........ —·—·—·

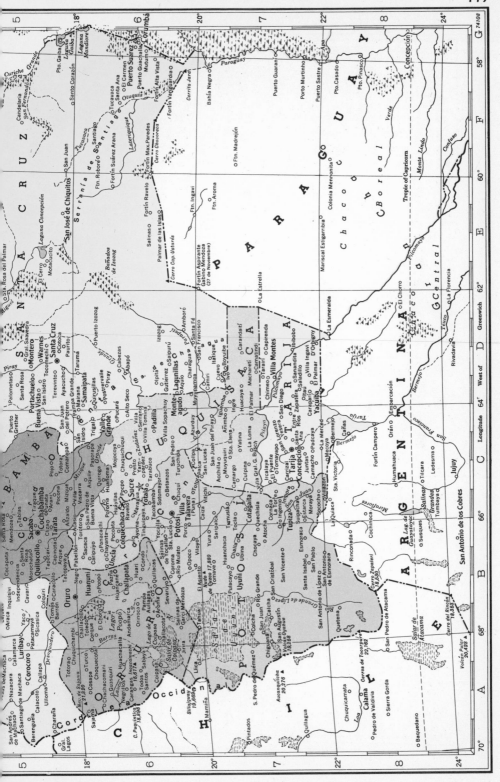

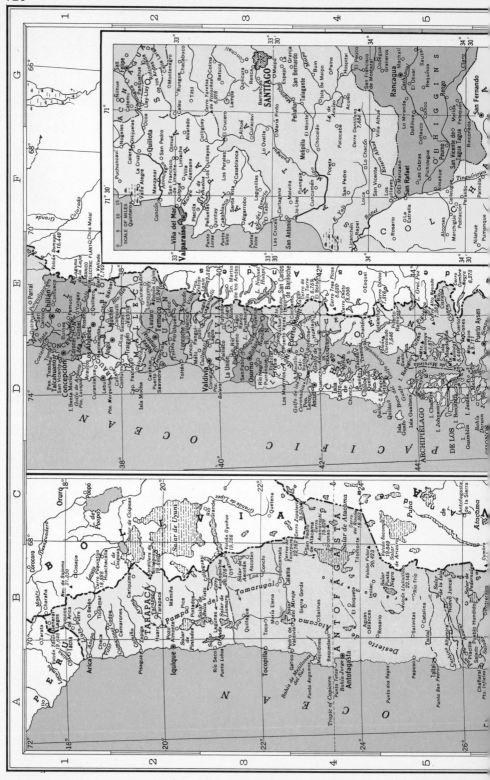

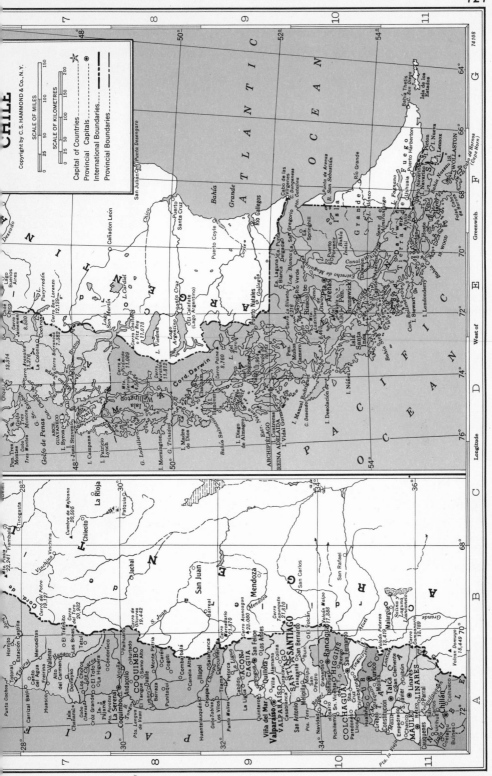

CHILE

Copyright by C. S. HAMMOND & Co., N.Y.

SCALE OF MILES
0   25   50   100   150

SCALE OF KILOMETRES
0   25 50   100   150   200

Capital of Countries
Provincial Capitals
International Boundaries
Provincial Boundaries

74108

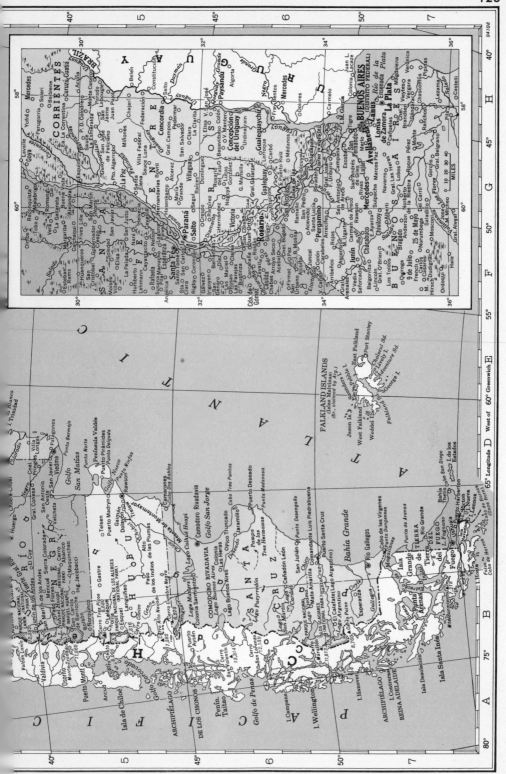

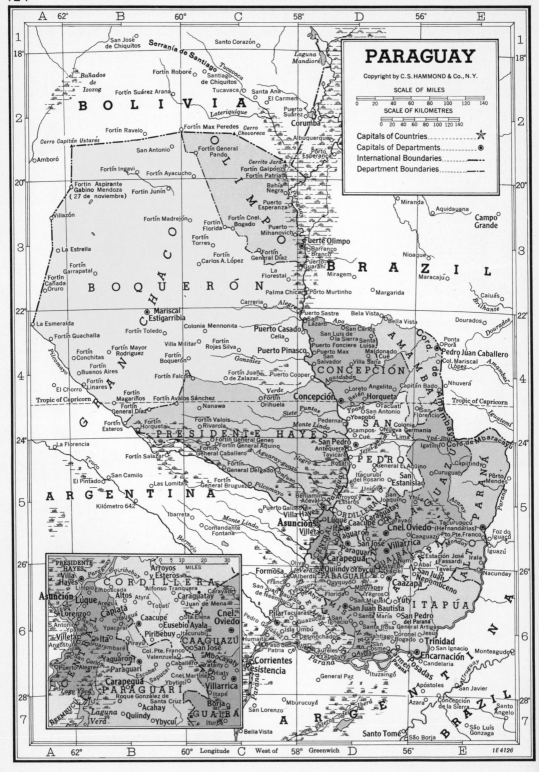

PARAGUAY

Copyright by C. S. HAMMOND & Co., N. Y.

SCALE OF MILES

0 20 40 60 80 100 120 140

SCALE OF KILOMETRES

0 20 40 60 80 100 120 140

Capitals of Countries.............. ☆
Capitals of Departments............. ◉
International Boundaries..............
Department Boundaries..............

1E 4126

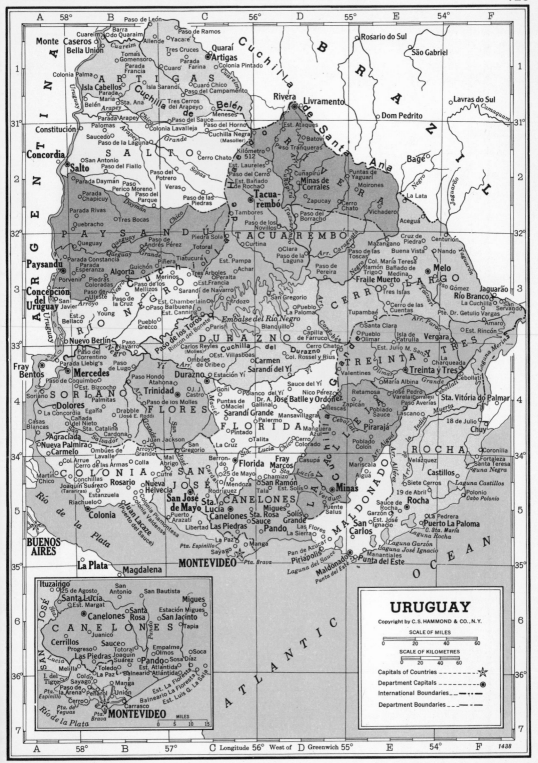

URUGUAY

Copyright by C. S. HAMMOND & CO., N.Y.

SCALE OF MILES

0   20   40   60

SCALE OF KILOMETRES

0   20   40   60

Capitals of Countries ⭐

Department Capitals ◉

International Boundaries ▬ ▪ ▬

Department Boundaries ▬ ▪ ▬

A 58°   B 57°   C Longitude 56° West of D Greenwich 55°   E 54°   F   1438

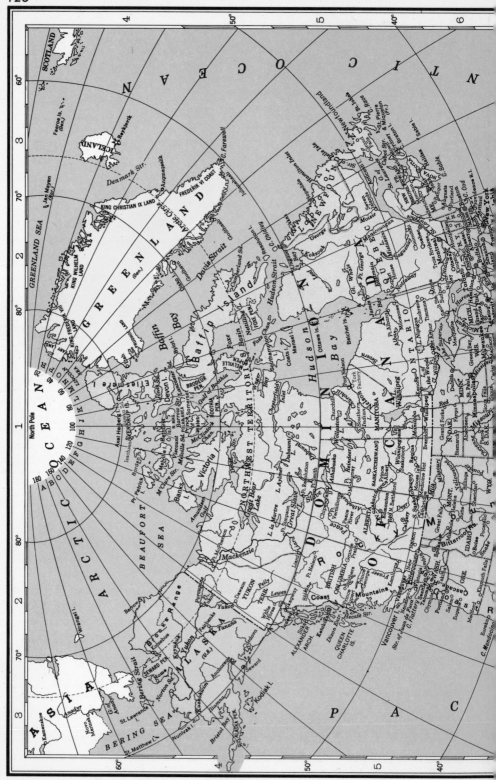

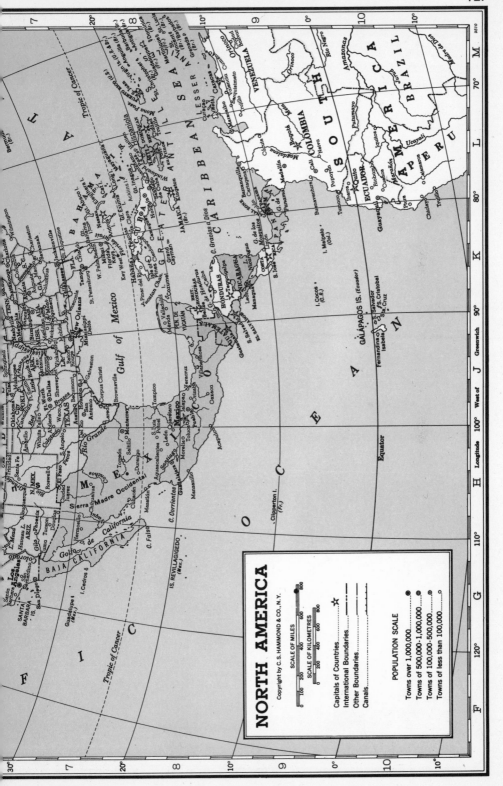

NORTH AMERICA

Copyright by C. S. HAMMOND & CO., N.Y.

SCALE OF MILES

SCALE OF KILOMETRES

Capitals of Countries .... ☆
International Boundaries ....
Other Boundaries ....
Canals ....

POPULATION SCALE

Towns over 1,000,000 .... ●
Towns of 500,000-1,000,000 .... ◉
Towns of 100,000-500,000 .... ◎
Towns of less than 100,000 .... ○

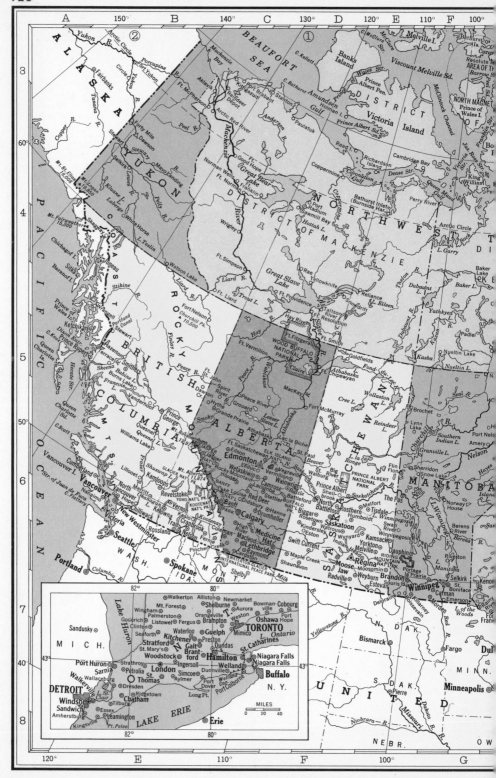

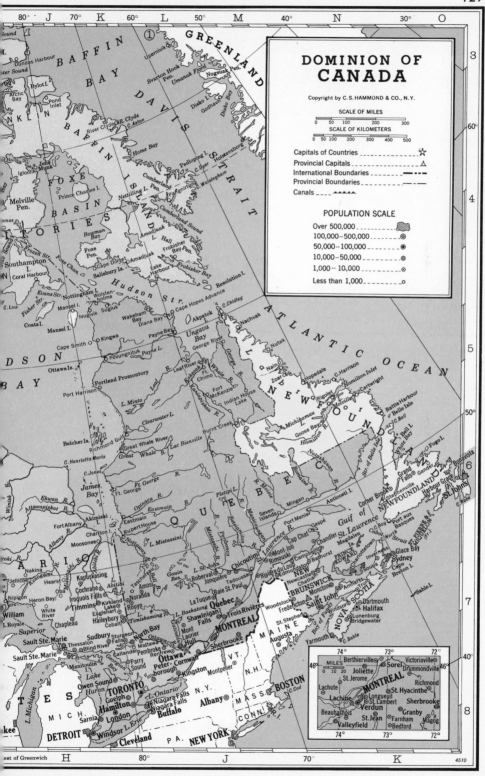

DOMINION OF CANADA

Copyright by C. S. HAMMOND & CO., N.Y.

SCALE OF MILES

0 50 100 200 300

SCALE OF KILOMETERS

0 50 100 200 300 400 500

Capitals of Countries	☆
Provincial Capitals	△
International Boundaries	— ∙ — ∙ —
Provincial Boundaries	— ∙∙ — ∙∙ —
Canals	

POPULATION SCALE

Over 500,000

100,000--500,000

50,000--100,000

10,000--50,000

1,000 -- 10,000

Less than 1,000

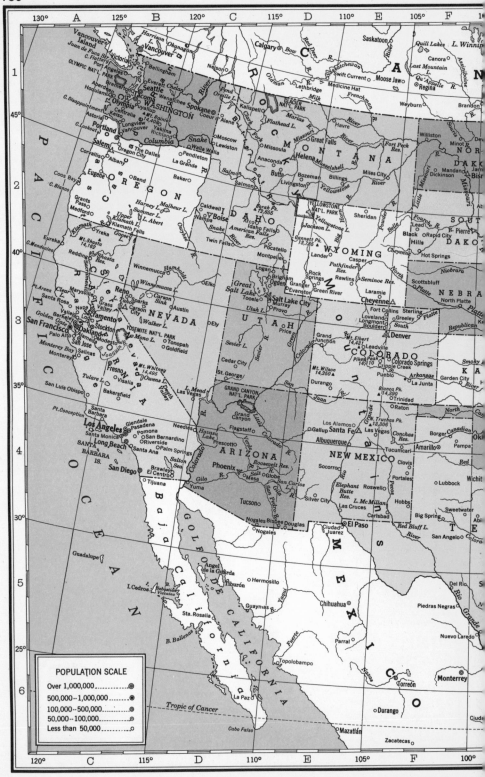

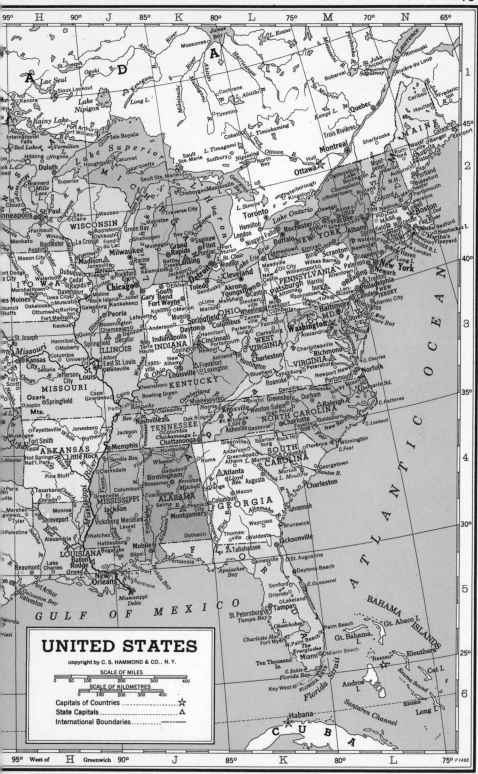

UNITED STATES

copyright by C. S. HAMMOND & CO., N.Y.

SCALE OF MILES

0   50   100   200   300   400

SCALE OF KILOMETRES

0   100   200   300   400

Capitals of Countries .... ☆
State Capitals .... △
International Boundaries ....

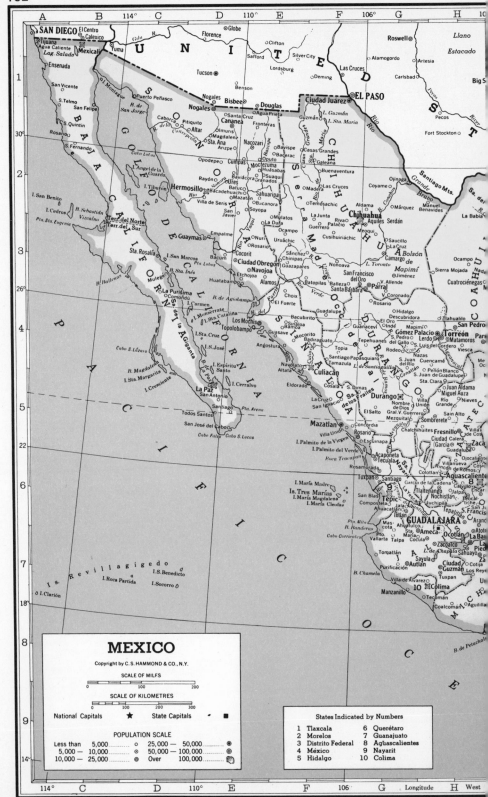

MEXICO

Copyright by C.S.HAMMOND & CO., N.Y.

SCALE OF MILES

0   100   200

SCALE OF KILOMETRES

0   100   200   300

National Capitals   ★   State Capitals   ■

POPULATION SCALE

Less than 5,000	○	25,000 — 50,000
5,000 — 10,000	○	50,000 — 100,000
10,000 — 25,000	◉	Over 100,000

States Indicated by Numbers

1	Tlaxcala	6	Querétaro
2	Morelos	7	Guanajuato
3	Distrito Federal	8	Aguascalientes
4	México	9	Nayarit
5	Hidalgo	10	Colima

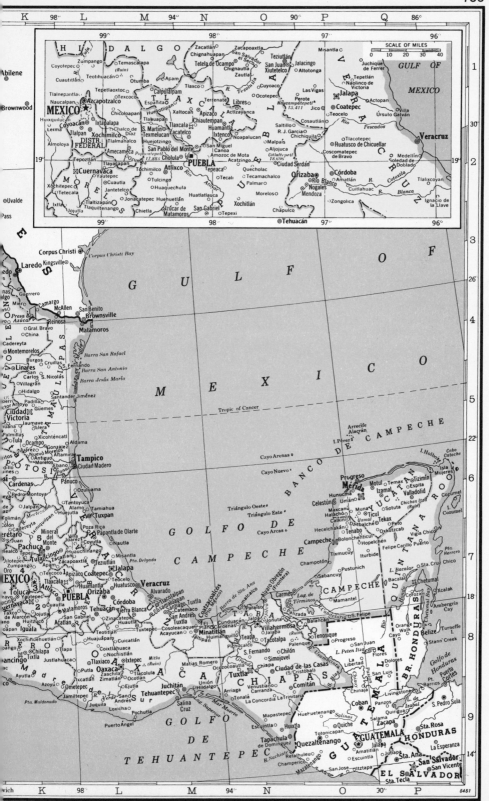

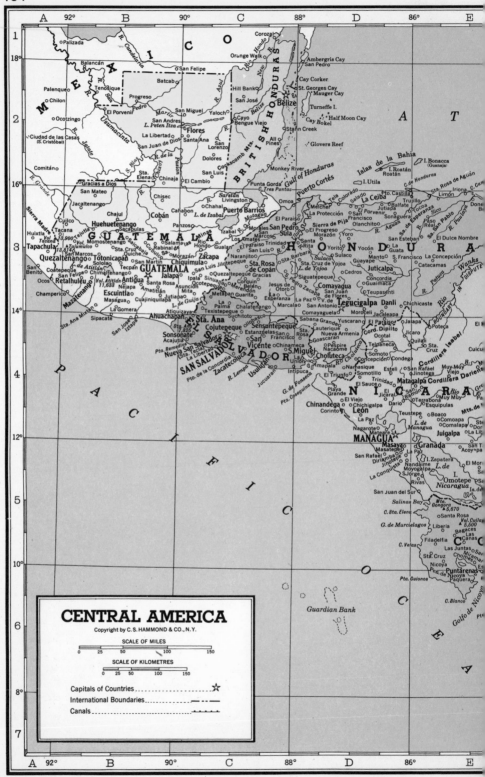

CENTRAL AMERICA

Copyright by C.S. Hammond & Co., N.Y.

SCALE OF MILES

0   25   50   100   150

SCALE OF KILOMETRES

0 25 50   100   150

Capitals of Countries .... ☆
International Boundaries ....
Canals ....

F 82° G 80° H 78° J 76°

Montego Bay
Falmouth
St. Ann's Bay
Annotto Bay
Port Maria
Port Antonio
S. Negril Pt.
Savanna la Mar
Ewarton
Black River
Spanish Town
Blue Mountain Pk.
7,388
Kingston
(U.S. Leased Base)
Morant Point
JAMAICA
Portland Point

Walton Bank

CARIBBEAN

Pedro Bank

Rosalind Bank

Pedro Cays
(Jamaica)

Morant Cays
(Jamaica)

Cay Gorda
Gorda Bank
Pigeon Cays
Half Moon Reefs
C. Falso
C. Gracias a Dios
Alargate Reef
Cabo Gracias a Dios

Serranilla Bank

Bajo Nuevo

Miskito Cays

Quita Sueño Bank
(Claimed by U.S. and Col.)

Serrana Bank *(Claimed by U.S. and Col.)*

Puerto Cabezas
(Bragman's Bluff)
Lag. de Karatá
Río Wawa

Lag. de Wounta
Prinzapolca

Roncador Bank
(Claimed by U.S. and Col.)

I.de Providencia
(Col.)

OCEAN

Tyra Cays
King Cays

SEA

Pearl Cays
Pen. de Perlas
Little Corn I.
(U.S. Lease)
Great Corn I.
(U.S. Lease)
uefields

I.San Andres
(Col.)

Cayos de Albuquerque
(Col.)

Monkey Pt.
Gorda
Bahia de
Juan del Norte
San Juan del Norte
(Greytown)

Carmen
Jácimo
Pta. Blanca
Siquirres
Limón
Matina
C. Blanco
11,696
Pta. Cahuita
Pta. Carreta
Beverly
Vesta
Suretka

CANAL ZONE
Portobello
Colón
Pta. Manzanillo
Miramar
Pta. San Blas
Golfo de San Blas
Archipiélago de las Mulatas
I.Fuerte

Golfo de Darién

Sixaola
I. de Colón
I. del Oro
I. Bastimentos
Guabito
Almirante
Chiriqui
Pen. Valiente
Escudo de Veragua
Pta. del Rincón

Mandinga
C. Brewster
Cord. de San Blas
3,018
Lagarto
Donoso
Cocle del Norte
Belén
Gatún
Cristóbal
La Chorrera
Pacora
Chepo
Pigeon Grande
Carreto
Pto. Caribana
Pta. Caribana
Golfo de Uraba

Golfo de los
Mosquitos
V. Chiriqui
10,991
Boquete
Chiriqui Grande
San Cristóbal
Sa. de Tabasara
Loma Escobaro
Capira
Alboa
I.Taboga
Panamá
Chimán
R. Chuquraqua
Nicocli
Acandi

David
Potrerillos
Dolega
Gualaca
Concepción
Alanje
Horconcitos
Canazas
Santa Fe
Ola
Antón
San Carlos
Penonomé
Nata
Agua Dulce
ARCH.
de las
PERLAS
San Carlos
de las
I. del
Rey
La
Palmarina
El Real
Obaldia
Turbo

Puerto
Armuelles
Pta. Burica
I. Parida
San Felix
Tole
Las Palmas
Sano
Francisco
Colobre
I.San José
Bahia San Miguel
Pta. Gorda
Garachine
Limones

G. de Chiriquí
Is.
Secas
Santiago
Montijo
Santa Fe
Sonao
Parita
G. de Parita
Chitre
Golfo de Panamá
Pta. Piñas

COLOMBIA

La
Ladrones
I.Coiba
I.Jicaron
G. de Montijo
I.Cebaco
Ocú
Las Tablas
Pen. de Azuero
Pedasi
Tonosí
C. Mala

Riosucio
R. Atrato

I.Santiago

Morro de Puercos
Pta. Mariato
Pta. Ardita
Jurado

F Greenwich 82° G 80° H 78° J 76°
P1483

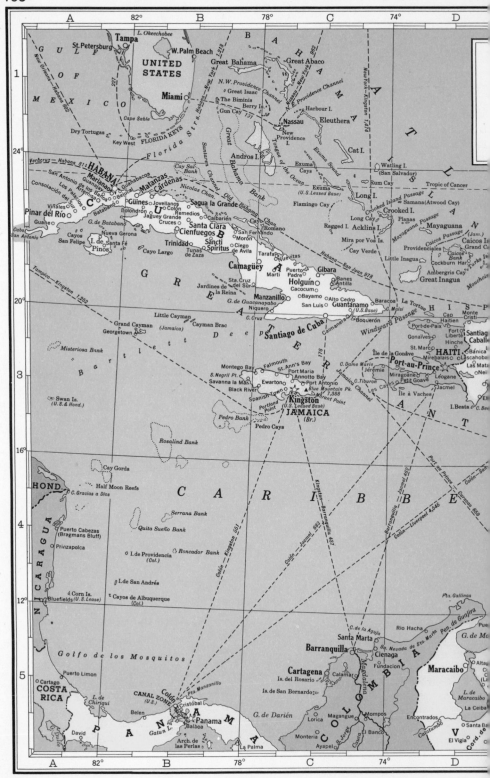

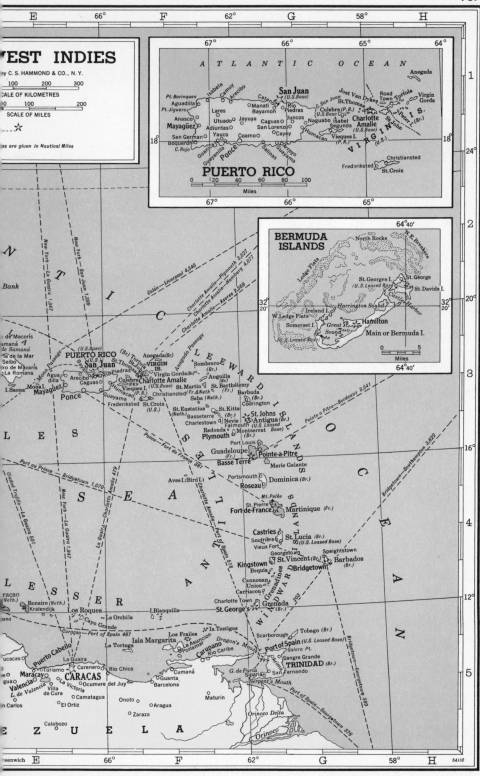

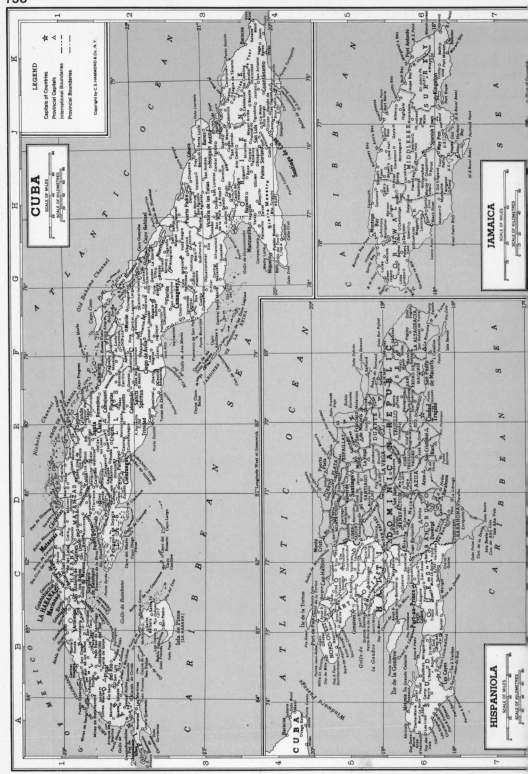

CUBA

SCALE OF MILES

SCALE OF KILOMETRES

JAMAICA

SCALE OF MILES

SCALE OF KILOMETRES

HISPANIOLA

SCALE OF MILES

SCALE OF KILOMETRES

LEGEND

Capitals of Countries ★

Provincial Capitals △

International Boundaries

Provincial Boundaries

Copyright by C. S. HAMMOND & Co., N. Y.

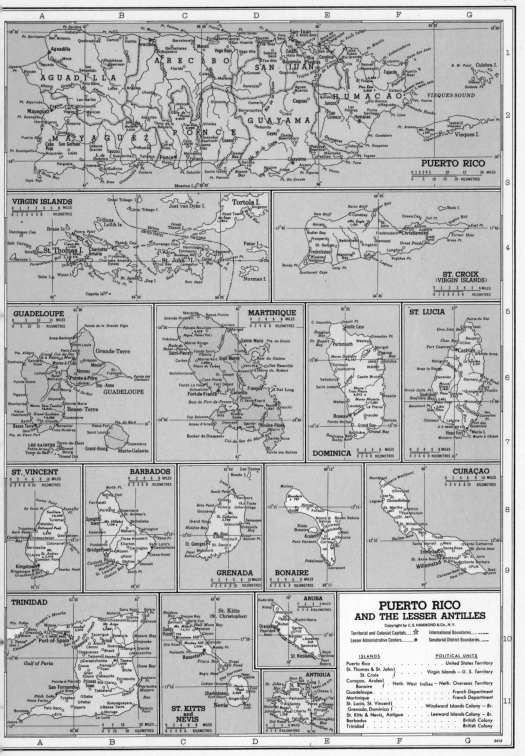

PUERTO RICO
AND THE LESSER ANTILLES

Copyright by C. S. HAMMOND & Co., N.Y.

Territorial and Colonial Capitals..........☆ International Boundaries........
Lesser Administrative Centers..........✸ Senatorial District Boundaries........

ISLANDS	POLITICAL UNITS
Puerto Rico	United States Territory
St. Thomas & St. John	Virgin Islands – U. S. Territory
St. Croix	
Curaçao, Aruba	Neth. West Indies – Neth. Overseas Territory
Bonaire	
Guadeloupe	French Department
Martinique	French Department
St. Lucia, St. Vincent	Windward Islands Colony – Br.
Grenada, Dominica	
St. Kitts & Nevis, Antigua	Leeward Islands Colony – Br.
Barbados	British Colony
Trinidad	British Colony

140

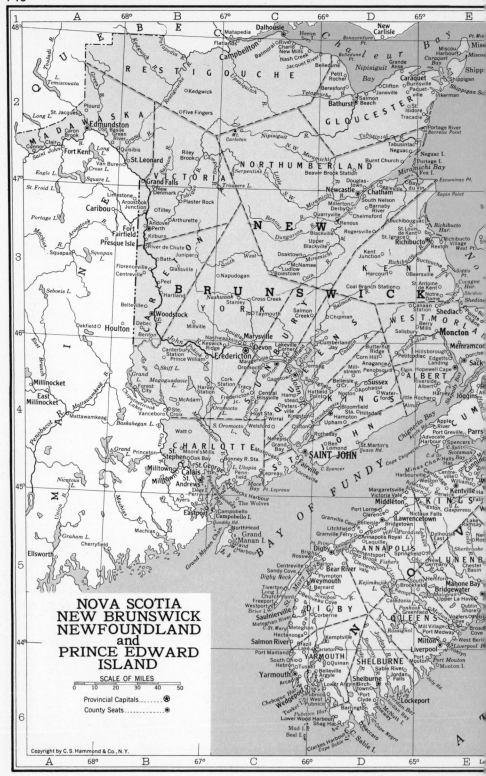

NOVA SCOTIA
NEW BRUNSWICK
NEWFOUNDLAND
and
PRINCE EDWARD
ISLAND

SCALE OF MILES

0   10   20   30   40   50

Provincial Capitals..........⊛
County Seats.............◉

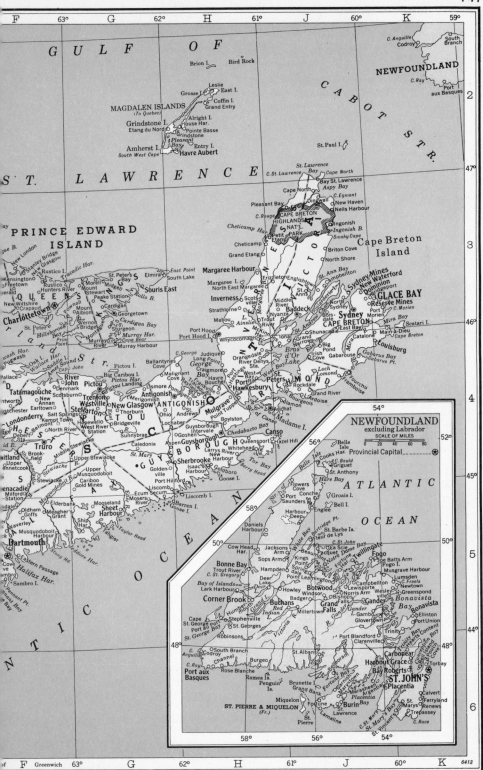

GULF OF

ST. LAWRENCE

Brion I.   Bird Rock

NEWFOUNDLAND

C. Anguille
Codroy   South Branch

C. Ray
Port aux Basques

Leslie
Grosse I.   East I.
Coffin I.
Grand Entry
MAGDALEN ISLANDS
(To Quebec)
Grindstone I.   Alright I.
Etang du Nord   House Har.
Pointe Basse
Grindstone
Pleasant
Bay
Amherst I.   Entry I.
South West Cape   Havre Aubert

St. Paul I.

CABOT STR.

ST. LAWRENCE

PRINCE EDWARD
ISLAND

St. Lawrence Bay
C. St. Lawrence   Cape North
Bay St. Lawrence
Cape North   Aspy Bay
C. Egmont
Pleasant Bay   Dingwall
New Haven
Neils Harbour
C. Rouge   CAPE BRETON
HIGHLANDS   Ingonish
Cheticamp Har.   NAT'L   Ingonish B.
PARK   Smoky Cape
Cheticamp   Briton Cove
Grand Etang   North Shore

Cape Breton
Island

Margaree Harbour
East Point
South Lake
Margaree I.
North East Margaree   Frizzleton
Englishtown
Inverness   Scots-   St. Ann Bay   Campbellton
ville   St.
Red   Ann's   Sydney Mines
River   New Waterford
Strathlorne   Nyanza   North   Dominion
Baddeck   Sydney   GLACE BAY
Mabou   Ainslie   Reserve Mines
McKin-   Port   C. Morien
Port Hood   non   Morien
Port Hood I.   Grand   CAPE BRETON
Whycocomagh   Narrows   East Bay   Mira Bay   Scatari I.
Bras   Big   Main-a-Dieu
C. George   Judique   d'Or   Pond   Gabarus   Cape Breton
Long Point   West   Irish   Cove   Gabarus Bay
Ballantynes   George   Bay   Cove   Louisburg
Pictou I.   Cove   River Denys   St.   Gabarus Pt.
Big Caribou I.   Bay   L'Ardoise   Loch   Fourchu
Cape John   Malignant   Havre   Bouchar   Peters   Lomond   Framboise
Pictou Har.   Cove   Boucher   Rockdale
River   Ilsmore   Port   Grand River
John   Denver   Hawkesbury   RICHMOND
Pictou   Port Tupper   St. Bourgeois   Ardoise
Merigomish   Arichat
Trenton   Ohio   St.   Madame I.
Westville   Andrews   Boylston
New Glasgow   ANTIGONISH   Mulgrave
Thorburn   Lochaber   Guysborough
Stellarton   Bridgeville   Intervale
Sunnybrae   Chedabucto Bay

Canso

PICTOU

Caledonia   Aspen   Queensport   Hazel Hill
St. Mary   Larrys
Upper Stewiacke   River   Whitehead
Golden-   New
ville   Harbour   Tor Bay   Ferry Head
Sherbrooke   Isaac's
Port Hilford   Harbour   Goldboro
Liscomb   Colabora   Goose I.
Liscomb I.
Mosers   Barren I.
River   Goose I.

ATLANTIC

OCEAN

NEWFOUNDLAND
excluding Labrador
SCALE OF MILES
0   20   40   60   80

Belle
Isle
Belle Isle
Cook's Har.   St. Anthony
C. Bauld   Provincial Capital
Griquet
St. Anthony
Hare Bay   ATLANTIC
Flowers   Conche
Cove   Groais I.
Port   Bell I.
Saunders   Englee
Harbour   OCEAN
Deep
Daniels
Harbour
C. St. John
Cow Head   White   Partridge Pt.
Har.   Bay   Fleur de Lys
Jacksons   La Scie   Twillingate
Arm   Pacquet   Fogo
Sops Arm   Kings   Spring   Fortune   Fogo I.
Bonne Bay   Point   Dale   Batts Arm
Trout River   Hampden   Leamington   Musgrave Harbour
C. St. Gregory   Deer   Lumsden
Bay of Islands   Lake   Norris Arm   Greenspond
Lark Harbour   Howley   Lewisporte   Newtown
Badger   Campbellton   Wesleyville
Corner Brook   Botwood   Gander   Bonavista
Buchans   Windsor   L. Gambo   Bay
Cape   Stephenville   Grand   Gloverton   Eliston
St. George   Millertown   Falls   Port Union
St. George Bay   Gander   Trinity
St. Georges   Victoria   L. Gambo
Robinsons   Glovertown   Hearts Content
South Branch   Bishops   Harbour Grace
C. Anguille   St. Albans   Carbonear
Channel   Belleoram   Bay Roberts
C. Ray   Burgeo   St. John   Torbay
Port aux   Rose Blanche   ST. JOHN'S
Basques   Ramea Is.   Brunette I.   Placentia
Penguin   Grand Bank   Calvert
Is.   Fortune   Ferryland
Miquelon   Burin   Renews
ST. PIERRE & MIQUELON   Lamaline   St.   Trepassey
(Fr.)   Lawrence   St. Marys   C. Race
St.   C. St. Marys   St. Vincents
Pierre   C. Race

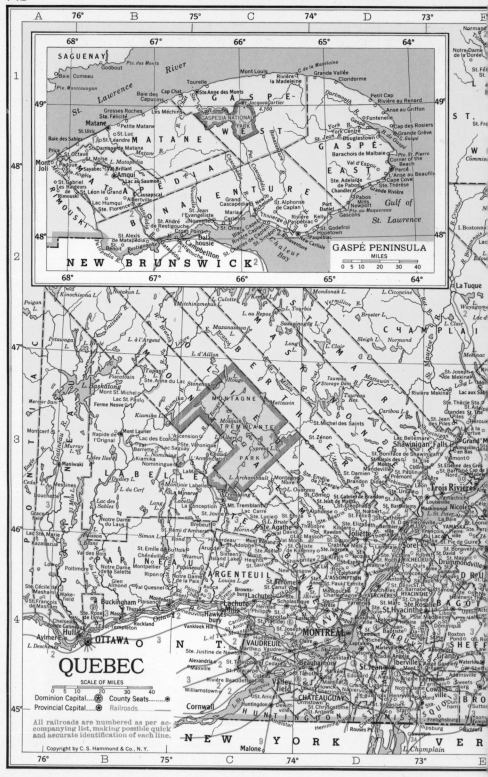

GASPÉ PENINSULA

MILES

QUEBEC

SCALE OF MILES

Dominion Capital ⊛   County Seats ◉
Provincial Capital ⊛   Railroads

All railroads are numbered as per accompanying list, making possible quick
and accurate identification of each line.

Copyright by C. S. Hammond & Co., N.Y.

7 Napierville Junction   10 Quebec Central   12 Roberval & Saguenay
9 New York Central   11 Quebec Ry., Light and Power   14 Temiscouata

143

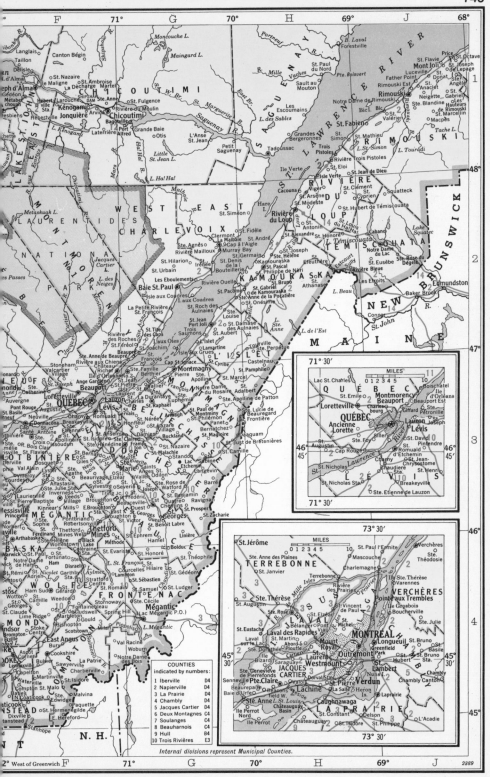

COUNTIES
indicated by numbers:

1 Iberville   D4
2 Napierville   D4
3 La Prairie   D4
4 Chambly   D4
5 Jacques Cartier   D4
6 Deux Montagnes   C4
7 Soulanges   C4
8 Beauharnois   C4
9 Hull   B4
10 Trois Rivières   E3

Internal divisions represent Municipal Counties.

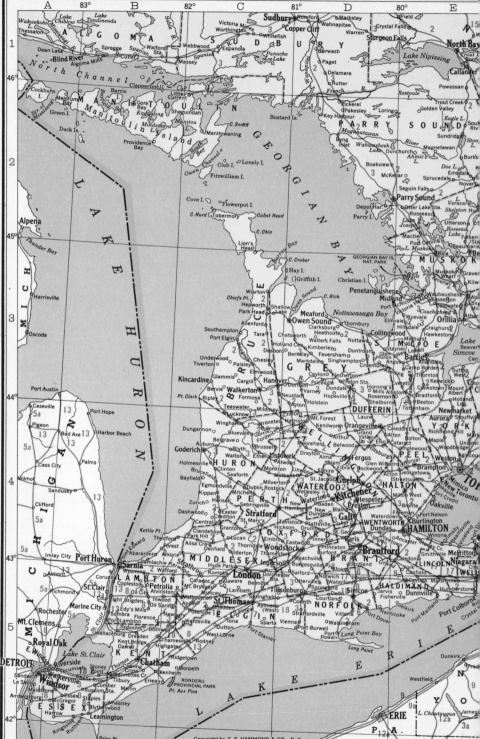

York Central
w York, Chicago & St. Louis
ario Northland

12a Pennsylvania
13 Chesapeake & Ohio
13a Port Huron & Detroit

17 Toronto, Hamilton and Buffalo
18 Wabash

145

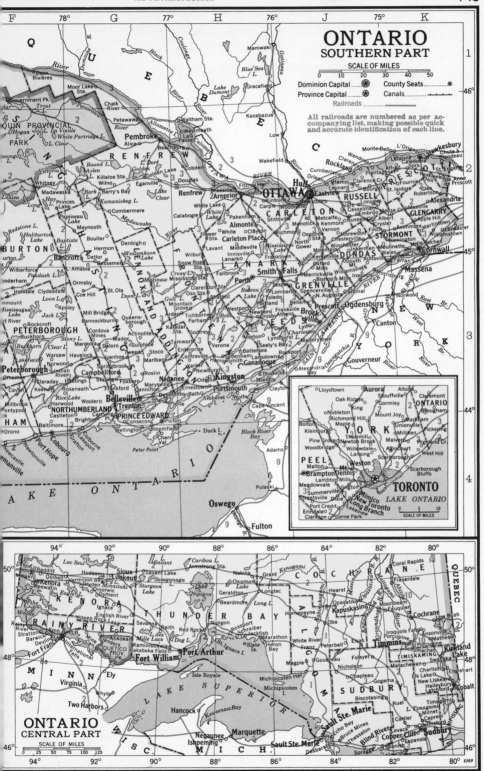

ONTARIO
SOUTHERN PART
SCALE OF MILES

| | | | | | |
| 0 | 10 | 20 | 30 | 40 | 50 |

Dominion Capital......⊛   County Seats..........◉
Province Capital.......⊛   Canals...........

Railroads ....

All railroads are numbered as per accompanying list, making possible quick and accurate identification of each line.

ONTARIO
CENTRAL PART
SCALE OF MILES

| | | | | |
| 0 | 25 | 50 | 75 | 100 | 125 |

6369

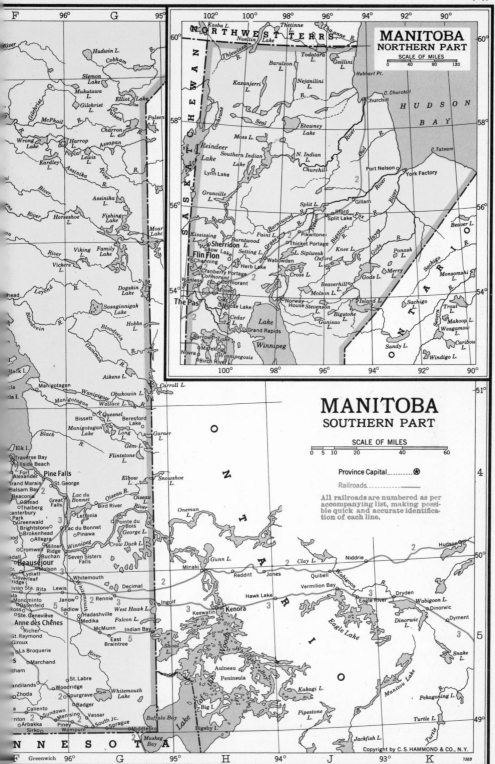

MANITOBA
NORTHERN PART
SCALE OF MILES
0 40 80 120

MANITOBA
SOUTHERN PART

SCALE OF MILES
0 5 10   20   40   60

Province Capital............⊕

Railroads...............

All railroads are numbered as per
accompanying list, making possible quick and accurate identification of each line.

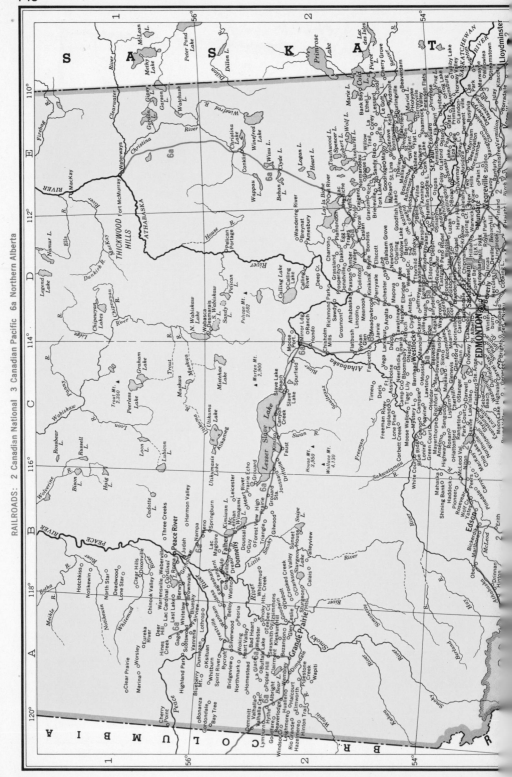

RAILROADS: 2 Canadian National 3 Canadian Pacific 6a Northern Alberta

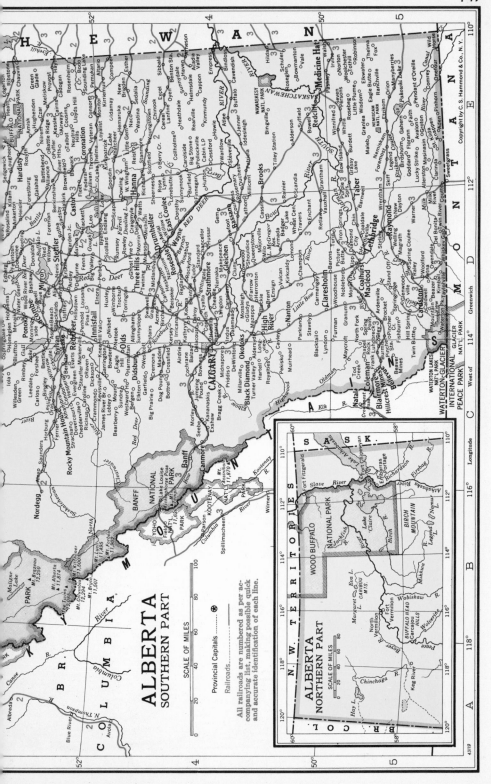

ALBERTA
SOUTHERN PART

SCALE OF MILES

Provincial Capitals .... ⊛
Railroads ....

All railroads are numbered as per accompanying list, making possible quick and accurate identification of each line.

Copyright by C. S. Hammond & Co., N.Y.

ALBERTA
NORTHERN PART

SCALE OF MILES

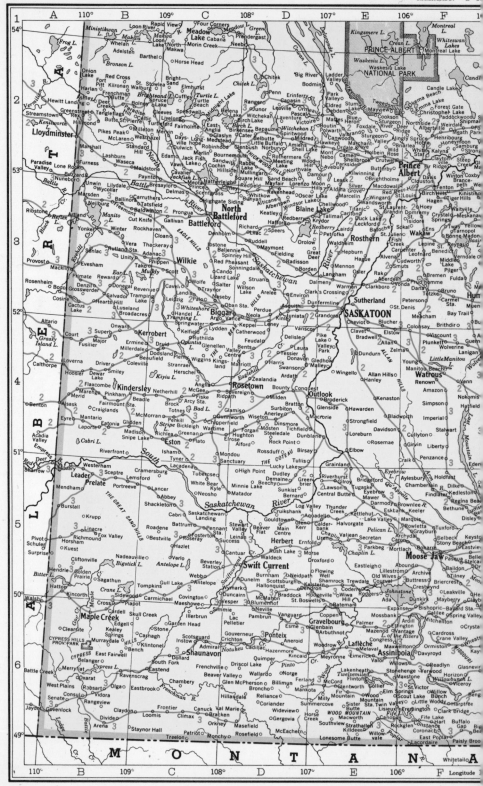

SASKATCHEWAN
NORTHERN PART

MILES
0 20 40 60 80 100

N. W. TERR'S

SASKATCHEWAN
SOUTHERN PART

SCALE OF MILES
0 5 10   20   40   60

Provincial Capital .... ⊛
Railroads.................

All railroads are numbered as per accompanying list, making possible quick and accurate identification of each line.

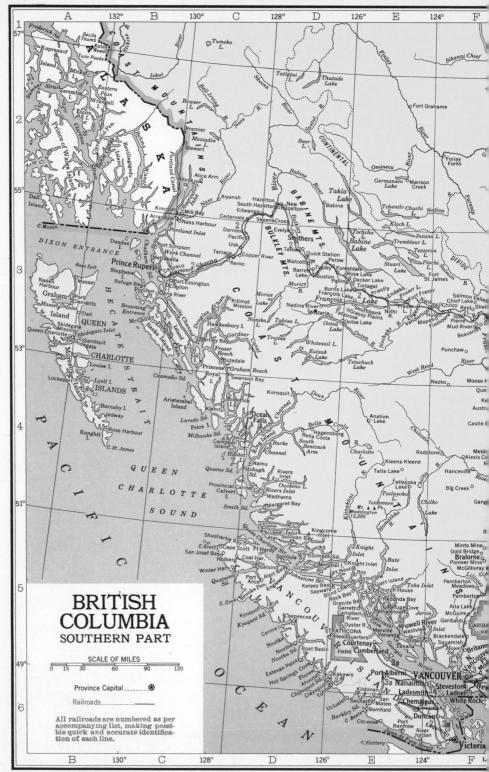

BRITISH COLUMBIA
SOUTHERN PART

SCALE OF MILES

0   15   30   60   90   120

Province Capital .... ⊛

Railroads ....

All railroads are numbered as per
accompanying list, making possible quick and accurate identification of each line.

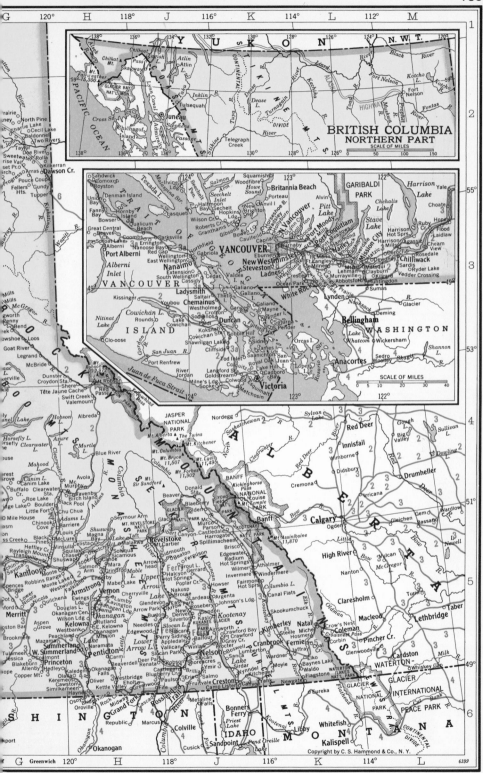

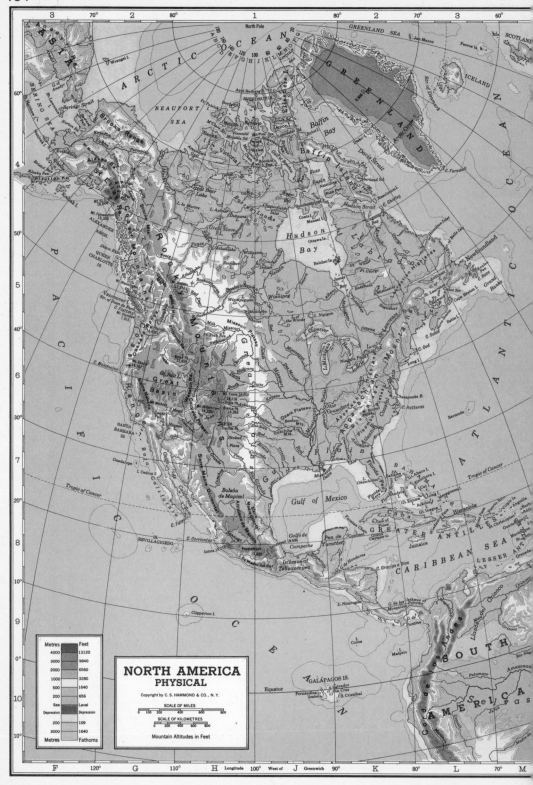

NORTH AMERICA
PHYSICAL
Copyright by C. S. HAMMOND & CO., N. Y.

SCALE OF MILES

SCALE OF KILOMETRES

Mountain Altitudes in Feet

Metres		Feet
4000		13120
3000		9840
2000		6560
1000		3280
500		1640
200		656
Sea		Level
Depression		Depression
200		109
3000		1640
Metres		Fathoms

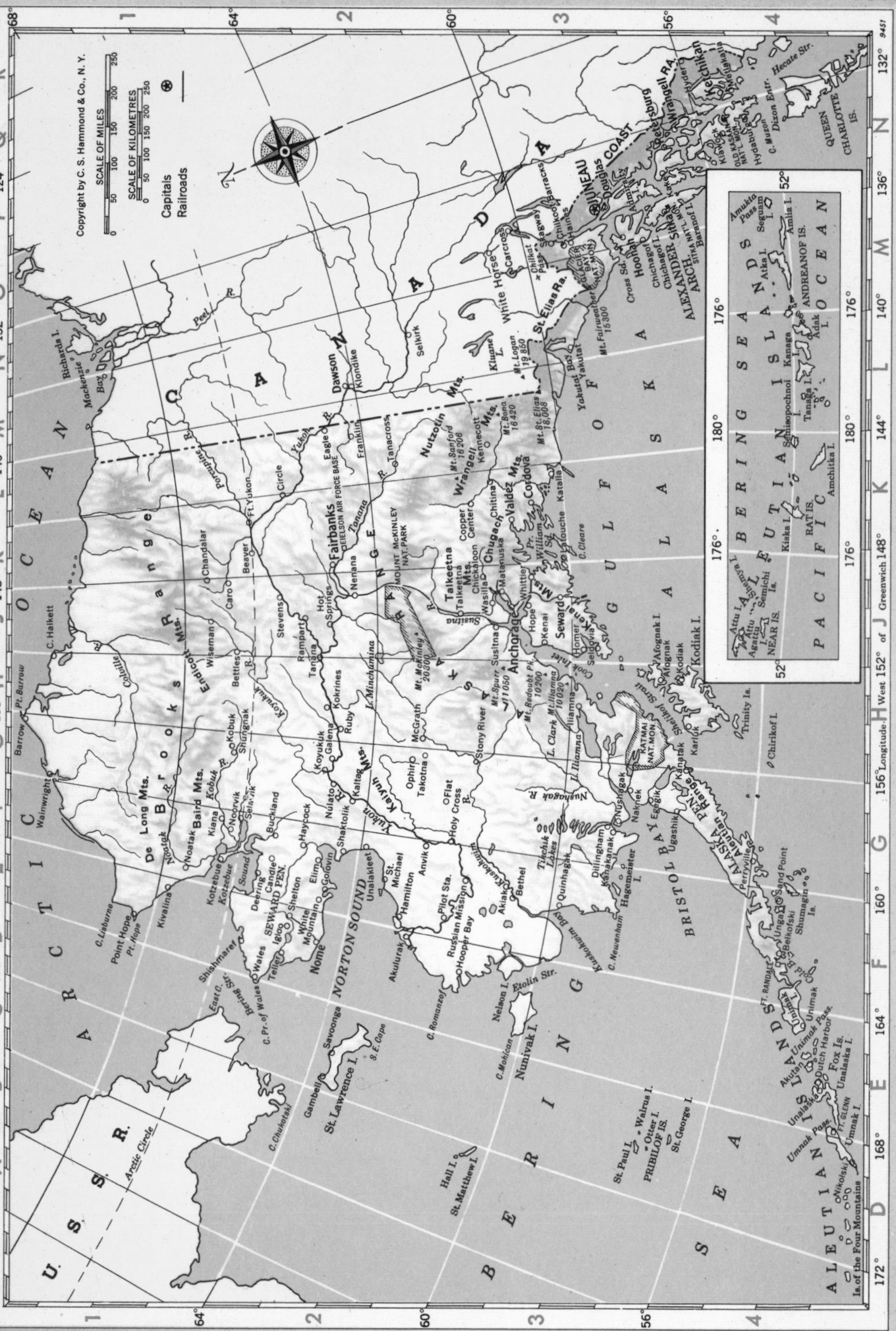

Copyright by C. S. Hammond & Co., N. Y.

SCALE OF MILES

SCALE OF KILOMETRES

Capitals
Railroads

CANADA

ARCTIC OCEAN

BERING SEA

GULF OF ALASKA

PACIFIC OCEAN

ALEUTIAN ISLANDS

Brooks Range

De Long Mts.

Endicott Mts.

Baird Mts.

ALASKA RANGE

St. Elias Mts.

Wrangell Mts.

NORTON SOUND

SEWARD PEN.

BRISTOL BAY

ALEXANDER ARCH.

QUEEN CHARLOTTE IS.

U. S. S. R.

Arctic Circle

JUNEAU
Douglas
Ketchikan
Skagway
Dawson
Fairbanks
Anchorage
Nome
Seward
Cordova
Valdez
Kodiak
Barrow
Wainwright
Kotzebue
Bethel
Dillingham

MOUNT McKINLEY NAT. PARK

MOUNT McKINLEY 20300

Mt. St. Elias 18,008

Mt. Logan 19,850

Yukon R.

Tanana R.

Kuskokwim R.

Nunivak I.
St. Lawrence I.
St. Matthew I.
Hall I.
Pribilof Is.
St. Paul I.
St. George I.
Kodiak I.
Afognak I.
Unimak I.
Unalaska I.

KATMAI NAT. MON.

BERING SEA ISLANDS

ATTU
AGATTU
NEAR IS.
RAT IS.
Kiska I.
Amchitka I.
ANDREANOF IS.
Atka I.
Adak
Amlia I.
Seguam I.
Amukta Pass

Ix. of the Four Mountains

RAILROADS

9	Alabama, Tennessee & Northern
12	Atlanta & St. Andrews Bay
13	Atlanta & West Point
14	Atlantic Coast Line
17	Atlantic Coast Line
20	Birmingham & Southeastern
24	Birmingham Southern
24	Central of Georgia
28	Chattahoochee Valley
73	Gulf, Mobile & Ohio
87	Illinois Central
107	Louisville & Nashville
107a	Meridian & Bigbee River
108	Manistee & Repton
110	Mississippi & Alabama
114	Mobile & Gulf
124	Gulf, Mobile & Ohio
127	Nashville, Chattanooga & St. Louis
160	St. Louis–San Francisco
168	Seaboard Air Line
168	Southern
169	Sumter & Choctaw
173	Tennessee, Alabama & Georgia
174	Tuskegee
179	Western Railway of Alabama

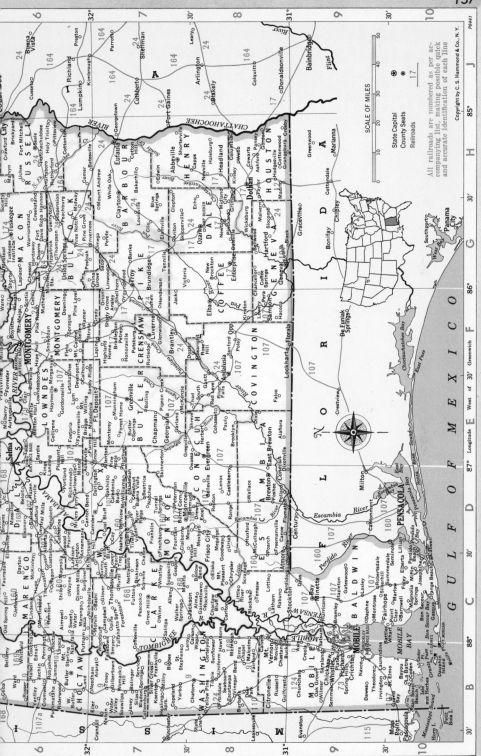

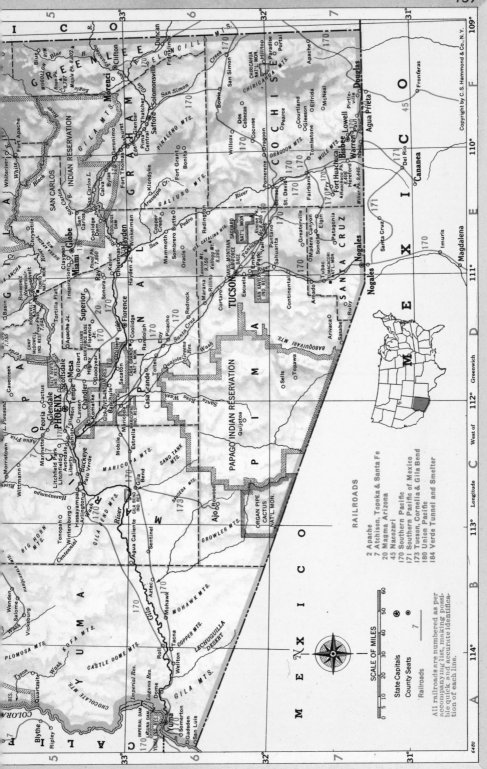

RAILROADS

2 Apache
7 Atchison, Topeka & Santa Fe
20 Magma Arizona
45 Nacozari
170 Southern Pacific
171 Southern Pacific of Mexico
173 Tucson, Cornelia & Gila Bend
180 Union Pacific
184 Verde Tunnel and Smelter

State Capitals
County Seats
Railroads

SCALE OF MILES
0 5 10 20 30 40 50 60

All railroads are numbered as per accompanying list, making possible quick and accurate identification of each line.

6450

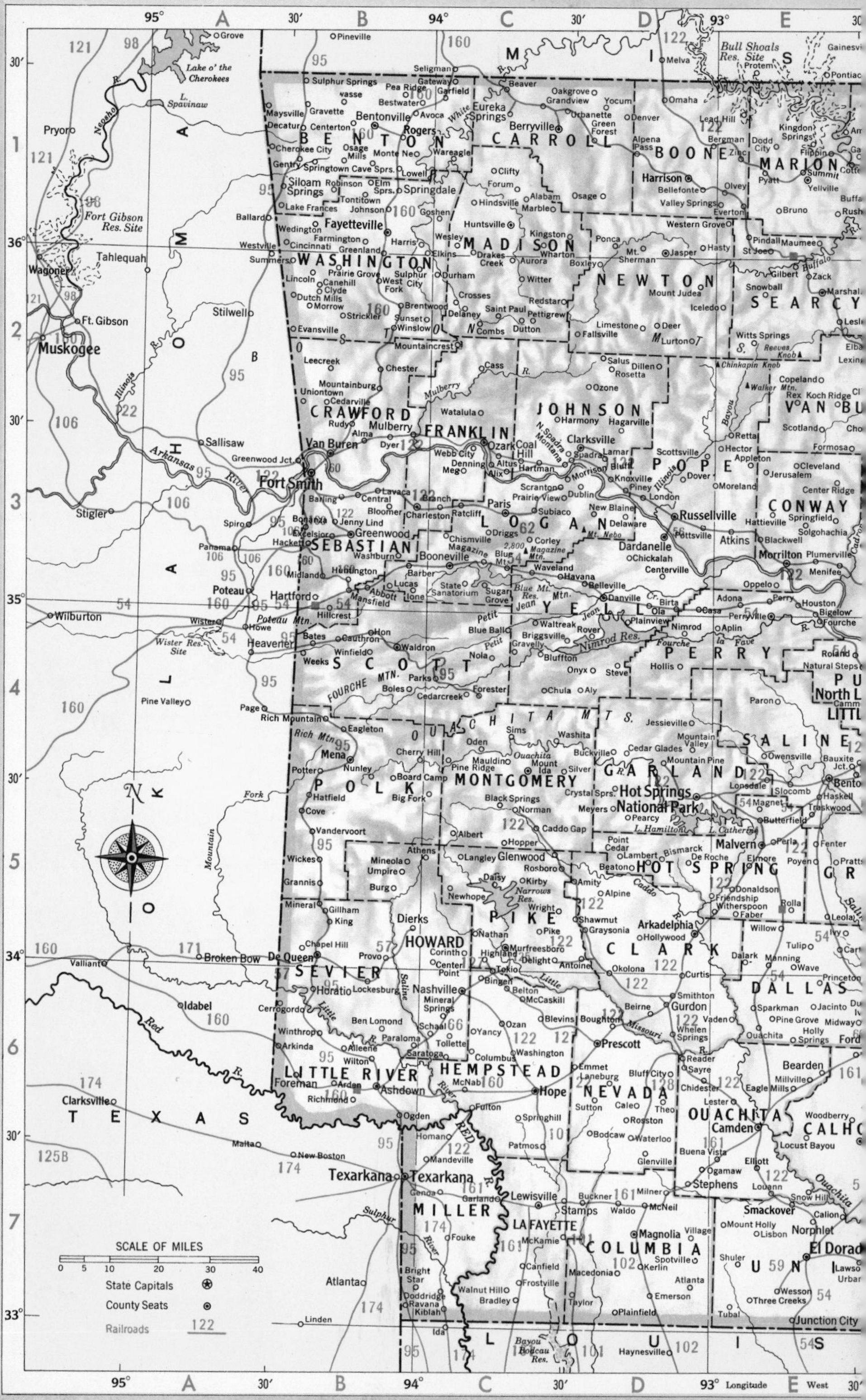

M I S S O U R I

Counties and places (north to south, west to east):

BENTON · CARROLL · BOONE · MARION · SEARCY

WASHINGTON · MADISON · NEWTON · VAN BUREN

CRAWFORD · FRANKLIN · JOHNSON · POPE · CONWAY

SEBASTIAN · LOGAN · YELL · PERRY · PULASKI

SCOTT · MONTGOMERY · GARLAND · SALINE

POLK · HOT SPRING · GRANT

SEVIER · HOWARD · PIKE · CLARK · DALLAS

LITTLE RIVER · HEMPSTEAD · NEVADA · OUACHITA · CALHOUN

MILLER · LAFAYETTE · COLUMBIA · UNION

O K L A H O M A

T E X A S

L O U I S I A N A

Fort Smith · Fayetteville · Bentonville · Springdale · Rogers · Harrison · Russellville · Hot Springs National Park · Malvern · Arkadelphia · Camden · El Dorado · Magnolia · Texarkana · Hope · Nashville · Mena · Paris · Clarksville · Van Buren · Poteau · Muskogee · Tahlequah · Fort Gibson

SCALE OF MILES

0 5 10 20 30 40

State Capitals ✪
County Seats ◉
Railroads ⎯122⎯

95°   30'   94°   30'   93° Longitude West 30'

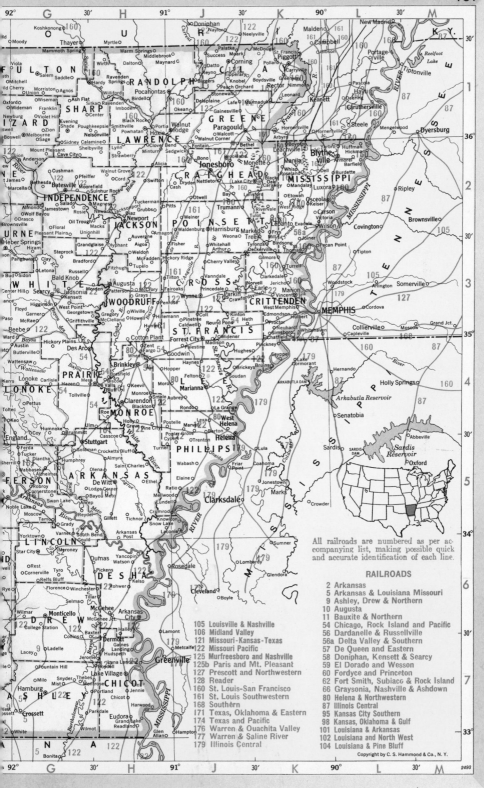

All railroads are numbered as per accompanying list, making possible quick and accurate identification of each line.

RAILROADS

2 Arkansas
5 Arkansas & Louisiana Missouri
9 Ashley, Drew & Northern
10 Augusta
11 Bauxite & Northern
54 Chicago, Rock Island and Pacific
56 Dardanelle & Russellville
56a Delta Valley & Southern
57 De Queen and Eastern
58 Doniphan, Kensett & Searcy
59 El Dorado and Wesson
60 Fordyce and Princeton
62 Fort Smith, Subiaco & Rock Island
66 Graysonia, Nashville & Ashdown
80 Helena & Northwestern
87 Illinois Central
95 Kansas City Southern
98 Kansas, Oklahoma & Gulf
101 Louisiana & Arkansas
102 Louisiana and North West
104 Louisiana & Pine Bluff

105 Louisville & Nashville
106 Midland Valley
121 Missouri-Kansas-Texas
122 Missouri Pacific
125 Murfreesboro and Nashville
125b Paris and Mt. Pleasant
127 Prescott and Northwestern
128 Reader
160 St. Louis-San Francisco
161 St. Louis Southwestern
168 Southern
171 Texas, Oklahoma & Eastern
174 Texas and Pacific
176 Warren & Ouachita Valley
177 Warren & Saline River
179 Illinois Central

Copyright by C. S. Hammond & Co., N. Y.

2493

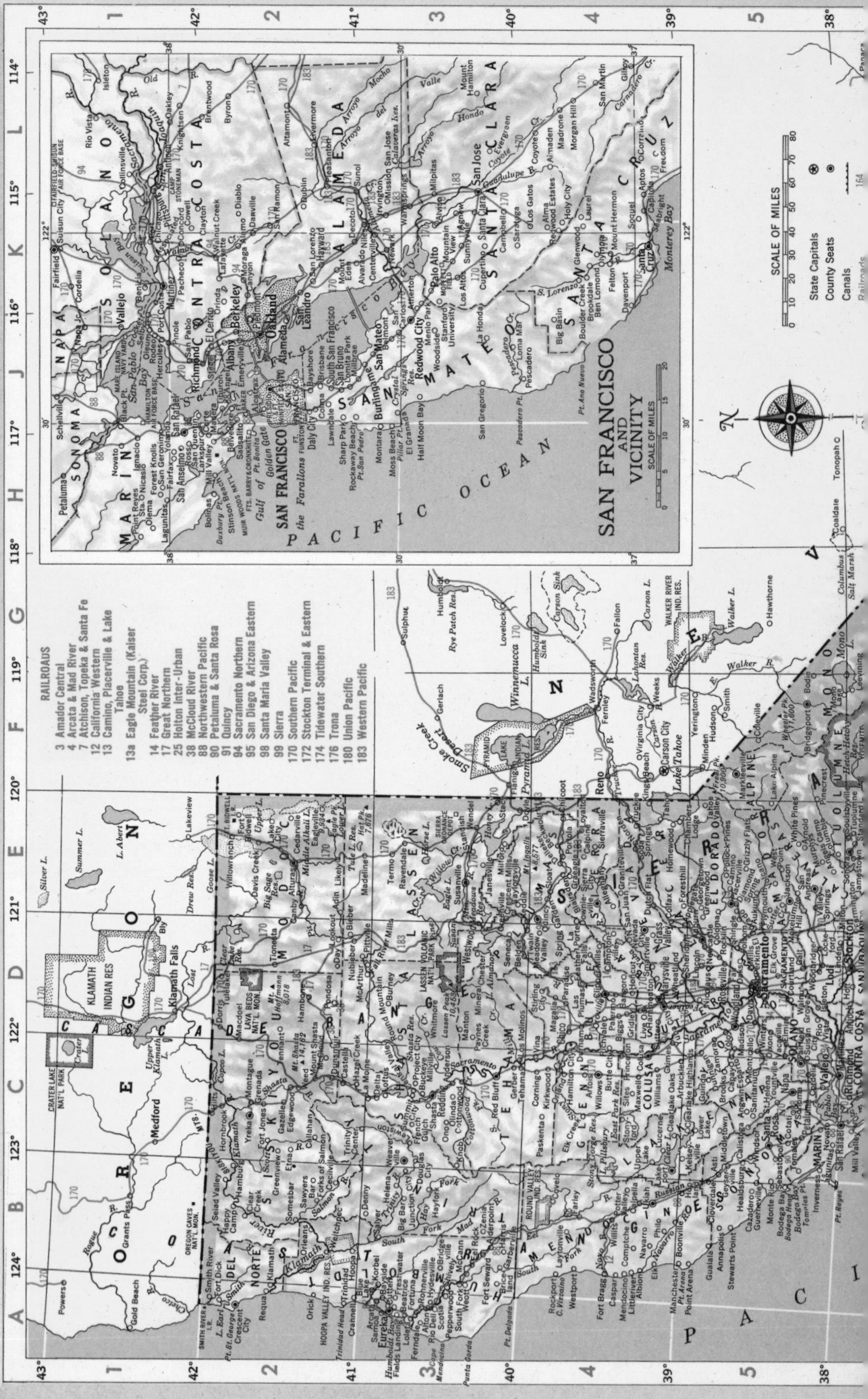

SAN FRANCISCO AND VICINITY

SCALE OF MILES

PACIFIC OCEAN

RAILROADS

3 Amador Central
7 Arcata & Mad River
7 Atchison, Topeka & Santa Fe
12 California Western
13 Camino, Placerville & Lake Tahoe
13a Eagle Mountain (Kaiser Steel Corp.)
14 Feather River
17 Great Northern
25 Holton Inter-Urban
38 McCloud River
80 Northwestern Pacific
88 Petaluma & Santa Rosa
90 Sacramento Northern
94 Sierra
95 San Diego & Arizona Eastern
99 Stockton Terminal & Eastern
170 Southern Pacific
172 Tidewater Southern
174 Trona
176 Union Pacific
180 Western Pacific
183

SCALE OF MILES

0 10 20 30 40 50 60 70 80

State Capitals
County Seats
Canals
Railroads

164

ARIZONA

Colorado R.

Lake Mead

LAKE MEAD RECREATIONAL AREA

Las Vegas

Boulder City

DEATH VALLEY NATIONAL MONUMENT

PANAMINT

Death Valley

INYO MTS.

JOSHUA TREE NATIONAL MON.

SAN BERNARDINO

Mojave Desert

Colorado Desert

Salton Sea

IMPERIAL VALLEY

El Centro

Mexicali

MEXICO

Ensenada

San Diego

SAN DIEGO

RIVERSIDE

San Bernardino

LOS ANGELES

Los Angeles

Long Beach

Santa Monica

Pasadena

VENTURA

Santa Barbara

Santa Barbara Channel

Santa Cruz I.

Santa Rosa I.

San Miguel I.

Santa Catalina I.

San Clemente I.

San Nicolas I.

San Pedro Channel

PACIFIC OCEAN

Gulf of Santa Catalina

Bakersfield

KERN

TULARE

SEQUOIA NATIONAL PARK

KINGS

Fresno

Visalia

MONTEREY

Salinas

Monterey Bay

Santa Cruz

SANTA CRUZ

SAN BENITO

SAN LUIS OBISPO

San Luis Obispo

Santa Maria

SACRAMENTO AND VICINITY

SCALE OF MILES

EL DORADO

PLACER

AMADOR

CALAVERAS

SAN JOAQUIN

SOLANO

SACRAMENTO

Sacramento

Lodi

Stockton

LOS ANGELES AND VICINITY

SCALE OF MILES

LOS ANGELES

ORANGE

RIVERSIDE

SAN BERNARDINO

Los Angeles

Long Beach

Santa Monica

Pasadena

Glendale

Burbank

Hollywood

Beverly Hills

Inglewood

Santa Ana

Anaheim

Riverside

San Bernardino

Pomona

Newport Beach

Balboa

Huntington Beach

Redondo Beach

Manhattan Beach

Hermosa Beach

San Pedro

Longitude West of Greenwich

Copyright by C. S. Hammond & Co., N.Y.

SCALE OF MILES

0 5 10 20 30 40

State Capitals ⊛ County Seats
Canals Railroads 60

All railroads are numbered as per accompanying list, making possible quick and accurate identification of each line.

W Y O M I N G

Bridgeport

Savery Slater Battle Creek King's Canyon Roach Foxpark Laporte Red Fea Lake

Columbine Mt. Zirkel 12,220 Cowdrey Walden Glendevey Glendwood Home

R O U T T Hahns Peak Clark Mystic

Greystone M O F F A T Zenobia Pk. DINOSAUR NAT'L MON. Sunbeam Lay Juniper Springs Craig Hayden Bear River Milner Steamboat Springs Spicer Gould Mt. Richthofen 12,953 Coalmont J A C K S O N ROCKY MOU

Jensen Yampa Maybell Mount Harris McGregor Sidney Rand Park View 11,432 Mt. Baker 12,406 NAT'L MO

Cross Mountain Juniper Mtn. 8,000 Hamilton Pagoda Dunkley Routt Haybro Rabbit Ears Pk. 10,119 Rabbit Ears Range Grand Lake Longs

BLUE MTN. Elk Springs Loyd Axial Willow Creek Pinnacle Oak Creek Phippsburg Granby Res.

Sand Springs Skull Creek Price Creek Pagoda Pk. 11,257 Yampa G R A N D Granby Arapaho 13,506. Hot Sulphur Springs Tabernash Fraser Winter Park 13,260 James 13,260

White Rangely Meeker Marvine Buford Trappers L. Toponas Kremmling Colorado Parshall Berthoud Pass Silver Plum Georgetown CLEA

R I O B L A N C O Yellow Cr. Piceance Cr. Burns McCoy Bond State Bridge Sheephorn Green Mtn. Res. Empire

Watson Dragon Rioblanco Riland Pershing Radium SUMMIT Montezuma Silver Plum

Atchee BOOK PLATEAU Rifle Cr. Dotsero Gypsum Eagle Wolcott Edwards Avon Minturn Frisco Dillon Tiger Santa Fe Pk.

G A R F I E Roan Rulison Rifle Antlers New Castle Silt Glenwood Springs E A G L E Gilman Redcliff Breckenridge Kokomo Mt. Baldy 13,964

De Beque Collbran Colorado Grand Valley Carbondale Basalt Sloss HOLY CROSS NAT'L MON. Tigiwon Pando Climax Alma Como

Mack Loma Fruita Holland Clifton Cameo Plateau Plateau City Molina Roaring Emma Snowmass Ruedi Troutville Meredith Tennessee Pass Jeffe

Fruitvale Palisade Bridges Skyway Woody Creek Malta Leadville Mt. Elbert 14,431 Fairplay

Westwater COLORADO NAT'L MON. Grand Junction Whitewater Grand Mesa Cedaredge Redstone Aspen P I T K I N Maroon Pk. 14,126 Grizzly Pk. 14,020 Twin Twin Lakes Res. Garo Hartsel

Glade Park M E S A Bowie Somerset Anthracite Marble Ragged Mountain L A K E Granite Antero Pea

D E L T A Eckert Austin North Paonia Crested Butte Castle Pk. 14,259 Taylor Pk. 13,419 La Plata Pk. 14,340 Buena Vista Trump

Delta Hotchkiss Lazear Baldwin Taylor Park Res. Mt. Yale 14,172 Saint Elmo Nathrop

Escalante Forks Read Crawford G U N N I S O N Almont Mt. Antero 14,172 Turret Salida

Gateway Olathe Maher BLACK CANYON OF THE GUNNISON NAT'L MON. Sapinero Gunnison Ohio Pitkin Monarch Garfield Poncha Spgs. Howard

Paradox Peagreen GUNNISON TUNNEL Cimarron Gunnison Tola Doyleville Waunita Hot Springs Parlin Marshall Coaldale

Uravan Oak Grove Montrose Sapinero Sargents Antero Mtn. 13,245 Bonanza Coalda

Bedrock M O N T R O S E Colona Ute Sheep Mtn. 13,180 Powderhorn Villagrove 14

Naturita Redvale Uncompahgre Pk. 14,306 Mineral Hot Springs Saguache Cresto

Norwood O U R A Y Ridgway Lake City San Luis Mtn. 14,149 Sogoo S A G U A C H E Moffat Creste

Summit Point Leonard Sanls Placerville Ouray Red Cloud Pk. 14,050 N. Creede L A G A R I T A MTS. Saguache

S A N M I G U E L Fall Creek Mt. Sneffels 14,143 Wetterhorn Pk. 14,020 Sunshine Pk. 14,018 Creede WHEELER NAT'L MON. La Garita GREAT SAND DUN NAT'L MON.

Egnar Cedar Vanadium Telluride Eureka Ophir CONTINENTAL Wagon Wheel Gap Center Hooper

Northdale Lone Cone Mt. Wilson 14,250 H I N S D A L E Rio Grande Res. Rio Grande Pyramid 13,830 M I N E R A L Freeman Spur Mosca Homelake

Dove Creek D O L O R E S Dunton Rico S A N J U A N Silverton Howardsville South River Mtn. 13,145 South Fork Del Norte Monte Vista A L A M

Cahone Hermosa Pk. 12,574 Tacoma Eolus Mtn. 14,079 R I O G R A N D E Del Norte Pk. 12,378 Summit Pk. 13,189 Alam

Ackmen Lewis McPhee Dolores Stoner Rockwood Graham Mtn. 12,517 Bennett Pk. 13,189 Summitville

Yellow Jacket Arriola Lebanon Hesperus Pk. 13,225 Vallecito Res. Pine River Dam Montezuma Pk. 13,131 Conejos Pk. 13,272 Nortonville

HOVENWEEP NAT'L MON. McElmo Cortez M O N T E Z U M A Trimble Sprs. A L A P L A T A Pagosa Springs Summit Pk. 13,272 La Jara

YUCCA HOUSE NAT'L MON. Towac Mancos MESA VERDE NAT'L PK. Hesperus Durango Animas Piedra A R C H U L E T A Capulin Bountiful

Only point in the UNITED STATES common to four state boundaries McElmo Cortez Breen Falfa Bayfield Dyke Conejos Romeo Manassa

Mesa Verde National Southern Ute Indian Res. Kline Oxford Ignacio Bondad Kearns Navajo Pk. 11,330 Mogote Conejos Antonito Ortiz

Redmesa Mancos Tiffany Allison Arboles Pagosa Junction Chromo C O N E J O S Canyon

ARIZ. NAVAJO INDIAN RESERVATION Riverside Cedar Hill JICARILLA IND. RES. Lumberton Chama Los Pinos

Copyright by C. S. Hammond & Co., N. Y.

Longitude 106° West

N E W M E

RAILROADS

7 Atchison, Topeka & Santa Fe

45 Chicago, Burlington & Quincy
54 Chicago, Rock Island & Pacific

54a Colorado
55 Colorado & South-Eastern

56 Colorado & Southern
57 Colorado & Wyoming

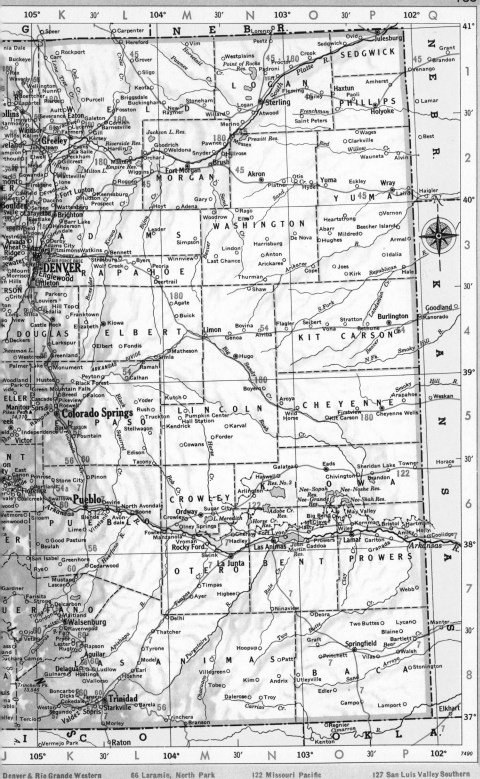

Map coordinates: 105° K 30' L 104° M 30' N 103° O 30' P 102° Q

41° — 30' — 40° — 30' — 39° — 30' — 38° — 30' — 37°

NEBRASKA

G Speer · Carpenter
Hereford · Vim · Lorenzo R.
Peetz · Sedgwick · Ovid · Julesburg
Buckeye · Rockport · Carr · Westplains · Proctor · 180 · Crook · Grant
nia Dale · Waverly · 56 · Point of Rocks Res. · Padroni · Ilif · Brandon
Nunn · Purcell · Grover · Sligo · Platte R. · **SEDGWICK** · 45 · Venango
Boettcher · Hereo · Keota · Logan · Fleming · Amherst · Lamar
Olaporte · Briggsdale · Buckingham · Stoneham · Atwood · **PHILLIPS** · Haxtun · Holyoke · Best
Aulto · Eaton · Galeton · Cornish · New · Willard · Merino · **LOGAN** · Sterling · Dailey · Paoli · Wages
Greeley · Kersey · Raymer · D · Saint Peters · Frenchman · Clarkville · Willow · Wauneta · Alvin
Evans · Gill · Hardin · Pawnee · Messex · Prewitt Res. · Red ·
La Salle · Orchard · Goodrich · Weldona · Snyder · Hillrose ·
Gilcrest · Empire Res. · **MORGAN** · Fort Morgan · 45 · Akron · Yuma · Eckley · Wray
180 · Masters · Wiggins · Otis · Platner · Hyde · **YUMA** · 45 · Laird · Haigler
Fort Lupton · Roggen · Gary · Hoyt · Adena · Rago · Vernon
Hudson · Prospect · Woodrow · Ella · Heartstrong · Beecher Island
Barr Lake · Leader · **WASHINGTON** · De Nova · Abarr · Mildred · Armel
Henderson · Derby · Simpson · Harrisburg · Anton · Hughes · Idalia
Watkins · Bennett · Lindon · Arickaree · Joes · Kirk · Hale
ARAPAHOE · Strasburg · Byers · Peoria · Last Chance · Copel · Republican R.
DENVER · Englewood · Winnwave · Thurman · Shaw ·
Littleton · Deertrail · 180 ·
Parker · Agate · Buick · Flagler · Seibert · Stratton · Bethune · **Burlington** · Goodland
Louviers · Hill Top · Franktown · Bovina · Genoa · Arriba · Vona · Kanorado
Elizabeth · Kiowa · Limon · 54 · **KIT CARSON** · Smoky Hill
DOUGLAS · Larkspur · Matheson · Hugo · Smoky · Arapahoe · Weskan
ELBERT · Elbert · Fondis · Simla · Ramah · Boyero · 180 · Firstview · Kit Carson · 180 · Cheyenne Wells · Horace
Monument · 54 · Calhan · **CHEYENNE** · Sheridan Lake · Towner
Black Forest · Peyton · Kutch · Yoder · Aroya · Wild · Chivington · Brandon · 122
Colorado Springs · Rush · Truckton · Hall Station · Karval · Horse · Galatea · Eads · **KIOWA** ·
EL PASO · Stellwagon · Kendrick · Forder · Haswell · Arlington · Nee-Sopah Res. · Nee-Noshe Res.
Fountain · Edison · Cowans · Res. No. 3 · Adobe Cr. Res. · Nee-Grande Res. · Nee-Shah Res.
56 · 60 · Tacony · **CROWLEY** · Sugar City · 122 · Big Bend · Max Valley
Penrose · Stone City · Pinon · Ordway · Olney Springs · Horse Cr. · McClave · Wiley · Kornman · Bristol · Amity · Holly
Pueblo · Devine · North Avondale · Crowley · L. Meredith · Hasty · Kornman · Coolidge
Florence · Boone · Fowler · Cheraw · Fort Lyon · **PROWERS** · Carlton
Swallows · 60 · Blende · Avondale · Manzanola · Hadley · Las Animas · John Martin Res. · Caddoa · **Lamar** · Granada · Arkansas R.
PUEBLO · Lime · Rocky Ford · Vroman · Prowers · Wiley
Good Pasture · 56 · Swink · **BENT** · Webb ·
Beulah · Greenhorn · **OTERO** · La Junta · Clay
San Isabel · Cedarwood · 60 · Timpas · Higbee · Rule · 7
Rye · Mustang · **HUERFANO** · Ayer · Ninaview · Deora
Farisita · Strong · Delcarbon · Delhi · Two Buttes · Lycano · Manter
Gordon · Maitland · Thatcher · Graft · Blaine · Bartlett · 7
Walsenburg · Ravenwood · Tyrone · Hoopup · Springfield · Vilas · Walsh
Pryor · Rapson · Model · Pattr · Pritchett
Aguilar · Rugby · **LAS** · Villegreen · Kim · Andrix · Utleyville · Stonington
Delagua · Ludlow · Earl · Tobe · **BACA** · Sand ·
Hastings · Hoehne · Dalerose · Troy · Edler · Lamport
Boncarbo · Dicks · Jansen · **Trinidad** · Barela · Carrizo · Campo
Cokedale · Starkville · 56 · Trinchera · Branson
Valdez · Sopris · Morley · Regnier · Cimarron · Elkhart
Raton · **OKLAHOMA** · Kenton

KANSAS

COLFAX · Vermejo Park

7490

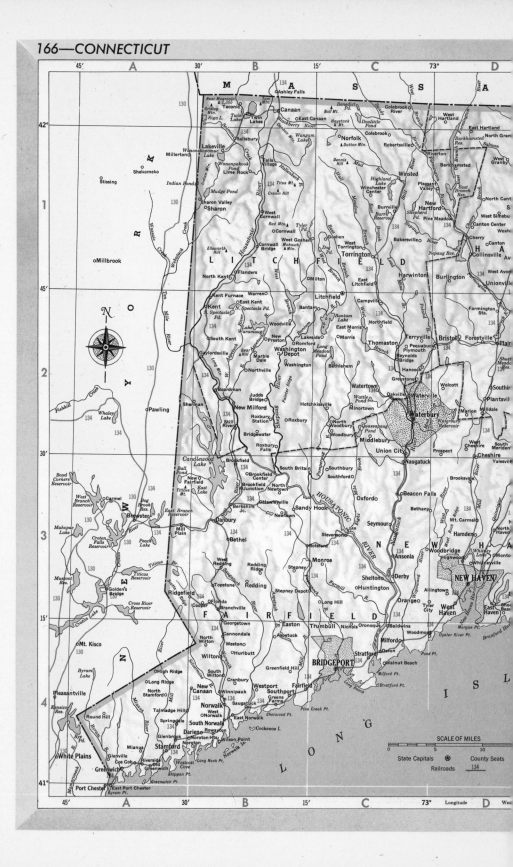

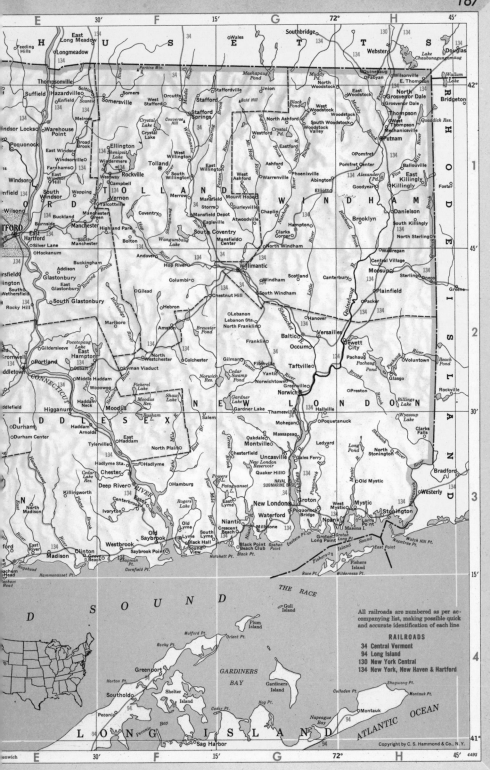

All railroads are numbered as per accompanying list, making possible quick and accurate identification of each line.

RAILROADS
34 Central Vermont
94 Long Island
130 New York Central
134 New York, New Haven & Hartford

Copyright by C. S. Hammond & Co., N. Y.

4498

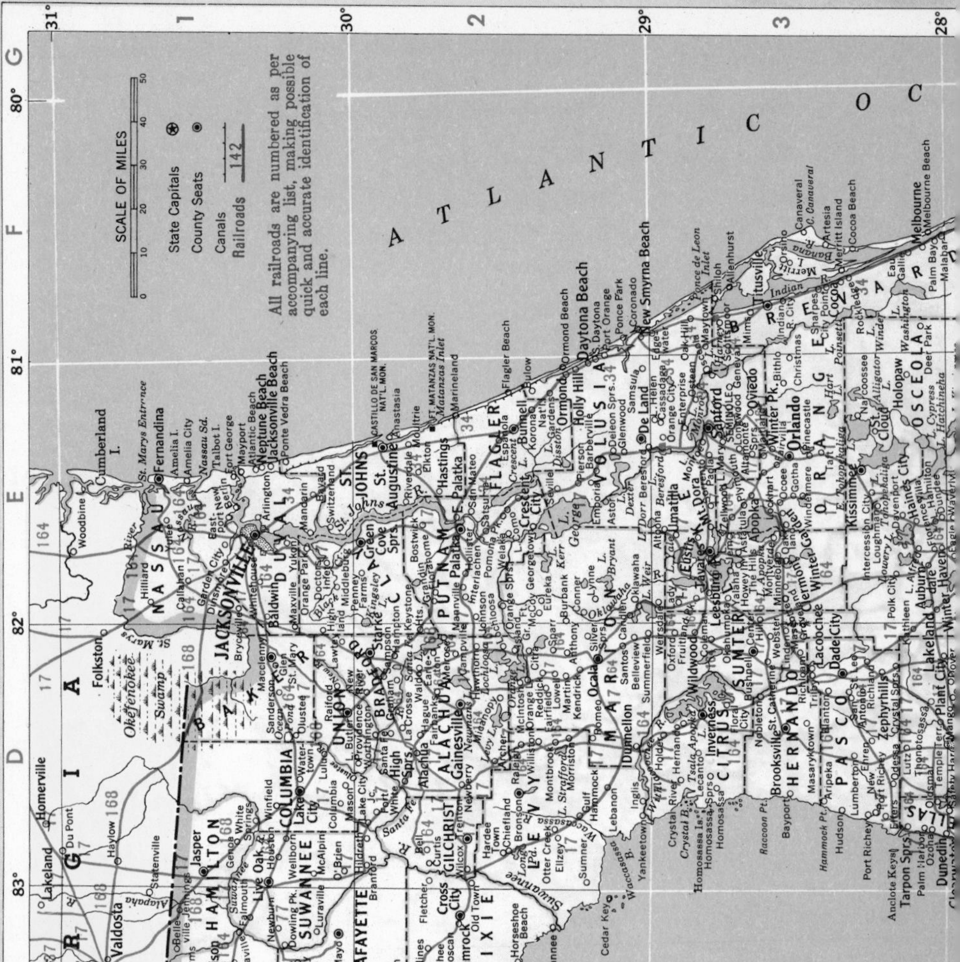

SCALE OF MILES

State Capitals ⊛
County Seats ⊙
Canals
Railroads 142

All railroads are numbered as per accompanying list, making possible quick and accurate identification of each line.

ATLANTIC OCEAN

GULF OF MEXICO

GEORGIA

ALA.

Thomasville
Cairo
Quitman
Valdosta
Bainbridge
Donalsonville
Homerville
Folkston
Cumberland I.

Chattahoochee River
Apalachicola

JACKSON
GADSDEN
LIBERTY
CALHOUN
LEON
WAKULLA
FRANKLIN
JEFFERSON
MADISON
HAMILTON
COLUMBIA
SUWANNEE
LAFAYETTE
TAYLOR
DIXIE
BAKER
NASSAU
DUVAL
CLAY
BRADFORD
UNION
ALACHUA
GILCHRIST
LEVY
MARION
PUTNAM
ST. JOHNS
FLAGLER
VOLUSIA
LAKE
ORANGE
SEMINOLE
SUMTER
CITRUS
HERNANDO
PASCO
OSCEOLA
POLK

Tallahassee
Monticello
Madison
Perry
Jasper
Live Oak
Lake City
Gainesville
Ocala
Palatka
St. Augustine
Jacksonville
Fernandina
Amelia City
Mayport
Neptune Beach
Jacksonville Beach
Ponte Vedra Beach
Hastings
Bunnell
Ormond Beach
Daytona Beach
New Smyrna Beach
De Land
Sanford
Orlando
Winter Park
Kissimmee
Bushnell
Brooksville
Dade City
Tarpon Springs
Dunedin
Inverness
Crystal River
Cedar Keys
Cross City
Horseshoe Beach
Steinhatchee
Mayo
Melbourne
Cocoa
Titusville
Lakeland

Okefenokee Swamp

Apalachee Bay

Suwannee River

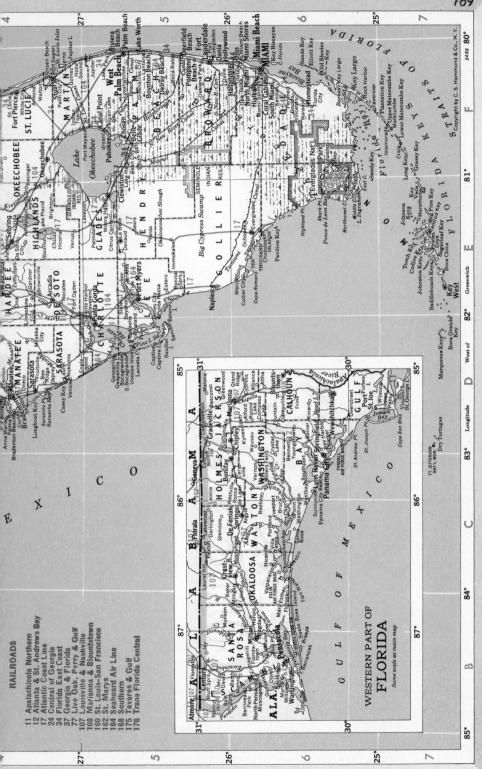

RAILROADS

11 Apalachicola Northern
12 Atlanta & St. Andrews Bay
17 Atlantic Coast Line
24 Central of Georgia
34 Florida East Coast
37 Georgia & Florida
77 Live Oak, Perry & Gulf
107 Louisville & Nashville
108 Marianna & Blountstown
160 St. Louis–San Francisco
162 St. Marys
164 Seaboard Air Line
168 Southern
175 Tavares & Gulf
176 Trans Florida Central

WESTERN PART OF
FLORIDA

Same scale as main map

Copyright by C. S. Hammond & Co., N.Y.

RAILROADS

All railroads are numbered as per accompanying list, making possible quick and accurate identification of each line

9	Albany & Northern	108	Louisville & Wadley
10	Apalachicola Northern	110	Macon, Dublin & Savannah
13	Atlanta & West Point	114	Milstead
14	Atlantic Coast Line	127	Nashville, Chattanooga & St. Louis
17	Atlantic Coast Line	128	St. Marys
21	Bowdon	129	Sandersville
22	Blue Ridge	132	Savannah & Atlanta
24	Central of Georgia	164	Seaboard Air Line
27	Charleston & Western Carolina	168	Southern
28	Chattahoochee Valley	169	South Georgia
33	Gainesville Midland	170	Sylvania Central
34	Georgia	171	Talbotton
37	Georgia & Florida	172	Tallulah Falls
38	Georgia, Ashburn, Sylvester & Camilla	173	Tennessee, Alabama & Georgia
40	Georgia Northern	175	Wadley Southern
44	Hartwell	179	Western Railway of Alabama
45	Lakeland	181	Wrightsville & Tennille
107	Louisville & Nashville		

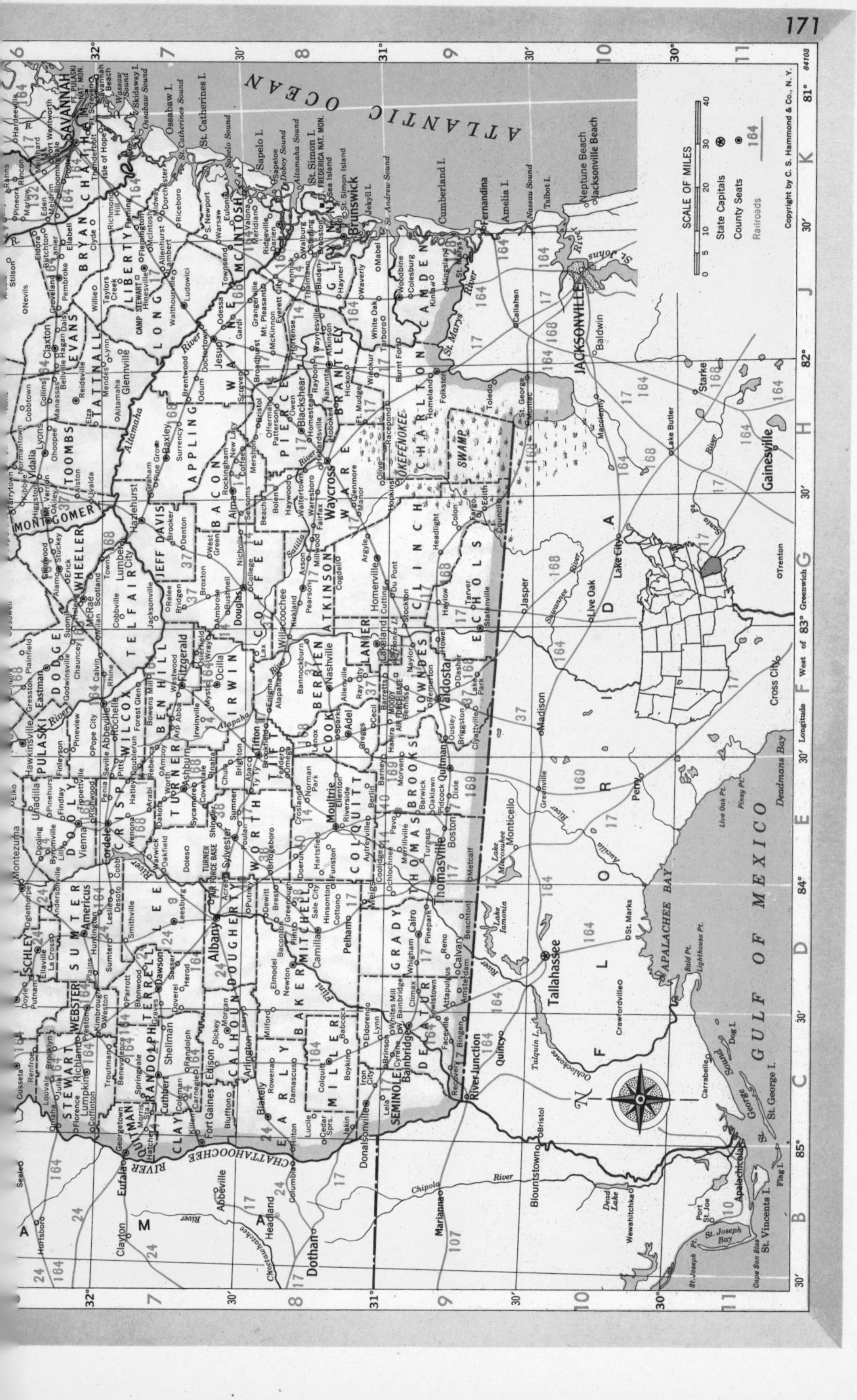

ATLANTIC OCEAN

GULF OF MEXICO

SCALE OF MILES

State Capitals
County Seats
Railroads

Copyright by C. S. Hammond & Co., N. Y.

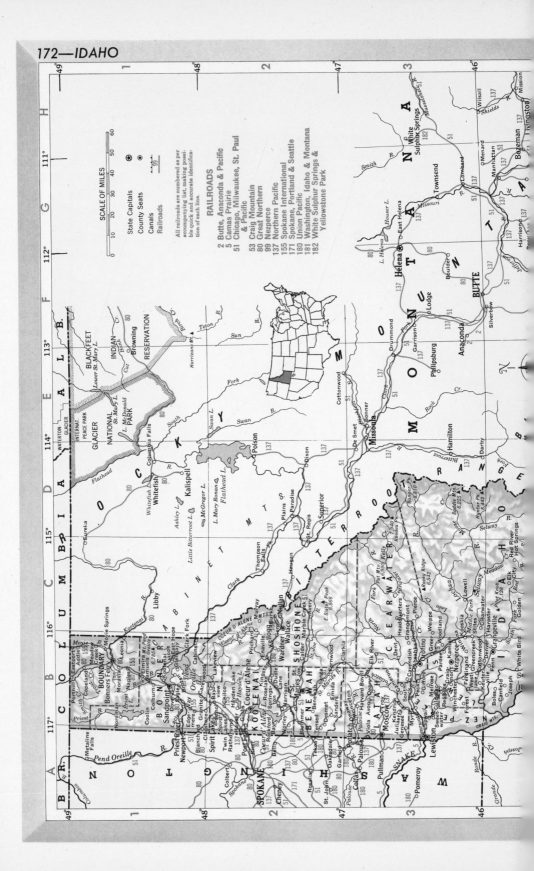

SCALE OF MILES

0 10 20 30 40 50 60

State Capitals ⊛
County Seats ⊚
Canals
Railroads ──99──

RAILROADS

All railroads are numbered as per accompanying list, making possible quick and accurate identification of each line.

2 Butte, Anaconda & Pacific
5 Camas Prairie
51 Chicago, Milwaukee, St. Paul & Pacific
53 Craig Mountain
80 Great Northern
99 Nezperce
137 Northern Pacific
155 Spokane International
171 Spokane, Portland & Seattle
180 Union Pacific
181 Washington, Idaho & Montana
182 White Sulphur Springs & Yellowstone Park

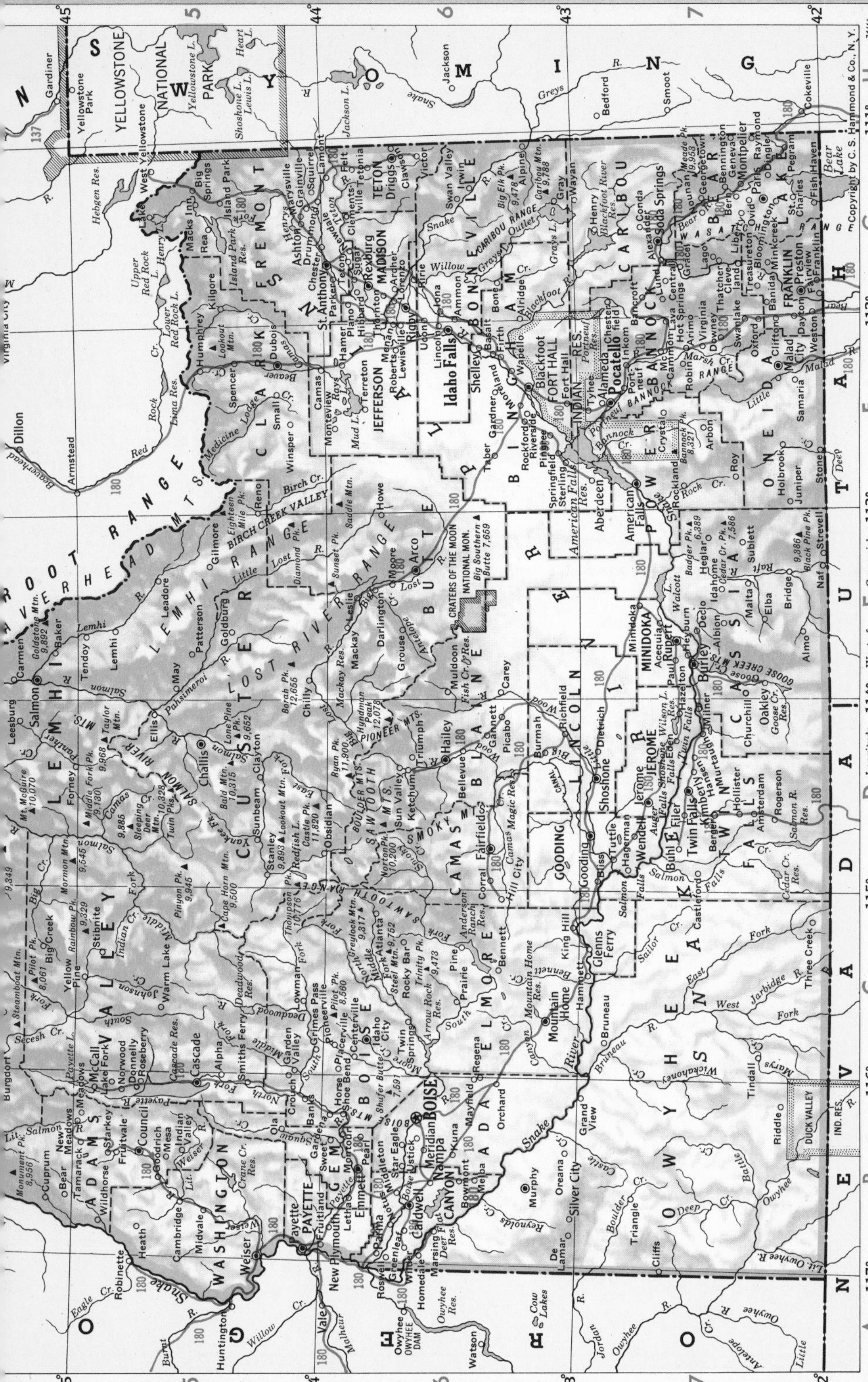

IDAHO

WYOMING

YELLOWSTONE NATIONAL PARK

NEVADA

OREGON

UTAH

BITTERROOT RANGE

BEAVERHEAD MTS.

LOST RIVER RANGE

SAWTOOTH MTS.

SALMON RIVER MTS.

LEMHI RANGE

CARIBOU RANGE

BEAR RIVER RANGE

CRATERS OF THE MOON NATIONAL MON.

Counties and towns: Boise, Nampa, Caldwell, Meridian, Idaho Falls, Pocatello, Twin Falls, Jerome, Gooding, Shoshone, Burley, Rupert, Paul, Hailey, Bellevue, Mountain Home, Glenns Ferry, Salmon, Challis, Mackay, Arco, Blackfoot, American Falls, Montpelier, Preston, Franklin, Malad, Soda Springs, Rexburg, St. Anthony, Ashton, Driggs, Victor, McCall, Cascade, Weiser, Payette, Emmett, Council, Cambridge, Grangeville

Counties: LEMHI, CUSTER, BLAINE, CAMAS, ELMORE, OWYHEE, ADA, CANYON, GEM, PAYETTE, WASHINGTON, ADAMS, VALLEY, BOISE, GOODING, LINCOLN, JEROME, MINIDOKA, CASSIA, POWER, BANNOCK, ONEIDA, FRANKLIN, BEAR LAKE, CARIBOU, BINGHAM, BONNEVILLE, MADISON, FREMONT, TETON, JEFFERSON, CLARK, BUTTE

Copyright by C. S. Hammond & Co., N.Y.

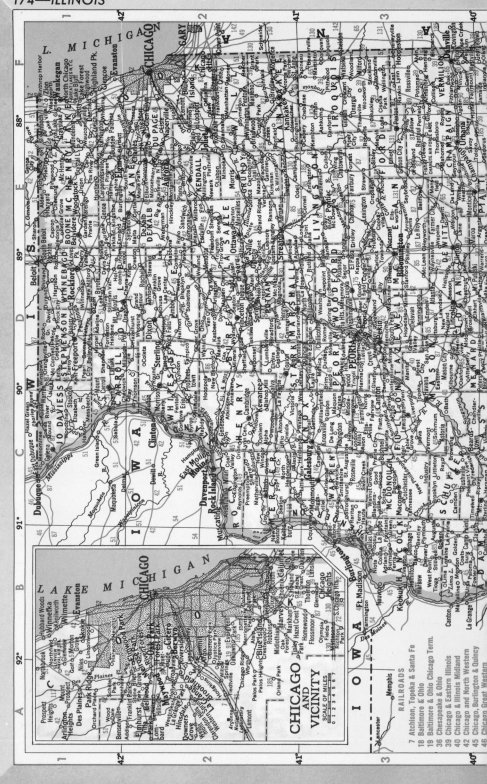

CHICAGO
AND
VICINITY
SCALE OF MILES
0 1 2 3 4 5 6 7

RAILROADS

7 Atchison, Topeka & Santa Fe
18 Baltimore & Ohio
19 Baltimore & Ohio Chicago Term.
36 Chesapeake & Ohio
39 Chicago & Eastern Illinois
40 Chicago & Illinois Midland
42 Chicago and North Western
45 Chicago, Burlington & Quincy
46 Chicago Great Western

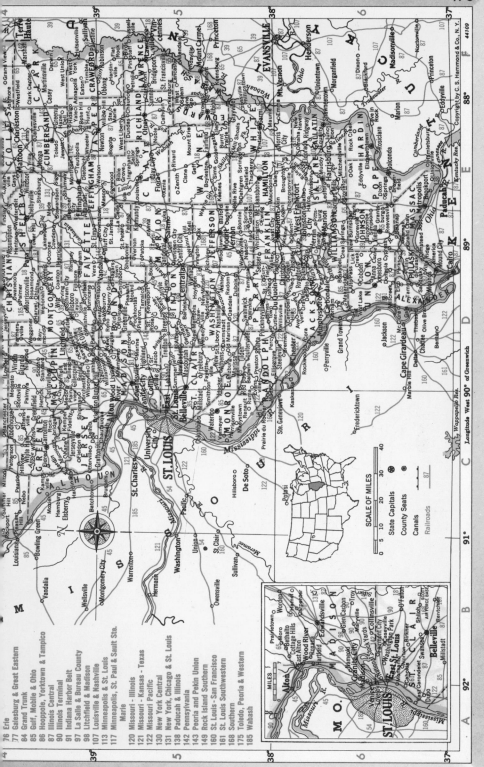

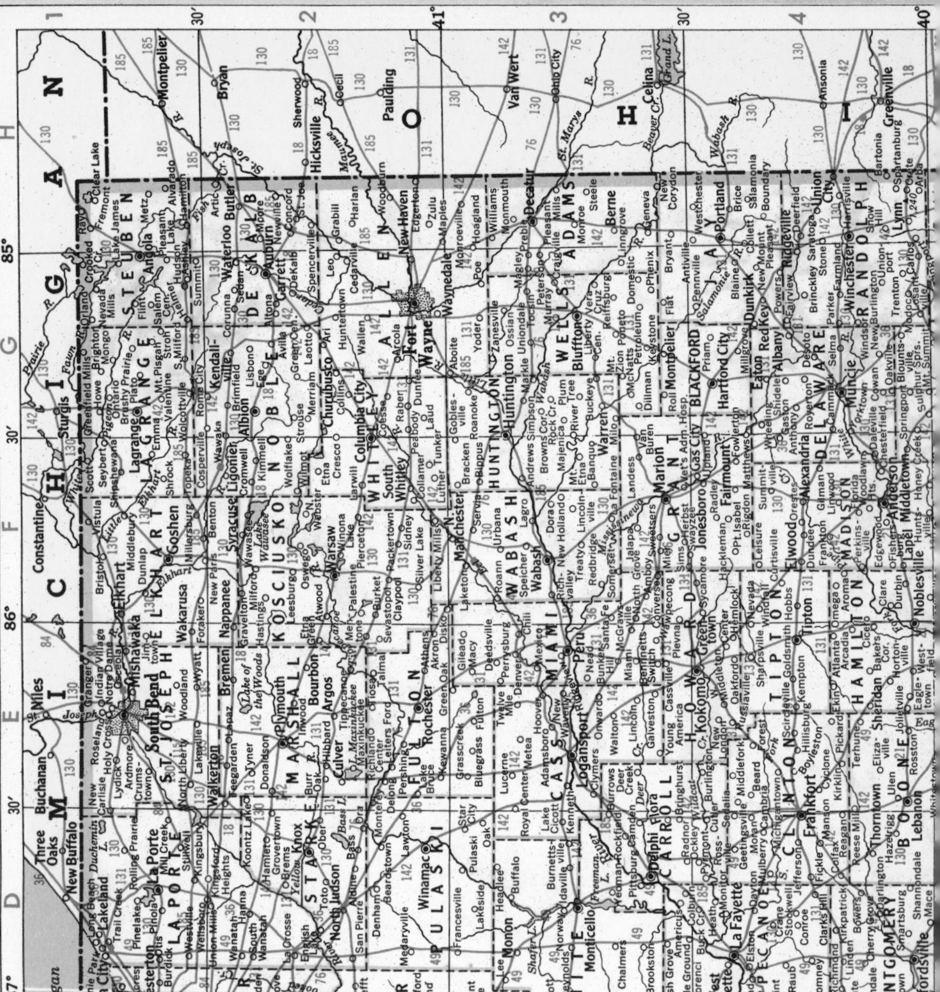
All railroads are numbered as per accompanying list, making possible quick and accurate identification of each line.
RAILROADS
1 Algers, Winslow & Western
6 Gulf, Mobile & Ohio
7 Atchison, Topeka & Santa Fe
18 Baltimore & Ohio
20 Carrollton
21 Central Indiana
36 Chesapeake & Ohio
39 Chicago & Eastern Illinois
45 Chicago, Burlington & Quincy
49 Chicago, Indianapolis & Louisville
51 Chicago, Milwaukee, St. Paul & Pacific
54 Chicago, Rock Island & Pacific
72 Elgin, Joliet & Eastern
76 Erie
79 Ferdinand
84 Grand Trunk
87 Illinois Central
90 Illinois Terminal
107 Louisville & Nashville
108 Louisville, New Albany & Corydon
115 New Jersey, Indiana & Illinois
130 New York Central
131 New York, Chicago & St. Louis
142 Pennsylvania
168 Southern
185 Wabash
MICHIGAN
OHIO
Lake Michigan
CHICAGO

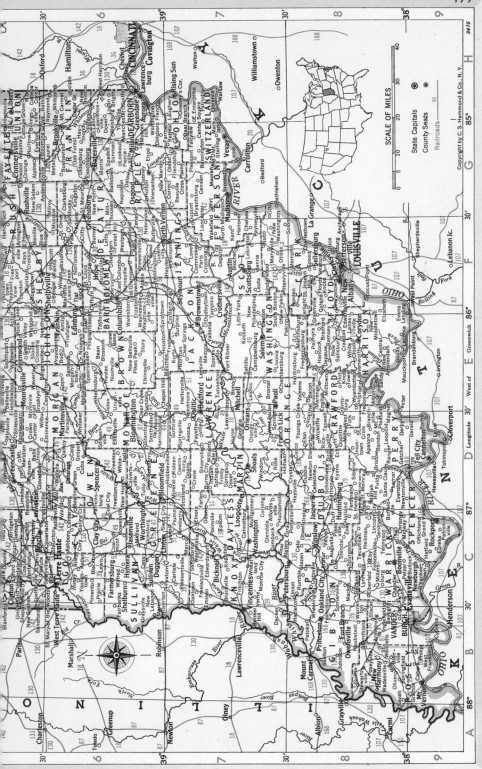

SCALE OF MILES

State Capitals
County Seats
Railroads

Copyright by C. S. Hammond & Co., N.Y.

SCALE OF MILES

0 5 10 20 30 40

State Capitals ⊛
County Seats ⊙
Railroads ——54——

RAILROADS

7 Atchison, Topeka & Santa Fe
42 Chicago & North Western
45 Chicago, Burlington & Quincy
46 Chicago Great Western
51 Chicago, Milwaukee, St. Paul & Pacific
54 Chicago, Rock Island & Pacific
55 Chicago, St. Paul, Minneapolis & Omaha
66 Davenport, Rock Island & Northwestern
67 Fort Dodge, Des Moines & Southern (Electric)
80 Great Northern
87 Illinois Central
97 Manchester & Oneida
113 Minneapolis & St. Louis
122 Missouri Pacific
175 Toledo, Peoria & Western
180 Union Pacific
185 Wabash

Copyright by C. S. Hammond & Co., N.Y.

3378

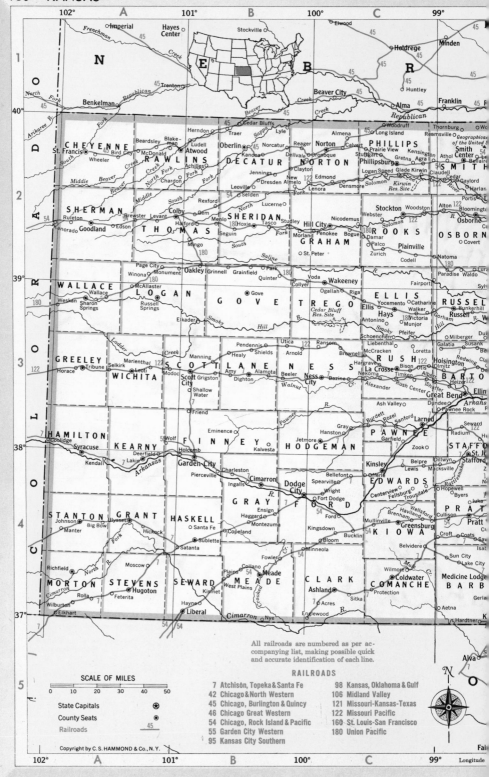

All railroads are numbered as per accompanying list, making possible quick and accurate identification of each line.

RAILROADS

7 Atchison, Topeka & Santa Fe	98 Kansas, Oklahoma & Gulf
42 Chicago & North Western	106 Midland Valley
45 Chicago, Burlington & Quincy	121 Missouri-Kansas-Texas
46 Chicago Great Western	122 Missouri Pacific
54 Chicago, Rock Island & Pacific	160 St. Louis-San Francisco
55 Garden City Western	180 Union Pacific
95 Kansas City Southern	

SCALE OF MILES

0 10 20 30 40 50

State Capitals ✪

County Seats ◉

Railroads 45

Copyright by C.S. HAMMOND & Co., N.Y.

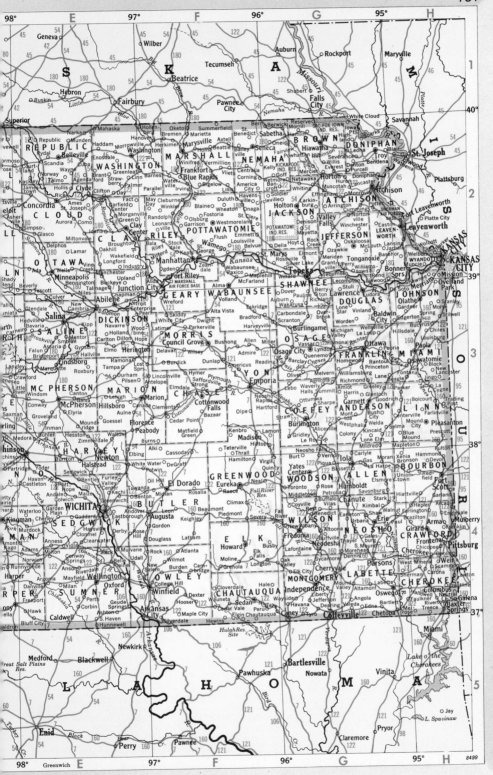

8499

A 88° B 30° C 87° D 30° E 86° F 30° G

All railroads are numbered on accompanying list, making possible quick and accurate identification of e...

WESTERN PART OF KENTUCKY
Same scale as main map.

ILLINOIS

Zeigler · West Frankfort · Eldorado · Smith Mills · Corydon · Waverly
Herrin · Marion · Harrisburg · Shawneetown · Uniontown · Morganfield · Grove Center · CAMP BRECKINRIDGE
New Burnside · South Fork · Henshaw · Pride · Tilden
Cobden · Anna · Jonesboro · Vienna · Elizabethtown · Rosiclare · Caseyville · Sturgis · Wheatcroft
Jackson · Golconda · Providence · Dixon · Clay · WEBSTER · Hope
Cape Girardeau · Thebes · Karnak · Cache R. · Bayou · CRITTENDEN · Marion · Shady Grove · Crider · Dawson Sprs. · CALDWELL
Mound City · Metropolis · Brookport · Birdsville · Salem · Fredonia · Olney · Princeton · Scottsburg
Cairo · Paducah · Smith land · Kuttawa · Eddyville · LYON
BALLARD · McCRACKEN · Calvert City · Grand Rivers · KENTUCKY DAM · Lamasco · Cobb
Charleston · Wickliffe · Blandville · Lovelaceville · Melber · MARSHALL · Golden Pond · TRIGG · Cadiz · Canton
CARLISLE · Bardwell · Milburn · Boaz · Viola · Benton · Brewers · Hardin
HICKMAN · Dublin · Mayfield · GRAVES · Kirksey · Dexter · Almo
Clinton · Pryorsburg · Farmington · Sedalia · CALLOWAY · Murray · New Concord
FULTON · Fulton · Water Valley · Lynnville · Wingo · Hazel · Hamlin

MISSOURI · MISSISSIPPI · Benton · East Prairie · New Madrid · Lilbourn

TENNESSEE

Main map:

ILLINOIS · INDIANA

New Harmony · Boonville · Corydon · LOUISVILLE · JEFFERSON
Mt. Vernon · Evansville · Tell City · Cannelton · MEADE · BULLITT · SPENCE
Henderson · Rockport · Hawesville · BRECKINRIDGE · Lebanon Jc. · Bardstown · NELSON · WASHIN
HENDERSON · Owensboro · HANCOCK · Cloverport · Hardinsburg · HARDIN · Springfield
Uniontown · Morganfield · DAVIESS · Calhoun · OHIO · GRAYSON · LARUE · MARIO
WEBSTER · McLEAN · Livermore · Hartford · Leitchfield · Hodgenville · Lebanon
CRITTENDEN · Madisonville · Central City · Beaver Dam · BUTLER · EDMONSON · HART · TAYLOR · GREEN
Marion · HOPKINS · MUHLENBERG · Greenville · Brownsville · MAMMOTH CAVE NAT'L PARK · Horse Cave · Greensburg · ADAI
CALDWELL · Princeton · Mortons Gap · Drakesboro · Woodbury · Cave City · Columbia
LYON · CHRISTIAN · Hopkinsville · TODD · LOGAN · Russellville · WARREN · Bowling Green · BARREN · Glasgow · METCALFE
TRIGG · Cadiz · Golden Pond · Elkton · Trenton · SIMPSON · Franklin · ALLEN · Scottsville · MONROE · CUMBERLAND
CAMPBELL AIR FORCE BASE · CAMP CAMPBELL · Guthrie · Adairville · Tompkinsville · Gamaliel
New Providence · Clarksville · Portland · Dale Hollow Res.
Kentucky Res. · Dover · Springfield · Hartsville · Livingston · Gallatin

TENNESSEE

Copyright by C.S. HAMMOND & Co., N.Y.

A 88° B 30° C 87° D 30° E 86° F 30° G

44109

RAILROADS

2 Artemus - Jellico	75 Detroit, Toledo & Ironton
18 Baltimore & Ohio	78 Flemingsburg & Northern
29 Cadiz	82 Frankfort & Cincinnati
32 Carrollton	86 Gulf, Mobile & Ohio
36 Chesapeake & Ohio	87 Illinois Central
39 Chicago & Eastern Illinois	90 Interstate
45 Chicago, Burlington & Quincy	107 Kentucky & Tennessee
49 Chicago, Indianapolis & Louisville	107 Louisville & Nashville
66 Clinchfield	122 Missouri Pacific
72 East Tennessee and Western North Carolina	125 Morehead & North Fork
	127 Nashville, Chattanooga & St. Louis
	130 New York Central
	133 Norfolk & Western
	134 Oneida & Western
	138 Paducah & Illinois
	142 Pennsylvania
	160 St. Louis - San Francisco
	161 St. Louis Southwestern
	168 Southern
	175 Tennessee Central

SCALE OF MILES

State Capitals
County Seats
Railroads

ARKANSAS

CADDO · **BOSSIER** · **WEBSTER** · **CLAIBORNE** · **UNION** · **MOREHOUSE** · **WEST CARROLL** · **EAST CARROLL**

DE SOTO · **RED RIVER** · **BIENVILLE** · **JACKSON** · **LINCOLN** · **OUACHITA** · **RICHLAND** · **MADISON**

SABINE · **NATCHITOCHES** · **WINN** · **CALDWELL** · **FRANKLIN** · **CATAHOULA** · **LA SALLE** · **GRANT**

VERNON · **RAPIDES** · **AVOYELLES** · **CONCORDIA**

BEAUREGARD · **ALLEN** · **EVANGELINE** · **ST. LANDRY** · **POINTE COUPEE** · **WEST FELICIANA**

CALCASIEU · **JEFFERSON DAVIS** · **ACADIA** · **LAFAYETTE** · **ST. MARTIN** · **WEST BATON ROUGE**

CAMERON · **VERMILION** · **IBERIA** · **ST. MARTIN**

Shreveport · Monroe · Alexandria · Pineville · Lake Charles · Lafayette · Opelousas · Natchitoches · Minden · Bastrop · Ruston · W. Monroe · Jonesboro · Winnfield · Leesville · De Ridder · Oakdale · Eunice · Crowley · Abbeville · Jennings · New Iberia · Franklin · Morgan City · Berwick

Beaumont · Port Arthur · Port Neches · Orange · Vidalia · Natchez

SCALE OF MILES
0 5 10   20   30   40

State Capitals ⊛
Parish Seats ⊙
Canals
Railroads

GULF OF MEXICO

SABINE LAKE · Louisiana Pt. · Calcasieu Pass · Grand Chenier · White Lake · Marsh Island · VERMILION BAY · WEST COTE BLANCHE BAY · ATCHAFALAYA BAY · Southwest Pass · South Pt.

NEW ORLEANS,
BATON ROUGE
AND VICINITY
SCALE OF MILES

0   5   10   15   20

RAILROADS

5 Arkansas & Louisiana
   Missouri
54 Chicago, Rock Island &
   Pacific
77 Gulf, Colorado & Santa Fe
80 Gulf, Mobile & Ohio
87 Illinois Central
95 Kansas City Southern
101 Louisiana & Arkansas
102 Louisiana & North West
106 Louisiana Southern
107 Louisville & Nashville
108 Mansfield Ry. & Transport.
113 Mississippi Central
122 Missouri Pacific
125 Natchez, Urania & Ruston
126 New Orleans & Lower
    Coast
134 North Louisiana & Gulf
139 Red River & Gulf
161 St. Louis Southwestern
168 Southern
170 Southern Pacific
174 Texas & Pacific
176 Tremont & Gulf

All railroads are numbered as per accompanying list, making possible quick and accurate identification of each line.

Copyright by C. S. Hammond & Co., N.Y.

24103

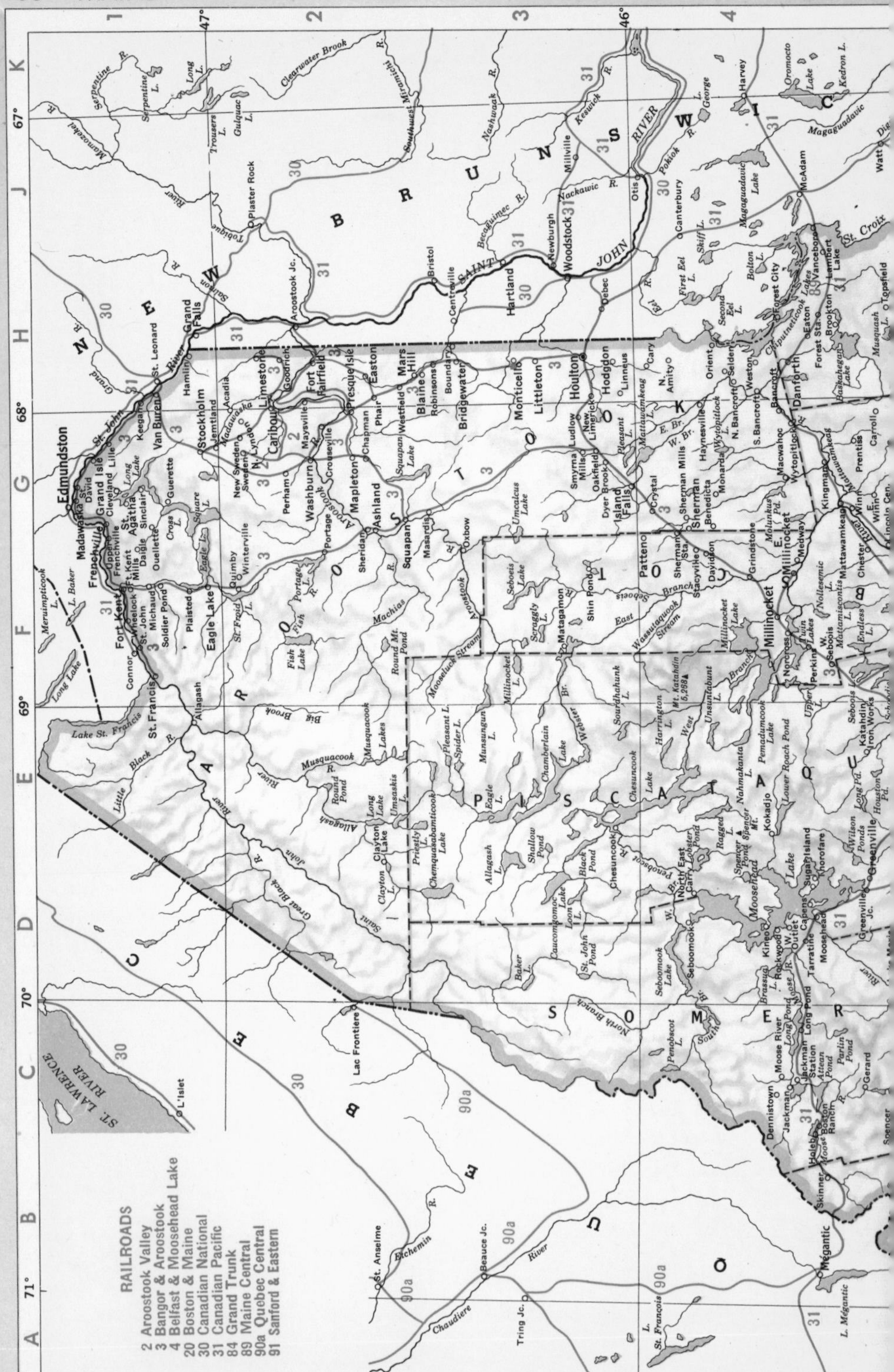

RAILROADS
2 Aroostook Valley
3 Bangor & Aroostook
4 Belfast & Moosehead Lake
20 Boston & Maine
30 Canadian National
31 Canadian Pacific
84 Grand Trunk
89 Maine Central
90a Quebec Central
91 Sanford & Eastern

NEW BRUNSWICK

SAINT JOHN RIVER

Edmundston
Madawaska
Frenchville
Fort Kent
St. Francis
Lake St. Francis
Connor
St. John
Grand Isle
Van Buren
Stockholm
Caribou
Presque Isle
Mars Hill
Easton
Blaine
Bridgewater
Monticello
Littleton
Houlton
Hodgdon
Washburn
Ashland
Mapleton
Squapan
Masardis
Oxbow
Patten
Sherman
Island Falls
Smyrna Mills
Crystal
Millinocket
Greenville
Jackman
Megantic

ST. LAWRENCE RIVER

AROOSTOOK

PISCATAQUIS

SOMERSET

Mt. Katahdin
5,268a

Moosehead Lake
Chamberlain Lake
Eagle Lake
Chesuncook Lake

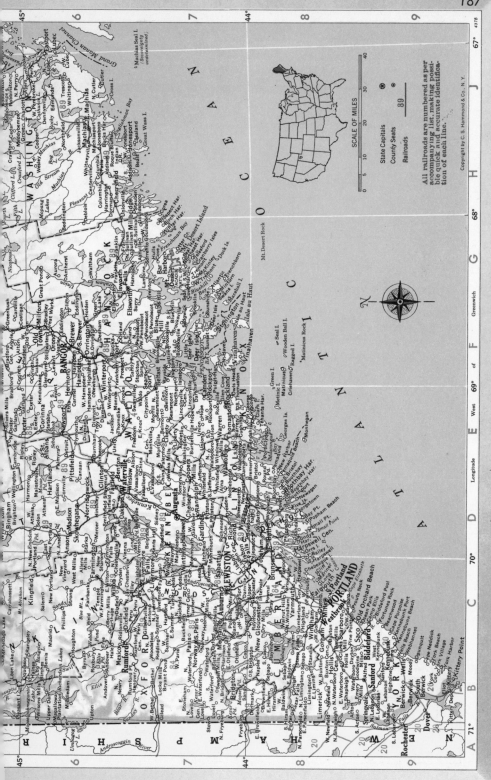

SCALE OF MILES

All railroads are numbered as per accompanying list, making possible quick and accurate identification of each line.

State Capitals ⊛
County Seats ⊙
Railroads 89

Copyright by C. S. Hammond & Co., N. Y.

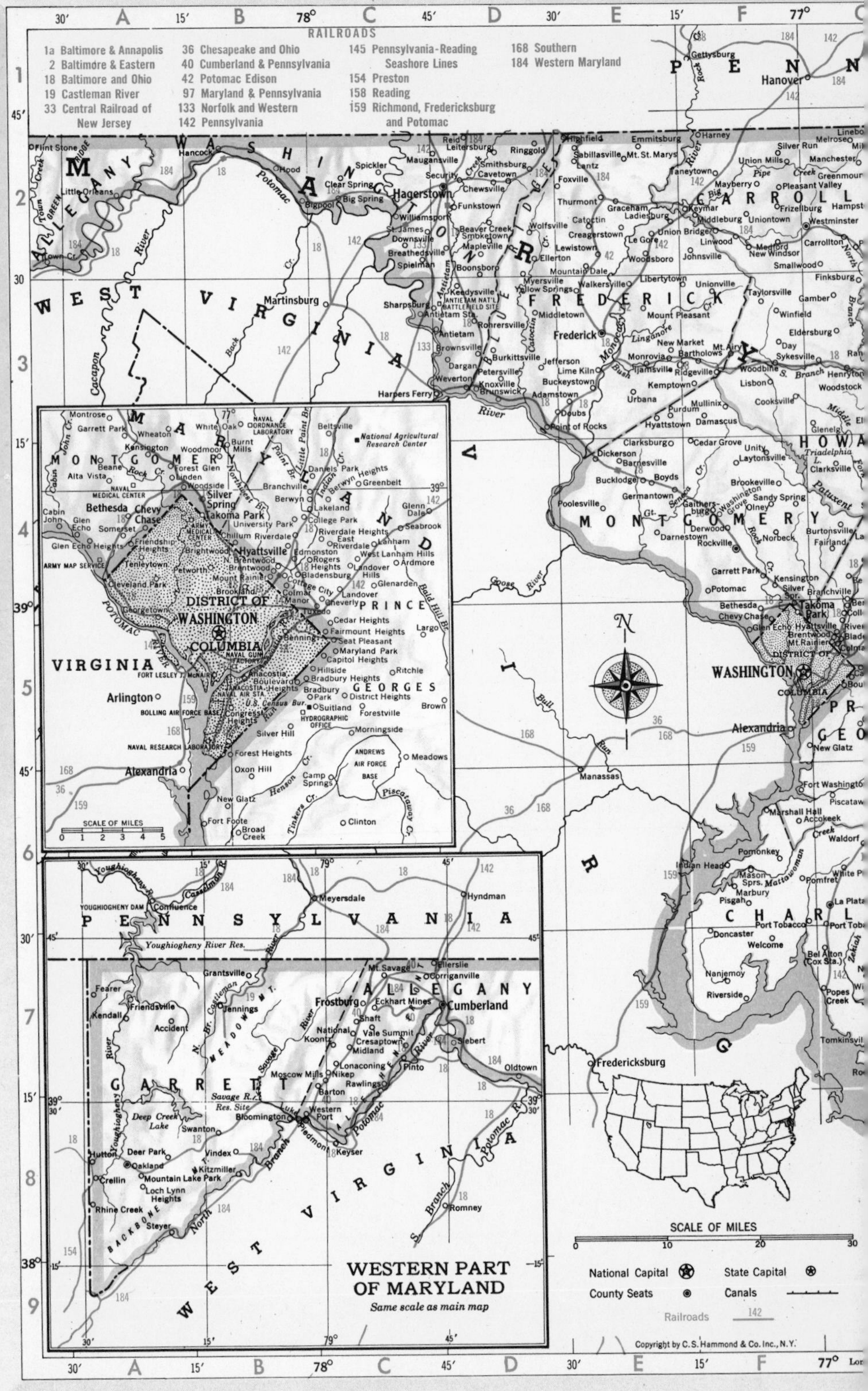

RAILROADS

1a Baltimore & Annapolis	36 Chesapeake and Ohio	145 Pennsylvania-Reading
2 Baltimore & Eastern	40 Cumberland & Pennsylvania	Seashore Lines
18 Baltimore and Ohio	42 Potomac Edison	154 Preston
19 Castleman River	97 Maryland & Pennsylvania	158 Reading
33 Central Railroad of	133 Norfolk and Western	159 Richmond, Fredericksburg
New Jersey	142 Pennsylvania	and Potomac
		168 Southern
		184 Western Maryland

WESTERN PART
OF MARYLAND
Same scale as main map

SCALE OF MILES

National Capital   State Capital
County Seats   Canals
Railroads   142

Copyright by C.S. Hammond & Co. Inc., N.Y.

Railroads are numbered as per accompanying list, making possible quick
accurate identification of each line.

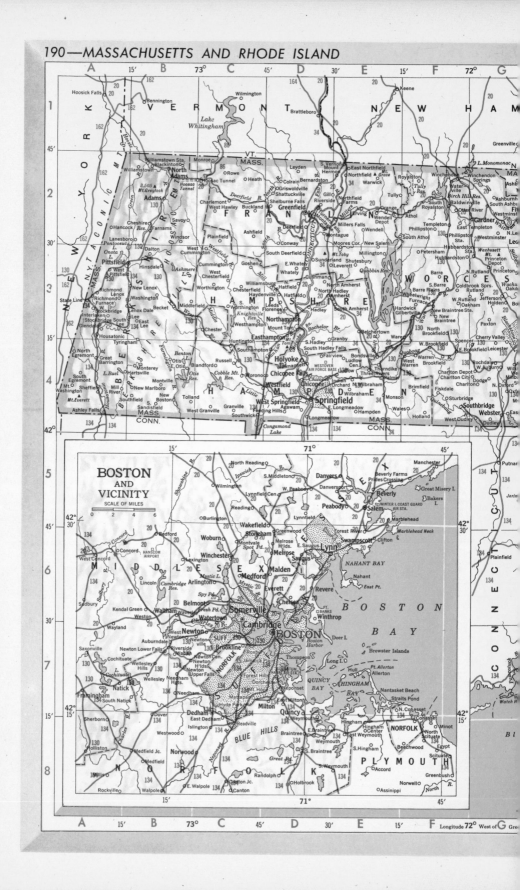

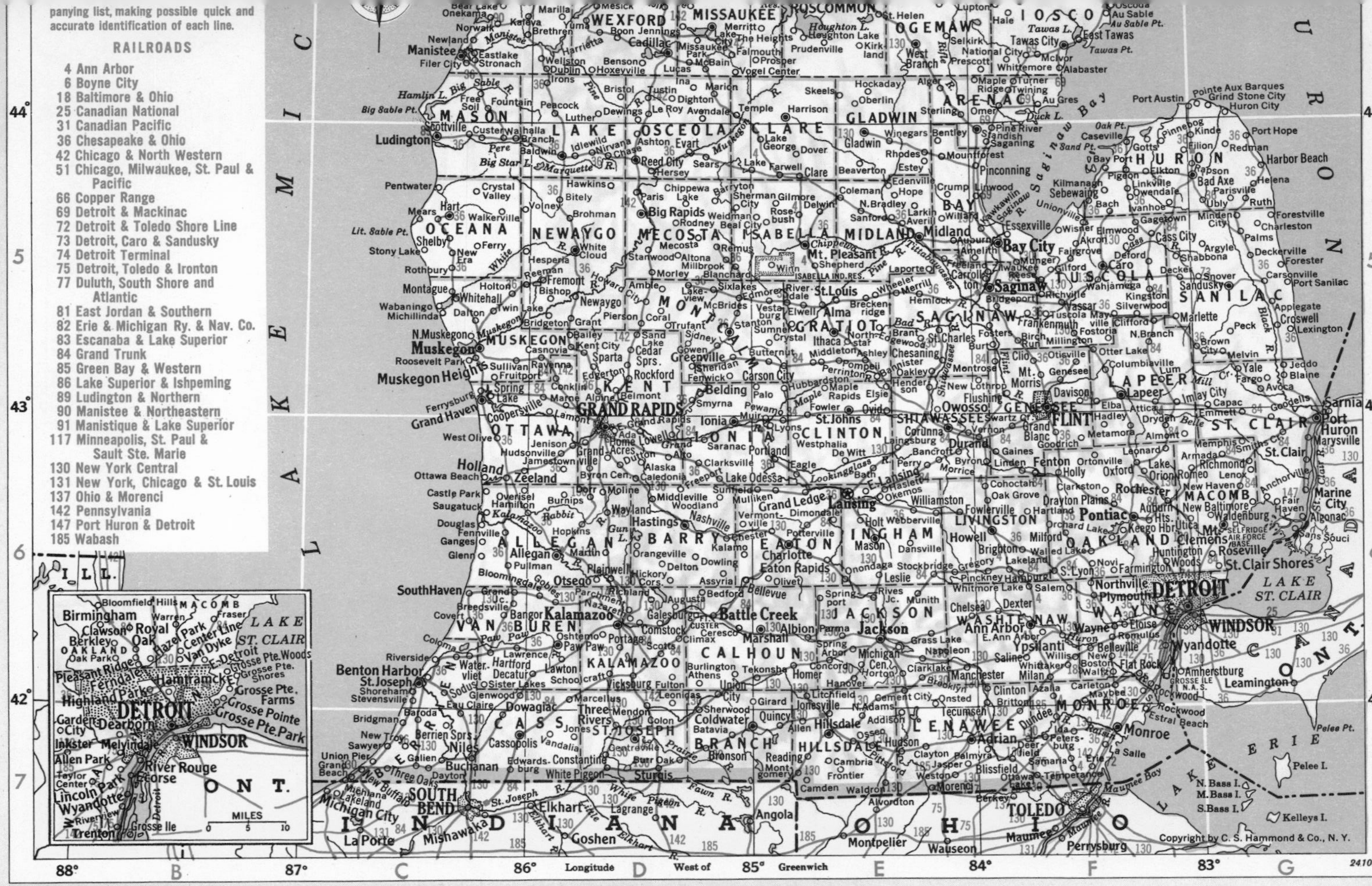
panying list, making possible quick and accurate identification of each line.
RAILROADS
4 Ann Arbor
6 Boyne City
18 Baltimore & Ohio
25 Canadian National
31 Canadian Pacific
36 Chesapeake & Ohio
42 Chicago & North Western
51 Chicago, Milwaukee, St. Paul & Pacific
66 Copper Range
69 Detroit & Mackinac
72 Detroit & Toledo Shore Line
73 Detroit, Caro & Sandusky
74 Detroit Terminal
75 Detroit, Toledo & Ironton
77 Duluth, South Shore and Atlantic
81 East Jordan & Southern
82 Erie & Michigan Ry. & Nav. Co.
83 Escanaba & Lake Superior
84 Grand Trunk
85 Green Bay & Western
86 Lake Superior & Ishpeming
89 Ludington & Northern
90 Manistee & Northeastern
91 Manistique & Lake Superior
117 Minneapolis, St. Paul & Sault Ste. Marie
130 New York Central
131 New York, Chicago & St. Louis
137 Ohio & Morenci
142 Pennsylvania
147 Port Huron & Detroit
185 Wabash
LAKE MICHIGAN
LAKE HURON
LAKE ERIE
LAKE ST. CLAIR
ILL.
INDIANA
OHIO
CANADA
ONT.
GRAND RAPIDS
DETROIT
FLINT
Lansing
Saginaw
Kalamazoo
Battle Creek
Jackson
TOLEDO
WINDSOR
SOUTH BEND
Longitude West of Greenwich
Copyright by C. S. Hammond & Co., N. Y.
24109

RAILROADS

30 Canadian National	77 Duluth, South Shore & Atlantic
31 Canadian Pacific	80 Great Northern
42 Chicago & North Western	82 Green Bay & Western
45 Chicago, Burlington & Quincy	87 Illinois Central
46 Chicago Great Western	113 Minneapolis & St. Louis
51 Chicago, Milwaukee, St. Paul & Pacific	115 Minneapolis, Northfield & Southern
54 Chicago, Rock Island & Pacific	117 Minneapolis, St. Paul & Sault Ste. Marie
55 Chicago, St. Paul, Minneapolis & Omaha	123 Minnesota Transfer
57 Duluth & Northeastern	125 Minnesota Western
75 Duluth, Missabe & Iron Range	137 Northern Pacific

NORTHEASTERN PART OF MINNESOTA
Same scale as main map.

CANADA

KOOCHICHING

LAKE OF THE WOODS

Rainy River

Lake Superior

DULUTH

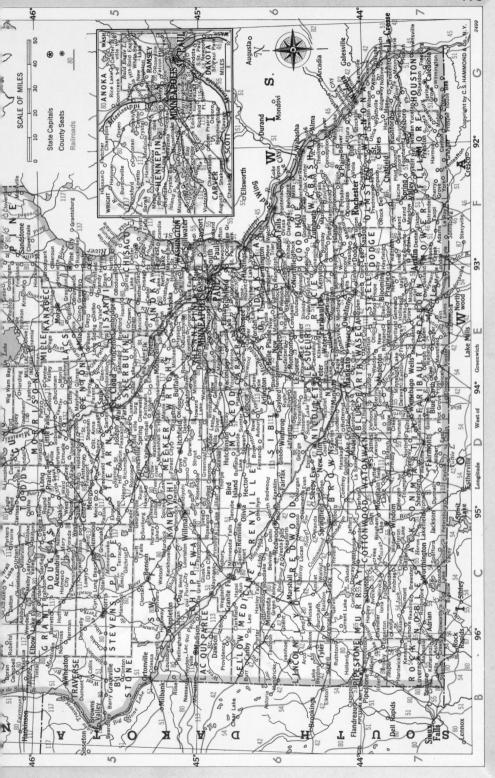

RAILROADS

All railroads are numbered as per accompanying list, making it possible to quickly and accurately identify each of the railroads in question.

- 10 Bonhomie & Hattiesburg Southern
- 10a Canton & Carthage
- 11 Columbus & Greenville
- 12 Dekalb & Western
- 13 Fernwood, Columbia & Gulf
- 73 Gulf, Mobile & Ohio
- 80 Helena & Northwestern
- 87 Illinois Central
- 101 Louisiana & Arkansas
- 107 Louisville & Nashville
- 107a Louisville & Nashville
- 108 Meridian & Bigbee River
- 109 Mississippi & Alabama
- 109a Mississippi & Skuna Valley
- 113 Mississippi Central
- 115 Mississippi Export
- 122 Missouri Pacific
- 124 Gulf, Mobile & Ohio
- 132 Pearl River Valley
- 160 St. Louis-San Francisco
- 161 St. Louis Southwestern
- 168 Southern
- 174 Sumter & Choctaw
- 174 Texas & Pacific
- 179 Illinois Central

LOUISIANA
MOBILE BAY
LAKE PONTCHARTRAIN
Lake Maurepas
MISSISSIPPI SOUND
MISSISSIPPI RIVER
JACKSON
BATON ROUGE
MOBILE
MONROE
Meridian
Hattiesburg
Vicksburg
Natchez
Laurel
Gulfport
Biloxi
Bogalusa
Longitude West of Greenwich
SCALE OF MILES
0 5 10 20 30 40
State Capitals
County Seats
Railroads
Copyright by C. S. Hammond & Co., N. Y.

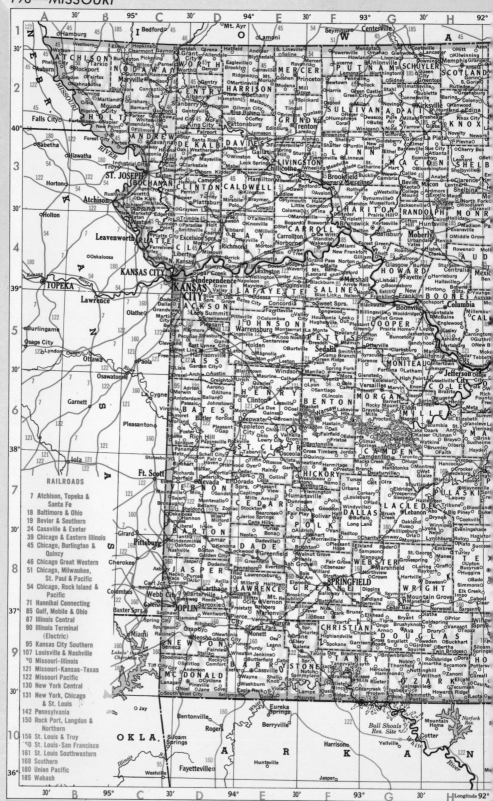

RAILROADS

7 Atchison, Topeka &
Santa Fe
18 Baltimore & Ohio
19 Bevier & Southern
24 Cassville & Exeter
39 Chicago & Eastern Illinois
45 Chicago, Burlington &
Quincy
46 Chicago Great Western
51 Chicago, Milwaukee,
St. Paul & Pacific
54 Chicago, Rock Island &
Pacific
71 Hannibal Connecting
85 Gulf, Mobile & Ohio
87 Illinois Central
90 Illinois Terminal
(Electric)
95 Kansas City Southern
107 Louisville & Nashville
90 Missouri-Illinois
121 Missouri-Kansas-Texas
122 Missouri Pacific
130 New York Central
131 New York, Chicago
& St. Louis
142 Pennsylvania
150 Rock Port, Langdon &
Northern
156 St. Louis & Troy
90 St. Louis-San Francisco
161 St. Louis Southwestern
168 Southern
180 Union Pacific
185 Wabash

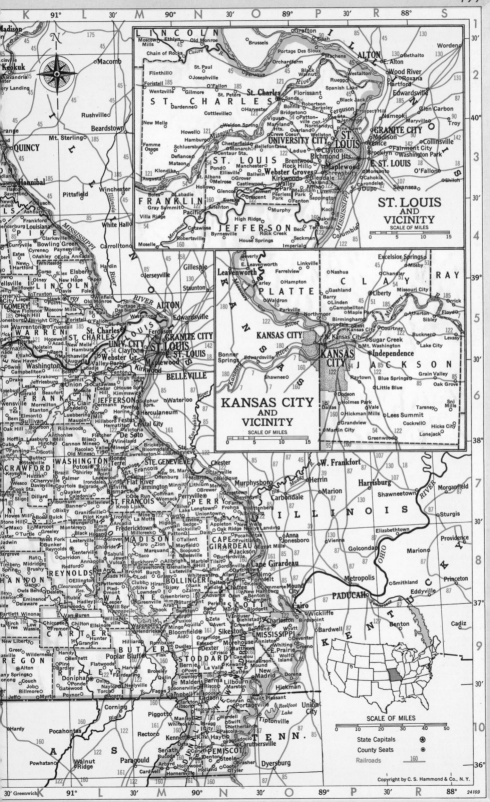

BRITISH COLUMBIA

ALBERTA

Medicine

Kimberley Cranbrook Fernie Blairmore Macleod Lethbridge Taber Bow Island

Pincher Creek Stirling Conrad Manyberries Pakowki Lake

Glenwoodville Cardston Whisky Gap Coutts Sweetgrass Whitlash Fairchild Gold Butte

LINCOLN

Yaak Rexford Eureka Trailcreek Kintla Babb Demers McDermott Goldbutte

Stonehill Fortine Trego Stryker Polebridge Radnor Olney Browning Kevin Ferdig Oilmont Grandview Alma

Troy Libby Warland Jennings Mock Lupfer Whitefish Columbia Falls Kalispell

TOOLE LIBERTY

Heron Noxon Manicke Marion Somers Bigfork

Shelby Galata Chester Inverness Rudyard

FLATHEAD

GLACIER NATIONAL PARK

BLACKFEET INDIAN RESERVATION

GLACIER

PONDERA TETON

SANDERS

FLATHEAD INDIAN RESERVATION

Poison Ronan Charlo Dixon

Wallace Saltese Thompson Falls Plains Paradise Perma

MINERAL MISSOULA

Superior Alberton Quartz

LEWIS AND CLARK

CASCADE GREAT FALLS

Missoula Milltown Bonner Clinton

POWELL

Helena East Helena MEAGHER White Sulphur Springs

GRANITE BROADWATER Townsend

Philipsburg Deer Lodge Anaconda

RAVALLI

Victor Corvallis Hamilton Grantsdale Darby Conner Sula

DEER LODGE JEFFERSON

Boulder Radersburg

BUTTE SILVER BOW Whitehall Cardwell Three Forks Bozeman

BITTERROOT RANGE

BEAVERHEAD MADISON

Wisdom Jackson Polaris Apex Dillon Twin Bridges Sheridan Ennis Virginia City

PARK

Livingston Emigrant Gardiner

Wise River Melrose Glen

Grant Armstead Lima Monida

YELLOWSTONE NATIONAL PARK Yellowstone

Gilmore Dubois Ashton

SCALE OF MILES
0 10 20 40 60 80

⊗ State Capitals
⊙ County Seats
137 Railroads

All railroads are numbered as per accompanying list, making possible quick and accurate identification of each line.

Copyright by C. S. Hammond & Co., N.Y.

RAILROADS

- 2 Butte, Anaconda & Pacific
- 30 Canadian National
- 31 Canadian Pacific
- 51 Chicago, Burlington & Quincy
- 51 Chicago, Milwaukee, St. Paul & Pacific
- 80 Great Northern
- 117 Minneapolis, St. Paul & Sault Ste. Marie
- 119 Montana Western
- 120 Montana, Wyoming & Southern
- 137 Northern Pacific
- 180 Union Pacific
- 181 White Sulphur Springs & Yellowstone Park

14109

104° A 103° B 102° C 101° D 100°

SOUTH DAKOTA

Custer 42
Fairburn
JEWEL CAVE NAT'L MON.
Scenic 51
Kadoka
White River
45
WIND CAVE NATIONAL PARK
45
Buffalo Gap
Hot Springs
FOSSIL CYCAD NAT'L MON.
Cheyenne
Edgemont
42
Wood
River

PINE RIDGE INDIAN RESERVATION

Keyapaha
ROSEBUD INDIAN RESERVATION

Martin
South Fork
White
Pine Ridge

43°

Montrose 45
Wayside
Orella
Dakota Jc.
Whitney
Chadron
Whiteclay
Albany
Merriman
Eli
Cody Nenzel 42
Kilgore
Crookston Sparks
Norden

Harrison
Andrews
White 42
Glen
Crawford
Fort Robinson
Belmont
Pine Ridge
Marsland
DAWES
Rushville
Hay Springs
Clinton 42
Gordon
Irwin
River
Melpha
Snake
Creek
Simeon
Wood Lake
Johns
Ainsw

Agate
Box Butte Res.
Niobrara
SHERIDAN
Balfe
Kennedy
Pelican Lake
Dods Lake
CHERRY
B

SIOUX
45
Nonpareil
Hemingford
BOX BUTTE
Berea
Wells
Gard
Brownlee

Alliance
Antioch 45
Ellsworth
Ashby
Whitman 45
Cherry
Cascade
Elsmere
Ma
Kosh

42°
Henry
Lake Alice
Morrill
Lyman
Mitchell
Lake Minatare
45
Lakeside
Bingham
Hire
Seneca
Purdum
Brew

SCOTTS BLUFF
SCOTTS BLUFF NAT'L MON.
Gering Scottsbluff
Minatare
Bayard
McGrew Melbeta
Riford
Angora
GRANT
Hyannis
Hecla
Mullen
HOOKER
Thedford
Halsey
THOMAS
BLA
Dune

MORRILL
Swan Lake
Mumper
Beaver Lake
Lena
Dismal
Middle
River

Pumpkin
Harrisburg
Northport
Bridgeport
Broadwater
Rackett
ARTHUR
Velma
Calora
MC PHERSON
Hoagland
LOGAN
Anse

BANNER
Redington
GARDEN
Lisco
Blue Cr.
180
Arthur
Bucktail
Carman
Flats
Tryon
Ringgold
Stapleton
Gandy
Arnold
C

45
Dalton
Oshkosh
Thune

Gurley
Lewellen
Belmar
Lemoyne
Sutherland
Callaw

Bushnell
180
CHEYENNE
Potter
McConaughy L.
Keystone
N.
Keystone
Sarben
Sutherland
Fallons
North Platte
180

Kimball Dix
Sidney
Sunol
Lodgepole
DEUEL
K 80 **E**
ITH
Hershey
Maxwell
Brady

KIMBALL
Lorenzo 45
Creek
Chappell
Big Springs
Brule
Roscoe
Paxton
R.
Maxwell

41°
COLORADO
Julesburg
South Platte
Ogallala
LINCOLN
Willow Island
Gothe

PERKINS
Grant
Elsie
Wallace 45
Somerset
Venango
Brandon
Madrid
Grainton
Dickens
Wellfleet
Ingham
Farnam

CHASE
Lamar
Chase
White
Maywood
Moorefield
Curtis
Eustis
FRONTIER
Stockville
Orafino

Champion
Frenchman
Imperial
Enders
HAYES
Hayes Center
Quick
St. Ann
Freedom
40°
Best
Enders Res.
Wauneta
45
Hamlet
Palisade
Indianola
Holbro
Bartley
Camb

DUNDY
Beverly
Culbertson
HITCHCOCK
Trenton
Red Willow
McCook
RED WILLOW
Lebanon
Wilson
FU
Hendle

Haigler
Benkelman
Parks
Max
Stratton
45
Marion
Danbury

Republican
St. Francis
Atwood 45
Oberlin
45
No
COLORADO
Beaver
Dog
54
Lenora North
A

N
K
Colby
Hoxie
180
South

Oakley
180
Quinter

A 103° B 102° C 101° D Longitude 1

WYOMING
COLORADO

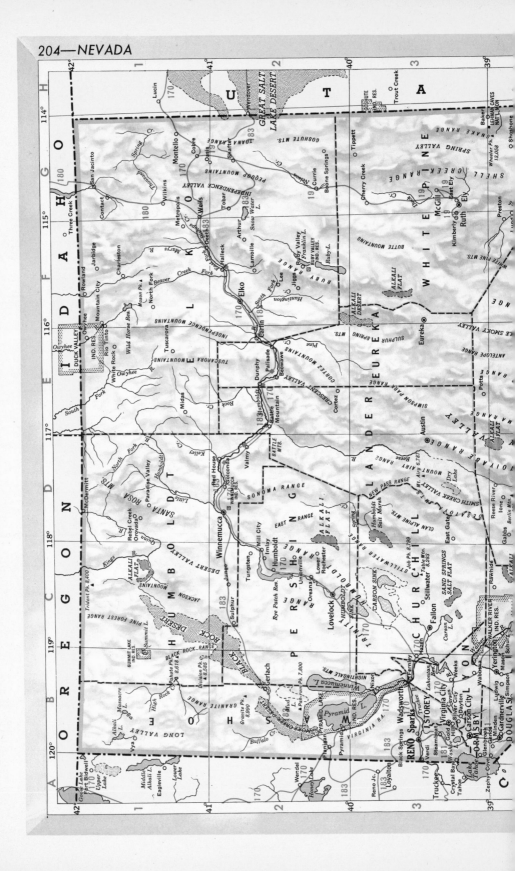

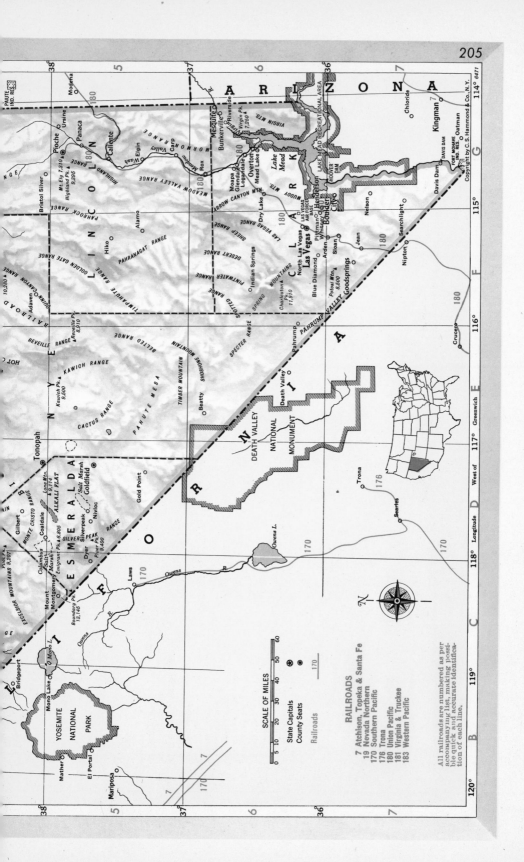

SCALE OF MILES
0 5 10 20 30 40 50 60

State Capitals ⊛
County Seats ◉
Railroads ___170___

RAILROADS

7 Atchison, Topeka & Santa Fe
19 Nevada Northern
170 Southern Pacific
176 Trona
180 Union Pacific
181 Virginia & Truckee
183 Western Pacific

All railroads are numbered as per accompanying list, making possible quick and accurate identification of each line.

Copyright by C. S. Hammond & Co., N.Y.

114° 6471

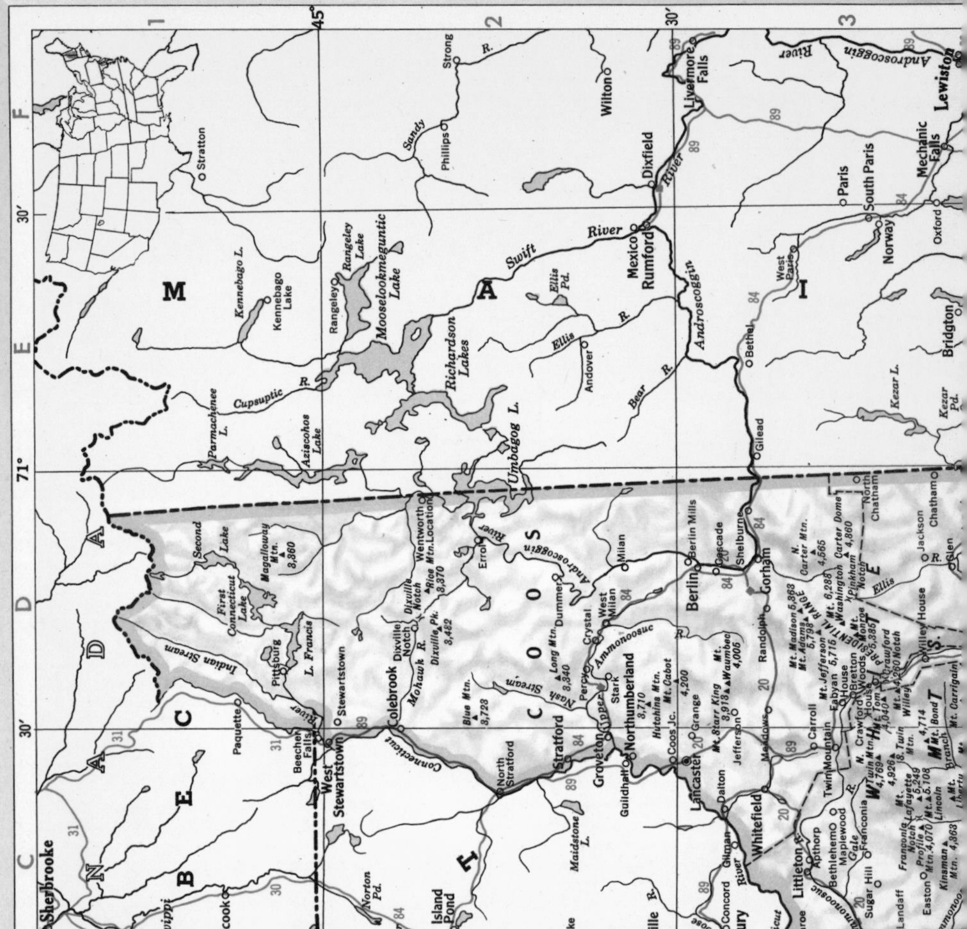

SCALE OF MILES
0 5 10 15 20 25

State Capitals ⊛
County Seats ◉
Railroads 162

All railroads are numbered as per accompanying list, making possible quick and accurate identification of each line.

RAILROADS
2 Barre & Chelsea
20 Boston & Maine
30 Canadian National
31 Canadian Pacific
34 Central Vermont
84 Grand Trunk
89 Maine Central
141 Quebec Central
162 Rutland
163 St. Johnsbury & Lake Champlain
163a Sanford & Eastern
164 Suncook Valley

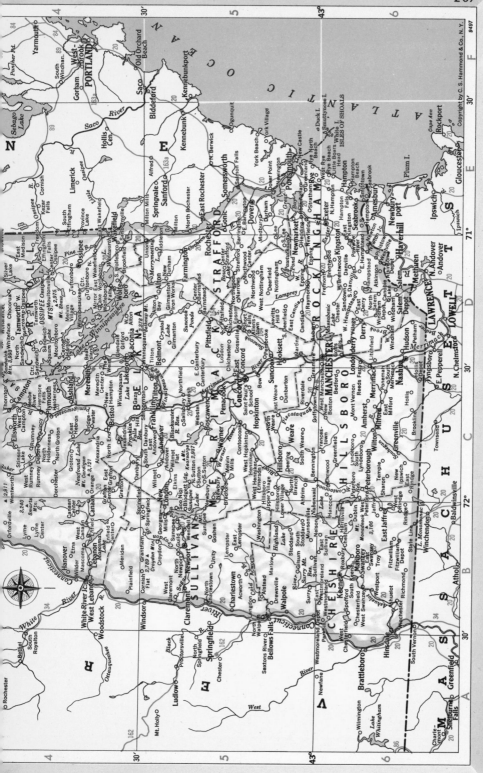

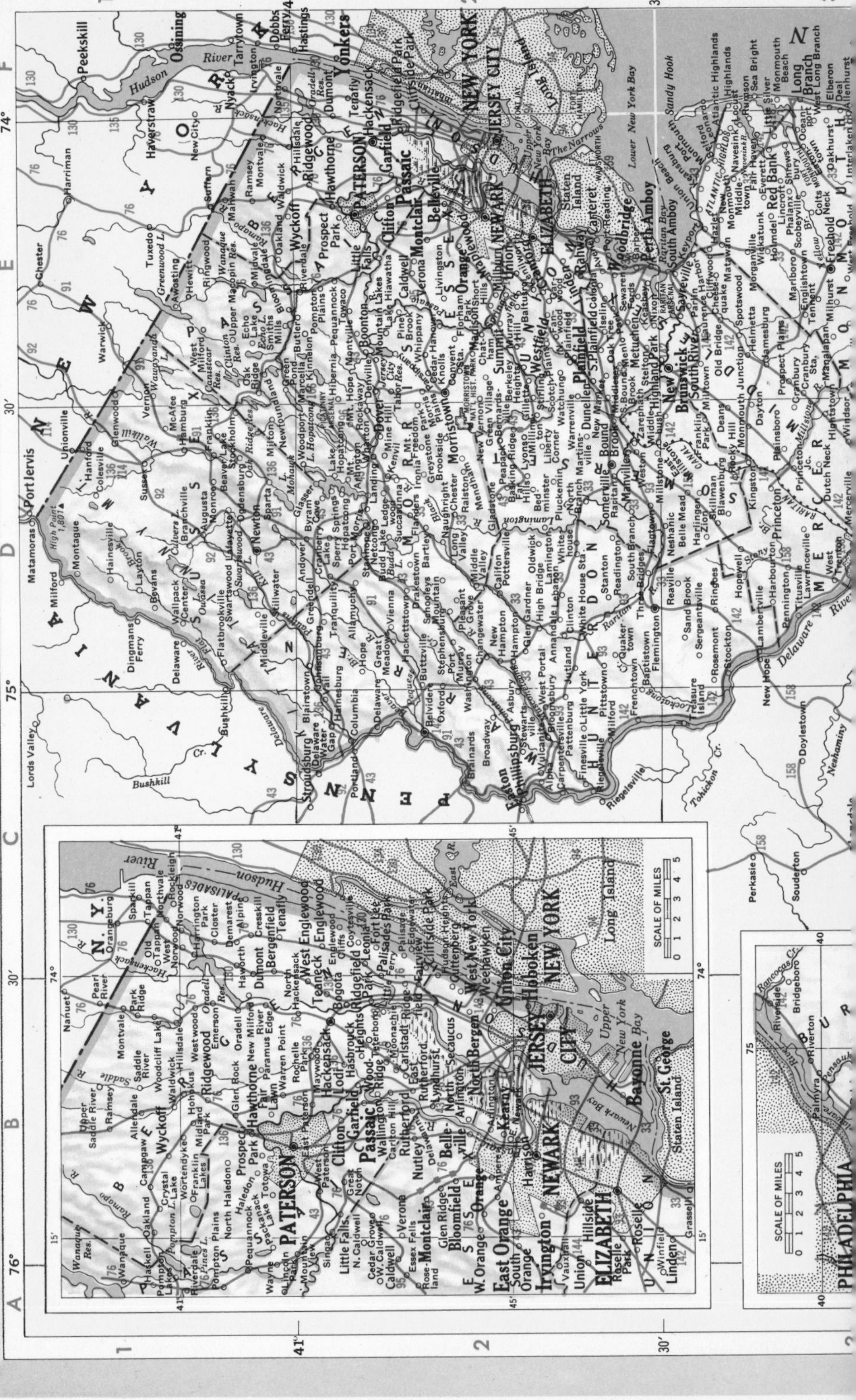

SCALE OF MILES
0 1 2 3 4 5

SCALE OF MILES
0 1 2 3 4 5

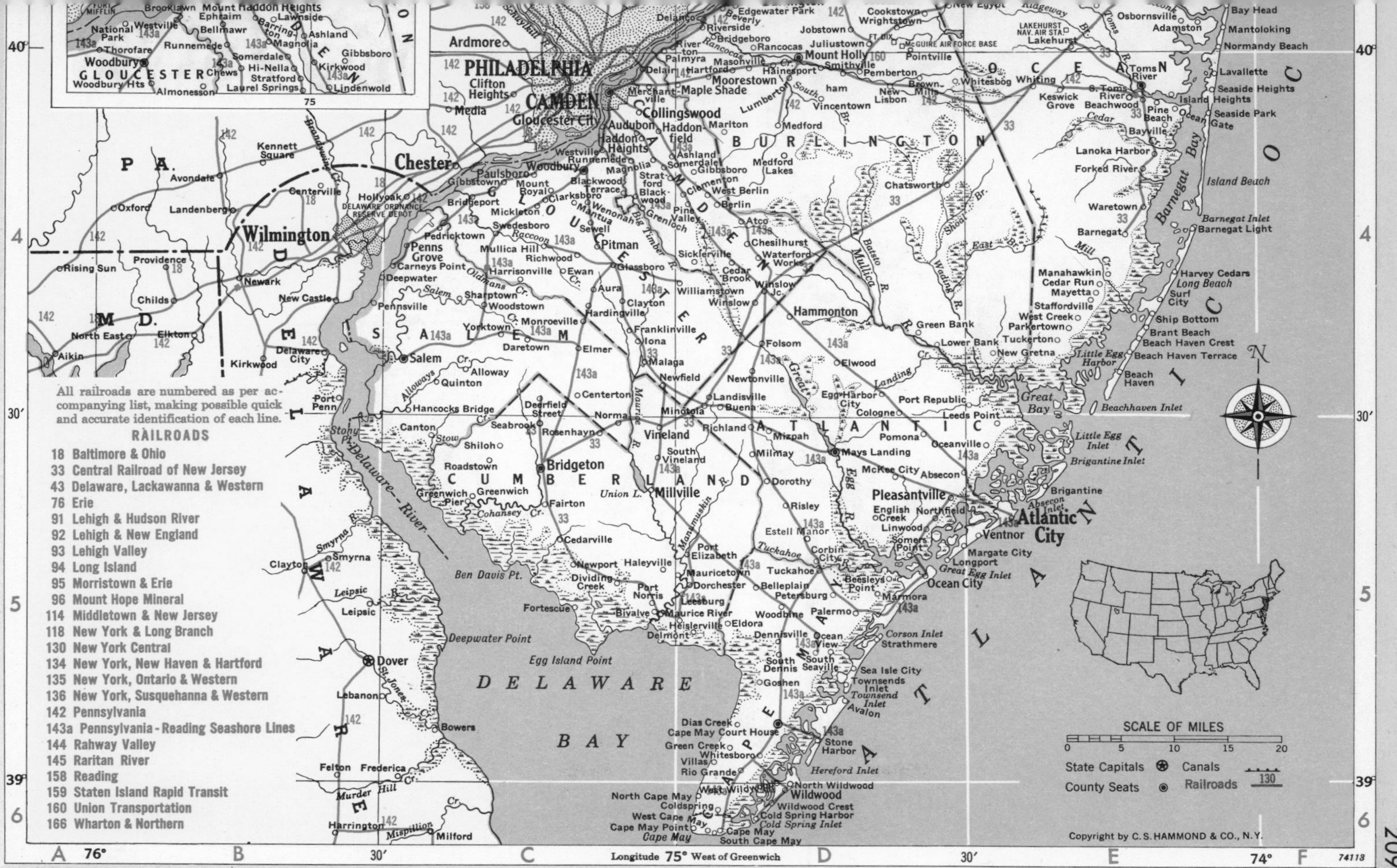

SCALE OF MILES

0	5	10	15	20

State Capitals ⊛   Canals

County Seats ⊙   Railroads

Copyright by C. S. HAMMOND & CO., N.Y.

74118

RAILROADS

All railroads are numbered as per accompanying list, making possible quick and accurate identification of each line.

18	Baltimore & Ohio
33	Central Railroad of New Jersey
43	Delaware, Lackawanna & Western
76	Erie
91	Lehigh & Hudson River
92	Lehigh & New England
93	Lehigh Valley
94	Long Island
95	Morristown & Erie
96	Mount Hope Mineral
114	Middletown & New Jersey
118	New York & Long Branch
130	New York Central
134	New York, New Haven & Hartford
135	New York, Ontario & Western
136	New York, Susquehanna & Western
142	Pennsylvania
143a	Pennsylvania–Reading Seashore Lines
144	Rahway Valley
145	Raritan River
158	Reading
159	Staten Island Rapid Transit
160	Union Transportation
166	Wharton & Northern

Longitude 75° West of Greenwich

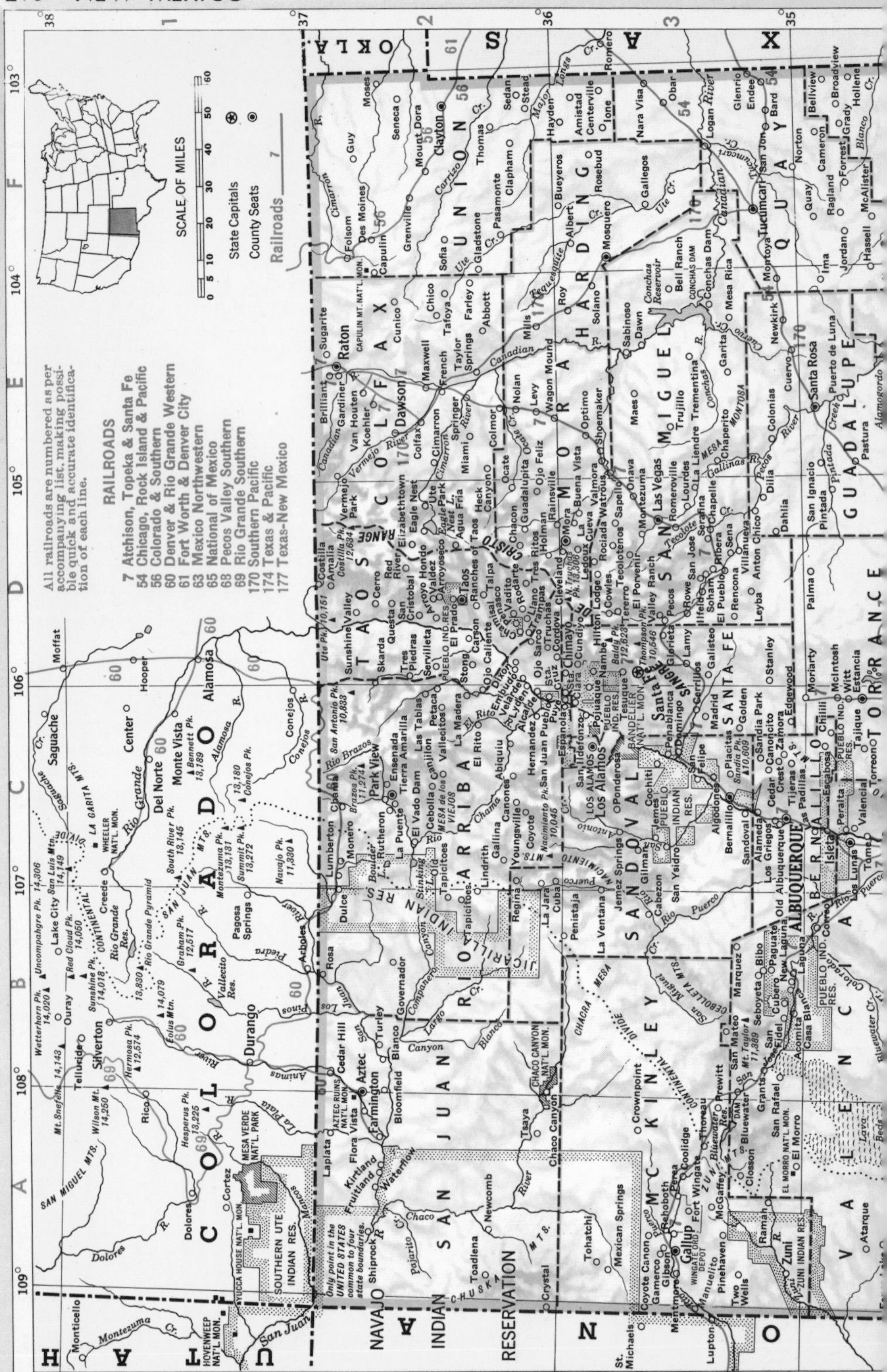

SCALE OF MILES

0 5 10 20 30 40 50 60

⊛ State Capitals

⊙ County Seats

Railroads _____ 7

RAILROADS

All railroads are numbered as per accompanying list, making possible quick and accurate identification of each line.

7 Atchison, Topeka & Santa Fe
54 Chicago, Rock Island & Pacific
56 Colorado & Southern
60 Denver & Rio Grande Western
61 Fort Worth & Denver City
63 Mexico Northwestern
65 National of Mexico
69 Pecos Valley Southern
170 Rio Grande Southern
174 Southern Pacific
177 Texas-New Mexico

Only point in the UNITED STATES common to four state boundaries

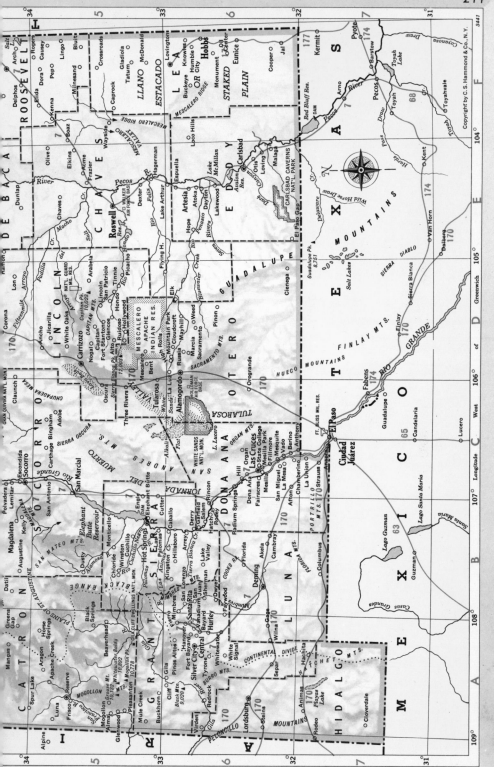

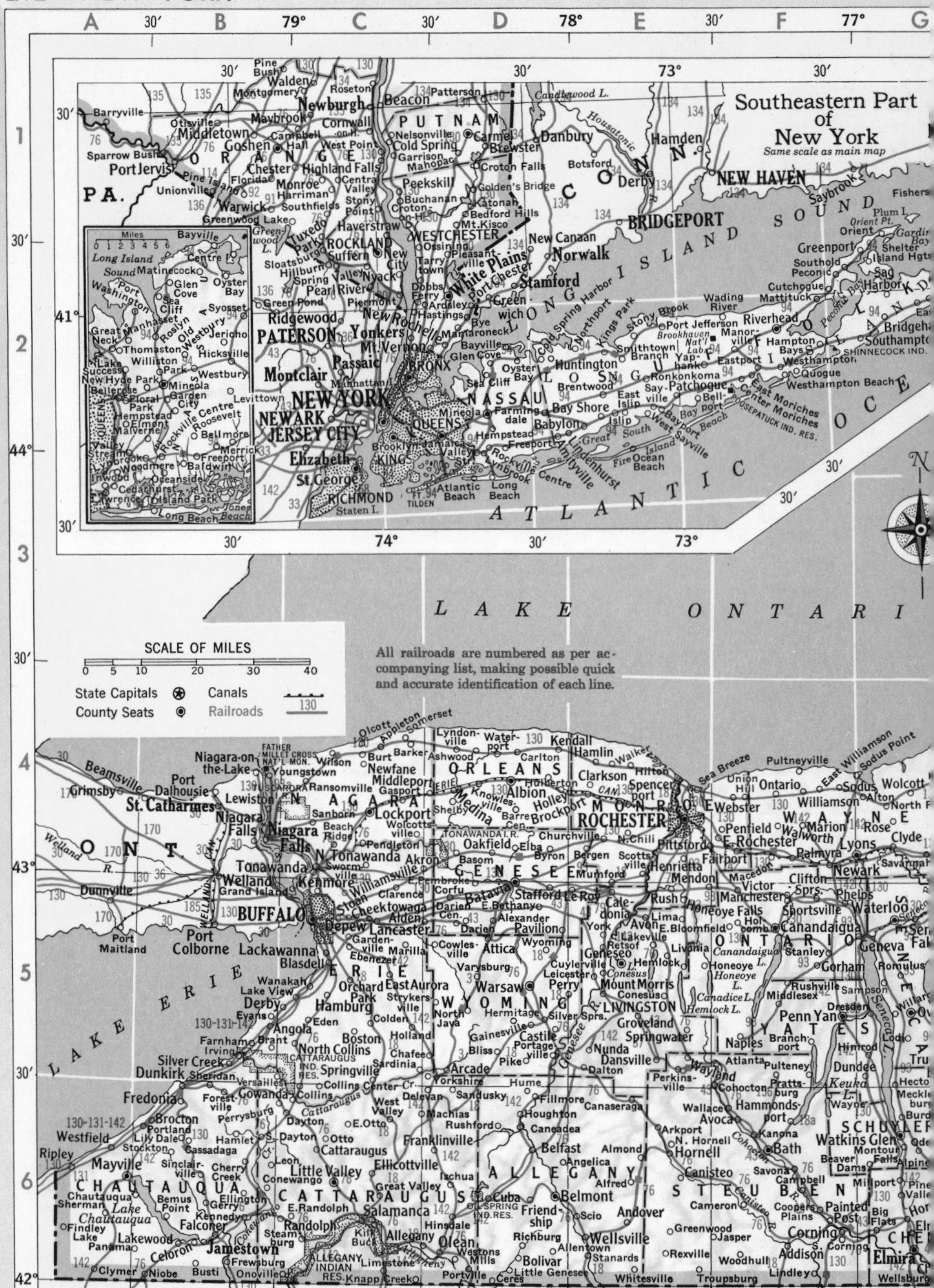

Southeastern Part of New York
Same scale as main map

SCALE OF MILES

0 5 10 20 30 40

State Capitals ⊛	Canals	
County Seats ◉	Railroads	130

All railroads are numbered as per accompanying list, making possible quick and accurate identification of each line.

LAKE ONTARIO

LAKE ERIE

ATLANTIC OCEAN

LONG ISLAND SOUND

RAILROADS

3 Arcade & Attica	93a Lewiston & Youngstown Frontier
18 Baltimore & Ohio	94 Long Island
18a Bath & Hammondsport	95 Lowville & Beaver River
20 Boston & Maine	96 Marcellus & Otisco
30 Canadian National	114 Middletown & New Jersey
31 Canadian Pacific	130 New York Central
33 Central Railroad of N. J.	131 New York, Chicago & St. Louis
34 Central Vermont	134 New York, New Haven & Hartford
36 Chesapeake & Ohio	135 New York, Ontario & Western
37 Dansville & Mt. Morris	136 New York, Susquehanna, & West.
41 Delaware & Hudson	138 Norwood & St. Lawrence
43 Delaware, Lackawanna & West.	142 Pennsylvania
76 Erie	156 Prattsburg
79 Genesee & Wyoming	162 Rutland
85 Grasse River	165 Skaneateles Short Line
86 Greenwich & Johnsonville	168 Staten Island Rapid Transit
91 Lehigh & Hudson River	169a Thousand Islands
92 Lehigh & New England	170 Toronto, Hamilton & Buffalo
93 Lehigh Valley	173 Unadilla Valley
	185 Wabash

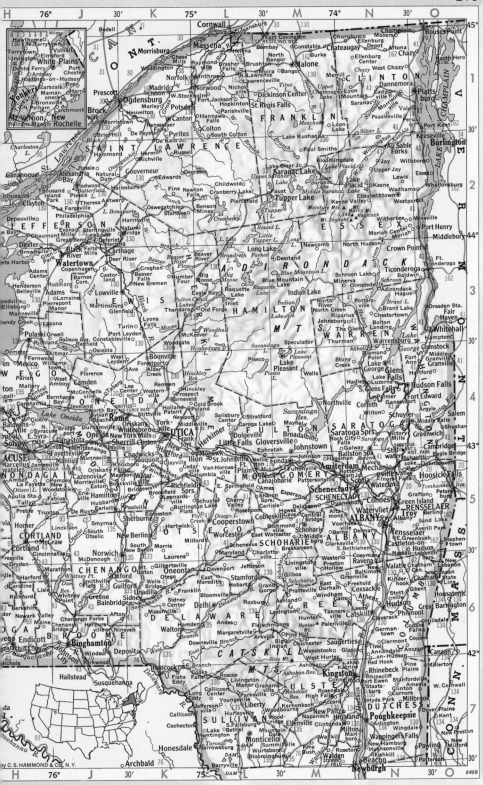

Grid columns: B 104° / C / 30' / D 103° / E / 30' / F 102° / G / 30' / H 101° / J 30'

SASKATCHEWAN

1 — Oxbow, Carnduff, Melita, Estevan, N

2 — Colgan, Alkabo, Westby, Fortuna, Ambrose, Crosby, Kermit, Noonan, Columbus, Portal, Northgate, Flaxton, Sherwood, Antler, Kuroki, Westhope, Roth, Souris, Carb, Bottineau, Stady, Larson, Stampede, Ligite, Woburn, Bowbells, Coteau, Norma, Tolley, Greene, Kenmare, Kenaston, Mohall, Truro, Hurd, Eckman, Lansford, Forfar, Glenburn, Deep, Upham, Bantry

DIVIDE, BURKE, RENVILLE, BOTTINEAU

3 — Grenora, Hanks, Appam, Corinth, Wildrose, Hamlet, Battleview, McGregor, Powers Lake, Lundsvalley, Lostwood, Coulee, Donnybrook, Aurelia, Carpio, Hartland, Deering, Rising, North Lake, Buffalo Lodge Lake, Denbigh, Zahl, Alamo, Temple, Tioga, White Earth, Manitou, Stanley, Palermo, Blaisdell, Tagus, Foxholm, Burlington, Surrey, Granville, Epping, Ray, Ross, Wheelock, Williston, Spring Brook, Hofflund, MOUNTRAIL, Belden, Des Lacs, Lonetree, Minot, Norwich, Simcoe, MCHEN, WILLIAMS, WARD, Trenton, MISSOURI, Dow, Charlson, Epworth, Drady, Logan, Sawyer, Velva, Voltaire, Rangeley, Bergen, Balfour

4 — Buford, Banks, Shell Cr., Plaza, Makoti, Ryder, Douglas, Benedict, Ruso, Butte, Kief, Fairview, Dore, Cartwright, Charbonneau, Alexander, East Fairview, Rawson, Arnegard, Schafer, Keene, Berg, Sanish, VERENDRYE NAT. MON., Van Hook, Parshall, Wabek, Maxo, Strawberry Lake, Long Lake, Sidney, Watford City, Croff, FORT, BERTHOLD, INDIAN, Raub, Roseglen, Emmet, Garrison, Crooked Lake, Skogm, Searing, Missouri, Little, RIVER, Blackwater, MCLEAN, SHE

5 — RESERVATION, Nishu, Ree, Elbowoods, Expansion, Mannhaven, GARRISON DAM, Underwood, Turtle L., Turtle Lake, Coleharbor, Mercer, Pickardville, McC, Oskaar, Trotters, Bicycle, Grassy Butte, Oakdale, Kildeer, Dunn Center, Werner, Halliday, Krem, Falkirk, Washburn, Alta, Mikkelson, Fairfield, Snow, Fayette, Dodge, Goldenvalley, Hazen, Beulah, Zap, Stanton, Hensler, Sanger, Wilton, Stilla, Westerheim, Gorham, Ukraina, Willmen, Emerson, Manning, Marshall, Fort Clark, DUNN, MERCER, OLIVER, Center, Price, Baldwin, Yucca

6 — Wibaux, Beach, Chama, Medora, THEODORE ROOSEVELT NAT'L MONUMENT, Fryburg, Belfield, Dickinson, South Heart, Zenith, Lehigh, Gladstone, Taylor, Richardton, Antelope, Hebron, Bluegrass, Youngstown, Rosebud, Harmon, New Salem, Judson, Sweetbriar, Mandan, Bismarck, Menoken, Sentinel Butte, New Hradec, Glen Ullin, Sims, Almont, Hannover, GOLDEN, BILLINGS, STARK, MORTON, BURLE, VALLEY, Golva, Alpha, Vim, Ranger, Gaylord, Schefield, Lefor, Heart, Muddy, Heart Butte, St. Anthony, Huff, Schmidt, Livor

7 — Marmarth, Ives, Rhame, Griffin, Bowman, Scranton, Gascoyne, Reeder, Bucyrus, Amidon, Black Butte 3,468, Rainy Butte, De Sart, Pierceo, Regent, Mott, Burt, Odessa, Leith, Elgin, Carson, Flasher, Fallon, Fort Rice, Midway, New England, Havelock, Watrous, Bentley, New Leipzig, Hell, Brisbane, Freda, Breien, Solen, Timmer, Cannon Ball, SLOPE, HETTINGER, GRANT, Clark Buttes, Clark, Raleigh, Whetstone Buttes, Buffalo Springs, Mound, Bessie, BOWMAN, ADAMS, Pretty Rock, Paradise, Shields, Porcupine, Winona, Fort Yates, Selfridge, Stowers, Emmo, SIOUX

8 — Haley, Hettinger, Haynes, Petrel, Lemmon, Cedar, McIntosh, McLaughlin, McClaughlino, Oak, North Fork, Grand River, SOUTH

SOUTH DAKOTA (S, O, U, T, H)

SCALE OF MILES

0   10   20   30

State Capitals ⊛
County Seats ⊙
Railroads ___117___

All railroads are numbered as per accompanying list, making possible quick and accurate identification of each line.

RAILROADS

30 Canadian National
31 Canadian Pacific
42 Chicago and North Western
51 Chicago, Milwaukee, St. Paul and Pacific
80 Great Northern
81 Midland Continental
113 Minneapolis & St. Louis
117 Minneapolis, St. Paul & Sault Ste. Marie
137 Northern Pacific

Copyright by C. S. Hammond & Co., N.Y.

24109

All railroads are numbered as per accompanying list, making possible quick and accurate identification of each line.

RAILROADS

2 Akron & Barberton Belt	76 Erie	152 Pittsburgh & West Virginia
3 Akron, Canton & Youngstown	77 Fairport, Painesville & Eastern	168 Southern
4 Ann Arbor	78 Federal Valley	169 Toledo, Angola & Western
18 Baltimore & Ohio	82 Lakeside & Marblehead	171 Toledo Terminal
23 Bessemer & Lake Erie	107 Louisville & Nashville	185 Wabash
25 Canadian National	130 New York Central	189 Wheeling & Lake Erie
30 Canadian Pacific	131 New York, Chicago & St. Louis	200 Youngstown & Southern
36 Chesapeake & Ohio	133 Norfolk & Western	
75 Detroit, Toledo & Ironton	142 Pennsylvania	

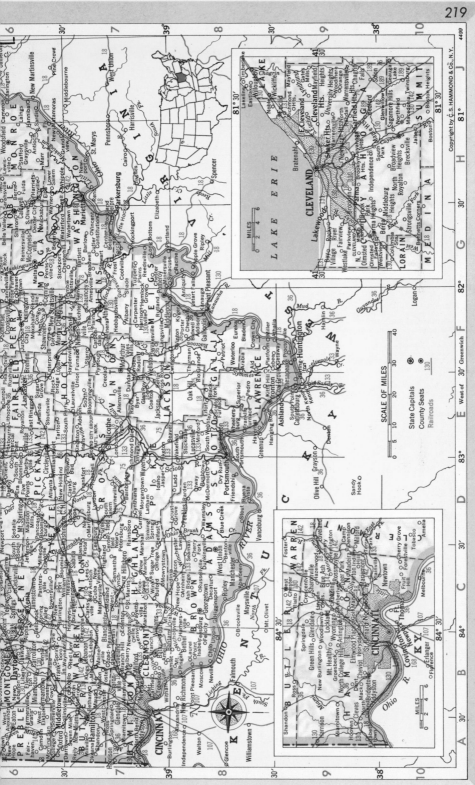

CLEVELAND

LAKE ERIE

SCALE OF MILES

State Capitals
County Seats
Railroads

CINCINNATI

KY.

Ohio R.

All railroads are numbered as per accompanying list, making possible quick and accurate identification of each line.

RAILROADS

- 7 Atchison, Topeka & Santa Fe
- 9 Beaver, Meade & Englewood
- 54 Chicago, Rock Island & Pacific
- 66 Fort Worth & Denver City
- 77 Gulf, Colorado & Santa Fe
- 95 Kansas City Southern
- 98 Kansas, Oklahoma & Gulf
- 106 Midland Valley
- 121 Missouri-Kansas-Texas
- 122 Missouri Pacific
- 128 Oklahoma City-Ada-Atoka
- 136 Okmulgee Northern
- 138 Osage
- 139 Panhandle & Santa Fe
- 160 St. Louis-San Francisco
- 162 Sand Springs
- 171 Texas, Oklahoma & Eastern
- 192 Wichita Valley

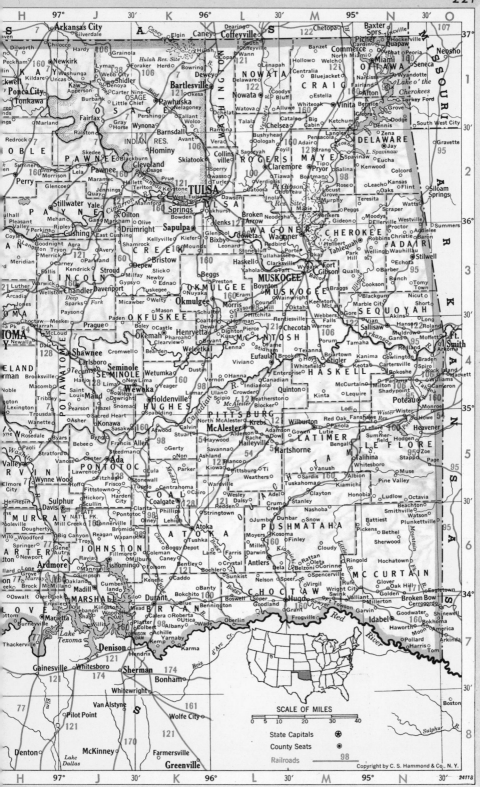

SCALE OF MILES

0 5 10 20 30 40

State Capitals   ⊛

County Seats   ◉

Railroads   98

Copyright by C. S. Hammond & Co., N.Y.

24118

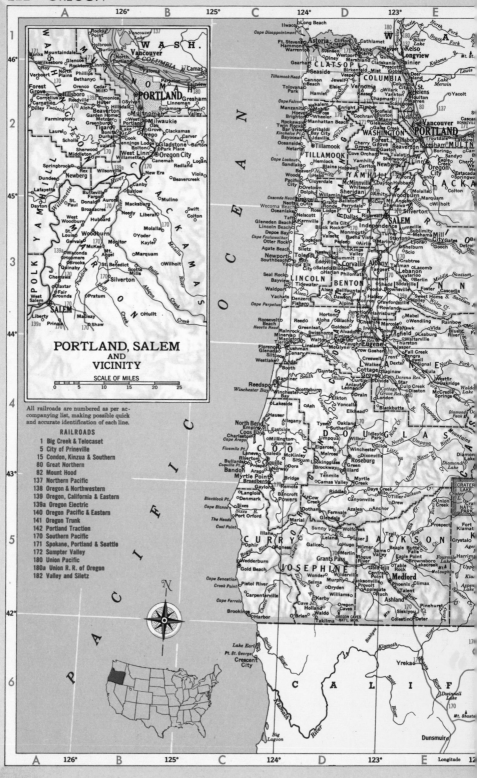

PORTLAND, SALEM
AND
VICINITY

SCALE OF MILES

0   5   10   15   20   25

All railroads are numbered as per accompanying list, making possible quick and accurate identification of each line.

RAILROADS

1 Big Creek & Telocaset
5 City of Prineville
15 Condon, Kinzua & Southern
80 Great Northern
82 Mount Hood
137 Northern Pacific
138 Oregon & Northwestern
139 Oregon, California & Eastern
139a Oregon Electric
140 Oregon Pacific & Eastern
141 Oregon Trunk
142 Portland Traction
170 Southern Pacific
171 Spokane, Portland & Seattle
172 Sumpter Valley
180 Union Pacific
180a Union R. R. of Oregon
182 Valley and Siletz

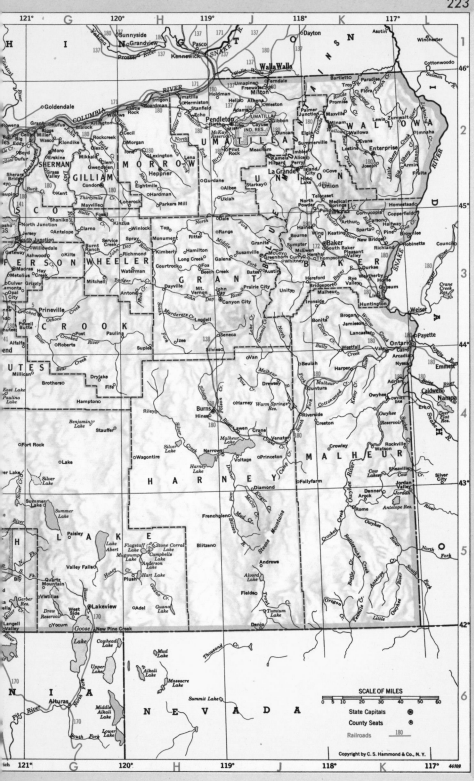

121° G **120°** H **119°** J **118°** K **117°** L

SCALE OF MILES
0 5 10 20 30 40 50 60

State Capitals ⊛
County Seats ⊙
Railroads ___180___

Copyright by C. S. Hammond & Co., N. Y.

44108

121° G **120°** H **119°** J **118°** K **117°** L

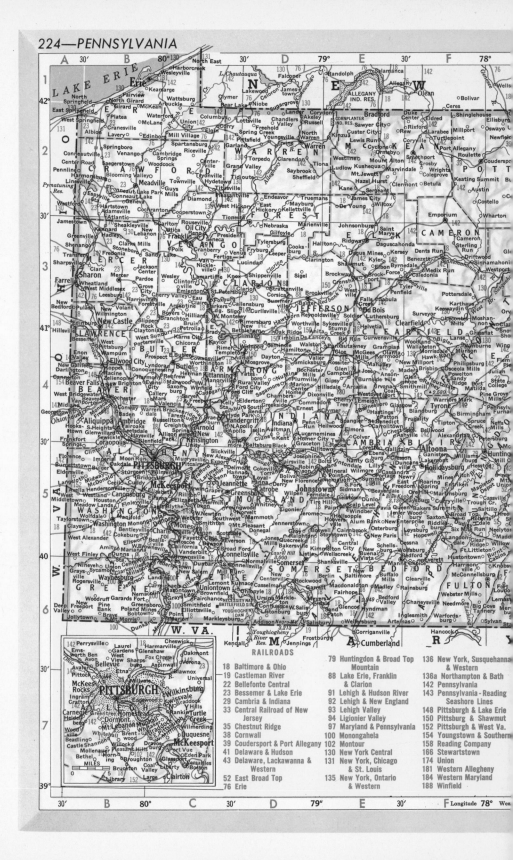

RAILROADS

18	Baltimore & Ohio
19	Castleman River
22	Bellefonte Central
23	Bessemer & Lake Erie
29	Cambria & Indiana
33	Central Railroad of New Jersey
35	Chestnut Ridge
38	Cornwall
39	Coudersport & Port Allegany
41	Delaware & Hudson
43	Delaware, Lackawanna & Western
52	East Broad Top
76	Erie
79	Huntingdon & Broad Top Mountain
88	Lake Erie, Franklin & Clarion
91	Lehigh & Hudson River
92	Lehigh & New England
93	Lehigh Valley
94	Ligonier Valley
97	Maryland & Pennsylvania
100	Monongahela
102	Montour
130	New York Central
131	New York, Chicago & St. Louis
135	New York, Ontario & Western
136	New York, Susquehanna & Western
136a	Northampton & Bath
142	Pennsylvania
143	Pennsylvania-Reading Seashore Lines
148	Pittsburgh & Lake Erie
150	Pittsburg & Shawmut
152	Pittsburgh & West Va.
154	Youngstown & Southern
158	Reading Company
166	Stewartstown
174	Union
181	Western Allegheny
184	Western Maryland
188	Winfield

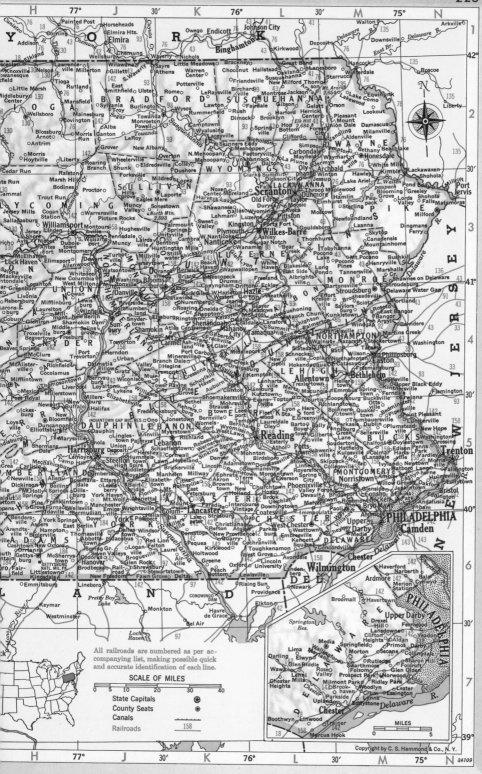

SCALE OF MILES

0 5 10   20   30   40

State Capitals
County Seats
Canals
Railroads   158

All railroads are numbered as per accompanying list, making possible quick and accurate identification of each line.

MILES

Copyright by C. S. Hammond & Co., N. Y.

34109

A 83° B 30' C 82° D 30' E

NORTH

BLUE RIDGE

Nantahala Res. Franklin Glenville Res. Lake Toxaway Brevard Columbus Cliffside Kings Mt. Gaste

Nantahala Tryon Landrum Chesnee Campobello Fingerville Cowpens Nat'l Battlefield Site Cowpens Nat'l Nat. Pk. Blacksburg Kings Mt. Nat'l Mil. Pk. Clov Cata

Sassafras Mt. 3,548 Caesars Head Gowensville Gramling Inman Mayo Gaffney Cherokee Falls Smyrna York

Nimmons Rocky Bottom Sunset Cleveland Tigerville Wellford Fairforest Converse CHEROKEE Hickory Sharon McConnells ville Ara Roc Ind

Nine Times Crow Creek Dacusville Marietta Travelers Rest Greer Lyman Arcadia Glendale Clifton Pacolet Mills Kelton Lowrys

PICKENS Pickens Mill Paris Pelham Reidville Switzer Moore Glenn Springs West Springs Buffalo Union Lock hart Monarch Mills Baldwin Mills

OCONEE Walhalla Seneca Central Norris Maulden Cashville Woodruff Enoree Cross Anchor Cross Keys Santuck Carlisle UNION CHES

Westminster Pendleton Clemson Piedmont Fountain Inn Owings Lanford Ora Sedalia

ANDERSON Anderson Belton Princeton LAURENS Renno Herbert Shelton FAI Winnsb

Honea Path Ware Shoals Laurens Lydia Clinton Whitmire Blairs Monticello Jenkins

Donalds Mountville Joanna Kinards Jalapa Oakland Strother Mill NEWBERRY Newberry Pomaria Peak White

ABBEVILLE Abbeville S. Greenwood Ninety Six GREENWOOD Greenwood Chappells Prosperity Little Mountain Chapin

McCORMICK Saluda SALUDA Murray Lexington LEXINGT

SCALE OF MILES
0 5 10 20 30 40

State Capitals
County Seats
Canals
Railroads

83° 30' 82° 30' Longitude E

RAILROADS

2	Aberdeen & Rockfish	75	Lancaster & Chester
17	Atlantic Coast Line	81	Laurinburg & Southern
21	Bennettsville & Cheraw	108	Louisville & Wadley
22	Blue Ridge	110	Macon, Dublin & Savannah
23	Buffalo, Union-Carolina	115	Norfolk Southern
24	Carolina & Northwestern	124	Pickens
25	Carolina Western	128	Piedmont & Northern
26	Central of Georgia	133	Rockingham
27	Charleston & Western Carolina	139	Sandersville
28	Cliffside	162	Savannah & Atlanta
46	Clinchfield	164	Seaboard Air Line
47	Columbia, Newberry & Laurens	168	Southern
50	Edgmoor & Manetta	169	Sylvania Central
63	Gainesville Midland	172	Tallulah Falls
66	Georgia	173	Virginia & Carolina Southern
67	Georgia & Florida	175	Wadley Southern
71	Greenville & Northern	179	Ware Shoals
72	Hampton & Branchville	180	Winston - Salem Southbound
73	Hartwell	181	Wrightsville & Tennille

7499

SCALE OF MILES

0   10   20   40   60

State Capitals ⊛

County Seats ⊙

Railroads 51

All railroads are numbered as per accompanying list, making possible quick
and accurate identification of each line

RAILROADS

42 Chicago & North Western
45 Chicago, Burlington & Quincy
51 Chicago, Milwaukee, St. Paul & Pacific
54 Chicago, Rock Island & Pacific
55 Chicago, St. Paul, Minneapolis &
   Omaha

80 Great Northern
87 Illinois Central
113 Minneapolis & St.
117 Minneapolis, St. Pa

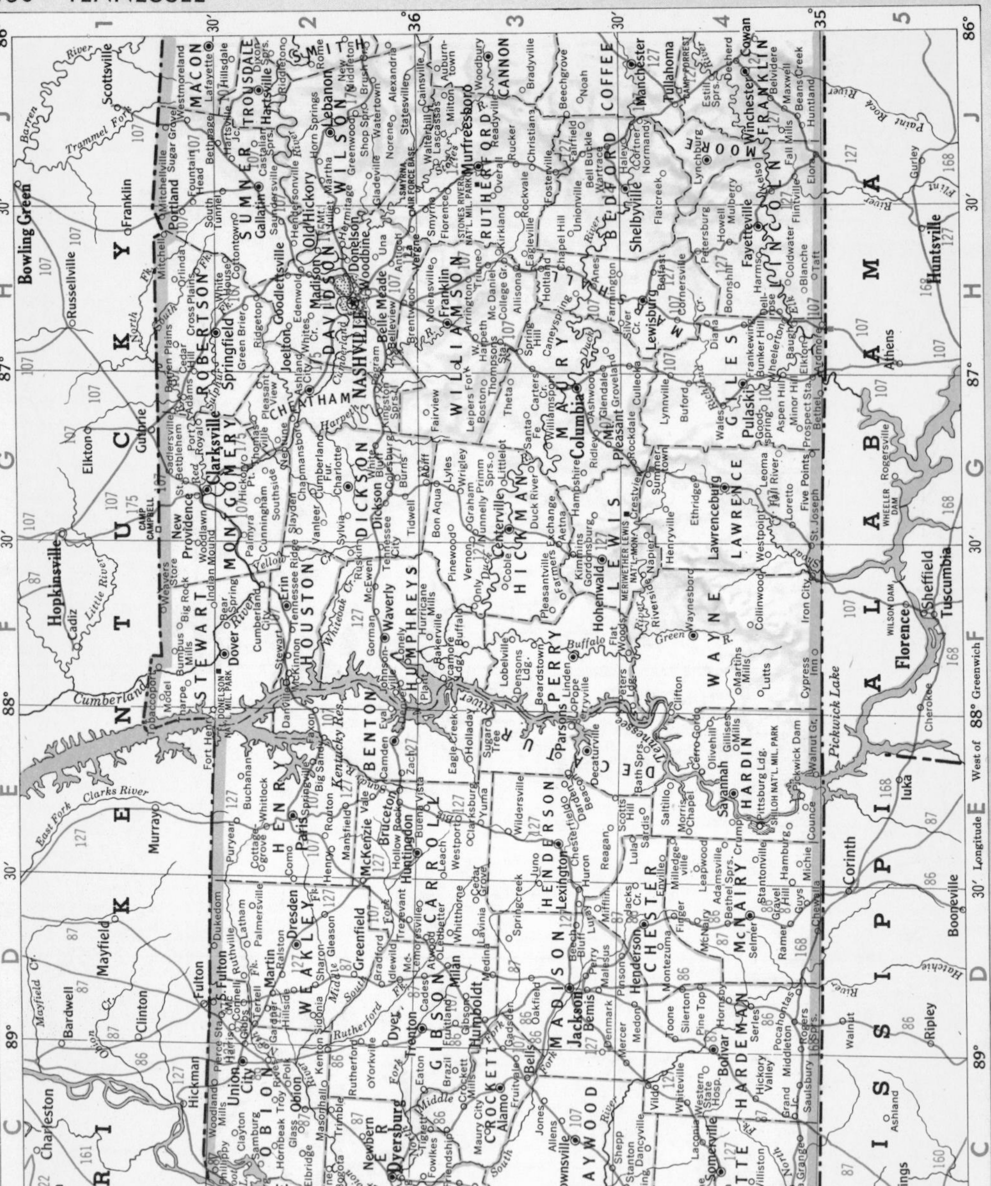

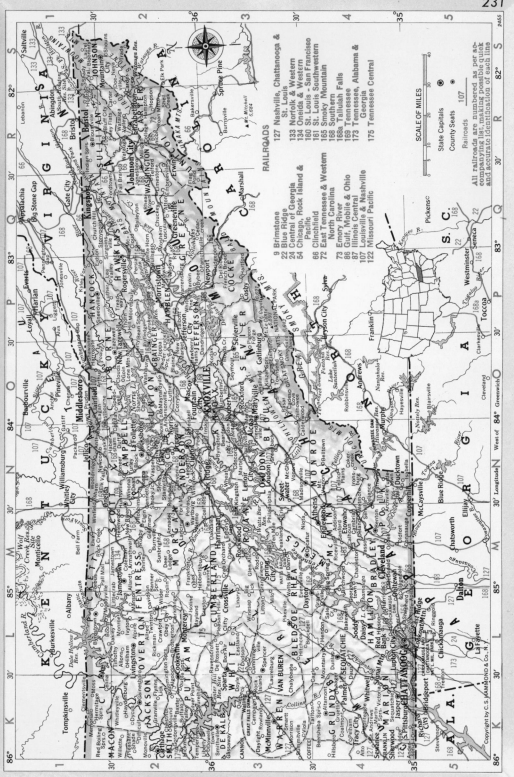

SCALE OF MILES

State Capitals ⊛
County Seats ⊙ 107
Railroads

All railroads are numbered as per accompanying list, making possible quick and accurate identification of each line

RAILROADS

127 Nashville, Chattanooga &
    St. Louis
133 Norfolk & Western
134 Oneida & Western
160 St. Louis – San Francisco
161 St. Louis Southwestern
165 Smoky Mountain
168 Southern
168a Tallulah Falls
169 Tennessee, Alabama &
    Georgia
173 Tennessee Central
175 Tennessee Central

9 Brimstone
22 Blue Ridge
24 Central of Georgia
54 Chicago, Rock Island &
    Pacific
66 Clinchfield
72 East Tennessee & Western
    North Carolina
73 Emory River
86 Gulf, Mobile & Ohio
87 Illinois Central
107 Louisville & Nashville
122 Missouri Pacific

Copyright by C. S. HAMMOND & Co., N. Y.

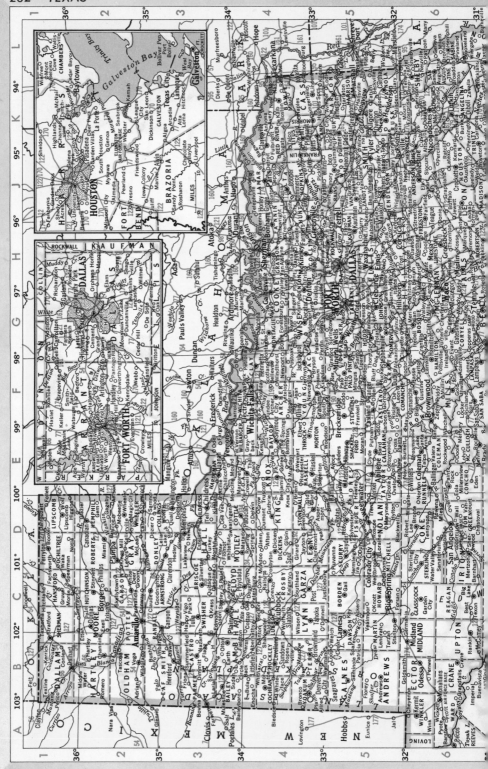

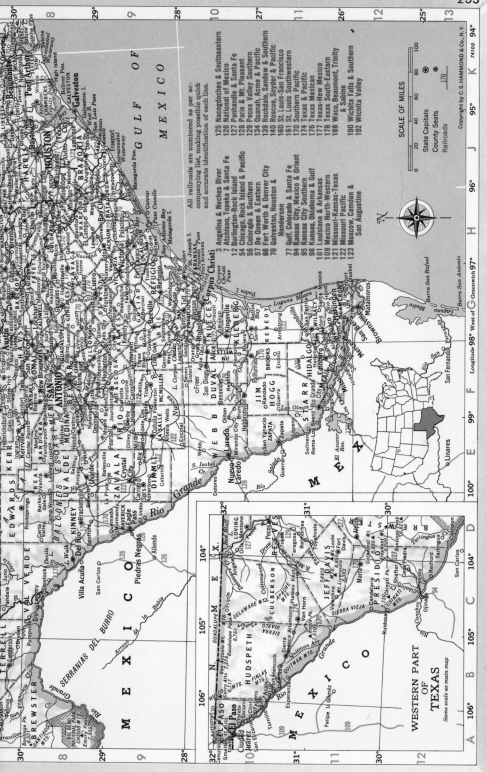

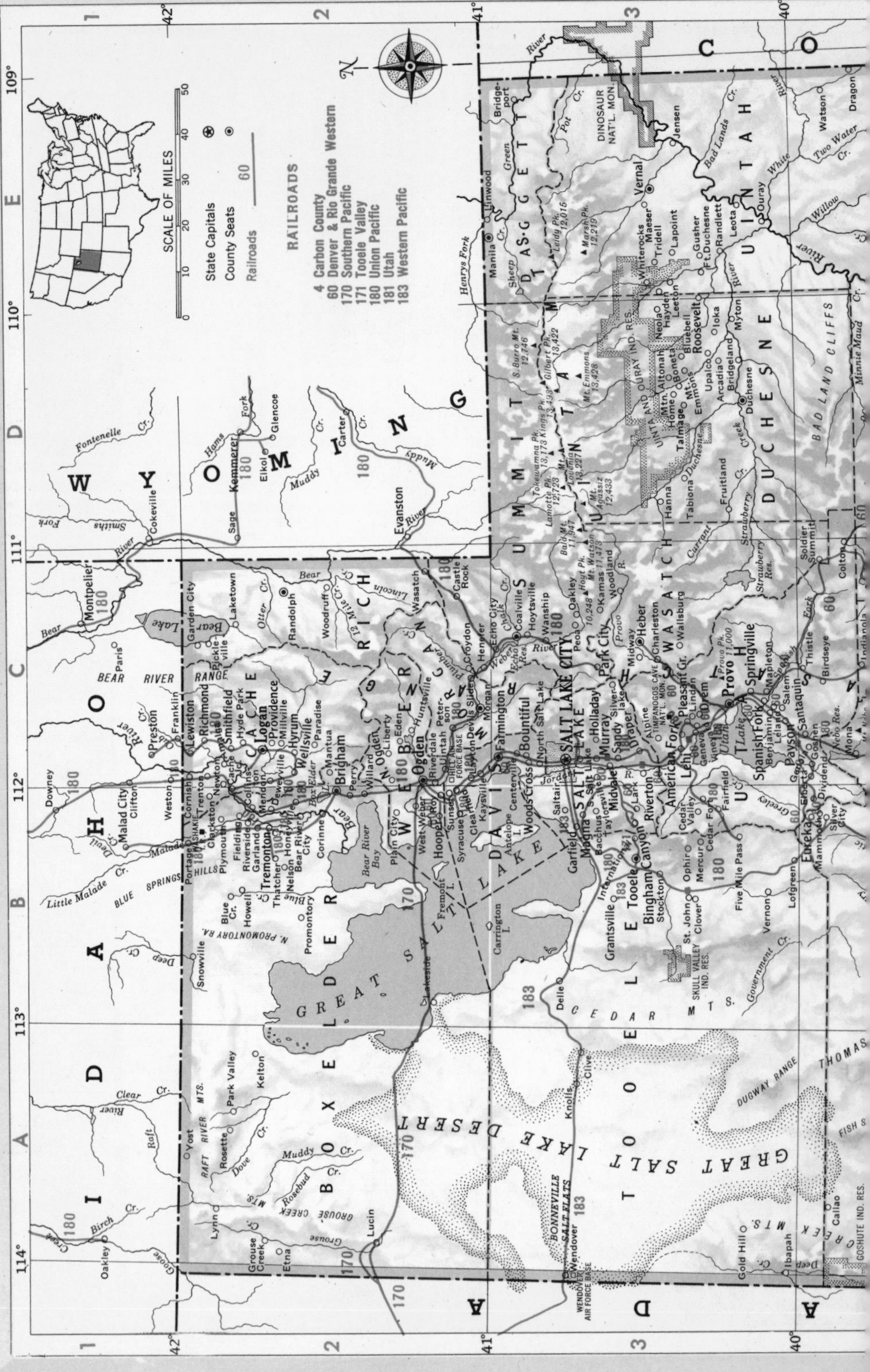

109°

SCALE OF MILES

0 10 20 30 40 50 60

State Capitals ⊛
County Seats ⊚
Railroads

RAILROADS

4 Carbon County
60 Denver & Rio Grande Western
170 Southern Pacific
171 Tooele Valley
180 Union Pacific
181 Utah
183 Western Pacific

W Y O M I N G

I D A H O

C O L O

U I N T A H

D A G G E T T

DINOSAUR NATL. MON.

DUCHESNE

BADLAND CLIFFS

SUMMIT

WASATCH

CACHE

BEAR RIVER RANGE

RICH

WEBER

MORGAN

DAVIS

SALT LAKE CITY

SALT LAKE

TOOELE

GREAT SALT LAKE DESERT

GREAT SALT LAKE

BOX ELDER

N. PROMONTORY RA.

CEDAR MTS.

DUGWAY RANGE

THOMAS

GREAT SALT LAKE

UTAH

WENDOVER AIR FORCE BASE

BONNEVILLE SALT FLATS 183

COLORADO

INDE PENDENT

UINTA & OURAY IND. RES.

ROAN BORDER

ROAN CLIFFS

GRAND

Deser L.

Westwater

Cisco Wash

Cisco

Thompson

Sego

Sagers

Dolores

Dolores River

Pack Cr.

Moab

Mt. Waas ▲ 12,586
Tomasaki ▲ 12,271
Mt. Peale ▲ 12,004
Mt. Tukuhnikivatz ▲ 13,089

La Sal

Wash Cr.

Summit Point

Hudson Cr.

ARCHES NATL. MON.

Colorado River

Indian Cr.

Hatch Cr.

Monticello

Blanding

Hallets

Montezuma

Cr.

HOVENWEEP NATL. MON.

SAN JUAN

Only point in the UNITED STATES common to four state boundaries.

Bluff

Butler Wash

Comb Wash

SAN JUAN RIDGE

MONUMENT

NATURAL BRIDGES NATL. MON.

San Juan River

CLAY HILLS

NAVAJO NATL. MON.

Mt. Navajo 10,416

Mt. Holmes 10,750

NAVAJO INDIAN RESERVATION

Copyright by C. S. Hammond & Co., N. Y.

Naugo Cr.

Navajo Mt. 10,416

RAINBOW BRIDGE NATL. MON.

COLORADO RIVER

Lees Ferry

Sentinel Rock

KAIPAROWITS PLATEAU

Paria River

A R I Z O N A

110°

111°

Greenwich

West of

112°

Longitude

113°

114°

E

D

C

B

A

San Rafael River

EMERY

SAN RAFAEL SWELL

Fremont River

COAL CLIFFS

Muddy Cr.

Salvation Cr.

Curtis Cr.

Moore

Emery

Fremont

Hanksville

Caineville

Mt. Ellen 11,485

HENRY MOUNTAINS

Mt. Pennell 11,320

Mt. Hillers 10,650

Pine Alcove Cr.

Hoxie Cr.

WAYNE

CAPITOL REEF NATL. MON.

Thousand Lake Mt. 11,260

Grover

Teasdale

Fremont

Tantalus Cr.

Escalante River

Boulder

Boulder Cr.

False Cr.

G A R F I E L D

Winslow Cr.

Birch Cr.

Escalante

Loa

Lyman
Bicknell

Mt. Hilgard 11,560
Mt. Marvine 11,600
Mt. Terrel 11,460
Fish Lake 11,002

Fremont

Burrville

Greenwich

Koosharem IND. RES.

Antimony

Angle

Kingston

Circleville

Mt. Dutton 10,800

PIUTE

Junction

Spry

PAUNSAUGUNT PLATEAU

Tropic

Cannonville

Henrieville

Ruby's Inn

BRYCE CANYON NATL. PARK

Bryce Cr.

Widtsoe

Sevier River

Johnsons Cr.

SEVIER

Salina

Redmond

Aurora

Sigurd

Sevier River

Richfield

Elsinore

Joseph

Monroe

Central

Annabella

Glenwood

Marysvale

Marysvale Pk. 11,600
Delano Pk. 12,240

Junction

Belknap Pk. 12,139

KINGSTON

Otter Cr. Res.

Otter Cr.

B E A V E R

Beaver

Minersville

Milford

Adamsville

Greenville

Green Birch Cr.

Sulphurdale

Minersville Res.

Beaver

WAH WAH MTS.

MINERAL MTS.

Nada

Frisco

Wild Cr.

BEAVER MTS.

Cove Fort

Black Rock

Manti

Mayfield

Axtell

Centerfield

Gunnison

Fayette

SANPETE

WASATCH

Spring City

Ephraim

Moroni

Cottonwood

Orangeville

Castle Dale

Ferron

Clawson

Perron

Huntington

Cleveland

Elmo

Moriland

Woodside

Green River

San Rafael

Green River

Sego

Crescent Junction

LABYRINTH CANYON

ORANGE CLIFFS

Dirty Devil River

Caineville

Salina Cr.

Clear Cr.

Crystal

Salina

Gunnison River

Fountain Green

MANTI

Wales

Chester

Fairview

Indianola

Thistle

Scipio

Holden

Fillmore

Meadow

Kanosh

Hatton

Kanosh Res.

Corn Cr.

Oak City

Delta

Oasis

Deseret

Hinckley

Abraham

Sutherland

Sugarville

M I L L A R D

Clear Lake

Pavant

Garrison

Baker

LEHMAN CAVE NATL. MON.

HOUSE RANGE

SION RANGE

Sevier Lake

Swan L.

Salt L.

Blue L.

PAVANT RANGE

Kanosh IND. RES.

I R O N

Paragonah

Parowan

Cedar City

Kanarraville

CEDAR BREAKS NATL. MON.

Little Creek Pk. 10,010

Panguitch

Panguitch L.

Hatch

Asay Cr.

Mammoth Cr.

Brian Head 11,315

Summit

Enoch

Iron Mt.

Lund

Beryl

Modena

Newcastle

Enterprise

ESCALANTE DESERT

Iron Springs

Little Salt Lake

Coal Cr.

Dry Cr.

Kanarra Cr.

W A S H I N G T O N

New Harmony

Pine Valley

Mt. 10,325

Pinto

Central

Veyo

Gunlock

Motoqua

Pintura

Leeds

Toquerville

La Verkin

Virgin

Rockville

Springdale

ZION NATL. PARK

ZION NAT. MON.

St. George

Washington

Santa Clara

Ivins

SHIVWITS IND. RES.

Hurricane

Virgin River

LaVerkin Cr.

Ash Cr.

Pierces Cr.

Beaver Dam

Santa Clara Cr.

Littlefield

Virgin River

K A N E

Alton

Mt. Carmel

Glendale

Orderville

Johnson

Kanab

Fredonia

KAIBAB IND. RES.

PIPE SPRING NATL. MON.

Kanab Cr.

Johnsons Cr.

37°

38°

39°

5

6

V

N

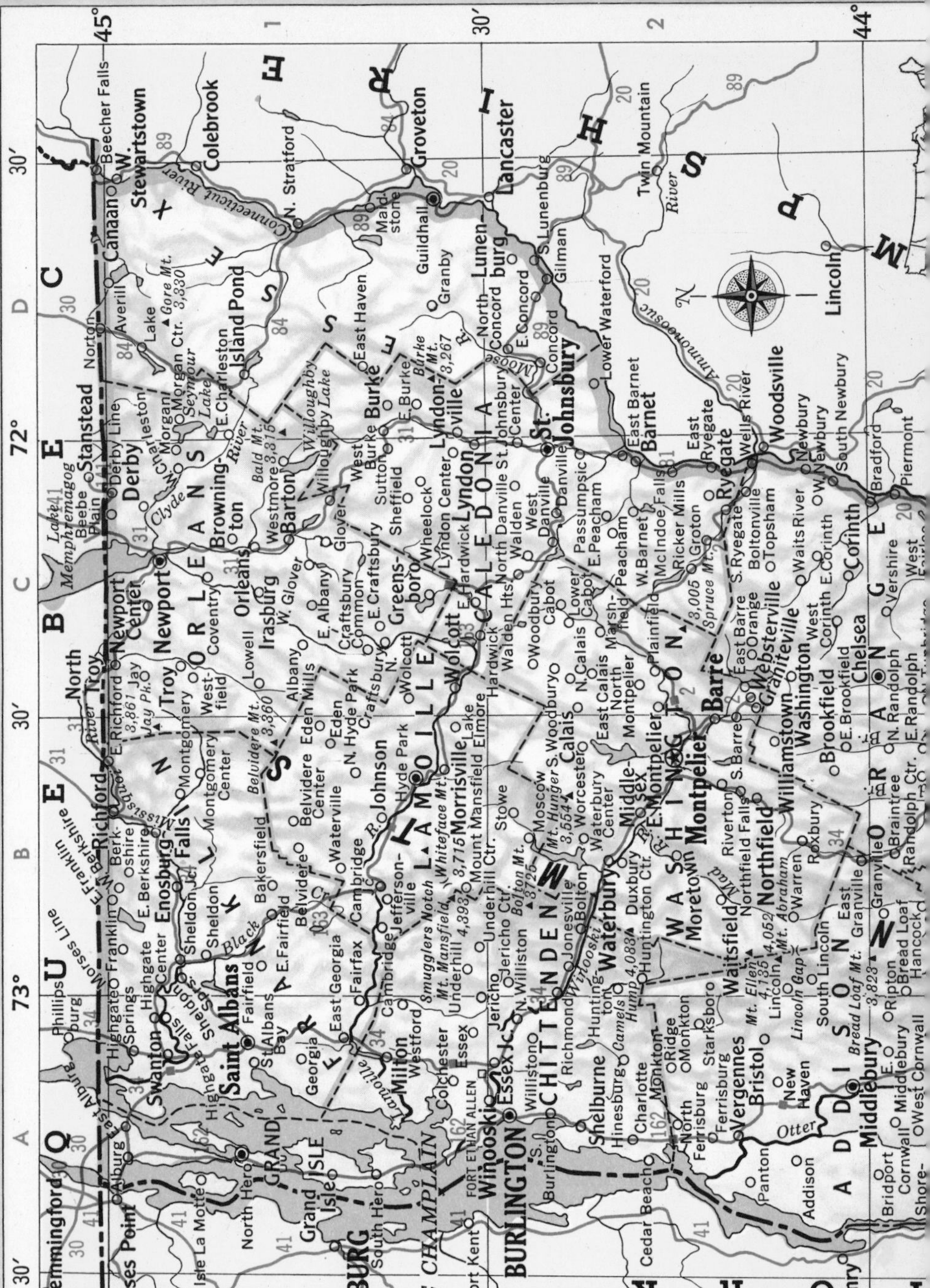
QUEBEC
ESSEX
ORLEANS
CALEDONIA
LAMOILLE
FRANKLIN
GRAND ISLE
CHITTENDEN
WASHINGTON
ADDISON
ORANGE
LAKE CHAMPLAIN
Lake Memphremagog
Connecticut River
Winooski
Lamoille
Missisquoi
Otter
Ammonoosuc
Moose
Clyde
Black
Hemmingford
Rouses Point
PLATTSBURG
Port Kent
Ausable Forks
Port Henry
Beecher Falls
W. Stewartstown
Colebrook
Groveton
Lancaster
Canaan
Norton
Averill
Island Pond
Derby Line
Stanstead
Derby
Newport
North Troy
Troy
Richford
Enosburg Falls
Swanton
Saint Albans
Alburg
North Hero
Grand Isle
South Hero
Milton
Essex Jc.
Winooski
BURLINGTON
FORT ETHAN ALLEN
Shelburne
Vergennes
Middlebury
Bristol
Waitsfield
Northfield
Montpelier
Barre
Waterbury
Stowe
Morrisville
Johnson
Hardwick
Lyndonville
St. Johnsbury
Barton
Orleans
Irasburg
Greensboro
Danville
Ryegate
Barnet
Woodsville
Wells River
Bradford
Corinth
Chelsea
Randolph
Brookfield
Williamstown
Washington
Websterville
Graniteville
Granville
Hancock
Lincoln
Twin Mountain
Guildhall
Maidstone
Granby
Burke
Lyndon
Mt. Mansfield 4,393
Camels Hump 4,083
Mt. Ellen 4,135
Mt. Abraham 4,052
Jay Pk. 3,861
Belvidere Mt. 3,360
Bolton Mt. 3,725
Mt. Hunger 3,554
Gore Mt. 3,330
Burke Mt. 3,267
Bald Mt. 3,315
Spruce Mt. 3,005
Bread Loaf Mt. 3,823
Whiteface Mt. 3,715
Smugglers Notch
Lincoln Gap
45°
44°
73°
72°
30′

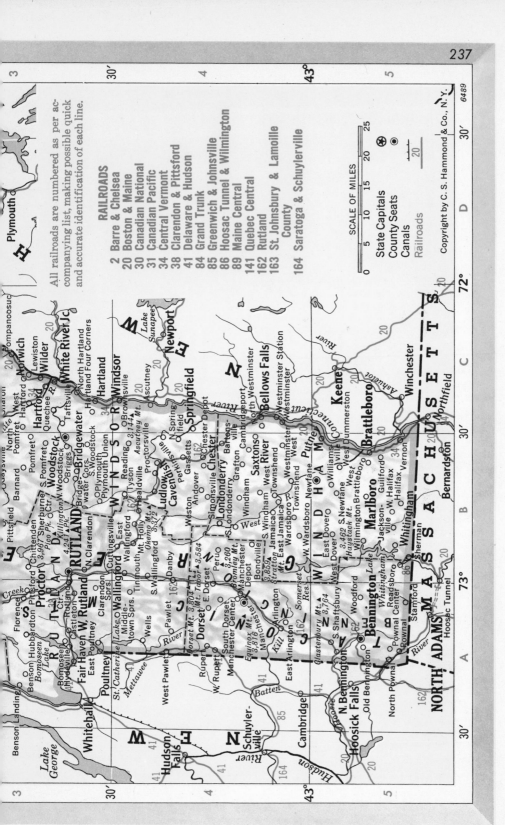

RAILROADS

All railroads are numbered as per accompanying list, making possible quick and accurate identification of each line.

2	Barre & Chelsea
20	Boston & Maine
30	Canadian National
31	Canadian Pacific
34	Central Vermont
38	Clarendon & Pittsford
41	Delaware & Hudson
84	Grand Trunk
85	Greenwich & Johnsville
86	Hoosac Tunnel & Wilmington
89	Maine Central
141	Quebec Central
162	Rutland
163	St. Johnsbury & Lamoille County
164	Saratoga & Schuylerville

SCALE OF MILES

0 5 10 15 20 25

State Capitals ⊛
County Seats ◉
Canals
Railroads

6489

WESTERN PART OF VIRGINIA
Same scale as main map.

SCALE OF MILES
0 5 10 20 30 40

RAILROADS

1	Atlantic & Danville	111	Nelson & Albemarle
2	Atlantic & Yadkin	133	Norfolk & Western
6	Baltimore & Eastern	135	Norfolk Southern
17	Atlantic Coast Line	142	Pennsylvania
18	Baltimore & Ohio	158	Reading
36	Chesapeake & Ohio	159	Richmond, Fredericksburg & Potomac
37	Chesapeake Western		
66	Clinchfield	164	Seaboard Air Line
67	Danville & Western	168	Southern
69	Interstate	171	Virginia Blue Ridge
107	Louisville & Nashville	183	Virginian
110a	Maryland & Pennsylvania	184	Western Maryland
		192	Winchester & Western

Copyright by C. S. Hammond & Co., N. Y.

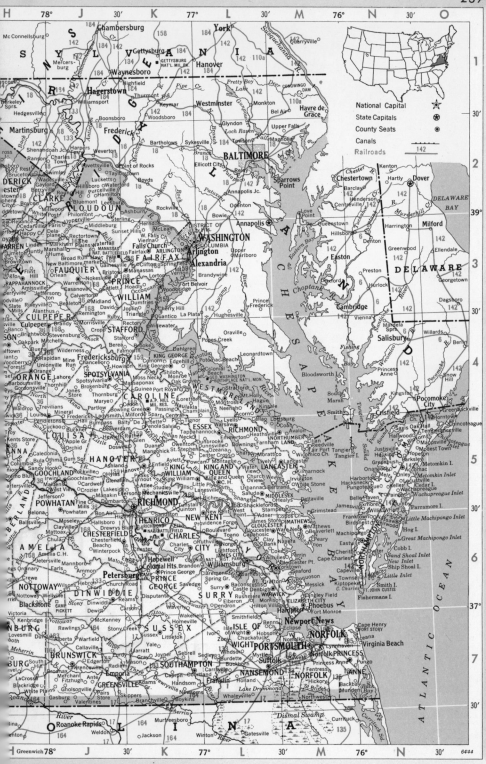

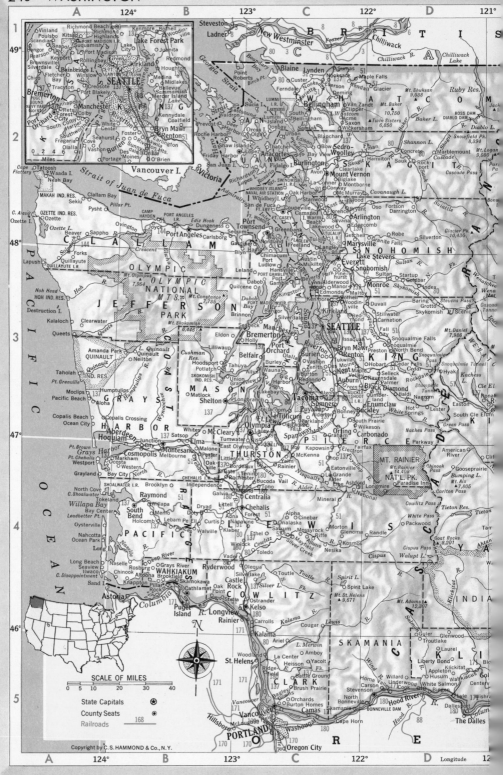

SCALE OF MILES

0 5 10 20 30 40

State Capitals
County Seats
Railroads

All railroads are numbered as per accompanying list, making possible quick and accurate identification of each line.

RAILROADS

3 British Columbia Electric	86 Longview, Portland & Northern
5 Camas Prairie	88 Mount Hood
6 Canadian National	137 Northern Pacific
8 Canadian Pacific	139a Oregon Electric
51 Chicago, Milwaukee, St. Paul & Pacific	141 Oregon Trunk
52 Cowlitz, Chehalis & Cascade	143 Pacific Coast
80 Great Northern	144 Port Angeles Western

145 Port Townsend
155 Spokane International
170 Southern Pacific
171 Spokane, Portland & Seattle
180 Union Pacific
181 Walla Walla Valley
182 Washington, Idaho & Montana
183 Waterville

All railroads are numbered as per accompanying list, making possible quick and accurate identification of each line

RAILROADS

18 Baltimore & Ohio
21 Buffalo Creek & Gauley
23 Campbell's Creek
36 Chesapeake & Ohio
37 Chesapeake Western
40 Cumberland & Pennsylvania
48 Kanawha Central
50 Kelley's Creek & Northwestern
64 Kelly's Creek
100 Monongahela
130 New York Central
133 Norfolk & Western
142 Pennsylvania
152 Pittsburgh & West Virginia
154 Preston
155 Rowlesburg & Southern
156 Southern
157 Strouds Creek & Muddlety

183 Virginian
184 Western Maryland
188 West Virginia Northern
189 Wheeling & Lake Erie
192 Winchester & Western
193 Winifrede

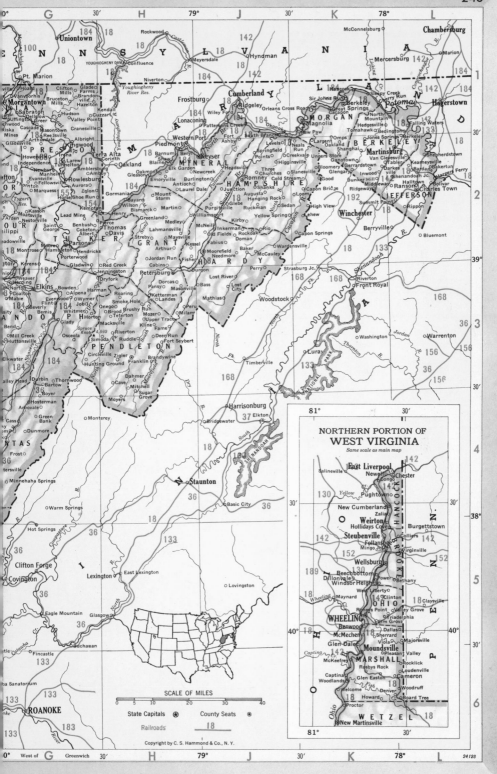

NORTHERN PORTION OF
WEST VIRGINIA
Same scale as main map

SCALE OF MILES

State Capitals ⊛   County Seats ⊙

Railroads   18

Copyright by C. S. Hammond & Co., N. Y.

West of G   Greenwich   30'   79'   30'   78'   24123

RAILROADS

2	Ahnapee & Western
42	Chicago, St. Paul, Minneapolis & Omaha
45	Chicago, Burlington & Quincy
46	Chicago Great Western
51	Chicago, Milwaukee, St. Paul & Pacific
54	Chicago, Rock Island & Pacific
55	Chicago, St. Paul, Minneapolis & Omaha
75	Duluth, Missabe & Iron Range
77	Duluth, South Shore & Atlantic
80	Great Northern
82	Green Bay & Western
85	Hillsboro & North-Eastern
87	Illinois Central
88	Kewaunee, Green Bay & Western
91	Laona & Northern
93	Marinette, Tomahawk & Western
117	Minneapolis, St. Paul & Sault Ste. Marie
137	Northern Pacific

SCALE OF MILES

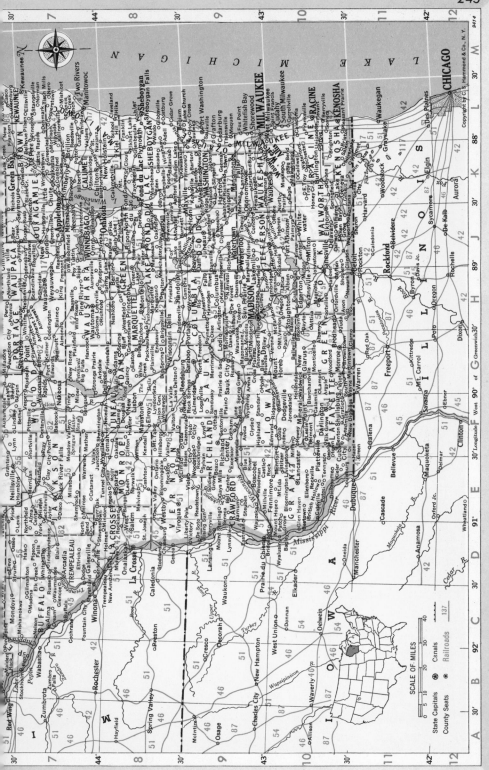

SCALE OF MILES

State Capitals ⊛

County Seats ⊙

Canals

Railroads

Copyright by C. S. Hammond & Co., N.Y.

A   111°   B   110°   C   109°   D   108°   E

M O N T A N A

45° — 45

Elk Me Pk. 11,155   Gardiner
Cooke   Chance   Warren
Yellowstone Park   Badger Basin   Elk Basin   Frannie
Gray Pk. 10,300   Tower Falls   Index Pk. 11,738   Clark   Deaver   Cowley
Hebgen Res.   Mt. Holmes 10,300   Mt. Washburn 10,346   Canyon   Painter   Garland   Lovell   Kane   Parkman Ra Day
W. Yellowstone   Powell   Byron
Ralston   45 R.
Hunt Mtn. 10,151

YELLOWSTONE   **BIG HORN**
Fishing Bridge   Holm Lodge   BUFFALO BILL DAM   Emblem   Shell
Big Springs   Lake Outlet   Cody   Burlington   45   Greybull
Old Faithful   Thumb   **NATIONAL**   North Fork   Wapiti   SHOSHONE CAVERN NAT'L MON.   Otto   Basin
180   Yellowstone Lake   Ishawooa   Manderson
Shoshone L.   **PARK**   Fortress Mtn. 12,073   **BASIN**   Hyattvi
Lewis L.   Heart L.   Eagle Pk. 11,360   Valley   South Fork   Fifteen   Mile   Cr.

44° — Lamont   Needle Mtn. 12,190   Pitchfork   Meeteetse   Dickie   Gooseberry   Cr.   Worland   **WASHAK**
Felt   Mt. Burwell 11,738   Sunshine   Grass Creek   45   Winchester
GRAND TETON NAT'L PARK   Moran   JACKSON HOLE   Mt. Crosby 12,435   Hamilton Dome   Gebo   Kirby   Lucerne   Bigtra
Tetonia   Buffalo Fork   Anchor
Driggs   Table Pk. 11,401   Jenny Lake   Grand Teton Pk. 13,766   **NATIONAL MONUMENT**   Diamond G Ranch   **HOT SPRINGS**
Victor   Moose   Gros   Govont   Mt. Leidy 10,317   North   Thermopolis
Kelly   Ventre   Du Noir   Duncan   Fork   **OWL CREEK MTS.**   Boysen

T   Wilson   Jackson   Diamond G   Dubois   Boysen
Jackson Pk. 10,707   **BACON RIDGE**   Bonneville   Lost Cabi
Green River Mtn. 10,175   Burris   Lenore   Morton   Shoshoni   Moneta   Lysite
Hoback   Doubleton Pk. 11,715   Crowheart   Pavillion   Pilot Butte Res.   Richar
Alpine   Hoback   Bondurant   Bull Lake Res.   **FREMONT**
Etna   Hoback Pk. 10,864   Kendall   New Fork Lks.   Fremont Pk. 13,730   WIND RIVER IND. RES.   Ethete   Riverton
43° — Freedom   Deadman Mtn. 10,365   Gannett Pk. 13,785   Fort Washakie   42
Thayne   Willow L.   Wind River   Arapahoe   Saint Stephens
Bedford   Merna   Cora   Fremont L.   Pope   Hudson
Turnerville   Mt. Bonneville 12,530   Lander
Auburn   Daniel   **SUBLETTE**   **WIND RIVER RANGE**
Grover   Halfway   Pinedale   Boulder Lake   **U**
Afton   Horse   Boulder   **GRANITE**
Fairview   Mason   Atlantic Pk. Little Popo   12,734
Smoot   Wyoming Pk. 11,363   Marbleton   Big Sandy   Atlantic City   Split Rock
Mt. Thompson 9,748   Big Piney   South Pass City
Geneva   Mt. Isabel 10,154   **CONTINENTAL**   **GREEN MTS.**   **ANTELOPE HILLS**
Calpet   St. Marys Pk.   Bairoil
Border   La Barge   Continental   **DIVIDE**
42° — Pegram   **LINCOLN**   Eden Reservoir   Farson   **GREAT DIVIDE BASIN**
Cokeville   Fontenelle   Eden
180   Fontenelle
Sublet   **SWEETWATER**
Nugget   180   Frontier   Winton   Superior
Fossil   Kemmerer   South Superior   Point of Rocks   Wamsutter
Sage   Diamondville   Oakley   Opal   Dines   180
Elkol   Blazon   180   Reliance   Thayer Junction   Bitter Creek
Brilliant   Gunn   Rock Springs   180
4 — Granger   180   Church Buttes   Qualy   Green River
UINTA   Evanston   Le Roy   Fort Bridger   Lyman   **ASPEN MTS.**   **SALT WELLS**
180   tunnel   Urie   Mountainview
Piedmont   Akwenasa   Robertson
Knight
41° — Lonetree   McKinnon   Baggs   Dixon
Manila
Bridgeport
U T A H   **C O L O**

111°   B   110°   C   109°   D   108°   E

SCALE OF MILES

0   10   20   40

State Capitals ✪
County Seats ◉
Railroads ——— 45

All railroads are numbered as per accompanying list, making possible quick and accurate identification of each line.

RAILROADS

42 Chicago and North Western
45 Chicago, Burlington & Quincy
56 Colorado & Southern
57 Colorado & Wyoming
66 Laramie, North Park & Western
137 Northern Pacific
165 Saratoga & Encampment Valley
180 Union Pacific
181 Wyoming

Copyright by C. S. Hammond & Co., N.Y.

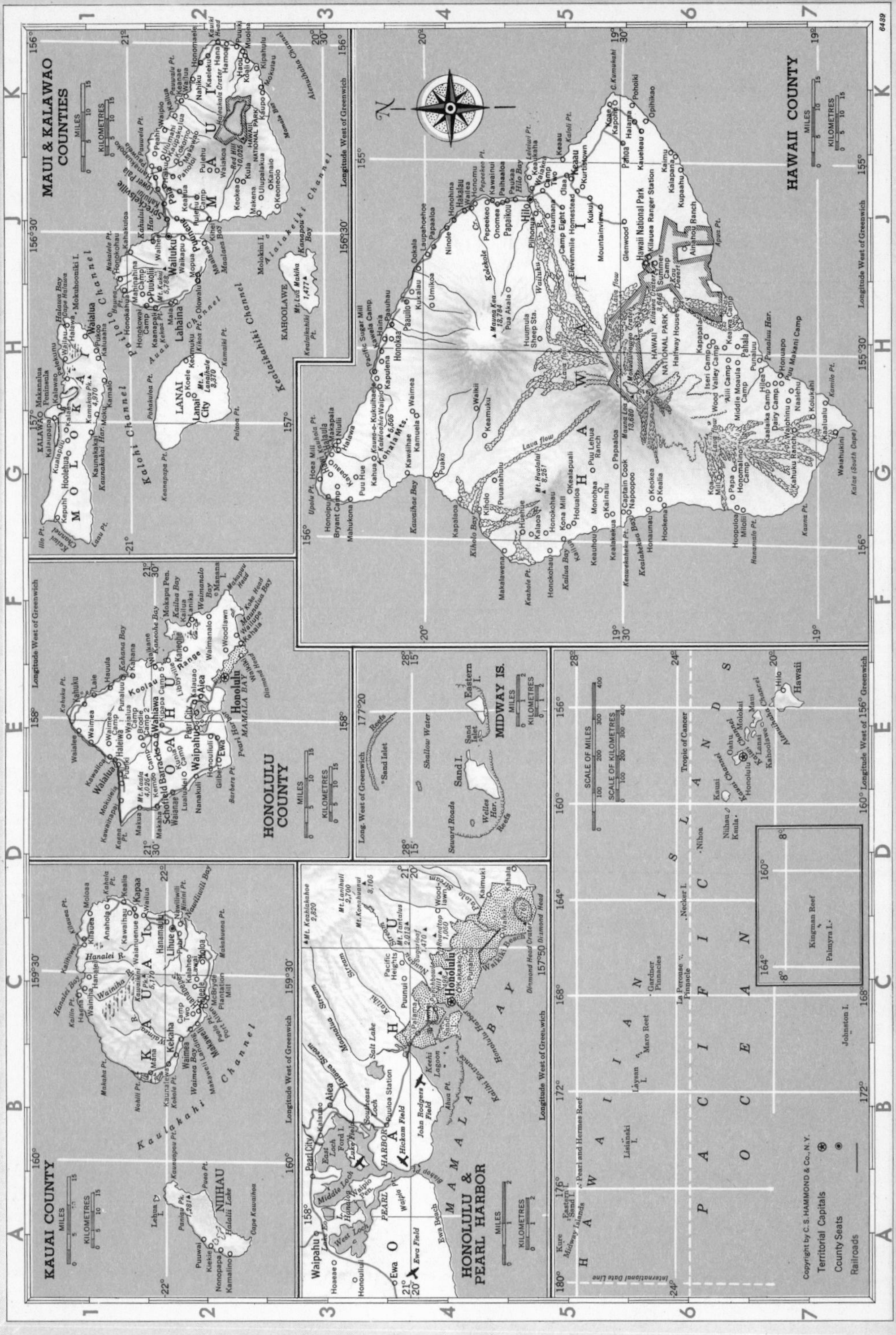
KAUAI COUNTY
NIIHAU
HONOLULU & PEARL HARBOR
HONOLULU COUNTY
MIDWAY IS.
MAUI & KALAWAO COUNTIES
HAWAII COUNTY
HAWAIIAN ISLANDS
PACIFIC OCEAN
Copyright by C. S. HAMMOND & Co., N.Y.
Territorial Capitals
County Seats
Railroads

Castle of Chillon, Switzerland.
A business street in Colombia.
Tomb of Yusuf, Egypt.
Flowerpot Island, Ontario.

5. Federal Parliament House, Australia.
6. Leaning Tower of Pisa, Italy.
7. Taj Mahal, India.
8. Mount Egmont, New Zealand.

9. Bay at Rio de Janeiro, Brazil.
10. Typical scene in Mexico.
11. The Great Wall, China.
12. Pyramids of Gizah, Egypt.

13. Church ruins near Panama City, Panama.

GAZETTEER

of

The WORLD

Countries are listed alphabetically. Information is given about the geography, area, form of government, natural resources, industries, commerce, communications, and principal cities. Dependencies, colonies, and other foreign possessions are treated under the country to which they belong or are attached: for example, Cypress appears under the heading "British Commonwealth of Nations: British Dependencies in Asia"; French Guiana appears under "France." British dominions such as Canada and Australia, however, are treated separately because of their independent status. Due to political upheavals, it is impossible to determine precisely the boundaries or political status of a number of countries. In such cases the traditional form of government is described, but the degree of foreign influence and territorial penetration is also noted.

AFGHANISTAN

The Country. The length of Afghanistan from the frontier of Iran to the Khyber Pass is about 600 miles and the extreme width north to south about 500 miles, estimated area being 250,-000 square miles. It is mainly mountainous, broken by deep ravines and fertile valleys.

Government. A constitutional monarchy with a parliament, which includes the king, a senate of, at most, 40 members, nominated for life by the king, and a national assembly of 120 elected members. A grand assembly, meeting at irregular intervals, deals with major questions of national policy. The country is divided into five major and four minor provinces, each under a governor.

The constitution of 1932 declared the country completely independent, and Islam the official religion. Slavery was abolished and state-controlled primary education made compulsory.

Commerce and Industry. The products are those of temperate regions varying in altitude such as tobacco, cotton, and fruits. The spring crop consists of **wheat, barley,** and lentils and the autumn harvest produces rice, millet, sorghum, tobacco, and corn. Cotton goods, indigo, tea, and sugar are the chief articles of import, whereas **wool,** skins, cattle, horses, timber, **fruit, silk,** and drugs are the principal *exports*

Communications. There is only one railroad in the country. The Khyber and Bolan roads are fit for light-wheeled traffic as far as Kabul and Kandahar, respectively. Merchandise is still transported on camel or horseback.

Principal Towns. Kabul, the capital, 6,396 feet above sea level; Herat, the chief town in the west, an important depot for the carpets of central Asia; Kandahar, the chief city in the south; Mazar-i-Sharif and Jalalabad.

ALASKA

See UNITED STATES OF AMERICA

ALBANIA

The Country. Albania is a mountainous country on the western side of the Balkan Peninsula, with a population of about 1,100,000 and an area of 10,629 square miles. In the center, part of the plateau is cultivable, and in the south there is fertile alluvial soil with grazing land on the slopes.

Government. Albania was proclaimed a republic in 1946. The government consists of a commander-in-chief assisted by a cabinet and the constituent assembly.

Commerce and Industry. Albania is mainly an agricultural and sheep- and cattle-raising country, although the methods used in agriculture are primitive. There are vast forest resources, and the mineral wealth is considerable, but undeveloped. Tobacco, timber, wool, hides, furs, olive oil, corn, cattle, and bitumen are the principal products. Copper mines are being exploited to some extent. Exports are unimportant. Principal industries are **flour** milling, cheese making, the manufacture of wool, and olive pressing.

Principal Towns. Durrës, a port; Tirana, the capital; Shkodër, Elbasan, Vlonë and Korcë.

ALGERIA

See FRANCE

ANDORRA

The Country. A small semi-independent republican state in the eastern Pyrenees, with an area of about 191 square miles and a population of approximately 5,500.

Government. Andorra is under the joint suzerainty of the president of France and the bishop of Urgel and its government is intrusted to a council of twenty-four members, holding office for four years, who elect the first and second syndic to preside. The executive power rests with the first syndic, while two civil judges and two magistrates exercise judicial power. In 1941, voting by heads of families replaced universal male suffrage. Catalan is the language of the country.

Commerce and Industry. Agriculture thrives where the soil is suited to tillage—rye, barley, vines, and **tobacco** being cultivated. There is also some mineral wealth, especially iron and lead, but transport difficulties make exploitation doubtful, there being only one good road between Urgel and Andorra-la-Vieja. Sheep-raising is the chief industry.

Principal Town. Andorra-la-Vieja.

ARGENTINA

The Country. A South American republic with a population of about 14,000,000 and an area of 1,079,965 square miles. The republic measures about twenty-three hundred miles from north to south. It is mountainous toward the west and the mountains extend to the western Andes. The remainder of the surface consists of grassy plains or forested hills, drained by the Paraná, Plata, Colorado, and other rivers flowing into the Atlantic.

Government. The constitution of the Argentine confederation resembles that of the United States. The republic consists of 14 provinces, 10 territories, and one federal district. The provinces elect their own governors and legislatures. The territories are under governors appointed by the president. The executive power, which is practically independent of the legislature, is in the hands of a president elected for six years by electors appointed by the provinces. The national congress consists of a senate and a house of deputies. There are 30 senators, two elected by each province and two by the capital; one-third of the senate is renewed every three years. The 158 deputies are elected directly by the people for four years; half the house retires every two years.

Commerce and Industry. Argentina is in the forefront among the countries in *exporting* food and raw materials, such as **wheat, corn, linseed,** oats, **alfalfa,** wool, chilled or **frozen meats,** and **hides.** The largest refrigerating plant in the world is at Buenos Aires, while near Bahía Blanca is the largest grain elevator in the Southern Hemisphere. Tobacco-growing is not inconsiderable and cotton-growing is increasing. The northern forests supply hard quebracho, excellent for building, but also exported for use in tanning. Petroleum production is growing. Textiles, foodstuffs, iron, glassware, chemicals, and oil are imported. The metric system of weights and measures is used.

Communications. There are about 28,600 miles of railroads in operation, all of which are owned by the government. Road mileage totals about 260,000, four of the highways forming part of the Pan American Highway system. The government also owns a fleet of oil tankers and cargo ships having a total of about 1,000,000 tons. The rivers Paraná, Plata and Uruguay also form important lines of communication. There is air service between Buenos Aires and Miami, Fla.

Principal Cities. Buenos Aires, the capital; Rosario, Córdoba, Tucumán, Santa Fé, Mendoza, La Plata, Bahía Blanca, Paraná and Salta.

AUSTRALIA

The Country. Australia, with a population of about 7,500,000, may be considered the largest island and the smallest continent in the world. It is the greatest isolated mass of land south of the Equator. Its total area, including the island of Tasmania, but excluding islands and other territory under trusteeship from the United Nations, is 2,974,581 square miles, with a coastline of about 12,210 miles. Its extreme measurements are about 2,000 miles from Cape York in the north, to Wilson's Promontory in the south, and 2,450 miles from Steep Point in the west, to

Cape Byron in the east. Its climate is partly temperate and partly subtropical. Tasmania, the island of the southeast, measuring roughly 200 by 200 miles is the most temperate area, with a climate similar to that of Ireland. A series of highlands runs along the eastern and north-eastern shores of Australia; coastal plains are the feature of the southeastern littoral. These broaden out in the eastern half of the interior into a great plain through which flow the main rivers of New South Wales, Victoria, and South Australia – the Darling, Murrumbidgee, and Murray. This plain covers nearly the whole of New South Wales and adjacent parts of Queensland and Victoria. Another large plain stretches inland along the Great Bight in the south, but both middle and southern plains give way to the western plateau, which reaches from the Indian Ocean to Eyre Peninsula and comprises over half the continent. Although the Darling, Murrumbidgee and Murray water the great area of the eastern plains and are navigable for hundreds of miles, the western half of the continent is almost waterless. The soil is generally fertile – even in the most arid districts a heavy rainfall favors a rapid growth of vegetation – but while the eastern shores are washed by a warm ocean current from the north, the western shores are washed by a cold current from the Antarctic. The eastern half is visited every few years by droughts causing heavy loss and suffering. In the northern tropical belt, where several short but torrential rivers run into the sea, growth is again luxuriant; but the whole of this great district, potentially wealthy in minerals as well as in pasture and arable land, awaits development. The eastern plains form one of the great stock-raising districts of the world.

Government. The Commonwealth of Australia is divided politically into six states: New South Wales, Western Australia, South Australia, Victoria, Queensland, and the Northern Territory, besides Tasmania and the Federal Capital Territory. In 1906 the administration of part of Papua (British New Guinea) was transferred to the Commonwealth. In 1920 the League of Nations gave a mandate for the administration of the Territory of New Guinea (formerly German New Guinea) to Australia. Australia is a self-governing dominion of the British Empire, and its constitution is defined by the Commonwealth of Australia Constitution Act as "an indissoluble Federal Commonwealth under the Crown of the United Kingdom." It is governed, like other British dominions, by a governor-general who appoints an advisory federal executive council—in practice, the commonwealth cabinet of the day. The Premier is the active head of the government. The Australian parliament consists of two houses, called the senate and the house of representatives.

Commerce and Industry. The main industry is the production of **wool**. General agriculture has long been the second industry, and **wheat** is grown for export. Other agricultural products are oats, barley, corn, hay, potatoes, sugarcane, beetsugar, wine and fruit. In recent years, wines have become an important subsidiary industry and cotton-growing is now being encouraged by the government. The discovery

of gold in Victoria first called attention to Australian minerals and induced the great stream of immigration. Since then, large quantities of gold have been found in every state except South Australia. **Gold** is the most important mineral resource and coal is second. The principal coal fields are near Sydney and Brisbane, and in eastern Tasmania. Other important minerals are **silver,** lead, zinc, manganese, copper, tin and iron. One of the most valuable silver, lead and zinc areas in the world is the Broken Hill mine in New South Wales. Australia is one of the great metal-producing countries of the world, both for precious and base metals. In the last twenty-five years, there has been a considerable increase in light and heavy industry. Manufacturing centers about the large cities; the leading industrial state is New South Wales. Concentrated in this southeastern section is most of the population of Australia.

Communications. There are over 27,000 miles of government railroads and over 800 miles of private railroads available for general traffic. The 636-mile long Darwin Road connects the railheads of Birdum and Alice Springs, completing the north-south transportation system. There are over 21,000 route miles of air services. Although the railway system is well developed, most of the country's goods is still carried by water.

Principal Cities. Melbourne, former capital; Canberra, the new capital of the Commonwealth, a modern city in the Federal Territory; Ballarat, gold field center; Bendigo, quartz crushing; Sydney, capital of New South Wales with Port Jackson, one of the world's most convenient harbors; Parramatta, in the orange district; Newcastle, coal mining town and place of coal export; Brisbane, capital of Queensland, important port; Adelaide, one of chief ports and capital of South Australia; Perth, capital of Western Australia; Fremantle, port for Perth; Albany, port; Hobart, capital of Tasmania, important port.

AUSTRIA

The Country. Republican Austria is but a small remnant of the old Austro-Hungarian Empire, consisting roughly of the German-speaking portion of what had been Austria in the dual monarchy. The country has a population of about 7,000,000 and an area of 32,369 square miles. While a part of Germany it was called Ostmark, and contained the former Hungarian province of Burgenland. The area of Ostmark was 34,064 square miles. Over 90 per cent of Austria is classified as mountainous. However, more than 80 per cent of the land is productive, and half of this is under cultivation. Beautiful alpine scenery characterizes much of the country.

Government. The government consists of a two house parliament—the Bundesrat and the Nazionalrat. Members of the Bundesrat are nominated by provincial assemblies and the 165 members of the Nazionalrat are elected by popular vote. The president is elected by the parliament for a six year term. Organized in 1945, this government was formulated on the basis of the constitution of 1920 which signified Austria a democratic republic constituted of Vienna and seven provinces. Approval and recognition by the Big Four occupying powers was accorded the government in 1946.

Commerce and Industry. Although agriculture employs over one third of the population, the country is primarily industrial. Austria depends heavily upon imported foodstuffs. The main crops are rye, oats, wheat, barley and potatoes, and there is some dairy-farming and stock breeding. The industries of greatest importance are metallurgical and engineering. The province of Styria, containing the Eisenerz-Vordenberg range with one of the largest iron ore deposits in Europe, produces most of the country's iron and steel. Manufactures include cottons, woolens, glass, paper, pottery, furniture and musical instruments. With nearly 40 per cent of Austria's area in forests, timber and related industries are of second importance. Included in Austria's valuable mineral resources are copper, lead, zinc, lignite, bauxite, graphite, sulphur and manganese. Small coal deposits make large imports of coal and coke necessary and place emphasis for sources of power upon the extensive available water power and the large petroleum deposits in the Isterdorf and Muhlenberg areas.

Communications. A land-locked state, where the construction and maintenance of railways and roads is rendered difficult by the mountainous terrain, Austria has over 4,000 miles of railways and over 53,000 miles of roads. Water transportation depends primarily upon the Danube, with Vienna and Linz the most important ports.

Principal Towns. Wien (Vienna), the capital; Graz, Linz, Innsbruck, Salzburg, Wiener-Neustadt, and Klagenfurt.

BAHAMA ISLANDS

See BRITISH COMMONWEALTH OF NATIONS: BRITISH DEPENDENCIES IN AMERICA

BELGIUM

The Country. Belgium is the most densely populated country in Europe with about 8,500,-000 people, occupying an area of 11,775 square miles. In the Ardennes Mts., which stretch over parts of the provinces of Namur, Luxemburg, and Liége, the average elevation is about 1,400 feet, while the highest points attain an altitude of a little over 2,000 feet. The country is well watered, and has two principal rivers, the Scheldt and the Maas. Four-fifths of the land is under cultivation, and more people are employed in agriculture than in all other trades.

Government. Belgium is a constitutional monarchy, with a two-chambered legislature—a chamber of deputies with 202 members, popularly elected, and a senate with a varying number of members elected in proportion to the population. The terms of both houses are four years.

Commerce and Industry. While agriculture and fisheries are important, Belgian prosperity is largely dependent upon industrial activity. The principal manufactures are rayon, linen, gloves, **lace, iron work,** locomotives and steam engines, motor cars, **arms,** bronze, **porcelain,** glass, etc. Belgian minerals include coal,

zinc, lead, and iron. The metric system of weights and measures is used.

Communications. The railroad system is the oldest on the continent; total mileage over 7,000. There are 1,000 miles of navigable waterways including a well developed canal system.

Principal Towns. Bruxelles (Brussels), the capital; Antwerpen (Anvers), Liége (Luik), Gent (Gand), and Mechelen (Malines).

Dependencies. *Belgian Congo* in Central Africa, with an area of 902,994 square miles. This colony is of great importance to the mother country, owing to its great yield of **rubber, copper,** gold, tin, cobalt, coal, iron, radium, palm nuts and palm oil. Principal towns are Léopoldville, the capital; Elisabethville and Likasi, the seaport. The districts of *Ruanda-Urundi,* area 20, 309 square miles, (once part of German East Africa), are administered as a trust territory. Capital: Usumbura.

BOLIVIA

The Country. The area of the republic of Bolivia, a land-locked country, is estimated at about 419,470 square miles. There are three main physiographic divisions, *Altiplano,* a tableland in the west, average elevation 12,500 feet, *Montañas,* valleys sloping to eastern lowlands, roughly between 5,000 and 10,000 feet , and the lowland forests, *Selvas.* The Gran Chaco War with Paraguay ended with the armistice of 1935. The peace treaty was signed, and the new boundary fixed in 1938, giving Paraguay 91,800 square miles of disputed territory. The population is about 3,500,000.

Government. The president is elected by direct popular vote for four years; the legislature consists of two houses, a chamber of deputies and a senate. La Paz, the capital, is the seat of the executive and the legislature. The supreme tribunal sits at Sucre, which is also the seat of the archbishop.

Commerce and Industry. The chief *imports* are textiles and clothing, provisions, petroleum products, mining machinery, drugs, leather and shoes, industrial chemicals, paper, tires and tubes, lumber, raw wool, explosives, auto trucks, dyes, iron and steel sheets and bars, railroad equipment. Ninety-five per cent of *exports* are metals, namely, **tin,** antimony, silver, zinc, copper. Other exports are crude rubber, cinchona bark, coca leaves, hides, quinine sulphate. The metric system of weights and measures is in use.

Communications. Three railroads descend from the highlands to the Chilean ports of Antofagasta and Arica, and to the Peruvian port of Mollendo, the total railroad mileage being about 1,200 miles. Airlines total 3,495 miles.

Principal Towns. La Paz, the actual seat of government, Sucre, Cochabamba, Potosí, Oruro, Santa Cruz, and Trinidad.

BRAZIL

The Country. Brazil, with a population of about 47,000,000, occupies more than half of the South American continent, an area of 3,275,510 square miles, and is the largest of the South American republics. From north to south, the extreme measure of its territory is 2,691 miles, and from east to west 2,500 miles. On the north and west are the great depressions of the Amazon and Paraguai Rivers which comprise large areas of flood-plains and swamps, heavily wooded and almost uninhabitable. The interior of the country is a high plateau with a general elevation of 1,000 to 3,000 feet, irregularly ridged by mountains and deeply cut by large rivers. The mountainous ranges of the maritime system form the eastern margin of this plateau. Brazil possesses three great river-systems; the Amazon, Plata, and the San Francisco. The Amazon and its tributaries drain fully half of the country. The Plata system drains nearly one-fifth of the country through its three branches—the Paraguai, Paraná, and Uruguai. Only the first of these is freely navigable for a long distance.

Government. The United States of Brazil is a federal union of twenty states, five territories, and one federal district. Its constitution resembles that of the United States. The federal congress is composed of the senate with 42 members and the chamber of deputies with 306 members.

Commerce and Industry. Industry now holds first place, ahead of agriculture in Brazil. Brazil is the chief **coffee** producer of the world. Production of rubber is on the increase. Rice, cotton, sugar, tobacco, yerba maté, and cacao are important products. Textiles amount to about forty per cent of the total manufactured articles. Both the forests and the mines of Brazil are important. Gold is found, and the greater part of the world's supply of monazite comes from Brazil. There has been lumber development in recent years. Pine has become an important *export*. Other exports are mica and talc, copper, manganese ore, platinum, and rock crystal. Steel manufacture and production of petroleum are beginning. The metric system of weights and measures is compulsory, but nevertheless certain local units are still used. Portuguese is the language of the country.

Communications. About 24,000 miles of railroads are open for traffic. The railroads of Brazil now join those of Uruguay, Argentina, and Paraguay. The republic has over 13,000 miles of navigable waterways open to river steamers and ocean-going vessels, and 30,000 miles additional which are navigable for light-draft and flat-bottom boats only. There are over 50,000 miles of airlines.

Principal Cities. Rio de Janeiro, the capital; São Paulo, Salvador (Baía), Recife (Pernambuco), Belém (Pará), Pôrto Alegre, Niterói, Bello Horizonte, Fortaleza (Ceará), Maceió, São Luis, Manaus, João Pessoa (Paraíba), and Santos.

BRITISH COMMONWEALTH OF NATIONS

UNITED KINGDOM

The Countries. The United Kingdom consists of England, Scotland, Wales, and Northern Ireland. Also under it are the Channel Islands and the Isle of Man. The governmental functions of Northern Ireland are treated under its respective heading. The Kingdom of Great Britain and Northern Ireland has an area of 94,279 square

miles. Within the small compass of the islands, there is a considerable variety of topography. In *Northern Ireland* are many lakes, including the largest one of the island, Lough Neagh, as well as a range known as the Mourne Mountains. A large portion of the country consists of the basalt plateau of Antrim. In *Scotland* three well-marked divisions stand out; the highlands, the southern uplands, and between these two, the central lowlands, into which four-fifths of the population is crowded. The lowlands contain the richest agricultural land, as well as the coal fields. They are penetrated by three great estuaries, the Firths of Tay and Forth on the east, and of Clyde on the west, so that communication coastwise or over-seas is everywhere easy. The *Welsh* upland is flanked to the north and east by small coal fields, but the greatest field lies to the south. A belt of limestone running from Bill of Portland to Tees Bay, and bearing at many points valuable iron ores, serves as a rough boundary of industrial *England*, for to the south and east of it, apart from the metropolis, agricultural interests predominate. Lying to the west of the limestone band is the Devon-Cornwall peninsula, where great bosses of granite and slate form the famous moors. The *Channel Islands*, lying across the English Channel off the coast of Normandy, and *Scilly Islands*, lying southwest of Land's End, enjoy an almost complete freedom from frost and severe weather.

Government. The government is vested in the Crown and Parliament. *England* is united with *Wales* in a system of local government, for which purpose the country is divided into fifty administrative counties, in each of which the crown is represented by a local lord-lieutenant. County affairs are administered by justices of the peace and county councils.

Commerce and Industry. The prosperity of the kingdom is due to its mineral wealth. **Soft coal** of the finest quality is found in central England and Wales; **iron** abounds in the same regions, and in Scotland and Ireland; tin has been mined in Cornwall since prehistoric times, and zinc, copper, gold and silver, with a large range of non-metallic minerals, are also present. Fisheries are conducted on an extensive scale and furnish a large proportion of the food of the people. The climate favors the breeding of horses, cattle and sheep, and the development of certain breeds has greatly improved the livestock of the world. An increase in land under cultivation and in mechanization permitted a substantial increase of home production of Britain's food. But in general, the vast supplies of coal, the geographical situation, and the deficiency in agricultural resources, have combined to favor and force an industrial development. Ships, machinery, metallic goods, iron, steel, textiles and leather goods are the chief products.

Communications. There are about 20,000 miles of railroads and 4,700 miles of canals. The Manchester Ship Canal, opened in 1894, is 35½ miles in length and 26 feet in depth. The canal connects directly with all the principal railroad systems and barge canals of the kingdom. All the principal cities of Europe are accessible over established airways radiating from London.

Principal Cities. London, the capital, is the largest city of Europe; Edinburgh, the capital of

Scotland; Glasgow, famous for its shipbuilding, general manufactures and great shipping trade; Manchester, the cotton manufacturing center, connected with the port of Liverpool by a ship canal. Birmingham, Sheffield, and Wolverhampton, manufacturing centers for machinery, cutlery, and hardware; Belfast, the capital of Northern Ireland, the seat of the Irish linen trade and of shipbuilding interests; Leeds and Bradford, woolen centers; Bristol, a manufacturing and commercial port; Hull and Dundee, important fishing centers; Newcastle and the Tyne ports, coal exporters; Nottingham, noted for laces, curtains, boots, and shoes; Cardiff and Swansea, the chief Welsh ports, exporting immense quantities of coal and ore.

The Dominions. (Australia, Canada, New Zealand, the Union of South Africa, India, Pakistan and Ceylon are described under their own headings). The Dominions are defined as "autonomous communities" within the British Empire, equal in status, in no way subordinate one to another in any respect of their domestic or foreign affairs, though united by a common allegiance to the crown, and freely associated as members of the British Commonwealth of Nations.

BRITISH DEPENDENCIES IN EUROPE

The Countries. These consist of the island of Malta, situated in the Mediterranean, and Gibraltar.

Malta. An Island off Sicily, with an area of 95 square miles, total area with the neighboring dependent islands, 122 square miles. Chief products: wheat, barley, potatoes, and fruit. Considerable fishing industry. Chief town and port: Valletta.

Gibraltar. A naval base commanding the entrance to the Mediterranean from the Atlantic Ocean and a position of great importance. Area, two square miles. The trade is chiefly transit.

BRITISH DEPENDENCIES IN AFRICA

The Countries. These consist of a number of colonies, protectorates, provinces, territories, islands, and groups of islands, Northern and Southern Rhodesia, and the self-governing Union of South Africa. The last is described under its own heading.

Government. The constitution of the British Empire is largely unwritten, but administration is based on three principles: Self-government, wherever and whenever practicable, self-support, and self-defense. The dependencies in Africa, apart from the self-governing Union of South Africa, are administered as follows:

1. By legislative assembly, partly or entirely elected, and an executive council nominated by the Crown, e.g., Mauritius.

2. By a governor with executive and legislative councils nominated by the Crown, e.g., Gambia, Sierra Leone, Gold Coast, Seychelles.

3. By a governor alone, e.g., St. Helena, Bechuanaland, Basutoland.

4. By governors or commissioners under the Colonial Office, with nominated advisory or ex-

ecutive councils, e.g., Nigeria, Kenya, Togoland, Tanganyika, Uganda, Zanzibar, Nyasaland, Somaliland, Swaziland.

Anglo-Egyptian Sudan. Administered by a governor-general appointed by Egypt with the assent of Great Britain, consists of 8 provinces, each under a governor. The provinces are subdivided into districts which are, in turn, administered by British district commissioners. The British and Egyptian flags are flown together. Area, about 967,500 square miles. It is the principal source of the world supply of gum arabic. Cotton growing is important. Other products are sesame, senna, groundnuts, hides, ivory and gold. Principal towns: Khartoum, the capital; Omdurman, Merowe, Suakin, El Obeid, and Port Sudan.

Ascension Island, in South Atlantic, a dependency of the colony of St. Helena. Area, 34 square miles.

Basutoland (Territory). Area, 11,716 square miles. Produces cattle, wool, wheat, corn, mohair, and Kaffir corn. Capital: Maseru.

Bechuanaland (Protectorate). Area about 275,000 square miles. Administered by the Union of South Africa. Cattle raising is the principal industry. Headquarters of administration are at Mafeking, Cape Province. Principal towns: Serowe, Francistown.

Cameroons (trust territory). Formerly a German colony. Area, 203,734 square miles, divided into French and British spheres. British Cameroon, a strip of 34,081 square miles, on Nigerian eastern border. Rich in forest produce. Near the coast are produced cacao, rubber, bananas, palm oil, and kernels. Capital: Buea.

Gambia (Colony and Protectorate). Area of the colony proper, St. Mary Island, etc., is 69 square miles; of the entire protectorate, 4,068 square miles. Capital: Bathurst.

Gold Coast Colony with *Ashanti, Northern Territories* and *Togoland* (tr. terr.). Area, 91,843 square miles. Chief products: cacao (about half the world's supply), gold, palm oil and kernels, kola nuts, manganese, and timber. Accra is the center of government. Other important towns: Kumasi, Sekondi, Cape Town and Tamale.

Kenya (Crown Colony and Protectorate). Area, 224,960 square miles. Coconuts, corn, sisal, sugar and other tropical products are grown in the lowlands; coffee, wheat, sheep, ostrich and dairy farming thrive in the highlands. Forests contain many valuable species of wood. Chief port: Mombasa, with a fine harbor. Other towns: Nairobi, the capital; and Lamu.

Mauritius with the dependencies of *Rodrigues, Diego Garcia*, and seven other islands in the Indian Ocean, east of Madagascar. Area about 720 square miles. Produces sugar, fibre, and coconut oil. Capital: Port Louis.

Nigeria (Colony and Protectorate). Area, 372,599 square miles. Chief products: palm oil, palm kernels, groundnuts, cacao, rubber, cotton, hides, and mahogany. It also has tin fields (about 9,000 square miles in Northern Provinces), and large coal fields. Lagos is the seat of government. Other trade centers are Kano, Warri, Ibadan, Opobo, and Katsina.

Northern Rhodesia (Crown Colony). Area about 287,950 square miles. Chief products: lead, copper, tobacco, coffee, grain, and cattle. Chief town: Livingstone, the old capital. The site of the new capital is at Lusaka, 65 miles south of Broken Hill.

Nyasaland Protectorate (formerly British Central Africa). Area, 38,000 square miles. Produces cotton, tobacco, groundnuts, tea, and coffee. Principal towns: Zomba, the seat of government; Blantyre, Kotakota and Fort Johnston.

St. Helena, solitary island in South Atlantic, 1,200 miles from west coast of Africa. Area, 47 square miles. Chief product: flax. Capital: Jamestown.

Seychelles, about 101 islands in the Indian Ocean. Total area estimated at 156 square miles. Chief products: coconuts, guano, and cinnamon.

Sierra Leone (Crown Colony and Protectorate). Area, 27,925 square miles. Produces palm kernels, palm oil, ginger, kola nuts, and piassava. Principal town: Freetown, capital and seaport.

Somaliland Protectorate. Area about 68,000 square miles. Exports: hides, gums and resins, cattle, and sheep. Principal town: Berbera.

Southern Rhodesia, self-governing colony of the British Empire. Area, about 150,350 square miles. Climate well suited for agriculture and European settlement. Great mineral wealth, including gold, coal, asbestos, and chrome. Corn, cotton, fruit, and tobacco are produced. Principal towns: Salisbury, the capital; Bulawayo, and Umtali.

Southwest Africa (former German Southwest Africa). See Union of South Africa.

Swaziland (Protectorate). Area, 6,704 square miles. Excellent grazing grounds and large cattle ranches. Sheep brought in large numbers from Transvaal for winter grazing. Rich mineral deposits. Principal town: Mbabane (Embabaan).

Tanganyika Territory (formerly German East Africa), now a trust territory of Britain. Area estimated as 350,000 square miles. Native products same as those of Kenya. European planters grow sisal, rubber, coffee, cotton, rice, sugar, etc. Chief ports: Dar-es-Salaam, capital; Tanga, Bagamoyo, Kilwa and Ujiji.

Togoland. Formerly German, now divided as French and British trust territories. Area, 13,041 square miles. Abundantly cultivated; products similar to those of the Gold Coast.

Uganda (Protectorate). Area, 93,981 square miles. Chief products: Coffee, cotton, cottonseed, gold, and hides. Seat of British administration: Entebbe.

Zanzibar (Protectorate) and **Pemba.** Two islands off the Tanganyika coast; area, 640 square miles and 380 square miles, respectively. They are administered by both a sultan and a British resident. The clove industry is practically a world monopoly. The coconut industry is also of great importance. The capital city, Zanzibar, is one of the finest ports in Africa.

BRITISH DEPENDENCIES IN AMERICA

The Countries. In addition to Canada, described separately, the British dependencies in America consist of some of the islands of the West Indies, Bermuda, Falkland Islands, British Guiana and British Honduras.

Government. All the islands and territories are crown colonies, and the crown is represented by a governor. Representative government, with partially or wholly elected legislative councils or executives, exists in Bermuda, Bahamas, Barbados, Jamaica, and Leeward Islands (except Antigua). In the Windward Islands, each island has its own form of government, either elected or appointed. The Falkland Islands, British Honduras, and Trinidad are ruled by governors with nominated councils.

Bahamas. Twenty inhabited, and a large number of uninhabited islands. Area, about 4,375 square miles. Principal Island, New Providence. Chief products: sponges, sisal, pearls, ambergris, and fruit. Capital: Nassau.

Barbados. Area, 166 square miles. Staple products: sugar, molasses, rum, and cotton. Capital: Bridgetown.

Bermuda. About 360 islands (twenty inhabited). Area, 19 square miles. Principal products are onions, potatoes, lily bulbs, and garden vegetables. Capital: Hamilton.

British Guiana. Area, 83,000 square miles. Principal products are sugar cane, rice, coconuts, coffee, para rubber, and timber. British Guiana is rich in gold and diamonds. Manganese ore and mica deposits have also been found. Capital: Georgetown.

British Honduras (Belize). Area, 8,867 square miles. Noted for the production of mahogany, logwood, bananas, coconuts, citrus fruits, and cacao. Capital: Belize.

Falkland Islands. East and West Falkland, with the adjacent islands, comprise an area of 4,618 square miles. Also included in the colony are South Georgia (estimated 1,000 square miles), the South Shetlands, the South Orkneys, the Sandwich group, and Graham Land (Antarctic). The Falkland Island Dependencies include all islands and territories between 20° and 50° west long. south of 50° south latitude, and between 50° and 80° west long. south of 58° south latitude. Principal products are whale produce and wool. Chief industries: sheep raising and horse breeding. Capital: Stanley.

Jamaica. Area, 4,450 square miles with *Turks* and *Caicos Islands* (166 square miles), *Cayman Island* (104 square miles), *Morant Cays*, and *Pedro Cays*. Principal products: sugar, bananas, rum, coconuts, logwood, coffee, and cacao. Chief industry in Turks Islands is salt raking; in Caymans, turtle catching. Principal towns: Kingston, capital; Spanish Town, and Port Antonio.

Leeward Islands comprise four administrative divisions. (1) *Antigua* (170 square miles), with *Barbuda* and *Redonda*. Products: sugar, cotton, and pineapples. Capital: St. John's. (2) *St. Kitts* (68 square miles) and *Nevis* (50 square miles), with *Anguilla* (35 square miles). Products: sugar syrup, and cotton. Capital: Basseterre. (3) *Montserrat* (about 32 square miles).

Chief products: cotton, lime juice, sugar. Chief town: Plymouth. (4) *British Virgin Islands* (about 58 square miles). Principal Islands: Tortola, Virgin Gorda, and Anegada. Chief products: cotton, sugar, tobacco, and coconuts. The others of the Virgin Islands belong to the U.S.A.

Trinidad, (1,862 square miles) and **Tobago** (114 square miles). Principal products are sugar, cacao, crude petroleum, asphalt, and coconuts. Capital: Port of Spain.

Windward Islands consist of four colonies with dependencies as follows: (1) *Grenada.* Area, about 133 square miles. Chief products: Sugar, rum, cacao, nutmegs, and spices. Chief town: St. George. (2) *St. Vincent.* Area, 150 square miles. Produces cotton, arrowroot, sugar, rum, cacao, and spices. Capital: Kingstown. (3) *St. Lucia.* Area, 233 square miles. Exports: sugar, cacao, lime juice, molasses, logwood, hides, and fuel. (4) *Dominica* (about 305 square miles). Products: limes, cacao, and coconuts. Chief town: Roseau.

BRITISH DEPENDENCIES IN ASIA

The Countries. These include Aden (with Perim, Socotra and the Kuria Muria Islands), Cyprus, Bahrein Islands, North Borneo, Brunei and Sarawak, Hong Kong, the Malayan Federation and Singapore. India with the Andaman, Nicobar and Laccadive Islands, Burma, Pakistan and Ceylon are described separately.

Government. Aden and its dependencies are protectorates with a British resident, Socotra having a native sheik. The **Bahrein Islands** have a native sheik under British protection. **North Borneo** is a crown colony with a British official in charge of administration. **Brunei** has a native sultan. **Sarawak** is a crown colony with a British governor. The last three are under the jurisdiction of the Governor-general of British Territories in Southeast Asia. **Hong Kong** is a crown colony with a governor and legislative council. The **Malayan Federation** consists of 9 states (Perak, Selangor, Negri Sembilian, Pahang, Johore, Kelantan, Trengganu, Kedah, and Perlis) and the two British settlements of Penang and Malacca. It was established in 1948, following the establishment in 1946 of the Malayan Union, to which the native sultans objected. Also in 1946, **Singapore** was set up as a separate crown colony.

Aden and Red Sea Territories. *Aden.* The area of Aden, on the southwestern tip of Arabia, is 75 square miles and combined with the protectorate areas totals 112,000 square miles. The population of Aden Colony is about 80,000 and that of the protectorate is about 600,000. Aden is primarily a commercial center for the Arabian peninsula and the African coast on the opposite shore. The free port of Aden with its excellent harbor, is an important coaling station and transhipment point for trade between the East and the West. The important exports, which are similar to the imports, consist of salt, sugar, coffee, hides and skins, tobacco, coal and cotton piece goods. Chief manufactures in Aden are salt, cigarettes and small native vessels called dhows. *Perim Island*, five miles square, is a fortified coaling station, and carries on a transshipment trade with the adjacent coasts. *Socotra.* Area, 1,400 square miles, is a pastoral country. Chief town: Tamrida. *Kuria Muria Islands.* Area, 29 square miles. Contain guano deposits used for fertilizer.

Bahrein Islands. *The Bahrein Islands* are an archipelago in the Persian Gulf off Arabia's east coast. The islands have an area of 250 square miles and a population of about 120,000. Bahrein is the center of the Persian Gulf **pearl fishing** industry and has an airport on the London-Australia route. Important **petroleum** deposits have been discovered there. Exports are rice, cotton goods, pearls, coffee and tea. Through Bahrein passes the major portion of the trade of the Saudi Arabian provinces of Nejd and Hasa.

Brunei. *Brunei,* on the northwest coast of Borneo has a population of about 31,000 and an area of 2,226 square miles with rich timber resources. Principal products are rubber, sago and cutch (mangrove extract). Petroleum is present and the field is being developed.

Cyprus. *Cyprus,* the most easterly island in the Mediterranean, lying south of Asia Minor, has an area of 3,572 square miles and a population of about 393,509. Chief products: timber, wheat, barley, cotton, tobacco, olives, raisins, wine and wool. Principal towns: Nicosia, the capital, and the seaports of Larnaka Limassol and Famagusta.

Hong Kong. *Hong Kong* is an island with an area of 32 square miles and a population of about 1,000,000. The area with *Kowloon* and *New Territories* comes to about 391 square miles. The capital, Victoria, an excellent harbor. Chief industries: sugar refining, shipbuilding and repairing, rope making, tin refining, manufacture of tobacco and cement and deep-sea fishing. Large trade in sugar, flour, rice, cotton, silk, leather, wolframite, iron and steel goods, tea, oils and matches.

Malayan Federation. The Federation, comprised of the former Federated and Non-Federated Malay States and the Straits Settlements, except Singapore and Labuan, has an area of 50,680 square miles and a population of about 4,700,000. About 80 per cent of the country is forest land. Both agriculture and mining are important. The country produces much of the world's natural rubber and nearly one-third of the world's tin. Exports include **tin, rubber,** gums, spices, copra, tarrans, sago, gambier, tapioca, preserved pineapples and phosphates of lime. Principal towns: Kuala Lumpur, the capital; Georgetown, Malacca, Ipoh and Taiping.

North Borneo. *North Borneo,* a region of highlands broken up by wide valleys and plateaus, has an area of about 29,400 square miles and a population of about 300,000. The chief products are timber, rubber, coconuts and copra, dried and salt fish, tobacco, rice, sago, cutch, hemp and rattans. Valuable minerals including gold, petroleum, copper, iron, manganese and tin exist but have not yet been exploited commercially. Principal towns: Jesselton, the capital; Sandakan, Kudat and Tawau.

Sarawak. *Sarawak* has an area of about 50,000 square miles and a population of about 500,000. Capital: Kuching. Large deposits of coal, petroleum and gold; chief *exports*: **rubber and petroleum.**

Singapore. *Singapore*, a crown colony, composed of the island of Singapore and its dependencies (the Cocos or   Keeling Islands and Christmas Island) has a total area of   280 square miles and a population of about 950,000. The island of Singapore is twenty-six miles long and fourteen miles wide. Singapore, midway between India and China, possesses a good harbor and is a very important center on the commercial route to the far east.

BRITISH DEPENDENCIES IN OCEANIA

The Countries. These include Australia and New Zealand, which are described separately, and the Pacific Islands. The latter, roughly grouped as Melanesia, Micronesia, and Polynesia, consist of colonies, protectorates, and Australian territories, formerly German, and the New Hebrides and Nauru. Total estimated area of the islands is about 208,000 square miles.

Government. The British high commissioner for the Western Pacific has jurisdiction over the islands, except those assigned by the United Nations to Australia and New Zealand. Papua has a legislative council, partly nominated by the governor-general of Australia; New Guinea is administered under the Commonwealth laws, as are the Papuan Islands. Fiji has a governor and legislative council. Tonga has a legislative council similar to Fiji's, but financial affairs are supervised by the high commissioner.

Fiji. Crown colony of about 250 islands, 80 inhabited, including *Viti Levu* (area 4,053 square miles), *Vanua Levu* (area, 2,130 square miles), and *Rotuma*. Population, 240,641. Chief products: sugar, molasses, gold, copra, rubber, breadfruit, plantains, and bananas. Capital: Suva.

Gilbert and Ellice Islands Colony. *Christmas Island* (occ. with the U.S.), area, about 56 square miles. *Ellice*, or *Lagoon* group, area, 14 square miles. *Fanning Island*, area, 15 square miles. *Gilbert Islands*, area, 166 square miles. *Phoenix Islands* (occ. with the U.S.), area, 16 square miles. *Washington Island*, area, six square miles. Chief products: **Phosphates,** coconuts, Colony headquarters: Tarawa.

Nauru or **Pleasant Island.** Formerly German, now administered by Great Britain, Australia, and New Zealand. There are valuable deposits of phosphates.

Bismarck Archipelago. Former German possession in the Western Pacific, now an Australian trust territory. Area of the component islands is 19,660 square miles. There are numerous coconut plantations.

New Hebrides. Under joint British and French administration. Area, 5,700 square miles. Chief products: copra, corn, cotton, and coffee.

Papua (British New Guinea). An Australian territory, consisting of the southeastern portion of New Guinea along with *D'Entrecasteaux* and the *Louisiade* groups. Area, 90,540 square miles. Products: gold, pearl-fishing, rubber, coconuts, and sisal-hemp. Trading center: Port Moresby.

North Eastern New Guinea. Formerly Kaiser Wilhelm's Land, it forms part of the Australian Trust Territory of New Guinea. Area, 69,700 square miles. Chief products: gold, coconuts, rubber, yams and bananas. Principal town Salamaua.

Pitcairn Island (Colony). Area, 2 square miles. Chief products: sugar cane, sweet potatoes, yams, pineapples, bananas, arrowroot, and coffee.

Solomon Islands. The British Protectorate includes *Guadalcanal*, *Malaita*, *Ysabel*, *San Cristobal* and numerous small islands, the *Lord Howe* group, the *Santa Cruz Islands*, and the *Wilson* group. Area, 11,000 square miles. Islands which are Australian trust territories are *Bougainville* 3,880 square miles; *Buka*, 190 square miles, and adjacent islands. Chief products: coconuts, rubber, pineapples, bananas, taro, and sweet potatoes.

Tonga or **Friendly Islands** (Protectorate). Area, 250 square miles. Products: copra, kava, and candlenuts.

BULGARIA

The Country. *Bulgaria* is a Balkan state with a population of about 6,800,000 and an area of 42,796 square miles. The country is hilly and well watered by numerous streams, of which the Isker, Struma and Maritza are the most important. Although nearly one-third of the country's area is in forests, only a small part of the wood is used commercially since about one-fourth of the forest area is completely unproductive. Many of the forests consist of scrub timber and a sizeable portion of the good forests are inaccessible.

Government. Bulgaria is a republic with a one house legislature, the Sobranje. The executive power rests in the prime minister and his cabinet. The country is divided into seven regional counties, each having its own appointed governor.

Commerce and Industry. Bulgaria is primarily an agricultural country of small farms with 80 per cent of the population employed in farming. Less than half of the land is cultivated or used for pasture and primitive farming methods prevail. Over one-half of the cultivated land is in **cereals,** with wheat, corn, barley, oats and rye the main grain crops. Other crops include **tobacco,** the leading export, alfalfa, cotton, flax potatoes and sunflower seeds. The southern valleys have large vineyards and rose gardens. Bulgarian industrial development is small with the exception of the industries preparing tobacco leaf, distilling **attar of roses,** and flour milling. There is also a highly developed **silkworm** cocoon industry and an important livestock industry. Bulgaria possesses little mineral wealth. The only important mineral is **soft coal** with most of the mines owned by the state. Other minerals are chromite, copper, iron, gold, silver rock salt and manganese ore.

Communications. There are about 2,200 miles of railroads in operation and about 19,700 miles of roads. There are about 3,800 miles of telegraph lines and about 13,000 miles of telephone lines.

Principal Cities. Sofiya, the capital; Plovdiv, a commercial center, Varna and Burgas, Black Sea ports, Ruse, chief Danube port, and Schumen.

BURMA

The Country. Formerly a dependency of Great Britain, Burma became an independent republic in 1948. It lies between India on the west and China and Siam on the east and has an area of 261,610 square miles; population, about 17,000,000. Burma proper occupies 192,158 square miles of the total area; the Federated Shan States, 62,335; and the unadministered area, 7,117 square miles. The country has a length of about 1,200 miles and a width of about 575 miles at its broadest point.

Government. The government is headed by a president elected by the parliament for a five-year term. Parliament consists of two chambers. The chamber of nationalities has 125 members, 53 of whom represent the Union proper, and 72 representing the states and tribal areas. There are twice as many members in the chamber of deputies who are elected for four years.

Commerce and Industry. Burma is primarily an agricultural country. The leading crops are: rice, sesame, groundnuts, corn and cotton. Minerals produced include tin, tungsten, silver and petroleum.

Communications. Important to Burma's transportation are the large rivers and navigable canals. The Irrawaddy River is navigable for about 900 miles inland, and the Chindwin is navigable for about 300 miles. There are about 10,500 miles of good roads, 3,800 miles of which are paved. Railroad mileage is about 2,300.

Principal Cities. Rangoon, the capital and largest city; Mandalay and Moulmein.

CANADA

The Country. The Dominion of Canada consists of the provinces Ontario, Quebec, Nova Scotia, New Brunswick, Prince Edward Island, Newfoundland, Manitoba, Saskatchewan, Alberta, British Columbia, Yukon Territory, and the Northwest Territories. Total area, 3,621,616 square miles and population, about 12,000,000.

Government. Executive authority is vested in a governor-general, appointed by the British Crown, and in an executive council; legislative power is vested in a federal parliament; the governor-general has the power of veto, but appeal lies to the privy council. The senate consists of 96 members nominated for life by the governor-general. The house of commons is elected every five years, the province of Quebec always having 65 members, and the other provinces proportionately according to population. The ten provinces have local legislatures, and control of local administration under a lieutenant-governor.

The territory of Yukon is under a chief executive officer and elective council. The Northwest Territories are administered by a commissioner and a nominated council.

Commerce and Industry. Canada is largely agricultural, though the value of manufactures now exceeds that of farm production: there is a great wheat belt in the prairie provinces; approximately 60,000,000 acres are under field crops. Area of land covered by timber is about 1,151,454 square miles. Pulp and paper production is important. Mineral products include **gold, silver, nickel,** copper, cobalt, chromite, iron, zinc, lead, coal, **asbestos,** and petroleum. There are large uranium ore deposits at Great Bear Lake. The fur industry is a very important one. Other industries include fishing and canning, and the production of fruit, wool, tobacco, maple sugar, agricultural implements, and motor vehicles. There is extensive use of water power.

Communications. Over 1,800 miles of canal, river, and lake navigation. There are eight rivers over 1,000 miles in length, including the Mackenzie, St. Lawrence, Nelson, and Saskatchewan. Railroads total about 56,584 miles. There are almost 565,000 miles of highways and extensive air lines.

Principal Cities. Ottawa, the capital; Montreal, Toronto, Winnipeg, Vancouver, Hamilton, Quebec, Calgary, Halifax, Edmonton, Saint John, Windsor, Regina, London, Victoria. St. John's.

CEYLON

The Country. The Dominion of Ceylon is located in the Indian Ocean at the southeast tip of India. It has an area of 25,332 square miles and a population of about 6,700,000. The Maldive Islands, lying about 400 miles southwest, are a dependency of Ceylon.

Government. A crown appointed governor-general heads the government of the new dominion. Advising him is a council of ministers headed by the prime minister. The parliament consists of a senate of 15 elected and 15 appointed members and a house of representatives of 95 elected members.

Commerce and Industry. Ceylon is essentially agricultural. Of its many products the most important are: rice, tea, coconuts, cacao, cinnamon and rubber. Graphite and precious stones constitute the major part of the mineral wealth.

Communications. Ceylon has about 900 miles of railroads, about 6,550 miles of roads, and is served by air lines.

Principal Cities. Colombo, the capital; Jaffna, Dehiwala-Mt. Lavinia, Kandy, and Galle.

CHILE

The Country. The republic of Chile, occupying the western coast of South America from 18° 30′ south latitude to Cape Horn, has a population of about 5,300,000 and an area of 296,717 square miles. The average width from east to west is only ninety miles and the length of the coastline is 2,900 miles. For about two-thirds of its total length, the Andes Mountains border Chilean territory. In Tierra del Fuego, the loftiest peaks barely reach 8,000 feet, but the heights generally increase northward up to Aconcagua (in Argentina), 22,834 feet, the highest peak of the whole continent.

Government. Chile now consists of 25 provinces. The administration is highly centralized, the local authorities being controlled by the executive in the capital. The franchise is extended to all literate male citizens 21 years of age. The congress consists of a senate of 45 members and a chamber of 143 deputies. The president is elected by direct popular vote for a term of six years.

Commerce and Industry. The varieties of Chilean products correspond with the immense geographical range. **Nitrates,** iodine, **copper,** iron, silver, gold, borax, and lead from the northern provinces; coal, **wheat,** fruit, wine, and pastoral products from central Chile; **timber** from the southern forests; meat and **wool** from the pastures north and south of the Strait of Magellan. The chief *exports* are nitrates, copper, wool, minerals, and pastoral products.

Communications. There are in Chile 26,795 miles of highway, including 8,778 miles of improved roads; 5,434 miles of railroads; three airlines are in operation.

Principal Cities. Santiago, the capital; Valparaiso, the principal port; Concepción, Antofagasta, Iquique, Viña del Mar, Yalca, and Chillán.

CHINA

The Country. China consists of thirty-five provinces and Tibet, a special territory under nominal Chinese control but politically independent. Formosa has been elevated to a provincial status. China has an area of 3,870,437 square miles and a population of about 461,000,000. A major part of the land is mountainous, particularly western China and Tibet, with the only extensive lowlands found in the lower regions of the Yellow (Hwang Ho) and Yangtze Rivers. These rivers, the Yellow draining northern China and the Yangtze draining central China, together with the Si Kiang River draining southern China, form the three great river systems of China proper.

Government. The new constitution, effective 1947, set up the first constitutional government in Chinese history. The government, replacing the revolutionary government established in 1928, has a constitution modeled partially on the United States and British systems. The constitution has a modern Bill of Rights. Both males and females over twenty years of age have the vote. A National Assembly elected for six years represents the people and elects the president and vice-president whose terms are six years. The government consists of five branches: the Executive Yuan (cabinet), the Legislative Yuan, the Judicial Yuan, the Examining Yuan and the Control Yuan.

Commerce and Industry. China is primarily agricultural with about 80 per cent of the population engaged in farming. Intensive cultivation prevails and farms are small with their fields scattered rather than contiguous. **Rice, wheat,** and **millet** are the most important food crops occupying about 70 per cent of the cultivated area. In the dry north, wheat and other cereals predominate; in the humid south, rice, **sugar** and **indigo** are the most important. Some of the most fertile soil in the world is found in the province of Manchuria. China follows the United States and India and ranks third among the world producers of cotton, with the chief Chinese cotton area along the Yangtze and Yellow River valleys. **Tea** is widely grown on the central uplands in the west and the coastal ranges in the south. **Silk** culture is widespread. Pigs are raised all over China and the export of **pig's bristles** is important. **Soybeans** form a large food export. China is well provided with mineral resources. It is one of the leading **coal** countries of the world. **Iron ores** are abundant in the anthracite fields of Shansi. **Tin,** mined in Yuan and Szechwan provinces, is a major export mineral. Normally, China is the world's foremost producer of some rarer minerals, particularly **antimony** and **tungsten.** Other minerals are bismuth ore, mercury, gold, silver, copper, lead, zinc and some oil. Industries on a large scale are carried on at the large ports; cotton spinning and weaving and wool mills at Shanghai; sugar refining at Canton; iron and steel works at Hanyang; docks, shipbuilding and engineering works at Shanghai and Hankow. Tanning factories, flour and rice mills, cement works, match manufacturing, porcelain and typical native industries such as lacquer-ware, enamel, carpets and rugs, mats and palm-leaf fans are other manufactures. One of the richest industrial areas in China is Manchuria.

Communications. China has an extensive system of waterways and canals which carry much of the internal trade. Its railway system totals about 13,000 miles, concentrated in north China and Manchuria, and there are 78,580 miles of roads.

Principal Towns. Nanking, Shanghai, chief port; Peiping, Tientsin, Canton, southern seaport; Chungking, Changchun, Mukden, and Harbin.

COLOMBIA

The Country. The republic of Colombia occupies the northwestern region of South America. Alone among the South American republics, Colombia has a coast line upon both oceans, its northern shores being washed by the Caribbean Sea, its western shores by the Pacific Ocean. The country lies wholly within the tropics, the equator traversing its southern region. The area is estimated at 439,885 square miles, and the population is about 10,000,000. The dominating feature of the whole country is the gigantic mountain system of the Andes.

Government. The president, elected by direct popular vote for a term of four years, possesses large centralized power, inasmuch as he appoints the governors of the fourteen departments, four intendencias, and six commissariats. Congress consists of a senate with members elected every four years, and a lower house, members of which are elected every two years.

Commerce and Industry. Only a small section of the country is under cultivation, but the soil is fertile and the productive acreage is increasing as the highway system improves. Coffee is the staple product. Tobacco is also grown; cotton, cacao, sugar, vegetable ivory, and dyewoods are produced, besides wheat and corn. **Banana** cultivation is increasing rapidly. The rubber tree grows wild, and its cultivation has begun. Tolu balsam is cultivated, copaiba trees are tapped. Dye- and cedarwoods are abundant on the Magdalena River but little or no wood of any sort is exported. Colombia is rich in **minerals,** and gold is found in all parts.

Communications. There are 88 miles of aerial cableways, while the total length of the railroad system is 2,121 miles. There are 10,594 miles of highway, five rivers are partly navigable, and air lines connect with United States and Panama.

Principal Towns. Bogotá, the capital, at an elevation of 8,660 feet above the sea; Medellín, Barranquilla, Cali, an important airport; Cartagena, a mining center; Manizales, Cúcuta, and Bucaramanga, center of coffee production.

COSTA RICA

The Country. A Central American republic with a population of about 750,000 and an area of 23,000 square miles. Costa Rica is traversed from northwest to southeast by a chain of mountains. The slopes of the mountains are heavily forested, much of the timber consisting of mahogany and other valuable cabinet woods.

Government. Legislative power is vested in congress, a chamber of 45 deputies, elected by manhood suffrage. The president is elected for four years.

Commerce and Industry. The principal industry is agriculture; **coffee, bananas,** cacao, and rubber are *exported*; horses, pigs, sheep, and goats are raised in considerable numbers. Gold and silver are mined; and there are deposits of other minerals.

Communications. The country has about 1,000 miles of highway and 450 miles of railroad, including one transcontinental railroad. At Limón there are excellent terminal facilities. At Puntarenas on the Pacific Ocean, the harbor has only fifteen feet of water at low tide. Two air lines connect with other countries.

Principal Towns. San José, the capital; Cartago, Heredía, Limón, Puntarenas, and Alajuela.

CUBA

The Country. Cuba, the largest and westernmost of the West Indies, has a population of about 4,800,000 and an area of 44,164 square miles (including the Isle of Pines and surrounding keys); its maximum length, east to west, is 730 miles, and its width varies from 20 to 100 miles, its coast line being about 2,500 miles. It is generally mountainous, though considerable flatlands, and marshy depressions extend along the south coast.

Government. Republic, modeled after the system of the United States, with a president, vice-president, senate, and a house of representatives.

Commerce and Industry. The foremost crops are **tobacco** and **cane sugar.** Other products are coffee, cacao, cereals, potatoes, market vegetables and fruits, bananas, guavas, oranges, grapes, etc. Cattle raising in the central and eastern districts is an ancient and extensive industry. The *exports*, largely to the United States, are **sugar, leaf tobacco, cigars,** iron ore, cattle products, forest products, and fruit. The *imports*, also largely from the United States, are meat products, iron and steel manufactures, wheat, lumber and timber products, coal, and coke. Copper, iron, and manganese mines are worked in the east, and petroleum, salt, and asphalt occur in useful quantities. Extensive forest lands yield mahogany, cedar, and other valuable cabinet woods, dye-woods, gums, resins, and other tropical forest products. The metric system of weights and measures is used.

Communications. Cuba has about 3,500 miles of steam railroads. Through trains run daily between Habana and Santiago, and many branch lines from this main trunk connect the principal ports on both the north and south coasts with the interior. The railroad system is supplemented by an elaborate system of highways, totaling 2,500 miles. There has been direct telephone communication with North and South America and Europe since 1921. There is an air mail and passenger service between Cuba and Mexico, Cuba and U.S.A., and to South and Central American countries.

Principal Towns. Habana (Havana), the capital; Camagüey, Cienfuegos, Santiago, Guantánamo, Santa Clara, Matanzas, Manzanillo, Pinar del Rio, Sancti Spíritus, Trinidad, and Cárdenas. There is a U. S. Naval Base at Guantanamo Bay.

CZECHOSLOVAKIA

The Country. The land-locked republic of Czechoslovakia has a population of about 13,000,000 and consists of Bohemia, Slovakia and Moravia with an area of 49,371 square miles. The country is about 600 miles in length from east to west with two large mountain ranges; the Carpathian in the east and the Sudeten in the west. The chief rivers are the Elbe (Labe), Oder (Odra) and the Moldau (Vltava). Czechoslovakia is famous for its subterranean caverns and its spas and mineral springs.

Government. A new constitution was drafted effective in 1948.

Commerce and Industry. Czechoslovakia is one of the richest countries in Europe in natural resources and industrial development. Since 1945, there has been extensive nationalization including all natural resources, public utilities, commercial banks and insurance companies. Over half of the country's industry was nationalized. The principal products of the mines are **coal, lignite, iron,** gold, silver and graphite. Famous deposits of pitchblende, a uranium ore, are found at St. Joachimstal. Manufactured products include textiles, shoes, gloves, glass, porcelain, sugar, metal goods, foodstuffs, toys and chemicals. Agriculture is highly developed, and extensive farming is carried on. The sugar beet is the foundation of an enormous **sugar** industry. Large quantities of **fruit** are exported. **Forests** comprise 32 per cent of the entire area, the country ranking among the most richly wooded in Europe.

Communications. Czechoslovakia has good

internal communications which tend to counterbalance some of the hindrances imposed by its land-locked position. Its railroads total about 8,700 miles and are an important direct link between eastern and western Europe. Highway mileage totals about 44,000, while there are about 260 miles of internal waterways.

Principal Towns. Praha (Prague), the capital; Brno (Brünn), Plzen (Pilsen), Bratislava (Pressburg) and Ostrava.

DENMARK

The Country. Denmark occupies a peninsula and numerous islands between the North and Baltic Seas. Its area, including the islands in the Baltic and the Faeroe Islands, is 16,575 square miles and its population 4,600,000. The highest elevation is the Himmelbjurg in Jutland which is only 560 feet high. The land is characterized by many lakes, ponds and short rivers.

Government. A constitutional monarchy. There is universal suffrage for all over twenty-five years of age. The legislative power is shared jointly by the king and the Rigsdag. The executive power is exercised by the king through his ministers. The Rigsdag is composed of two houses, the Landsting or senate and the Folketing or house of representatives. The term of the legislature is four years and its members are elected by proportional representation. The Statsraadet or cabinet consists of ministers who are individually and collectively responsible to the Folketing.

Commerce and Industry. The principal industries are agricultural with 90 per cent of the land productive. Many of the farms are small. Nearly 40 per cent of the cultivated land is in **cereals** with barley the foremost crop, followed by mixed grain, oats, rye and wheat. **Root crops** for fodder and potatoes and beets are also important. Denmark's most valuable industry is **dairy-farming** and the production of bacon, pork, butter and eggs. These products compose most of the country's exports. There are also thriving livestock and fishing industries.

Communications. In the kingdom, 3,300 miles of railroads are open for traffic, half of which belong to the state. There are about 5,000 miles of roads.

Principal Towns. Köbenhavn (Copenhagen), the capital, and clearinghouse for all of Scandinavia; Aarhus, Aalborg, Odense, Horsens and Randers.

Colonies. *Greenland* is the chief colonial possession of Denmark. Over 80 per cent of its 736,518,square miles is covered by *glaciers*. It has a population of about 18,000. Greenland is an important source of cryolite, a mineral used in the manufacture of aluminum. The trade of Greenland is a Danish monopoly. *The Faeroe Islands*, administered as a county of Denmark, have an area of 540 square miles and a population of about 26,000. *Iceland* declared its independence of Denmark in 1944.

DOMINICAN REPUBLIC

The Country. The Dominican Republic embraces the eastern and larger portion of the Island of Hispaniola. (Haiti comprises the rest of the island). It has an area of 19,332 square miles and a population of about 2,000,000. Mt. Tina (10,300 ft.) is the highest peak in the island and in the West Indies.

Government. Under the revised constitution of 1942, the government consists of a president, elected for five years; a senate composed of 19 members elected for five years, and a chamber of deputies (38 members), also elected for five years.

Commerce and Industry. The chief industry is agriculture, the products being **sugar,** tobacco, **cacao,** coffee, and molasses. There are large forested tracts throughout the country, yielding enormous quantities of cedar, mahogany, satinwood, and dyewoods. **Cattle raising** is extensively carried on, and the minerals include gold, silver, platinum, mercury, coal, iron, and rock salt.

Communications. There are three main highways, with branches extending from Ciudad Trujillo eastward for 105 miles, northward 204 miles, and westward 160 miles. The railroad lines, government-owned, total 168 miles.

Principal Towns. Ciudad Trujillo, formerly Santo Domingo, the capital; Puerto Plata, chief north coast port; Santiago and San Pedro de Macoris.

ECUADOR

The Country. This South American republic is so named because the equatorial line runs through the country. It is bounded on the west for 500 miles by the Pacific Ocean. Its area is about 275,936 square miles including the Galápagos Islands (2,868 square miles) in the Pacific Ocean, 600 miles from Ecuador. The population is about 3,200,000. Ecuador contains the volcanoes of Chimborazo and Cotopaxi, and others of great altitude. The most valuable and productive part of the country is the broad coastal plain.

Government. The president is chosen by direct popular election. His term is four years. The 32 senators and 56 deputies are elected upon limited franchise, which is withheld from illiterates. Women voted for the first time in 1939. In 1929 a model child-labor law and an eight-hour labor law were put into effect.

Commerce and Industry. The greater portion of the land is covered by virgin forest, rich in dyewoods, cinchona, wild rubber, and balsa, only about 11,000,000 acres being under cultivation. The staple products of Ecuador are cacao, and ivory nuts. Coffee is grown and largely exported. Other products are rubber, tobacco, sugar, rice, and cotton, "Panama" or "Jipijapa" hats are made very largely in Ecuador. Some gold is produced in the Andes and petroleum production is in the neighborhood of 1,500,000 barrels annually. Copper, iron, lead, coal, and sulphur exist, but are as yet unexploited. Salt, including that which is mined domestically, and that which is imported, is a government monopoly.

Communications. There are about 3,000 miles of highways. The total length of the railroads in operation is 761 miles. The rivers are navigable in the western lowlands. Two air lines are in service.

Principal Towns. Quito, the capital; Guayaquil, chief port; Cuenca, Riobamba, Ambato, and Loja.

EGYPT

The Country. The total area, including the Libyan Desert, the region between the Nile and the Red Sea, and the Sinai Peninsula, is about 386,000 square miles. The valley of the Nile constitutes a highly cultivated and populated region. The remainder of the country is largely desert. The population is about 17,000,000.

Government. Egypt is a kingdom, with a hereditary monarch and representative government. The parliament is composed of a senate and a chamber of deputies. All deputies and three-fifths of the senators are chosen by popular election. The rest of the senators are directly appointed by the king. In the Anglo-Egyptian treaty of alliance of 1936, England recognizes Egypt as a sovereign state, having no connection with the British Empire, and enjoying the same status as any other sovereign state in the world.

Commerce and Industry. The cultivable area is estimated at about 13,500 square miles and the agricultural population forms about 60 per cent of the whole. The great reclamation projects on the Nile irrigate some 5,400,000 acres, which may be increased to 7,500,000 or more. The great dam at Aswan is a mile and a quarter long. Two or three crops yearly of cotton, cereals, beans, lentils, sugar cane, and vegetables are grown. The fisheries are of considerable importance. Chief *imports* are textiles, and vegetable, mineral and chemical products.

Communications. The Nile is the great highway of the country. There are some 3,600 miles of state-owned and operated railroads, and about 850 miles of privately-owned light railroads. There are regular weekly air services between Egypt, Europe, India and South Africa. The Suez Canal, principally controlled by Great Britain, cuts through Egypt west of the Sinai Peninsula, and connects the Mediterranean and Red Seas. The length of the Suez Canal, including approach channels, is 103 miles.

Principal Towns. Cairo (El Qahira), the capital· Alexandria (El Iskandariya), Port Said (Bor Sa'id), Ismailia (Isma'iliya), Tanta, El Mansura, Asyut, Damanhur, El Faiyum, Zagazig (El Zaqaziq), El Minya, Suez (El Sweis), and Damietta (Dumyat).

ERITREA

The Country. The former Italian Colony lies along the southwest coast of the Red Sea between *Anglo-Egyptian Sudan* and *French Somaliland*, and north of *Ethiopia*. There is considerable irrigation, particularly in the lowlands, and enough rain in both lowlands and highlands for the raising of crops.

Commerce and Industry. Agricultural products and cattle, salt, pearl-fishing and gold. Some petroleum is found.

Communications. There are 320 miles of railroads, and about 200 miles of motor roads.

Principal Towns. Asmara, the capital; Massaua, Cheren, Agordat, Assab.

ESTONIA

The Country. Estonia comprises the former Russian province of Estonia, the northern part of Livonia, the northwestern portion of the Pskov government, and the islands of Saare Maa (Oesel), Hiiu Maa (Dagoe), and 'Muhu Maa in the Baltic Sea. Its area is 18,353 square miles. Except for the southeast which is hilly, the mainland is low and swampy. The population is about 1,000,000.

Government. Estonia became a constituent, nominally autonomous republic of the U.S.S.R. in 1940.

ETHIOPIA

The Country. The Kingdom of Ethiopia has an area of about 350,000 square miles and a population of approximately 9,000,000. East of the 40 deg. meridian the land is low and of semi-desert character, but west of it is a series of elevated plateaus with an average height of 7,000 to 8,000 feet, between which lie deep valleys and above which rise irregular ranges and peaks.

Government. Ethiopia is divided into twelve provinces, each administered by a governor-general under the direct control of the Minister of the Interior. The Emperor heads the government.

Commerce and Industry. Mainly pastoral and agricultural. Horses, donkeys, oxen, sheep, and goats are reared. Cereals, sugar cane, several kinds of coffee, and many fruits are raised in a primitive agriculture. Gold, copper, coal, rock salt, and iron are among mineral deposits found. Great forests contain valuable trees, including rubber. Chief *exports* are coffee, hides and livestock. *Imports* are cotton goods, gasoline, and manufactured articles.

Communications. There are about 500 miles of railroad, and 4,340 miles of new roads.

Principal Towns. Addis Ababa, the capital; Diredawa and Harar.

FINLAND

The Country. The Republic of Finland has an area of 130,500 square miles and a population of about 4,000,000. The country consists of a great plateau, ranging from 400 to 600 feet in elevation. The southern half of the plateau has about 25 per cent of its area occupied by thousands of shallow lakes, many of them linked by short natural or artificial channels.

Government. Finland is a republic. The president is elected for six years, and there is a house of representatives (*Kunta*) elected for three years by universal suffrage of citizens over the age of 24. The cabinet is appointed by the president.

Commerce and Industry. Agriculture is the chief occupation of the people, although the cultivated area covers less then nine per cent of the land. The principal crops are oats, rye, wheat, barley, potatoes and hay. Livestock is raised on the considerable grazing lands. Butter is another farm product. The **forests**, which cover over one-third of the land, are Finland's most valuable natural resource. Mineral resources are copper, sulfide ore, limestone, soapstone and red granite.

Chief manufactures include **wood, paper,** machinery and textiles.

Communications. The southern half of the country is well served by railways which are linked with those of the U.S.S.R. and those of Sweden, total mileage being about 3,670, of which 3,512 are state-owned. Numerous canals connect the lake districts in the interior with the coast. There are about 3,000 miles of navigable canals. Road mileage totals about 39,000.

Principal Towns. Helsinki (Helsingfors), the capital; Tampere (Tammerfors), Turku (Abo), Vaasa (Nikolaistad), and Oulu (Uleaborg).

FRANCE

The Country. France is a republic of western Europe with an area, including Corsica, of 212,659 square miles, and a population of about 40,000,000. The total length of the coast line is about 2,000 miles. The surface is diversified, but much of it is lowland, with a few level plains. In the center is a triangular plateau called the Auvergne Mountains, with a height of something over 3,000 feet. The Cevennes form the eastern edge of this plateau, and from them to the Vosges, the tableland continues. There is a mountainous area in Brittany, but the greatest heights are on the frontiers, the Jura, the Pyrenees, and the Alps separating it respectively from Switzerland, Spain, and Italy. The Ardennes in the northeast are less lofty. The Seine drains the north, the Loire and the Garonne the west, and the Rhone the east and south.

Government. The 1946 constitution of the Fourth Republic provides for a two house legislature composed of the National Assembly and the Council of the Republic. The Assembly has legislative power. Its 618 members are elected for five years by proportional representation. The 315 members of the Council are elected for four years by an electoral college. The president's term is seven years. Suffrage is given to all twenty years of age and over.

Commerce and Industry. First among the industries of France are textile products. Leading the list of *exports* are **chemical products, iron and steel,** textiles (silk and cotton), automobiles, and wine. French coal mines, of which the most productive are in the north, do not yield sufficient for the manufacturers' needs. The making of soap, cheese, and beet sugar are important industries. The state maintains manufacturing and industrial monopolies in tobacco and matches. **Coal, iron ore,** lead, rock salt, potash salts, and lignite are the chief mineral products. Fisheries and oyster culture form a large item in the wealth of the coast population. Agriculture is the basis of the French economy and France is normally self-sufficient in basic foodstuffs. The principal crops are **wheat,** rye, oats, barley, potatoes, vines and sugar beets. France is the world's foremost **wine** producer. Dairy products are an important export item. The nationalized industries include the railroads, coal mines, air transport, the Bank of France, larger insurance companies and public utilities.

Communications. The total length of railroads, all state operated, is about 26,400 miles, of which about 2,000 miles are electrified. The canals of France are a most valuable auxiliary to the railroads and are used regularly for transporting merchandise. There are in all about 6,000 miles of navigable waterways, with an annual traffic of approximately 50,000,000 tons. French roads are excellent.

Principal Cities. Paris, the capital and metropolis; Marseille, the chief Mediterranean port; Lyon, a leading industrial and commercial center; Bordeaux, an important port and coaling station on the Garonne River with a large export trade; Lille, center of important coal fields; Strasbourg, an important Rhine port in Alsace; Nantes, an important port on the Loire; Toulouse, a large manufacturing and market center; St. Etienne, a mining and manufacturing city; Nice, pleasure and health resort on the Riviera; Le Havre, an important port on the English Channel.

THE FRENCH UNION

France has the second greatest colonial empire in the world. Its world-wide possessions, from which it derives a great part of its wealth and power, cover a total area of about 4,548,000 square miles and have a population of about 60,000,000.

Government. The French Union has a federated system of government for France and its overseas territories. The Union employs three levels of government:

1. French Departments—each headed by a Prefet; total ninety-seven, including the ninety departments of France proper, the three of Algeria, and one department each for Martinique, Guadaloupe, Guiana and Réunion.

2. French Overseas Territories—headed by a Governor-General and have a colonial-like status.

3. Associated States—headed by native governments. The national defence and foreign policy are controlled by France.

4. Trust Territories—governed under trusteeship sanctioned by the League of Nations.

5. Anglo-French Condominium—administered jointly by France and Britain.

The Departments, Territories and Associated States send representatives to an Assembly of the Union which studies all legislation concerning the Union as a whole.

The French possessions in Africa are—the **Departments** of: Algeria with about 850,000 square miles and a population of about 7,300,000 and Réunion with 970 square miles and a population of about 250,000; the **Overseas Territories** of: French Equatorial Africa with about 960,000 square miles and a population of 4,000,000; French West Africa with 1,815,000 square miles and a population of about 16,000,000; Madagascar with 241,000 square miles and a population of about 4,000,000; Mayotte and Comoro Islands with 790 square miles and a population of 120,000; Somaliland with 8,500 square miles and 44,800 population; the **Associated States** of: Morocco, area, 154,000 square miles and population, about 8,600,000; and Tunisia with 48,300 square miles and a population of 3,000,000; and the **Trust Territories** of: Togo with 21,000 square miles and a population of 900,000; and Cameroun with 166,489 square miles and 2,800,000 population.

The French possessions in Asia are—The **Associated States** of: Indochina (Viet Nam, Cambodia and Laos) with an area of 286,000 square miles and a population of about 27,000,000; and the **Overseas Territory** of French India with 198 square miles and a population of about 324,000.

The French possessions in America are: in the West Indies—the **Departments** of: Martinique with 425 square miles and a population of about 244,000; and Guadaloupe with 688 square miles and a population of about 300,000. On the northeast coast of South America, is the Department of Guiana (including Inini Territory) with 35,000 square miles and, population, 26,000. Near the southern coast of Newfoundland are the **Overseas Territories** of St. Pierre and Miquelon with an area of 93 square miles and, population, about 4,500.

The French possessions in Australasia and Oceania are the **Overseas Territories** of New Caledonia with 8,548 square miles and a population of about 61,000; the French Pacific Settlements (Gambier, Makatea, Marqueses Islands, Rapa, Rurutu and Runatara, Society Islands, Tuamotu Archipelago and Tubuaia and Raivavae) with 1,545 square miles and a population of about 45,000; and the Anglo-French Condominium of New Hebrides with an area of 5,700 square miles and a population of 45,000.

GERMANY

The Country. Germany is the largest state of Central Europe. The greater part of the country is flat. Throughout the northern districts the coastal plain bordering the North Sea, Denmark and the Baltic Sea, is scarcely broken. In the south there are several low mountain systems. The rivers, in order of importance, are the Rhine, Elbe, Weser, and Oder. The area of Germany is 142,243 square miles and the population is about 63,200,000.

Government. The United States, Great Britain, France and the Union of Soviet Socialist Republics are all represented on the Allied Control Council for Germany which assumed the government in June, 1946. The occupation zones of the U. S., Great Britain and France are now united as the Federal Republic of Germany (Western German State) with its capital, Bonn. Eastern Germany, under Soviet occupation, is now the German Democratic Republic. An Inter-Allied Governing Authority has charge of Greater Berlin.

Commerce and Industry. About 90% of the area of Germany is agriculturally productive, the principal crops being wheat, rye, barley, oats, potatoes, and beets. Potatoes are produced in enormous quantities, and sugar beets also. Forestry is an industry of great importance. Germany's desire for economic self-sufficiency led to the production of many substitutes (Ersatz) products, including synthetic gasoline, rubber, textiles, soap, fish sausages, wood sugar, pumpkin milk, etc. **Coal**, lignite, **iron**, copper, zinc, lead, and **potash** are mined. **Textiles** are largely manufactured in Saxony, and Westphalia. The **steel** and iron, **electrical** and **chemical** industries are of primary importance; woolens, silk, glass, porcelain and earthenware are produced.

Communications. The total railroad mileage is about 33,500. The Rhine, Ems, Weser, Elbe, and Oder form natural highways for water transport, all of which have been canalized.

Principal Cities. Berlin, one of the great railway centers of Europe; Hamburg, München (Munich), Leipzig, Dresden, Köln (Cologne), Frankfurt-am-Main, Düsseldorf, Nürnberg, Hannover, Essen, Potsdam, and Bonn.

GREECE

The Country. Greece lies in the south of the Balkan Peninsula, with a very long coast line on the Aegean and Ionian Seas, and a large number of islands, including Crete (3,195 square miles), Mitylene (675 square miles), Dodecanese and Chios. The area of Greece is about 50,147 square miles. It is generally mountainous. The mountains, though not very high, divide the country into a number of small districts, between which communication is difficult. It is the sea which links the different regions of Greece.

Government. By a plebescite of 1946, Greece was again proclaimed a constitutional monarchy.

Commerce and Industry. Greece is an agricultural country, but only one-fifth of its area is cultivable. The draining of Lake Copais and the reclaiming of the Vardar River marshes has added 375,000 acres of arable land. Chief crops are **wheat, barley, currants,** oats, corn, and rice. Olives, tobacco, oranges, lemons, and figs are important products. Industrial products include olive oil, wine, textiles, chemicals, and articles of food.

Communications. Total length of railroads 1,668 miles; improved roads 7,064 miles. The Corinth ship canal is four miles long. There are one Greek, and several foreign air lines.

Principal Towns. Athenai (Athens), the capital and ancient city, now an important railway center; Thessalonike (Salonika), a great port near the mouth of the Vardar; Peiraievs (Piraeus), the port of Athens, and an important manufacturing center; Khania (Canea), chief town of Crete.

GUATEMALA

The Country. A Central American republic with a coast line on the Pacific, and a short coast line on the Caribbean Sea. It has a population of 3,500,000 and a total area of 45,452 square miles. The surface is mountainous, except near the northeast coast where it is low-lying and marshy forest land. Several mountain ranges, mainly belonging to the Antillean system, traverse the country. The coast line is unbroken on the Pacific side, and the only indentation on the Atlantic side is the Gulf of Amatique, an extension of the Gulf of Honduras.

Government. The legislative power is vested in a one-house national assembly consisting of representatives (one for every 50,000 inhabitants) chosen by universal suffrage for four years, and a council of state of 7 members partly elected by the national assembly, partly appointed by the president of the republic. The president is elected for six years.

Commerce and Industry. The most important crops are **coffee**, honey, **bananas**, sugar, **corn**, rice, and potatoes. The cotton-growing industry is being developed. The country raises and exports most of the chicle used in the United States for the manufacture of chewing gum. In the plateau region, horses, mules, **cattle,** sheep, goats, and pigs are reared in large numbers. Gold, chromite, and sulphur are produced in small quantities. The forests abound in valuable trees, producing mahogany, dyewoods, oak, pine, and spruce.

Communications. There are 650 miles of railways, privately owned, but subsidized by the government, and 4,025 miles of highways, including the Inter-American Highway. Air mail and passenger service connect Guatemala City with Puerto Barrios, San Salvador, Tegucigalpa, Managua, Panama, and Mexico City.

Principal Towns. Guatemala City, the capital; Quezaltenango, an industrial center; Cobán, center of a coffee producing district; and Antigua.

HAITI

The Country. The republic of Haiti, occupying the western portion of the island of Hispaniola (formerly the island of Haiti), has an area of 10,204 square miles and a population of about 3,000,000. It is a land of mountains and valleys. The coast line is greatly indented on the west by the Gulf of Gonaïves or Léogane.

Government. Under the constitution of 1935, the senate and the chamber elect the president for a term of seven years. Senators (21) are elected for six year terms; deputies (37) for four years.

Commerce and Industry. Nearly all the trade is with the United States. Logwood, **coffee,** cotton, and cacao are *exported.* Most of the people depend on agriculture. Gold, iron, and copper are known to exist, but have not been greatly exploited.

Communications. Port-au-Prince is connected with Cap Haïtien by a road 169 miles long, and with Mirebalais and Lascahobas by a road 33 miles long. Total length of automobile roads about 1,500 miles. Total mileage of railroads about 160 miles.

Principal Towns. Port-au-Prince, the capital, with a large shipping trade; Cap Haïtien, with considerable export trade.

HONDURAS

The Country. A Central American republic with an area of about 45,000 square miles and a population of about 1,175,000. The boundary dispute with Guatemala was settled in 1933, air-photo maps being used for the demarcation. The boundary dispute with Nicaragua has not been entirely settled. The surface of the country is mainly mountainous, especially in the west and southeast, interspersed with elevated plateaus, plains, and valleys. The coastal regions are low-lying and swampy. The loftiest peaks are found in the volcanic ranges on the Nicaraguan boundary, rising to nearly 10,000 feet. Most of the rivers are unsuitable for navigation. The Gulf of Fonseca on the southern coast contains numerous islands.

Government. At the head of the government is the president who, assisted by an executive council of five members, serves for years. Legislative power is vested in a congress of deputies, 38 in number, serving for six years, who are elected at the ratio of one per 25,000 inhabi-

tants. Education is free and compulsory between the ages of seven and fifteen years.

Commerce and Industry. Stock-raising is extensively practiced. The chief agricultural product is **bananas.** Lemons, oranges, corn, rice, tobacco, coconuts, and coffee are also produced. The minerals include gold, silver, lead, zinc, tin, antimony, and copper, but the mining industry has not yet been extensively developed.

Communications. There are about 1,150 miles of railroad on the north coast. In general, traveling and transport are accomplished by means of mules and oxcarts. Two air lines now serve Honduras.

Principal Towns. Tegucigalpa, the capital and mining center; San Pedro Sula, Choluteca, La Esperanza, Nacaome, and Santa Rosa; the ports of Amapala on the Pacific and Puerto Cortés, La Ceiba, Trujillo, Tela and Puerto Castilla on the Atlantic.

HUNGARY

The Country. Hungary is one of the states of Europe formed out of the old Austro-Hungarian Empire. It has a population of about 9,100,000 and an area of 35,875 square miles, having returned 4,886 square miles to Czechoslovakia, the northern half of Transylvania to Rumania, and Burgenland to Austria. It is almost entirely lowland. The shallow Lake Balaton is fed by springs, has brackish waters, and drains into the Danube.

Government. Hungary has a unicameral legislature, the National Assembly, composed of about 400 members elected for four years by the people. Males vote at eighteen years of age and females at nineteen. The president is selected by the National Assembly for a five-year term.

Commerce and Industry. The cultivation of the soil is the chief industry of Hungary. **Coal** and **lignite** are extensively mined, and large bauxite deposits are worked. The Magyars still retain the bulk of the agricultural land, the products of which made Hungary the chief granary of the old dual empire. **Corn** and **wheat** are the chief cereals, although barley and oats are grown. The vineyards north of Lake Balaton are extensive, and the grapes for the world-renowned Tokay wines are grown in the northeastern section of the country. **Horses** are reared in large numbers, and great efforts have been made to improve the breeds of cattle.

Communications. Hungarian railroads radiate from Budapest, the total mileage being about 6,307, of which some 4,787 miles are state-owned and operated. There are about 23,641 miles of roads.

Principal Towns. Budapest, the capital and great railroad center; Szeged, important trading center; Debrecen, chief city of the northeast; Kecskemét, an important agricultural and cattle market; Hódmezövásárhely, an agricultural center.

ICELAND

The Country. An island of the north Atlantic with a population of about 126,000 and an area of 39,709 square miles, of which about one-fourth is covered with glaciers and lava fields. Iceland is a great tableland averaging 2,000 feet above sea level. Of its whole area barely a quarter is habitable. The surface is dotted by over 100 volcanic peaks. There are many boiling springs and the geysers are world-famous.

Government. In 1944 Iceland became a free republic, severing all ties with Denmark. The legislative branch of the government consists of the fifty-two member Althing or parliament which is divided into two houses, the upper and lower. Executive power is exercised by a ministry of six departments, headed by the President of the Republic. The country is divided into sixteen provinces, each having its local government, directly elected by universal suffrage.

Commerce and Industry. Apart from sheep and cattle raising, the principal industry is **fishing.** Herring abound, but the chief wealth of Icelandic waters is cod. Whales are hunted by the Icelanders, and seals are numerous. The minerals are lignite, sulphur, and Iceland spar.

Communications. There are no railroads in Iceland, but some 2,728 miles of road in the vicinity of the towns.

Principal Towns. Reykjavik, the capital and largest city; Akureyri and Hafnafjördhur.

INDIA

The Country. The Dominion of India has an area of about 1,100,000 square miles and a population of about 315,000,000.

Government. The government is headed by a president, elected for a five year term. Parliament consists of two houses, the Council of States and the House of the People. Under the new constitution "untouchability" is abolished.

Commerce and Industry. Agriculture is the chief industry, the principal crops being rice, tea, wheat, jute, sugar cane and cotton. Other important industries include weaving of cotton and silk cloth and carpets, woodcarving, and metal working. Among the minerals found the most important are coal, gold, mica, salt, petroleum, and copper, iron and manganese ores.

Communications. There are about 41,000 miles of railroads. Inland steam navigation is well established on the lower courses of the main rivers, the most important being the Ganges.

Principal Cities. Calcutta, principal port of the east coast; Madras, the great cotton manufacturing and shipping port of the south; Bombay, New Delhi, the capital; Jamshedpur, Hyderabad, and Lucknow.

IRAN

The Country. Iran (called Persia until 1935) is a kingdom of southwestern Asia, with a population of about 15,000,000 and an area of about 628,000 square miles. Most of the country is plateau, from 3,500 to 6,500 feet above sea level, surrounded by mountain chains, except in the east, where huge salt deserts are found. An extension of the mountain ranges, locally known as the Khorasan Mountains of the Hindu Kush, enters on the northeast from Afghanistan and merges into the Elburz Range south of the Caspian, the highest peak being Mt. Demavend, 18,603 feet.

Government. The king or shah divides his power with a cabinet and an elective assembly.

Commerce and Industry. Deposits of coal and iron in the Elburz Mountains; copper, lead, and other metallic ores in the Kerman Desert; copper and turquoise in Khurasan; and rock salt near the Persian Gulf are known to exist, but have been little exploited. **Oil fields** are very rich, and are being exploited in increasing quantity. The chief *exports* are **petroleum,** opium, fruits, **lambskins,** raw cotton, rice, wool, and carpets; *imports* include cotton textiles, sugar, machinery, and tea.

Communications. Well-designed and constructed automobile roads are everywhere rendering the camel caravan obsolete. There are some 4,000 miles of first-class motor roads. A new road from Tehran to the Caspian Sea crosses the Elburz Range at an altitude of nearly 10,000 feet. The Trans-Iranian railroad, completed in 1938, is 900 miles long, and connects the Persian Gulf and the Caspian Sea. There is tug and barge navigation on Lake Urmiah and small steamers ply the Karun River.

Principal Towns. Tehran, the capital; Tabriz, manufacturing and chief commercial center; Isfahan, the former capital; Meshed, principal city of the northeast; Resht and Kerman.

IRAQ

The Country. After World War I, Mesopotamia, till then under Turkish rule, was recognized as an independent state and placed under the mandatory power of Great Britain. In 1927, by treaty with Great Britain, her independence was recognized. The country is a great alluvial plain, bounded on the north by Kurdistan, on the east by Iran, on the south by the Persian Gulf, and on the west by the Syrian and Arabian Deserts. Area, 116,600 square miles and population, about 4,800,000.

Government. The Organic Law of 1924 provides for a limited monarchy and a responsible government. There is a senate of 20 nominated "elder statesmen" and a lower house of 115 elected deputies.

Commerce and Industry. Watered by the Tigris and Euphrates, Iraq is a land of great potentialities with extremely fertile soil, awaiting irrigational development. Wheat, barley, and millet are grown. The annual *export* of **dates** is in the neighborhood of 150,000 tons. The **petroleum** resources are being steadily developed, and wool is also an important *export*.

Communications. A railroad runs from Basra (near the head of the Persian Gulf) to Baghdad, 354 miles. About 5,000 miles of automobile roads.

Principal Towns. Baghdad, the capital; Mosul; Basra, the port.

IRELAND

The Country. The Republic of Ireland has an area of 26,601 square miles and a population of about 2,954,000. Except for coastal hills and mountains, the country is largely an ill-drained plain dotted with lakes and peat-bogs, and crossed by the sluggish Shannon.

Government. Ireland became a free and independent Republic in 1949. The President, who is elected by direct vote for a 7 year period, appoints a prime minister on nomination of the House of Representatives. This House with 147 members and the Senate with 60 members comprise the Parliament. The country is divided into four provinces which are in turn divided politically into 27 counties and 4 county boroughs.

Commerce and Industry. A large part of the population is engaged in agriculture and live stock raising. The chief crops are wheat, oats, barley, rye and potatoes. The principal industries include brewing and distilling, grain milling and baking, clothing and textiles, tobacco and dairy products.

Communications. There are about 3,000 miles of railroads. There are extensive navigable inland waterways and a number of good ports.

Principal Cities. Dublin (Baile Atha Cliath), the capital; Cork, Kingstown (Dun Laoghaire), and Limerick.

ISRAEL

The Country. The Republic of Israel, established in 1948, on the eastern shores of the Mediterranean, lies between Egypt and Jordan. Its area is about 7,100 square miles; population, 850,000.

Government. The government is made up of a president, a prime minister and a 120 member constituent assembly elected by universal suffrage.

Commerce and Industry. Over half the people are engaged in farming. Citrus fruits, olives, wheat, and barley are the principal crops. The chief products are textiles, cement, light metal, and chemicals. Railroads connect principal cities and extend into Egypt. Israel has about 1,700 miles of asphalt roads.

Principal Cities. Jerusalem and Tel-Aviv, the capitals; Jaffa and Haifa.

ITALIAN SOMALILAND

The Country. The country has an area of about 194,000 square miles and a population of about 1,000,000. For a period of ten years it is to be a trust territory administered by Italy. At the end of this time it is to become an independent sovereign State.

Commerce and Industry. Cattle raising and agriculture flourish. Southern part of country is highly cultivated. Chief exports are sesame oil, gum, hides, butter, cotton and cotton-seed oil, resin, kapok, bananas and other fruits.

Communications. New motor roads are being built to take the place of wagon tracks. There is steamer service on the Giuba River from Chisimaio to Bardera.

Principal Towns. Mogadiscio, the capital; and Chisimaio.

ITALY

The Country. Italy consists of the Apennine Peninsula, and the islands of Sicily and Sardinia, and has a population of about 45,000,-000. The area comprises about 116,764 square miles. The Apennines, extending southward from the Alps, form the backbone of the penin-

sula, the southern and western parts of which have been subjected to volcanic eruptions; and Vesuvius, Etna, and Stromboli are still active volcanoes. The Alpine lakes are long and narrow, and the lakes of central Italy are in the craters or pipes of extinct volcanoes. The principal rivers are the Adige, 230 miles in length; the Arno, 150 miles; the Po, 420 miles; and the Tiber, 250 miles.

Government. Italy became a republic in 1946, as a result of a referendum in which the Italian people voted to dissolve the monarchy.

Commerce and Industry. Italy is predominantly agricultural; one-sixth of the area is forested. Valuable work has been and is being accomplished by the draining of the Pontine Marshes, and a new province, Litorria, with model towns and villages, has sprung up where formerly was swampland. The chief food products are **wheat, grapes, corn,** tobacco, potatoes, beets, barley, olives, and rice. Silk culture is general, but is of special importance in the north. The chief minerals are **sulphur, marble,** and iron. The chief imports are wheat, coal, raw cotton, cereals, iron and steel, mineral oils, and wool. The prime exports are raw silk, vegetables, fruit, rayon, cotton and silk goods, woolens, hemp, **wine,** and **motor cars.**

Communications. There are 14,000 miles of railroads, three-fourths of which belong to the state. There are over 120,000 miles of roads.

Principal Towns. Napoli (Naples), the most important port; Milano (Milan), great railroad and industrial center; Roma (Rome), the capital; Torino (Turin), manufacturing center; Palermo, on the island of Sicily, the center of a great fruit producing industry; Genova (Genoa), the port on the Ligurian coast, headquarters of the iron trade; Venezia (Venice), the historic port on the Adriatic; Firenze (Florence), and Bologna.

JAPAN

The Country. The Japanese Empire now consists of only the home islands, namely: Honshu (the mainland), Shikoku, Kyushu, and Kokkaido. The area is about 145,000 square miles and the population, about 81,000,000. The chief feature of the country is its mountainous character, for each island has a mountainous backbone. Fujiyama, the highest mountain, reaches 12,395 feet. One of the most notable physical features is the Inland Sea or Japanese Mediterranean. It is almost entirely landlocked and surrounded by chains of volcanoes, of which few are now active. The climate is temperate and healthful, with abundant rainfall.

Government. The government of Japan underwent many radical changes at the end of World War II. A new constitution was drafted on the pattern of western governments. It abolished oligarchic control (the Emperor became a mere figurehead), established a system whereby political parties were allowed to campaign and compete for government office, and, for the first time in Japan's history, provided for the enfranchisement of women. Is also renounced war "for ever" and prohibited the maintenance of an army, navy or air force. The Japanese Diet consists of two houses: a house of peers, which has 300 members under the new regime as opposed to the former 404 members, and a house of representatives of 466 representatives who are elected for a four year term by universal suffrage. Women first exercised their right to vote in the 1946 elections. This government is under the supervision of the United States occupation authorities.

Commerce and Industry. Agriculture is the chief industry, but only about 20,000 square miles of Japan proper can be cultivated; of this 57 per cent is under rice and 12 per cent under wheat. **Tea** plants are produced on nearly 200 square miles. Over 3,000,000 households are occupied with the production of **silk,** the yield of raw silk equaling that of the whole of Europe. About 75 per cent of the silk is exported. Tobacco, soybeans, and fruits are extensively produced. The fishing industry is important. Coal, copper, gold, petroleum, iron, and silver are mined. Chief manufactures are textiles, silk, earthenware, glass, lacquered goods, matting and hemp. Trade in matches and paper is important. A large amount of timber is produced. *Chief exports* are raw and manufactured **silks, cotton yarns,** and **piece goods,** coal, pottery, glassware, machinery, tea, toys, camphor, and sugar. *Imports* are **raw cotton,** machinery, wool, petroleum, rubber, and dyes.

Communications. The whole country is covered with a network of railroads with a total length of over 15,000 miles, and it is possible to travel continuously by train from the extreme north of Hokkaido to the extreme south of Kyushu, except in crossing the straits of Tsugaru and Shimonoseki.

Principal Towns. Tokyo, the capital and great industrial center; Osaka, seaport and textile manufacturing city; Kobe, seaport with extensive shipbuilding; Kyoto, with silk, porcelain and lacquer goods factories; Nagoya, port with large textile industries; Yokohama, port of Tokyo; Nagasaki, a seaport and winter resort.

JORDAN

The Kingdom of Jordan has a population of about 400,000 and an area of about 35,000 square miles. The country is largely a desert plateau with an elevation of about 3,000 feet. Jordan, which became completely independent in 1946, is a constitutional monarchy. The administration of the country is in the hands of the king, assisted by department heads and a legislative council of twenty elected members. Since the land is suitable for little else, a primitive pastoral economy prevails with camels, goats and sheep being raised. Only a small portion of the land is cultivated. Crops are grains, tobacco, and some vegetables and fruits. Only 5% of the country is inhabited.

KOREA

The Country. Under Japanese control prior to World War II, the country is now divided into two separate governments. The total area is 85,246 square miles and the population, about 26,000,000.

Government. In North Korea was established the "Korean People's Republic" in 1948. In the same year, the "Republic of Korea" was proclaimed in South Korea.

Commerce and Industry. Korea is essentially agricultural. The chief crops are rice, barley, wheat, beans, miscellaneous grains, tobacco, and cotton. Fishing has been intensively developed. Gold, iron ore and coal are abundant. Textile (including cotton, silk and rayon), hyrdoelectric power, nitrogenous fertilizers and chemical manufacture are the leading industries.

Principal Cities. Seoul, capital of the southern part; P'yŏngyang, capital of the northern part; Pusan, Taegu, and Inch'ŏn

LATVIA

The Country. Latvia is a Soviet Socialist Republic on the Baltic Sea, with a population of about 2,000,000 and an area of about 25,402 square miles. It has about 340 miles of seacoast. The land is flat and low-lying, and is watered by many rivers, the chief of which is the Dvina. There are many marshy tracts and lakes. A quarter of the country is covered with forests.

Government. Latvia became a constituent, nominally autonomous republic in the U. S. S. R. in 1940.

LEBANON

The Country. The Republic has a population of about 1,050,000 and an area of 3,475 square miles. Lebanon is a narrow coastal plain broken by steep mountains in the north. There are no large rivers.

Government. The Republic is headed by a president who is elected by parliament. The president appoints the cabinet of ministers which is responsible to the parliament.

Commerce and Industry. The principal occupations are the production of **tobacco,** the mulberry and silk, olives and grapes, fruits, cereals and cotton. The olives, wine and silk industries are the only ones of importance. Tripoli is an important terminus of the oil pipeline from Iraq. Rich iron ore deposits are found in northern Lebanon, and deposits of lignite exist in southern Lebanon. *Exports* are silk, fruit and carpets; *imports*: machinery and tin plate.

Principal Cities. Beirut (Beyrouth), the capital; Tripoli.

LIBERIA

The Country. Liberia is an independent Negro republic with a population of about 2,000,000 and an area of 43,000 square miles. It occupies about 350 miles of the West African coast and extends inland 200 miles at its widest part. Many rivers are navigable in stretches. The interior rises into mountains of from 2,000 to 6,000 feet in height.

Government. The constitution of the republic is modeled on that of the United States. The executive power is vested in a president and a council of 6 ministers, and the legislative power in a parliament of two houses, called the Senate and the House of Representatives. Electors must be of Negro blood and owners of land.

Commerce and Industry. The *exports* include **rubber,** palm oil, palm kernels, piassava fiber from the raffia palm, **coffee,** cacao, ginger, chillies, ivory, annatto seed, dye- and camwood, a hard dyewood. The chief *imports* are rice, textiles, tobacco, building timber, galvanized iron roofing, ready-made clothing, and dried and preserved fish.

Communications. There are no railroads. The means of transportation are oxcarts and automobiles. There are about 400 miles of motor roads in the coastal area.

Principal Towns. Monrovia, the capital and chief port; Robertsport, and Badawe.

LIBYA

Libya was granted its independence in 1949. The country's area is about 680,000 square miles and the population, about 888,000. In the area near the coast agriculture is carried on extensively, the principal crops being barley, wheat, olives, grapes, dates and figs. Tuna fishing and sponge fishing are major industries, and next to these in importance to the country's economy is the growing of tobacco and manufacture of tobacco products. Tripoli, Benghasi, Misurata, Homs, and Derna are the principal cities.

LIECHTENSTEIN

A small, independent principality, extending along the right bank of the Rhine opposite the Swiss canton of St. Gall and the Austrian province of Vorarlberg. It has a population of about 11,000 and an area of 65 square miles. The monarchy is hereditary in the male line. It has a diet of 15 members, elected by direct vote, and universal suffrage. Agriculture is important, especially cattle raising. Industries include spinning, weaving, and the manufacture of leather goods and pottery. It has a customs treaty with Switzerland which includes administration by Switzerland of the post and telegraph lines. Vaduz is the capital and principal town.

LITHUANIA

The Country. Lithuania is a Soviet Socialist Republic on the Baltic Sea with a population of about 2,880,000 and an area of 22,959 square miles. The country is flat and low-lying with a short coast line. It has numerous lakes, marshes and many rivers, the largest being the Neman (Niemen). About 16 per cent of the land is forest.

Government. Lithuania was admitted into the U. S. S. R. in 1940 as a constituent, nominally autonomous republic.

LUXEMBURG

The Country. A grand duchy surrounded by France, Germany, and Belgium. It has an area of about 999 square miles, and a population of about 300,000.

Government. Legislation is performed by a chamber of deputies, and executive power is vested in a president of government and a cabinet of not less than three directors-general. Luxemburg is in a customs union with Belgium and the Netherlands.

Commerce and Industry. The wealth of the country lies in its iron ore. Three-fifths of the area is cultivated; wheat, rye, oats, and potatoes are the main crops. There are many vineyards in the Moselle valley; horses and cattle are raised.

Principal Towns. Luxemburg, the capital; Esch-Alzette, the mining center.

MEXICO

The Country. Mexico has a population of about 20,000,000 and an area of 760,290 square miles. Two mountain chains traverse the country, forming between them a number of valleys and plateaus. The plateau of Anahuac, on which the capital is situated, is the largest and most important. The eastern edge of this plateau is formed by the Sierra Madre Oriental; the western edge, the Sierra Madre Occidental, shows a steep front and narrow ridges broken by canyons. In both sierras the highest peaks are about 10,000 feet. At the southern edge of the plateau confused ranges of mountains fall sharply to the Isthmus of Tehuantepec, where the lowest point on the watershed between the Atlantic and the Pacific is a little over 700 feet. The physical divisions eastward of the Isthmus of Tehuantepec include the highlands of Chiapas and the narrow, low plain of Soconusco on the Pacific side. These highlands range from 6,000 to 8,000 feet in extreme elevation. Northeast of them is the peninsula of Yucatan.

Government. Mexico is a federal republic composed of 28 states, one federated district and three territories. Each of the states has a right to manage its local affairs. The powers of the national government are divided into legislative, executive, and judicial branches. The legislative power is vested in a congress consisting of a chamber of deputies and a senate; the executive power, in a president. The 147 deputies are elected for three years by universal suffrage. The senate consists of 58 members, two for each state and federal district, elected for six years in the same manner as the deputies.

Commerce and Industry. Mexico is a country of immense natural wealth, with **oil fields,** gold, **silver, copper,** iron, and other minerals, and a great variety of vegetable products. Among these last may be especially mentioned, hemp, bananas, logwood, and other tropical forest products of the southeast; coffee, tobacco, and cotton in the more northerly localities, with a variety of fruit and all usual grain crops. Rubber plants are being raised experimentally. Mexico is one of the chief **petroleum**-producing countries, of the world. Coal is mined in the state of Coahuila and opals in the state of Querétaro.

Communications. Mexico has in operation about 15,000 miles of railroads, most of which are owned by the government. There are about 43,500 miles of roads, 9,500 miles good for all-year-round motoring, including the new Inter-American Highway.

Principal Towns. Mexico City, the capital and chief commercial center; Guadalajara, an agricultural and manufacturing center; Puebla de Zaragoza, with cotton spinning and other manufactures; San Luis Potosí, an agricultural and mining center; León, a mining and manufacturing town; Veracruz, principal port; Tampico, principal oil port.

MONACO

This principality, the second smallest state of Europe, situated on the Mediterranean coast, has a population of about 19,000 and an area of 370 acres and is encircled by the French department of the Alpes Maritimes and the Mediterranean Sea. The government is carried out under the authority of the Prince by a minister assisted by a council of state. The legislative power is exercised by the Prince and the National Council, which consists of 12 members elected for four years. The museum of oceanography is world famous. A large number of the inhabitants are employed in the celebrated gambling-house known as the "Casino." The climate is very mild. Revenue is derived chiefly from the gambling concessions.

NEPAL

An independent kingdom, Nepal lies in the Himalayas bounded on the north by Tibet and on the south and west by India. Its area is 54,000 square miles and its population, about 6,300,000. Several of the world's highest mountains, including Mount Everest, are in southern Nepal. The chief occupation is agriculture, with rice, corn, wheat and jute the main crops. The forests are extensive; the minerals as yet untapped. The nominal ruler is the maharajadhiraja; the actual one is the prime minister, who is always a member of the ruling Rana family. The capital of Nepal is Katmandu.

NETHERLANDS

The Country. The population is 9,000,000 and the total area of the country, including interior waters, gulfs, and bays, totals 15,771 square miles. The land area, amounting to 12,712 square miles (mostly flat), lies to a large extent below sea level. Along the canals, the meadows are often ten or twelve feet below the water line, and between the land and the sea at high tide there may be a difference of twenty-five feet or more. The land is protected by embankments and dikes, and it may be pictured as a great trough, the floor of which slopes down from east and southeast toward the North Sea. The rivers which flow across the country from the higher continent beyond, are at their mouths, frequently below the level of the sea, into which they have to be lifted by canals and locks across the dams or dikes. At all times the precarious river levels threaten internal floods. In 1933 the Zuider Zee was closed off from the North Sea by a huge dam, and made into a fresh-water lake.

Government. The Netherlands form a constitutional monarchy, governed by a sovereign, and a States-General, of two houses. Members of the upper house are elected by the States, the lower house by the people. The executive power of the sovereign is wielded by a council of ministers.

Commerce and Industry. The chief *exports* are **dairy produce,** vegetables, and bulbs, flax, **fish,** and sugar beets. Shipbuilding is an important industry and textiles are extensively manufactured. Amsterdam is a world center of the diamond-cutting industry. Chief *imports* are **textiles,** cereals, flour, mineral oil, iron and steel. Intensive methods are largely used in horticulture as well as in agriculture. The metric system of weights and measures is used.

Communications. Total length of railroads in operation is about 2,250 miles. Total extent of navigable rivers and canals is about 4,500 miles. There are about 16,000 miles of roads. There is a government subsidized air service from Amsterdam to London, Brussels, Paris, Malmö and Batavia, and between Rotterdam and Berlin.

Principal Towns. Amsterdam, the capital and second seaport; Rotterdam, chief port, with a large foreign trade; 's Gravenhage (The Hague), the seat of government; Utrecht, university city; Groningen, chief city of the north; Haarlem, famous for horticulture and the bulb trade; Arnhem, on the Rhine near the German frontier; Leiden, the famous university town; Nijmegen, a historic fortified city on the Waal.

Dependencies. The Netherlands has a large colonial empire of about 790,000 square miles in Asia and America, the population of which is about 69,000,000. One of the principal areas is the *United States* of *Indonesia* consisting of *Java* with 51,000 square miles and *Sumatra* with 164,000 square miles; the islands *Bali* and *Lombok* with 4,000 square miles, the *Molucca Islands* with 30,000 square miles, the *Celebes* with 73,000 square miles, the *Timor Archipelago* with 24,500 square miles, and the autonomous territories of the *Riouw-Lingga Archipelago* with 12,235 square miles, *Bangka* with 4,611 square miles, *Billiton* with 1,866 square miles, *Borneo, West,* with 56,664 square miles, and *Borneo, South* and *East* with 151,622 square miles. Another territory in the East Indies is *Netherlands New Guinea* with 161,514 square miles. It occupies the western half of the island of New Guinea. Products of the Indies are rubber, sugar, tea, rice, coffee, spices, corn, tobacco, fibers, petroleum, and tin.

In America are *Surinam* on the north coast of South America with 55,000 square miles and the *Netherlands Antilles* which include two widely separated groups of islands, *Curaçao* and three small islands in the Leeward Islands. The Antilles group has an area of 403 square miles. Surinam produces sugar, coffee, cacao, rice, bananas, balata, gold and bauxite. Aruba, in the Curacao group, has the world's largest petroleum refinery.

NEW ZEALAND

The Country. New Zealand is a British Dominion in the South Pacific. Politically, it embraces North Island and South Island, the small Stewart Island, and many islands in the neighboring seas. Area, 103,934 square miles and a population of about 1,800,000.

Government. The Dominion is governed by a governor-general and a general assembly, consisting of a legislative council of 34 paid members, and a house of 80 paid representatives.

Commerce and Industry. The dominant industry is sheep raising. Dairy farming, mainly for the production of butter and cheese, is of growing importance. Crops of wheat, oats, and barley are grown for local consumption. **Kauri gum** is dug in the Auckland Peninsula. **Coal** is mined on the western coast of South Island, and **gold** in the Thames Peninsula; some alluvial gold is dredged. The principal *exports* are **wool, frozen meat, butter, cheese,** tallow, hides, skins, and flax.

Communications. A growing railroad system is supplemented by a coastal steamer service. Total railroad mileage, about 3,400. The telegraph and telephone system is government owned and operated. New airfields have been developed, partly due to the war.

Principal Towns. Wellington, the capital; Auckland, Christchurch, Dunedin, Wanganui, Invercargill, and Palmerston North.

Dependencies. *Cook Islands, Niue Island, Union* or *Tokelau Islands* and the *Kermadec Islands.* The *Western Samoan Islands* are under trusteeship; *Nauru Island* is administered jointly by New Zealand, the United Kingdom and Australia.

NICARAGUA

The Country. This Central American republic has an area of about 57,145 square miles and a population of about 1,150,000. The east coast is backed by an alluvial plain, beyond which lie the central mountains, which rise to 7,000 feet. From the Gulf of Fonseca on the northwest coast, a depression extends southeast across the country, comprising the basins of Lakes Managua and Nicaragua and the San Juan River. Between the lakes and the Pacific coast is a range of low mountains, the chief center of volcanic activity in the country.

Government. Executive power is vested in the president, elected for six years. Legislative power is vested in a congress of two houses, consisting of 40 deputies, elected for six years by universal suffrage, and 15 senators, elected for six years, (plus ex-presidents).

Commerce and Industry. The **banana** is the principal agricultural product in the east. Coconuts are also of some importance, and a few plantains, oranges, and pineapples are raised. Rice is grown to a small extent, and some wheat in the hilly districts, while tobacco is cultivated around Masaya. The most important products of the western half are **coffee,** sugar cane, cacao, corn, and beans. Extensive forests yield mahogany, cedar, gums and medicinal plants. Chief *imports* are **textiles,** machinery, chemicals, and flour; *exports* are **coffee,** sugar, **bananas,** timber, and hides. Gold and silver are mined.

Communications. The republic has 367 miles of railroads. The principal line runs from Corinto to Granada and Diriamba. Transportation is largely by pack train and oxcart. The country is served by two air lines.

Principal Towns. Managua, the capital; León, Granada, Matagalpa, Bluefields, and Masaya.

NORTHERN IRELAND

The Country. The present Ulster border was determined by the Government of Ireland Act in 1920, which contemplated the division of Ireland between the Nationalist South and the Unionist North. For centuries, Ireland has been geographically divided into four provinces: Ulster, Munster, Leinster, and Connaught, of which the first was predominately Unionist, and the remainder Nationalist, the latter term being used to include Sinn Fein. But upon closer examination the framers of the act discovered that three of the counties of Ulster, namely Donegal, Monaghan, and Cavan, contained a population with a considerable majority of Nationalists. These counties were therefore included in southern Ireland, and the Ulster border became the line circumscribing the remaining six counties of Ulster. Area of Northern Ireland, 5,237 square miles. Population, about 1,300,000.

Government. Under the act of 1920, the government of the territory comprising the six counties of Down, Londonderry, Armagh, Tyrone, Antrim and Fermanagh is intrusted to a parliament consisting of the King of England, the Senate of Northern Ireland and the House of Commons of Northern Ireland. The powers of the parliament and government of Northern Ireland are wholly domestic. For description of physical features, principal towns, etc., see British Commonwealth of Nations.

NORWAY

The Country. Norway, occupying the western half of the Scandinavian Peninsula, has an area of 124,556 square miles and a population of about 3,000,000. It is 1,100 miles in length and the coast line, including fjords and greater islands, is 12,000 miles long. It is separated from Sweden by the Kjölen Mountains, which form the backbone of the peninsula. These mountains rise in many parts to over 6,000 feet, the highest peaks being over 8,000 feet. Norway's long coast line, facing the Atlantic, is edged with lofty cliffs and seamed with deep fjords. Islands, countless in number, fringe the coast. These archipelagoes cover a total area of no less than 8,600 square miles. Seventy per cent of Norway's area is barren land. Of the whole area only 4,300 square miles are fit for agriculture, and nearly 5,000 square miles are water. The rivers are short and torrential, but provide the finest salmon fishing in Europe.

Government. Norway is a constitutional and hereditary monarchy. Executive power is exercised by the King through a council of state (*Statsraad*). Parliament, called the *Storting,* consists of an upper and lower house, having in all 150 members, one-quarter forming the *Lagting* or senate, three-fourths the *Odelsting* or house of commons. Questions relating to the laws are considered by each house separately, but if the two houses do not agree, they resolve themselves into a common sitting for discussion, and a two-thirds vote is then required for decision. Members are chosen by universal suffrage.

Commerce and Industry. Agriculture is practiced only in eastern and southern Norway. The chief crops are potatoes, oats, barley, rye, wheat, and hay. Dairy farming on co-operative lines is making great progress; butter and condensed milk are exported. Norway is essentially a maritime country, and the fisheries of cod, herring, mackerel, and salmon, are important; fish and fish products constituting about one quarter of the total *exports*. The forest resources are very large, and the wood pulp, and paper industries, together with the canning and electrochemical industries are operated by electric transmission of the country's enormous water power. It is proposed to transmit hydroelectric power from Norway to Central Europe. **Iron, bauxite,** zinc, lead, and tin are mined.

Communications. The total railroad mileage is about 2,500 miles, of which 2,154 miles are state-owned. Coastwise steamers serve all ports.

Principal Towns. Oslo, the capital; Bergen, an important seaport with fishing and shipbuilding industry; Trondheim, and Stavanger.

Dependencies. *Svalbard (Spitzbergen)*, total area 24,294 square miles, a mountainous group of islands in the Arctic Ocean, has important coal deposits which are being progressively exploited. *Jan Mayen*, an island lying between Northern Norway and Greenland. *Bouvet Island* in the South Atlantic and *Peter I Island* in the Antarctic, the latter being declared a dependency in 1933.

PAKISTAN

The Country. The Dominion of Pakistan is divided into two sections, western Pakistan which is northwest of India on the Arabian Sea, and eastern Pakistan on the Bay of Bengal. Western Pakistan, composed of the Baluchistan States, West Punjab and the provinces of Baluchistan, Northwest Frontier, and Sind has an area of about 306,920 square miles. About a thousand miles east is East Pakistan made up of East Bengal and the former Sylhet District of Assam Province, with an area of about 54,000 square miles. The total population is about 70,100,000. Most of the people are Moslems. The Indus in western Pakistan is the most important river.

Government. The state is headed by a governor-general, an assembly, and the cabinet of federal ministers.

Commerce and Industry. Pakistan is primarily an agricultural country, although not enough food is produced for its own needs. Irrigation projects are reclaiming desert areas in Sind and West Punjab. About 85% of the people are farmers. Cereals, cotton, jute, oilseeds, and tobacco are the chief crops. Road mileage is about 45,800; railways, about 6,600.

Principal Cities. Karachi, the capital, is the major sea and air port; Lahore, Multan, Peshawar, Dacca, capital of the eastern zone, Chittagong and Hyderabad.

PANAMA

The Country. Panama, a Central American republic, has an area, excluding the Canal Zone, of 28,576 square miles and a population of about 623,000 It occupies the narrowest portion of the connecting link between North and South America, known as the Isthmus of Panama. The interior is elevated and is drained by short rapid streams to both coasts. The peninsula of Azuero projects into the Pacific Ocean.

Government. The constitution provides for a national assembly of 32 members, and for a president of the republic elected by direct vote for six years and not eligible for the succeeding term. There are three vice-presidents and a cabinet of six ministers.

Commerce and Industry. The chief agricultural products are bananas, cacao, coconuts, coffee, sugar, rubber, tobacco, and sarsaparilla. The forest resources include mahogany and other valuable woods. Cattle raising is successful and provides hides for *export*. Mother-of-pearl, tortoise shell, and ivory nuts are *exported*. Mining is unimportant, but resources of gold, manganese, coal, iron, and asbestos are reported.

Communications. The U. S. government railroad between Colón and Panama, 48 miles in length, with a branch 3 miles long to Balboa, the Pacific entrance to the Canal, is the most important transportation route of the Isthmus.

Principal Towns. Panama, the capital and chief port on the Pacific; Colón, the chief port on the Caribbean.

PARAGUAY

The Country. Paraguay, a South American republic and one of the two inland countries of South America, has a population of about 1,000,000 and an area of 157,000 square miles, including the Gran Chaco area between the Paraguay and Pilcomayo Rivers. The Gran Chaco Peace Settlement in 1938 ended the nation's war with Bolivia, and more than doubled Paraguay's territory.

Government. The legislative authority is vested in a Chamber of Representatives, elected under the Constitution of 1940. The executive authority is entrusted to a president, elected for five years, and a Council of State of nine ministers.

Commerce and Industry. Excellent grazing land is abundant and pastoral industries have made great advance in recent years. The chief *exports* are **hides, yerba maté** (Paraguay tea), oranges, cotton, tobacco, timber, meat, cattle, and quebracho (tannin) extract. Chief *imports* are textiles, wheat, flour, petroleum products, provisions, hardware, and fancy goods.

Communications. Total railroad mileage is about 713 miles. Asunción, the capital, is now in direct communication with Buenos Aires. The main channel of communication is the navigable system of the Plata.

Principal Towns. Asunción, the capital and chief river port; Villarrica, the center of tobacco growing; Concepción, and Luque.

PERSIA
See IRAN

PERU

The Country. A South American republic with a population of about 7,000,000 and an area of 482,000 square miles. This area takes into account the boundary settlements of 1929 and 1930 with Chile and Colombia; and the settlement of the 125 year old boundary dispute with

Ecuador, 1942. The Cordilleras of the Andes divide Peru into three natural divisions. The first or coastal strip includes the Pacific ports, the cotton and sugar valleys, the rice and petroleum fields. The second, the *Sierra*, includes the chief mining towns and upland plateaus, suitable for grazing. Lake Titicaca is in this region, which ranges from 4,000 to 20,000 feet in height. The third, or *Montanas*, includes the eastern slopes of the Andes and the low basin of the Amazon.

Government. The constitution of 1933 provides for a president, to whom is entrusted the executive power. He is elected for five years, but is not eligible for a consecutive term. The legislative power rests in a senate and chamber of deputies, both elected by direct vote. The franchise is exercised by literate males over 21 years of age.

Commerce and Industry. The mineral deposits, which are found in the mountainous regions, consist of gold, silver, **copper,** iron, lead, vanadium, zinc, sulphur, and **petroleum.** Of these, **copper** and **petroleum** are the chief minerals worked and *exported.* Peru produces 55 per cent of the world's supply of **vanadium,** and is probably the only country where it is mined for itself alone. **Cotton, sugar,** and wheat are the principal products; coffee, cacao, and coca (from which cocaine is made) are also cultivated. Cinchona bark and castor oil are produced. Rubber and balata production has greatly declined. The annual output of guano from the Peruvian islands has been sharply cut. The *exports* consist chiefly of minerals, sugar, wool, cotton, and hides. The principal *imports* are manufactured goods and machinery.

Communications. The Andean Plateau is connected with the sea by two mountain railroads. One of these, the Callao-Oroya line, traverses the western cordillera and is linked by a north extension to the great copper mines of Pasco. The southern railroad mounts over the western cordillera to the north shore of Lake Titicaca at Puno, whence steamers connect it with the Bolivian railroad system. These two mountain railroads with their extensions total about 900 miles. The total length of the Peruvian railroads is about 2,600 miles.

Principal Towns. Lima, the capital and industrial center; Callao, Arequipa, a cathedral town.

PHILIPPINES, REPUBLIC OF

The Country. The Philippine Republic has a population of about 19,234,182 and an area of 115,600 square miles. There are about 7,100 islands in the group comprising the Republic. Fewer than 500 of the islands have an area of over one mile square, and only eleven of the islands have more than 1,000 square miles. The largest islands are Luzon, Mindanao, Samar, Negros, Palawan and Panay. The Philippine Islands are the tops of a submerged mountain chain of volcanic origin. There are well-watered fertile plains between the mountains.

Government. The Republic achieved full sovereignty in 1946. The constitution provides for a government similar to that of the United States. The president and vice-president are popularly elected for a four-year term. Congress,

also popularly elected, consists of a twenty-four member senate and a 120 member House of Representatives. There are forty-eight provinces for administrative purposes.

Commerce and Industry. The chief industry is agricultural; most farms are small, but there are also many large plantations. The main agricultural crops are rice, **copra, sugarcane, hemp** (abaca), corn, tobacco and maguey. The Philippines rank among the world's foremost producers of copra and coconut oil. Manufacturing includes products made in the home (fine embroidery, woven clothes, pottery and mats), sugar refineries and centrals, textile mills, distilleries, cigar and cigarette factories, lumber and rice mills. The extensive forests, covering about three-fifths of the area and mostly government owned, are the basis of many industries. Mineral resources are large, but not fully developed. The more important ones are gold, chromite, copper, iron ore and manganese ore. Some coal, asbestos, rock asphalt and silica deposits also exist.

Communications. There are about 800 miles of railroads, mostly on Luzon and 14,000 miles of roads.

Principal Cities. Quezon City, the capital; Manila, Cebu, Zamboanga, Davao, Iloilo, and Baguio.

POLAND

The Country. Poland, with a population of about 24,000,000 and an area of 121,131 square miles, is mostly a plain. Low hills are found in Pomerania in the northeast. The lower regions of the Vistula have marshes, sand dunes and lakes. The central plain of Poland with an elevation of about 500 feet is traversed by great rivers. The Oder and the Vistula are the most important rivers.

Government. The Republic of Poland has a one house parliament: the National Council. The 1946 government was based on the principles of the 1921 constitution. One important deviation was the elimination of the senate. The Council of Ministers initiates legislation and sends it to the National Council for approval. This government nationalized all basic industries.

Commerce and Industry. Prior to World War II, Poland was primarily agricultural. However, with the addition of former German areas east of the Oder, industry became almost equally important. The chief crops are potatoes, rye, sugar beets, oats, flax, wheat, barley and corn. Industrial production includes textiles, wood and paper, steel, metals and chemicals. Resources include extensive **coal** deposits, which make Poland one of the foremost world coal producers, iron, lignite, zinc, lead, salt and potash. Much of Poland is valuable **timber** land.

Communications. Total railroad mileage is about 17,000 including normal and narrow gauge. There are about 60,000 miles of highways and about 3,100 miles of inland waterways.

Principal Towns. Warszawa (Warsaw), the capital; Lódź, a great textile center; Kraków, the old capital; Poznań (Posen), Katowice, Lublin, and Wrocław (Breslau); Gdynia and Gdańsk (Danzig) are the chief ports.

PORTUGAL

The Country. Portugal, a republic in the extreme southwest of Europe, has a population of about 7,800,000 and an area of 34,254 square miles. Including the Azores and Madeira Islands in the Atlantic Ocean, which politically form an integral part of the republic, the total area is 35,490 square miles. The length of Portugal from north to south is approximately 300 miles, and its average width is a little less than 100 miles. Physically, Portugal is an integral part of the Iberian Peninsula, its mountains and rivers being mainly prolongations of those of Spain. The longest river rising in Portugal is the Mondego. The chief rivers are the Minho, which forms part of the northern boundary; the Guadiana, which forms part of the southeastern frontier; the Douro, and the Tagus (Tejo).

Government. A new constitution, adopted in 1933, set up a corporative state and provided for a president elected by males who are literate or taxpayers, and females with a secondary school diploma; and for a 120-member National Assembly which the president can dissolve at will. Strikes and lockouts are illegal.

Commerce and Industry. Vineyards are cultivated throughout the land, and **wine** is an important product. In the mountainous regions, rye is grown, and sheep and goats are raised; in the north, corn and cattle are raised; in the south, wheat and swine. **Olive trees** cover a large area; figs, tomatoes, potatoes, **oranges**, and nuts are grown. Fish, especially **sardines** and **tunny fish,** are caught, cured, and canned for *exportation*. The principal manufacturing industry is the production of textiles, the second being the fisheries. Articles manufactured of **cork** are *exported*. Other industries are silk, leather, glass, paper, and gold and silver filigree manufactures. Salt, gypsum, and marble are *exported*.

Communications. About 2,000 miles of railroads are in operation, of which about 800 miles are state-owned.

Principal Towns. Lisboa (Lisbon), the capital and chief seaport; Porto (Oporto), with an extensive port wine trade; Setúbal, noted for its sardine fisheries and export of fruit and salt; Braga, noted for its manufactures of firearms; Coimbra, an inland city with a famous university.

Colonies and Dependencies. Portugal has a large colonial empire in Africa, totaling about 800,000 square miles, and minor possessions in Asia, extending over 8,873 square miles. Thus the total area of the colonies is about 808,000 square miles.

In Africa, the colonies are: *Cape Verde Islands*, 1,557 square miles, with the capital Praia; *Portuguese Guinea* on the coast of Senegal with 13,948 square miles; *Principe* and *São Tomé Islands* with 372 square miles; *Angola* (Portuguese West Africa) with 481,351 square miles, and a coast line of 1,000 miles; capital, Loanda, and *Mozambique* (Portuguese East Africa) with an area of 297,731 square miles; capital, Lourenço Marques.

In Asia, the possessions are: *Gôa* and *Diu*, 1,537 square miles, in India; *Macao*, 6 square miles, in China; and in Malaysia, Portugal owns 7,330 square miles of the island of *Timor*.

PUERTO RICO

See UNITED STATES OF AMERICA

RUMANIA

The Country. Rumania has a population of about 17,000,000 and an area of about 91,671 square miles. In western Rumania the Carpathian Mountains from the northwest and the Transylvanian Alps from the southwest meet in the center to form a crescent. To the north and west of this crescent is the Transylvanian plateau; to the south and east are the plains of Moldavia and Walachia. The principal rivers are the Danube in the south which enters the Black Sea at Sulina, and the Prut in the northeast and the Siret in the southeast—both of which connect with the Danube.

Government. Rumania has a one-house legislature, the National Assembly. The only party opposing government parties was dissolved in 1947.

Commerce and Industry. Rumania is an agricultural country with about four-fifths of the people cultivating the soil. It is one of the chief grain producers of southeast Europe. Principal crops are **wheat,** rye, barley, corn and tobacco. The mulberry, vine and olive are extensively cultivated. Rumania's most valuable mineral is **oil** with production centered in the Ploesti region. **Natural gas** is the second most important mineral. Other minerals are coal, lignite, salt, iron ore, copper, silver and gold. About one-fifth of the country is forested. The lower Danube fisheries are important. Exports: **petroleum products, cereals,** wood and wood products and livestock. Imports: iron, machinery and vehicles.

Communications. Railroad mileage is about 6,000, and there are about 43,163 miles of roads.

Principal Towns. Bucureşti (Bucharest), the capital; Iaşi, Galaţi (Galatz), chief port on the Danube; Constanţa, chief Rumanian port on the Black Sea.

RUSSIA

See UNION OF SOVIET SOCIALIST REPUBLICS

SALVADOR, EL

The Country. El Salvador, the smallest and most densely populated of the American republics, and the only one of the Central American states lying wholly on the Pacific, has a population of about 2,000,000 and an area of 13,176 square miles. The Pacific coast plain is narrow and is backed by the coast range of mountains which rises above 7,000 feet. The chief river is the Lempa.

Government. The constitution provides for a National Assembly elected for one year by universal suffrage. Executive power is vested in a president elected for 4 years.

Commerce and Industry. The population is largely engaged in agriculture. **Coffee** is the chief crop and the chief *export*; others are balsam of Peru, railway ties, rice, indigo, palm hats, and henequen. **Cattle** are numerous. Gold, **silver,** copper, zinc, and mercury are mined.

Communications. Total railroad length is about 350 miles. Direct railroad communication between San Salvador and Puerto Barrios, Guatemala, is now open. Road making has progressed rapidly under a well planned government system. The Inter-American Highway runs through the country. From San Salvador, there are air communications with Central American points and North and South America.

Principal Towns. San Salvador, the capital; Santa Ana, center of the sugar growing district; and San Miguel, an agricultural center.

SAN MARINO

This small, independent republic, lies entirely within the territory of Italy, area 38 square miles and a population of about 12,100 The Grand Council of 60 elected members acts as a legislature, two members of the council being appointed regents every six months. Chief *exports* are wine, cattle, and building stone. The city of San Marino is connected with Rimini, Italy, by an electric railway twenty miles long.

SAUDI ARABIA, KINGDOM OF

Saudi Arabia, occupying the central two-thirds of the Arabian Peninsula, has a population of about 5,000,000 and an area of 350,000 square miles. The Kingdom, consisting of the provinces of Hejaz, Nejd and Asir, is largely desert with scattered oases. In the west, parallel with the Red Sea is a mountain chain; to the east the country is largely a plateau. The population is mostly nomadic and engaged in pastoral pursuits, breeding camels, sheep and goats. There are no rivers, forests or railroads, and very few roads. An important source of income to the kingdom is the royalties from the **oil wells** which are entirely controlled by United States interests. Saudi Arabia has 3,000,000 barrels of proved reserves of petroleum or one-twentieth of the world's reserves. Mecca and Riyadh are the capitals.

SIAM

The Country. An independent kingdom of southeastern Asia in the Indo-Chinese peninsula, with a population of about 18,000,000 and an area of 200,148 square miles. The climate is hot, but not unhealthy, and the country is mountainous and covered with forests.

Government. Siam is a constitutional monarchy. Under the constitution of 1946, supreme power belongs to the nation and the king exercises legislative power through an assembly of 182 people's representatives, and executive power through a state council of 14 to 24 members. The assembly is elected under direct suffrage by all citizens over 20, regardless of literacy.

Commerce and Industry. Rice is the staple crop and the main *export*. Other produce includes pepper, sesame, cardamoms, areca nut, gamboge, and tobacco. Rubber plantations are increasingly important. **Teak** is the chief commercial product of the forests. The mineral resources are extensive and varied, including **tin**, tungsten, wolfram, coal, iron, zinc, manganese, and antimony.

Communications. About 1,900 miles of railroads are in operation. The Menam is navigable by deep-draught launches at high water for 275 miles. There is direct commercial radio communication with Germany, England, France, Java, Philippine Islands, Hong Kong, Japan, and India.

Principal Towns. Bangkok, the capital, is the principal port and an important trading center; Ayudhya, a trading center on the Menam River.

SPAIN

The Country. Spain, a republic in the southwest of Europe, occupying about five-sixths of the Iberian Peninsula, has an area of 195,504 square miles and a population of about 26,000,000. The Balearic and Canary Islands form three of its fifty provinces; the province of Cádiz includes Ceuta, a fortified station on the north coast of Morocco. The greater part of the surface is a tableland ranging in height from 2,000 to 3,000 feet above sea level. This great tableland is enclosed by the Cantabrian Mountains and the Pyrenees on the north and the Sierra Morena on the south. Outside the plateau lie the highest summits of the whole country, the Pico de Aneto in the Pyrenees being over 11,000 feet. The plateau itself is traversed by four mountain ranges which separate the valley of the Ebro from that of the Duero. All important rivers, except the Ebro flow westward to the Atlantic.

Government. Spain is ruled by a nationalist government under a dictatorship. The *Cortes* has been re-established as the state organ for the preparation and enactment of laws, but most of its 438 members are appointed as a result of positions already held. No provision exists whereby legislation can be introduced by a member. Spain was declared a monarchy in 1947. Franco remains chief of state, and after his death the country will choose its king. Each province in Spain has its own assembly. Roman Catholicism has been re-established under Franco as the state religion.

Commerce and Industry. Spain is largely an agricultural country. Wheat, barley, corn, rye, oats, and rice are the chief crops; the annual production of red and white wines exceeds 607,000,000 gallons, and of olive oil 93,000,000 gallons. Silk culture and stock raising are also important industries. **Coal, iron, copper,** lead, zinc, mercury, iron pyrites, and lignite are mined. The chief *imports* are cotton, machinery, coal coke, chemical products, and fish; the chief *exports* are **mineral ores, wine, olive oil, oranges** and **cork.**

Communications. The total length of railroads is 10,783 miles. The normal gauge lines total 7,920 miles, and have passed into state ownership.

Principal Towns. Madrid, the capital; Barcelona, the chief seaport on the Mediterranean Valencia, important center of tobacco and pottery; Sevilla (Seville), a thriving port and chief city of Andalusía; Málaga, an important seaport and health resort; Zaragoza, capital of the former kingdom of Aragon; Cartagena, Murcia, and Granada.

Colonies and Dependencies. The former great empire of Spain is now considerably reduced All colonies are in Africa and occupy a total are of about 132,000 square miles. They consist of *Spanish Morocco* with about 18,000 square miles, with the fortified towns of Ceuta and Melilla, and including the territory of *Ifni*; *Spanish Sahara*, a colony including two zones: *Rio de Oro* and *Saguia el Hamra* with an area of 103,000 square miles; and *Spanish Guinea*, which comprises *Rio Muni*, *Fernando Poo* and other small islands, 10,900 square miles.

SWEDEN

The Country. Sweden, occupying the eastern and larger portion of the Scandinavian Peninsula, has an area of 173,403 square miles. It has a length of nearly 1,000 miles, and a coast line of over 1,500 miles. Besides the large number of small islands which fringe the coast, Sweden includes the two large Baltic islands of Gotland and Öland. Its islands cover an area of 3,000 square miles. The whole country is a tableland sloping from the Kjölen Range to the Baltic. No less than 8 per cent of the surface of Sweden is water, the immense number of lakes covering almost 15,000 square miles. The two largest, Vänern and Vättern, in the southern portion of the country, are connected by a system of canals.

Government. Sweden is a constitutional monarchy, the king's power being exercised in conjunction with a council of state and a diet. There are two legislative chambers, the upper one consisting of 150 members and the lower one of 230. Suffrage is universal for all over 21.

Commerce and Industry. Principal crops are oats, potatoes, barley, rye, and wheat. **Livestock** is widely raised. A large amount of butter is *exported*. Forests of pine, fir, and larch cover more than half of the area, and its output of **imber** and **paper pulp** is very large. The mining of iron ore and the production of **iron** and **steel** is important, and also the timber and woodworking industry. Cream separators, **matches,** lighthouse apparatus, telephone supplies, motors, and many kinds of electrical machinery are among the highly specialized products of industry.

Communications. Sweden has about 10,000 miles of railroad, all of which are now state-owned. This is supplemented by an excellent system of canals. The work of electrifying the state-owned railroads is progressing, all those south of Stockholm having been changed.

Principal Towns. Stockholm, the capital; Göteborg, the chief seaport; Malmö, a seaport and air field opposite Copenhagen; Norrköping, an important manufacturing city.

SWITZERLAND

The Country. Switzerland, an inland mountainous country in the central portion of the Alps, surrounded on the north by Germany, on the south by Italy, on the east by Austria, and on the west by France, has a population of about 4,345,000 and an area of 15,940 square miles. Between Lake Constance on the Rhine and Lake Geneva on the Rhone are Lakes Neuchâtel, Zurich, Lucerne, Brienz, Thun, all of which drain to the Aar. Lake Geneva and Lake Constance each exceed 200 square miles in area; Lake Neuchâtel covers 85 square miles. Many of Switz-

erland's mountains are permanently covered with snow. Four languages are officially recognized and used: German, French, Italian, and Romansch.

Government. Switzerland is a federal republic consisting of twenty-two cantons. The parliament consists of the state council (44 members) and the national council (194 members). The referendum is used when legislative measures are submitted directly to the people. The chief executive authority is vested in a federal council of seven members elected by the federal assembly for three years. The president is elected yearly by the federal assembly and cannot serve for two consecutive years. Franchise is exercised by all citizens over 21. The separate cantons have an independent system of local government.

Commerce and Industry. The thousands of tourists who visit Switzerland have made hotel keeping one of the principal industries of the country. Switzerland is highly industralized: **silk**, cotton, and **textile** mills employ thousands; the manufacture of machinery, **clocks, watches,** and dairy farming are the most important economic factors of Switzerland. Large quantities of milk are consumed in **chocolate** factories and **milk condensing** concerns, and in the manfacture of **cheese** for *export*.

Communications. About 3,245 miles of railroads are in operation, all state-owned.

Principal Towns. Zürich, an industrial center; Basel, producer of silk ribbons; Bern, the capital; St. Gallen (St. Gall), an industrial center south of Lake Constance; Lausanne, an educational center; Genève (Geneva), noted for its watches; Luzern (Lucerne), a great tourist center.

SYRIA

The Country. Syria, with a population of about 2,800,000 and an area of 72,587 square miles, consists of a coastal plain bounded by a chain of mountains with a steppe area in the interior.

Government. The Syrian Republic, which became completely independent in 1945, is headed by a president who is elected for five years by the legislature. Executive power is exercised by the prime minister and his cabinet. There is a one house legislature composed of about 138 representatives elected by male voters over twenty years of age.

Commerce and Industry. Syria is primarily agricultural with farming and cattle breeding the main occupations of the people. The principal crops are wheat, barley, maize, sorghum, sesame, chickpeas, lentils and hemp. There is little known mineral wealth; however, marble and good building stone are plentiful. Industrial development is limited and confined mostly to the production of consumers goods. Manufactures include flour, oil, soap and silk thread. *Exports* are textiles, fruits and vegetables, and animal products; *imports* food and drink, textiles, vegetables and animal products and metals.

Principal Cities. Dimishq (Damascus), the capital; Haleb (Aleppo), a trade center; Homs and Hama.

TRIESTE, FREE TERRITORY OF

The Free Territory of Trieste was provided for in 1947 by the United Nations. It has an area of 250 square miles and a population of about 300,000 Trieste's independence is assured by the Security Council of the United Nations which also appoints the governor.

TURKEY

The Country. Turkey, which has an area of about 296,000 square miles, comprises a portion of Thrace adjacent to Istanbul (Constantinople); the bulk of it, however, is confined to the Anatolian Peninsula in Asia Minor. Much of the district is an elevated plateau, the altitude varying from 2,500 to 6,000 feet above sea level. Among the chief mountains are the Taurus Range, stretching from the southwestern shore of the Aegean to the north of Syria, their principal peaks rising from 7,000 to 10,000 feet; the Bulgar Mountains rising over 10,000 feet; and the Ala Mountains, north of Seyhan, rising 8,000 to 10,000 feet high. The highest peak in the country is Mt. Ararat, 16,916 feet. Flowing into the Black Sea are the Coruh, the Yesil Irmak, the Kizil Irmak and the Sakariya. Into the Mediterranean flow the Seyhan and Ceyhan. In the east of Asia Minor are the headwaters of both the Euphrates and the Tigris as well as of the Araks. Important lakes are the Tuz, 60 miles long; the Beyschir, 30 miles long; the Egridir, 30 miles long, and Lake Van, 80 miles long. Turkey has a population of about 18,860,000.

Government. Turkey is a constitutional republic with a national assembly elected by the people every four years. The executive power is exercised by the assembly through the president (elected by the assembly), and a council of ministers chosen by him. In 1937 the Grand National Assembly (Kamutay) made the principles of the dominant Republic Peoples Party part of the constitution. Their principles are nationalism, democracy, evolutionism (adaptation to change), separation of church and state, and nationalization of the chief means of communication, industries, mines and public utilities.

Commerce and Industry. Agriculture is primitive, but modern methods are being rapidly adopted and the soil, where cultivable, is fertile and produces considerable crops of wheat, **barley,** cotton, **tobacco,** nuts, **figs,** olives, grapes, and other fruits. A large quantity of opium is grown, but in 1933 laws were passed limiting the production of drug-producing plants to a quantity sufficient only for medicinal purposes. The fisheries are important. The *exports* include cereals, cotton, fruit, olive oil, tobacco, carpets, and wool. Asia Minor is rich in minerals, which however, are only slightly worked. The principal minerals produced are coal, lignite, copper, chrome, antimony and mercury. Turkish industries include iron and steel, textile, mining, paper, glass, sugar and cement.

Communications. Railroads total 4,609 miles. Ankara, the capital, is connected to Sivas by rail, furnishing an outlet to the Bosphorus, and an extension to Samsun on the Black Sea was opened in 1933. Regular air service links Istanbul and Ankara with most European capitals. There are approximately 10,370 miles of roads.

Principal Towns. Istanbul (Constantinople), the former capital; Izmir (Smyrna), an important seaport; Bursa (Brusa), the ancient capital and center of silk manufacture; Sivas, a mining center; Ankara (Angora), the capital.

UNION OF SOUTH AFRICA

The Country. The Union of South Africa, a self governing dominion within the British Commonwealth of Nations, has a population of about 11,068,000 and an area of 472,494 square miles. The Union of South Africa consists of four provinces: the Cape of Good Hope, Natal, Transvaal, and the Orange Free State. South Africa is a vast tableland with a lofty rim to the east and south, represented by the Drakensberg and other mountains. The country is drained westward by the Orange and Vaal Rivers. Vegetation in the Cape region consists of evergreen trees, shrubs, and heaths; the well watered eastern terraces are clothed with a richly wooded savanna. Over acres of the eastern tableland, there is an almost treeless grassland (the veldt), which merges westward into scrub and bush composed of thorn bushes and other drought resisting plants. In the north, the grassland is wooded, and is known as the bush veldt. *Southwest Africa*, formerly German, with an area of 322,394 square miles, is now administered by the Union.

Government. The Union of South Africa is a dominion within the British Commonwealth of Nations, enjoying the status of an independent state, free of any control by the British Government or Parliament. Under the act constituting the Union, the sovereign appoints a governor-general, who with an executive council, administers the executive government of the Union. Departments of state have been established, the governor-general appointing officers to administer them. Legislative power is vested in a parliament consisting of the King, a senate and a house of assembly. The senate consists of 40 members, 8 being nominated by the governor-general, and 32 elected. The house of assembly has, in accordance with the 1941 census results, 150 members. There must be a session of parliament every year.

Commerce and Industry. The most important crops are **mealies, wheat,** oats, and barley. Tobacco is widely grown, and in Natal and Transvaal, cotton is being increasingly cultivated. Fruit growing is one of the leading agricultural industries. The leading pastoral occupation is **sheep raising.** Dairy farming is carried on successfully on the higher and cooler eastern terraces of Natal, and is similarly situated in parts of the Cape Provinces. The mineral wealth is enormous; of this **gold** represents considerably more than half, and constitutes over 50 percent of the world's production. Ranking second to the gold mines, as regards the monetary value of their output, are the **diamond** mines Coal is mined in the Transvaal and the Orange Free State. Among the metals of secondary importance are **copper** and **tin,** asbestos, silver and platinum. As regards manufactures, the products include biscuits, jams and preserves beer, cement, soap, candles, matches, furniture leather, boots, shoes, explosives, chemicals **tobacco,** and vehicles.

Communications. There are 13,244 mile

of government owned railroads, and about 410 miles of privately owned railroads. Road mileage totals about 80,000.

Principal Towns. Johannesburg, the center of the densely populated gold mining region; Capetown, the chief port of South Africa and joint capital; Durban, second port and principal port for Johannesburg; Pretoria, the capital; Port Elizabeth, and East London.

UNION OF SOVIET SOCIALIST REPUBLICS

The Country. The U.S.S.R. is a federation of sixteen Union Republics: the Russian Soviet Federated Socialist Republic (which includes over half of the area and of the population of the Soviet Union); the Ukrainian Soviet Socialist Republic; the White Russian S.S.R.; the Armenian S.S.R.; the Georgian S.S.R., the Azerbaidzhan S.S.R.; the Uzbek S.S.R.; the Turkmen S.S.R.; the Tadzhik S.S.R.; the Kazakh S.S.R.; the Kirghiz S.S.R.; the Karelo-Finnish S.S.R.; the Moldavian S.S.R.; the Lithuanian S.S.R.; the Latvian S.S.R.; and the Estonian S.S.R. In addition to these republics there are autonomous republics within certain of the Union Republics. Most of these are in the Russian S.F.S.R. The total area of the Soviet Union in 1945 after the territorial acquisitions of 1939-1945 was about 8,548,000 square miles; the population was about 193,000,000.

In its large area the U.S.S.R. has vast plains, high mountain ranges, and great rivers. A distinctive feature is the steppes, which are broad rolling plains of sandy formation. The European portion of the Soviet Union may be considered as a series of low tablelands, gradually sloping to the Baltic, Black, and Caspian Seas, and northward to the Arctic Ocean. For nearly 200 miles north of the Caspian Sea, the land is below sea level. The greatest of the rivers, the Volga, rises in the central tablelands, and flows in an easterly direction to Kazan and thence south to the Caspian, receiving the Kama group of tributaries from the Urals. The Don and the Dnepr flow to the Black Sea, the Dvina to the Baltic, and the Volkhov to Lake Ladoga, which drains by the Neva to the Gulf of Finland.

Government. The highest legislative power is exercised by the Supreme Council of the U.S.S.R. It consists of two chambers, the Council of the Union and the Council of Nationalities, each elected for a term of four years. Each deputy of the Council of the Union is elected by the citizens for every 300,000 of the population; the deputies of the Council of Nationalities are also elected, twenty-five for each Union Republic, eleven from each autonomous republic, five from each autonomous region and one from each national area. The highest executive and administrative body in the state is the Council of Ministers of the U.S.S.R. The highest judicial body is the Supreme Court of the U.S.S.R. The franchise is extended to all citizens over twenty-one years of age who are engaged in productive labor. Employers of labor for profit (except farmers), and persons deprived of civil rights, may not vote. The Union Republics and the autonomous republics are governed by their own Supreme Council and Council of Ministers; the autonomous regions and areas are governed by local executive committees. Since 1944, each of the Constituent Republics of the Union may have separate Ministeries for Defense and for Foreign Affairs.

Commerce and Industry. The Soviet Union, formerly predominantly agricultural, is developing a planned industrial-agricultural state. The organization of industry is based on state ownership and control, and is administered by state trusts and combines. As the area controlled by the Soviet Union possesses every form of climate except the actual tropical, and includes all variations of topography, almost every natural resource is present. **Coal, iron,** copper, manganese, gold, silver, zinc, graphite, and lead are all profitably worked; and in **petroleum** production, the country ranks second to the United States. The steel industry has been widely expanded. The forest resources are immense, those of the Caucasus alone being capable of furnishing the markets of the world with an inexhaustible supply of valuable timber. All the cereals are grown and most fruits except tropical varieties, also a form of wild rubber plant. The river fisheries are of considerable importance. Chief *imports* are metals, machinery, electrical and engineering products, foodstuffs, and textiles; chief *exports* are **petroleum products,** grain, lumber, textiles, and furs. The foreign trade of the U.S.S.R. is organized as a state monopoly.

Communications. Railroads total some 59,000 miles. Inland waterways total 68,000 navigable miles. Highway mileage is about 220,000.

Principal Cities. Moskva (Moscow), the capital; Leningrad; Kiev; Kharkov; Baku, the center of the Caucasian oil fields;Gor'kiy(formerly Nizhni Novgorod), center of manufacture of automotive parts; Odessa, great seaport on the Black Sea; Tashkent; Tbilisi; Rostov-on-Don; Dnepropetrovsk; Stalino; Stalingrad and Kaliningrad. In addition to the above, there are 69 cities with populations of more than 100,000, including the new ice-free port of Murmansk, and new industrial centers such as Magnitogorsk, which have been developed in the last decade.

UNITED STATES OF AMERICA

The Country. Area of the continental United States is 3,026,789 square miles, and population is about 131,000,000. Length from north to south is 1,598 miles, width from east to west about 3,000 miles, coast line 21,354 miles. Mountains and highlands cover the eastern and western coastal areas; the Rocky Mountains in the west and the Appalachians in the east. Short slopes and coastal plains drained eastward by the Hudson, Delaware, Susquehanna, Potomac and other rivers, and westward by the Columbia, and Colorado, extend from the mountains to the seaboards. Between the mountain systems is the great central valley of the Ohio-Missouri-Mississippi river system. Waterfalls, chief of which is Niagara, are found in many parts of the country. The climate varies in different regions owing to the size of the country. Its northern regions are in a zone where winters are severe; its southern extremities lie near the tropics. But for the most part the country is temperate, though the summers are much hotter and the winters are much colder than in western Europe. The prevailing winds of the northwest are from the Pacific Ocean; they give the western coast a mild and fairly uniform climate. In Florida and Texas, there are regions where tropical vegetation flourishes; in California and the states along the Gulf of Mexico and the Atlantic, as far north as Virginia, sub-tropical plants are found.

Government. The country, a federal republic of forty-eight sovereign states, is bound together by the Constitution, adopted in 1787, and put in effect in 1789. The Federal Government, from its seat at Washington, D. C., deals with only such matters as the states have delegated to it, and each state retains complete authority over all enumerated categories. The government looks after foreign relations, the Army and Navy, and the administration of dependencies, and controls interstate commerce, customs, the post office, currency, bankruptcy, patents, and copyrights. The ordinary civil and criminal law are state matters; but income tax, suits between residents of different states, and the majority of banks and interstate carriers are controlled by Washington. The President and Vice President are elected every four years. The Vice President presides over the Senate, and in case the President dies, fills out his term. The President is commander-in-chief of the Army and Navy, and until it comes to treaty making, is supreme in foreign affairs. He can, within ten days of its passage, veto any bill. The Senate representing the states as sovereign entities, has two members from each state, regardless of its population; the House has state delegations proportionate to their population. Senators hold office for six years and, as one-third retire every second year, the life of the Senate is never interrupted, and is periodically renewed. Representatives are elected for two years, a general election being held every presidential year, and again two years later.

Commerce and Industry. The country is rich in natural mineral wealth, and leads the world in its output of **coal, iron, oil,** and silver. The deposits of gold, mercury, lead, and copper are also extensive. In the west and northeast are dense forests of pine, spruce, birch, and maple; in the southeast, cedar, pine, and valuable hardwoods; in the east central part, oak, maple, hickory, and elm. The great agricultural region, raising about 13% of the **wheat** and over 35% of the **corn** crops of the world, is in the northern and central part of the Mississippi Valley. Forty per cent of the **cotton** supply of the world, and one-third of the tobacco crop, together with corn, rice, and tropical fruits, grown in the south; grains, vegetables, and fruits (including grapes), are cultivated extensively in California. The raising of cattle, sheep, hogs, and poultry, is an important industry, yielding an immense product for *export*. Some of the foremost American industries are meat packing, fruit and vegetable canning, automobiles, petroleum refining, steel and iron production, electrical apparatus, textiles and clothing, paper, locomotives, shoes, and motion pictures.

Communications. Total railroad mileage is about 241,000. American shipping, excluding about 1,500,000 tons of canal boats and barges, totals more than 15,000,000 tons. The New York Barge Canal from Buffalo on Lake Erie to Troy on the Hudson River is 352 miles long, to

which its Oswego and Cayuga-Seneca tributaries add another 100 miles. The Great Lakes are connected with each other, and by canals, with the Atlantic Ocean, St. Lawrence and Mississippi Rivers. Nearly a million miles of highways are reported, of which half have been improved.

Principal Cities. New York, Chicago, Philadelphia, Detroit, Los Angeles, Cleveland, Baltimore, St. Louis, Boston, Pittsburgh, Washington, the nation's capital; San Francisco, Milwaukee, Buffalo, New Orleans, and Minneapolis.

Dependencies. The total area of dependencies and non-contiguous territories of the United States is 713,459 square miles, divided as follows: on the continent of North America, *Alaska*, with an area of 586,400 square miles, forms a territory of the United States, governed jointly by Congress at Washington and the local legislative assembly, consisting of 8 senators and 16 representatives. The seat of government and the largest city is Juneau. Other dependencies in America are the *Panama Canal Zone*, with an area of 554 square miles including the canal between the Atlantic and Pacific Oceans; the *Virgin Islands* (formerly Danish West Indies), with an area of 133 square miles, capital, Charlotte Amalie; and the island of *Puerto Rico*, with an area of 3,435 square miles, capital, San Juan.

In the Pacific Ocean are the island of *Guam*, area 206 square miles; *Hawaiian Islands*, including *Midway*, 6,406 square miles, capital, Honolulu; and *American Samoa*, 75 square miles; also *Wake, Baker, Jarvis,* and *Howland*.

Trust Territory of the Pacific Islands include the *Caroline Islands*, 525 square miles; the *Mariana Islands*, 247 square miles; the *Marshall Islands*, 74 square miles; and the *Palau Islands*, 175 square miles. In addition, the U.S. holds jointly with Britain a number of other Pacific islands among which are the islands of *Canton, Enderbury* and *Christmas*.

URUGUAY

The Country. Uruguay, the smallest South American republic, has an area of 72,153 square miles. It is bounded on the north by Brazil, on the west and south by Argentina, and on the east by the Atlantic Ocean. The entire country consists of rolling, grassy plains, occasionally broken by low mountain ranges, and copiously watered by numerous streams. Population, 2,220,000.

Government. On March 31, 1933, the president effected a coup d'état, upsetting the government existing under the terms of the Constitution of 1919, and a new constitution was drawn up. A plebiscite held in April, 1934, approved the new constitution providing for a senate of 30 members elected by universal and compulsory franchise, and a lower house of 99 elected by the provinces on the basis of population. The president is elected by both houses and has a council of nine ministers.

Commerce and Industry. Sheep and cattle raising are the principal industry. Agriculture is also practiced to a considerable extent, nearly all cereals being grown. Wine is produced in considerable quantities, and tobacco and olives are cultivated. In the northern departments, gold mines are worked. Silver, copper, lead, manganese, and lignite are found. The *exports* consist almost entirely of **animal products.**

Communications. The railroads all converge on Montevideo, and have a total length of 1,527 miles. Two lines connect with the Brazilian system, and there is an international train through to São Paulo. There are both shipping and air services between Montevideo and Buenos Aires, and Pan-American stops here on its Miami-Buenos Aires run. Most of the large ocean liners stop at Montevideo. The roads are among the best in South America and total 2,611 miles.

Principal Towns. Montevideo, the capital and chief seaport; Paysandú, seaport on the Uruguay River, with meat packing interests; Salto, also on the Uruguay, with a large trade in hides

VATICAN CITY

The smallest independent state in Europe, Vatican City consists of 108.7 acres including the Vatican Palace, St. Peter's and the grounds surrounding these buildings. The Pope is the supreme ruler over a community of about 1,000 people. He has his own secretary of state, and is represented diplomatically in most major countries. The new pope is always elected by the College of Cardinals, who also run the daily affairs of the Church after the death of the pope, and before the election of his successor. Membership in the Sacred College is limited to 70 members.

VENEZUELA

The Country. Venezuela, the northernmost country in South America, is bounded on the north by the Caribbean Sea, on the east by British Guiana, on the south by Brazil, and on the west by Colombia, and has an area of 352,143 square miles and a population of about 3,850,000. It comprises roughly the basin of the Orinoco and the district surrounding the Gulf of Maracaibo. It contains many high mountains.

Government. Legislative authority of the republic is vested in a congress of two chambers, the senate and the chamber of deputies. The former consists of 40 members, two for each state; the latter consists of 90 members. Both houses are elected for four years. The executive power is exercised by the president in conjunction with the cabinet ministers, through whom he acts. The president is elected by congress for five years, and cannot succeed himself.

Commerce and industry. **Coffee** and **cacao** are largely grown and *exported*; sugar and tobacco are important crops. Cattle raising is important. The mountains are heavily wooded and many useful trees and plants are found. **Petroleum** is a leading product, Venezuela coming next after the United States and the U.S.S.R. in production. The mines produce **gold,** silver, copper, and lead; various lakes yield the best quality of **ashpalt;** and along the coast, pearls are obtained. *Imports* are chiefly textiles, machinery, and hardware.

Communications. Venezuela has about 600 miles of railroads. There are 5,883 miles of road, of which about 3,600 miles are improved surface highways. The waterways of Venezuela form important means of communication and transportation, there being 70 navigable rivers in the country with a total navigable length of 11,000 miles, of which the Orinoco with its tributaries furnishes nearly 4,000 miles. A regular steamship service is maintained on the Orinoco, between Ciudad Bolívar and the interior, as well as points along the coast.

Principal Towns. Caracas, the capital; Maracaibo, a city with extensive export trade in coffee, cacao, and rubber, and the shipping point for much of the crude petroleum; special tank steamers of shallow draft being necessary because of the shallowness of the water over the bar at the entrance to Maracaibo Lake; Valencia, Barquisimeto, Ciudad Bolívar, on the right bank of the Orinoco, with export trade in coffee, hides, etc.; Puerto Cabello, and La Guaira, seaports.

YUGOSLAVIA

The Country. Yugoslavia, the land of the Serbs, Croats, and the Slovenes, occupies the northwest corner of the Balkan Peninsula. It consists essentially of a mountainous core, most of it over 3,000 feet in elevation, which stretches from the Dinaric Alps in the northwest to the Balkan Mountains on the Bulgarian frontier. The only valley which cuts the mountains and forms a passageway is that of the Marava River, which with that of the Vardar, leads from Beograd to Thessalonike. Beyond the Sava-Danube, as far as the northern boundary, the land is low and swampy near the rivers, with a few minor elevations. The chief concentrations of people are around Zagreb and Beograd. Following World War II, the addition of approximately 1,000,000 people and about 3,000 square miles from parts of the former Italian departments of Venezia Giulia and Zara increased Yugoslavia's population to about 15,750,000 and area to about 98,576 square miles.

Government. Yugoslavia became The Federal Peoples Republic of Yugoslavia in 1945. The Republic is composed of the six republics of Serbia, Croatia, Montenegro, Slovenia, Macedonia and Bosnia-Hercegovina and the two autonomous provinces of Voyvodina and Kosovo-Mitohiyan. Parliament, which elects the commander-in-chief for four years, consists of two chambers—the Federal Assembly and the 175-member House of the Peoples, elected for four years. The constitution enfranchised women, separated church and state, and established land reforms which fixed maximum individual holdings at ninety acres.

Commerce and Industry. Agriculture is the chief industry. Fruit, chiefly plums, and tobacco are successfully grown. **Swine** are raised in the oak and beech forests; **cattle,** sheep, and goats are also raised. Some wheat is grown, and hemp is an important crop. The considerable mineral resources include coal, iron, copper, gold, lead, zinc, and bauxite.

Communications. Yugoslavia has about 6,655 miles of railroads, mostly state operated. Total length of navigable waterways, principally the Danube and Sava, amounts to 1,282 miles. Considerable attention is being paid to highway construction. There are air services between Beograd and Zagreb and between Beograd and Skopje.

Principal Cities. Beograd (Belgrade), the capital; Zagreb, the University city; Sarajevo, former capital of Bosnia; Bitola (Monastir), trade center near the Greek frontier; Skopje (Üsküb), on the Vardar; Niš, an important railroad center; Rijeka (Fiume), seaport; and Ljubljana.

NIGHT VIEW OF THE CAPITOL

ILLUSTRATED GAZETTEER OF THE UNITED STATES AND TERRITORIES

ALABAMA

ALABAMA, one of the East South-Central States of the Union, lies between latitudes 30° 13' and 35° N., and longitudes 84° 48' and 88° 30' W. It is bounded on the N. by Tennessee; on the E. by Georgia and Florida: on the S. by Florida and the Gulf of Mexico; on the W. by Mississippi. Alabama is 336 m. in extreme length, 220 m. in width, and ranks twenty-eighth in area (51,998 sq. m., of which 719 sq. m. are water surface) among the states.

Cotton, corn, peanuts, sweet potatoes, cotton goods, coal, iron ore, lumber, naval stores and cement are this state's chief products.

History. Alabama was settled by the French in 1702. The territory north of latitude 31° was ceded to Great Britain in 1763, and to the United States in 1783; the remaining territory was ceded by Spain to the United States in 1819, in which year it was admitted to the Union. It seceded January 11, 1861, and was readmitted in July, 1868.

ARIZONA

ARIZONA, one of the Mountain States of the Union, lies between latitudes 31° 20' and

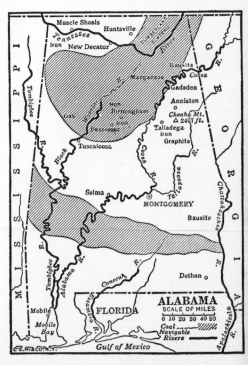

37° N., and longitudes 109° and 114° 44′ W. It is bounded on the N. by Nevada and Utah; on the E. by New Mexico; on the S. by Mexico; and on the W. by Mexico, California, and Nevada. Arizona has an extreme length from north to south of 390 m. and extreme width from east to west of 355 miles. In area, it ranks fifth among the states, having a gross area of 113,956 sq. m., of which 146 sq. m. represent water surface.

Arizona's chief industries are copper, gold and silver mining; the smelting and refining of copper; stock raising; and intensive fruit, vegetable, hay, alfalfa and wheat raising by means of extensive irrigation systems.

History. Pueblo ruins and aboriginal remains are found in the river basins of Arizona, notably in those of the Colorado, Little Colorado, and Gila. Arizona was explored by Spaniards from Mexico in the 16th Century. Jesuit and Franciscan missionaries labored among the Indians from the days of the early explorers until about 1820, when they finally abandoned the country because of Indian wars, and there was little attempt on the part of the Spaniards to settle the

In 1861, Arizona was occupied by a Texan force and joined the Confederacy. In 1862, the Texans were driven out. In 1863, Congress organized Arizona as a territory, with the meridian of 109° W. longitude as its eastern boundary. It was admitted as a state on February 14, 1912.

COURTESY, CHAMBER OF COMMERCE, PHOENIX

Giant Sahuaro Cacti, Arizona.

country for the same reason. American traders and explorers began to visit Arizona about 1820. As a result of the Mexican War, New Mexico, which then included all of Arizona north of the Gila, was ceded to the United States. The strip of territory known as the Gadsden Purchase was added to New Mexico in 1854. The progress of American settlement was slow and the removal of troops during the Civil War, led to the outbreak of Indian hostilities and prolonged wars.

ARKANSAS

ARKANSAS, a West South-Central State of the Union, lies between latitudes 33° and 36° 30′ N., and longitudes 89° 40′ and 94° 40′ W. It is bounded on the N. by Missouri; on the E. by Tennessee and Mississippi, from which it is separated by the Mississippi River; on the S. by Louisiana; and on the W. by Texas and Oklahoma. In gross area, Arkansas ranks twenty-sixth among states (53,335 sq. m., of which 810 sq. m. are water surface).

Agriculture is by far the leading industry, with cotton the chief crop among many; followed by lumber and timber products, cotton seed products; oil, gas, bauxite and coal extraction.

History. The first settlement of Europeans in what is now Arkansas was made by the French (1686) at Arkansas Post, important as a trading post in the earlier days of the American occupation, and the first territorial capital, 1819-20. In 1717, a grant on the Arkansas was made to John Law as a part of what turned out to be the "Mississippi Bubble"; in 1763, the territory

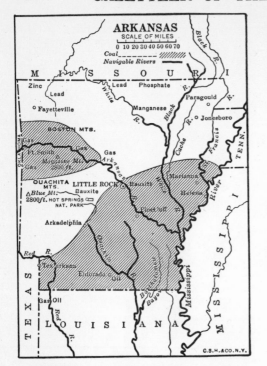

42° N., and longitudes 114° 10′ and 124° W. It
is bounded on the N. by Oregon; on the E. by
Nevada and Arizona; on the S. by Mexico; and
on the W. by the Pacific Ocean. It ranks second
in size among the states, with a gross area of
158,297 sq. m., of which 2,645 sq. m. represent
water surface.

California's chief industries are the production of motion pictures; extraction of petroleum
and gas; mining of gold and silver; forestry,
fishing and their products; and unusually diversified agriculture—specializing in fruits.

History. California was formerly a part of
Mexico, and the Franciscan Fathers made several settlements here between 1769 and 1776.
In 1846, during the war between the United
States and Mexico, it was occupied by the
former country and annexed by it in 1848. The
gold discoveries later in 1848, caused a rush of
immigrants to the territory, which in 1850 was
admitted to the Union. The prosperity of the
state was greatly stimulated by the opening of
the Union Pacific Railway in 1869. In April,
1906, a disastrous earthquake and the resultant
fires destroyed a great part of San Francisco and
injured many other towns. Visitors to the
Panama-Pacific Exposition, held in San Francisco in 1915, found a new and more beautiful
city built upon the ruins of the old town.

passed to Spain; in 1800, it reverted to France,
and formed a part of the French Colony of
Louisiana which was purchased by the United
States in 1803. It was organized as a territory
in 1819, became a state in 1836, seceded in 1861,
and was readmitted in 1868.

CALIFORNIA

CALIFORNIA, one of the Pacific Coast States
of the Union. lies between latitudes 32° 28′ and

COLORADO

COLORADO, a Mountain State of the United
States, lies between latitudes 37° and 41° N.,
and longitudes 102° and 109° W. It is bounded
on the N. by Wyoming and Nebraska; on the E.
by Nebraska and Kansas; on the S. by Oklahoma and New Mexico; and on the W. by Utah.
Colorado has an extreme length from east to

The Will Rogers' Memorial, Colorado Springs,
Colorado.

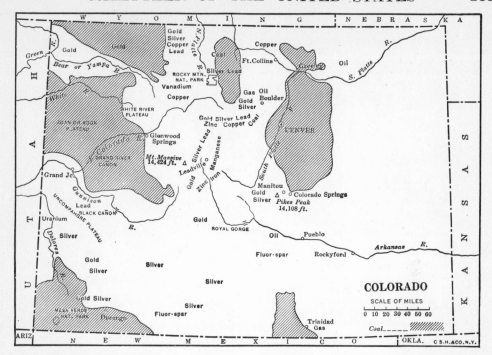

COLORADO

SCALE OF MILES

0 10 20 30 40 50 60

C.S.H.&CO.N.Y.

west of 390 m., and an extreme width from north to south of 270 m. In gross area, it ranks seventh among the states (103,948 sq. m., of which 290 sq. m. represent water surface).

Despite the great production of molybdenum, gold, silver and coal, agriculture, through extensive irrigation, has become the leading industry (sugar beets leading) and live stock raising next.

History. Within Colorado are pueblos and cave dwellings which are survivals of the Indian period and culture of the southwest. Coronado may have entered Colorado in 1540. There are records of Spanish exploration in the south in the latter half of the 18th century. In 1806, while exploring for the Federal government, Zebulon M. Pike discovered the famous peak

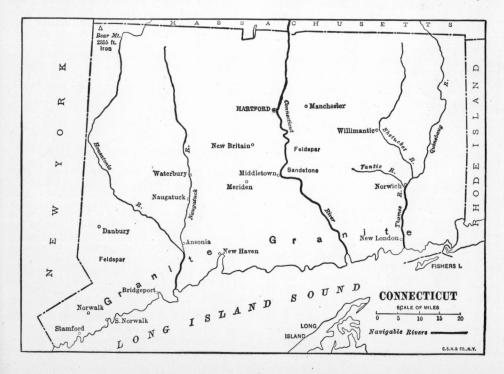

CONNECTICUT

SCALE OF MILES

0 5 10 15 20

Navigable Rivers ———

C.S.H.& CO., N.Y.

that bears his name. From 1804 to 1854, the whole or parts of Colorado were included nominally under some half dozen territories carved successively out of the trans-Mississippi country. It was practically an unknown region when, in 1858, gold was discovered on the tributaries of the South Platte near Denver. During 1860, '61 and '62, it received a continuous stream of immigration. The territory was organized in 1861, and was admitted as a state in 1876.

CONNECTICUT

CONNECTICUT, one of the New England States, and one of the original thirteen states of the Union, lies between latitudes of 40° 54' and 42° 3' N., and longitudes 71° 47' and 73° 43' W. It is bounded on the N. by Massachusetts; on the E. by Rhode Island; on the S. by Long Island Sound; and on the W. by New York. Connecticut ranks forty-sixth in area (4,965 sq. m. of which 145 sq. m. is water surface) among the states.

This is primarily a manufacturing state, specializing in iron and steel and nonferrous metal products, machinery, textiles, and fur-felt hats. Tobacco, dairy products, poultry and fisheries are valuable—but secondary to wholesale and retail trade, finance and insurance.

History. The first settlement in Connecticut was made by English colonists on the site of Hartford in 1633. Trading and exploring parties from Massachusetts soon opened the way for the immigration into the Connecticut Valley of Puritan colonists from Dorchester, Watertown, and New Town (now Cambridge). This colony may be said to date from the secession in 1634 of the more democratic element from Massachusetts. Its constitution of 1639 was "the first written democratic constitution on record." The Royal Charter of 1662, mainly a confirmation of the older one, was superseded only in 1818 when the present state constitution was framed and adopted. Prominent events in Connecticut history were the bloody war with the Pequot Indians, 1637; the governorship of Sir Edmond Andros (during a part of which, 1687-88, the colonial charter was in abeyance), and the abolition of slavery in 1818.

DELAWARE

DELAWARE, one of the South Atlantic States and one of the original thirteen states of the Union, lies between latitudes 38° 27' and 39° 50' N., and longitudes 75° 2' and 75° 47' W. It is bounded on the N. by Pennsylvania; on the E. by the Delaware River and Delaware Bay, which separate it from New Jersey, and by the Atlantic Ocean; and on the S. and W. by Maryland. Next to Rhode Island, it is the smallest state, its area being 2,370 sq. m., of which 405 sq. m. represent water surface.

Delaware's leading industries are concerned with the fisheries (notably oysters); fruit growing (notably peaches); cereals; diversified chemical products; ships; leather goods; paper and textiles.

DELAWARE
SCALE OF MILES
0 5 10 15 20
Canals
Navigable Rivers

History. Delaware River and Bay were explored by Henry Hudson in 1609. As a result of that voyage, the territory was claimed by the Dutch who planted a settlement near the present town of Lewes in 1631. The Dutch settlement was soon destroyed by the Indians, and the first permanent white settlements were made by Swedes and Finns in 1638; Dutch and Swedes contended for this region until 1655 when it passed under Dutch sway. After the transfer of New Netherland (New York) to the English in 1664, Delaware became English also. Though a slave state until the Civil War, Delaware took no part in the secession movement.

DISTRICT OF COLUMBIA

DISTRICT OF COLUMBIA, the Federal District which contains the national capital of the United States. It lies on the eastern bank of the Potomac, at the head of tide and navigation, in latitude 38° 53' 25" N., and longitude 77° 00' 34" W. Area, 70 sq. m., of which 8 sq. m. represent water surface. It contains, besides Washington with Georgetown, several small villages. The District is administered by the Federal Government through three commissioners who are appointed by the President and confirmed by the Senate.

History. It was originally formed of cessions of territory made by Maryland in 1788 and Virginia in 1789, comprising 100 sq. miles. It was organized in 1790-1791 and the seat of government was removed thither in 1800. The Virginia portion of the district was retroceded in 1846. Territorial government was established in 1871; a provisional government followed in 1874; the present form was established in 1878.

FLORIDA

FLORIDA, the most southern of the South Atlantic States of the U.S.A., lies between latitudes 24° 30′ and 31° N., and longitudes 79° 48′ and 87° 38′ W. It is bounded on the N. by Georgia and Alabama; on the E. by the Atlantic Ocean; on the S. by Florida Strait, and the Gulf of Mexico; and on the W. by the Gulf of Mexico and Alabama. Florida ranks twenty-first in area (58,666 sq. m., of which 3,805 sq. m. are water) among the states.

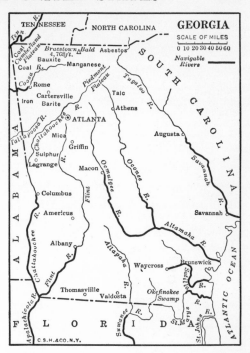

Florida's leading industries are citrus fruits, vegetables, swine and graded cattle; lumber and naval stores; a valuable fish catch, and phosphate rock. The state is famous for its winter resorts.

History. Florida was discovered by Ponce de Leon in 1513, settled by Huguenots in 1562, and permanently settled by Spaniards in St. Augustine in 1565. It was ceded to Great Britain in 1763 and to Spain in 1783. In 1818, General Jackson invaded Florida, attacked the Seminoles, and captured Pensacola which was then restored to Spain. It was ceded to the U.S.A. in 1819. The state was admitted to the Union in 1845; seceded in 1861; was readmitted in 1868.

GEORGIA

GEORGIA, one of the South Atlantic States and one of the original thirteen states of the Union, lies between latitudes 30° 25′ and 35° N., and longitudes 80° 48′ and 85° 54′ W. It is bounded on the N. by Tennessee and North Carolina; on the E. by South Carolina and the Atlantic Ocean; on the S. by Florida, and on the W. by Alabama. Georgia ranks twentieth in area (59,265 sq. m., of which 540 sq. m. represent water surface) among the states.

Georgia's leading products are cotton, tobacco, peaches, sugar cane syrup, sweet potatoes, peanuts, soybeans; swine and cattle; lumber and naval stores; textiles, and raw clay products.

History. Georgia, named in honor of George the Second, was settled by a chartered company of English colonists under Oglethorpe in 1733, as a refuge for poor whites and persons seeking religious freedom. Georgia became a Royal Province in 1763, and was the fourth state to ratify the Federal Constitution (January 2, 1788). It seceded in January, 1861, and was readmitted to the Union in 1870. It has experienced a rapid industrial growth.

Cotton Picking in Georgia.

PHOTO BY ACKERMAN, COURTESY U S. D. A.

IDAHO

IDAHO, one of the Mountain States of the Union, lies between latitudes 42° and 49° N., and longitudes 111° and 117° W. It is bounded on the N. by British Columbia and Montana, on the E. by Montana and Wyoming, on the S. by Utah and Nevada, and on the W. by Oregon and Washington. The state has an extreme length of 490 m., and an extreme width of 305 miles. In gross area, it ranks twelfth among the states (83,888 sq. m., of which 534 sq. m. represent water surface).

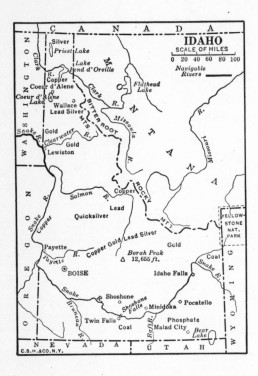

Idaho's chief industries are silver, lead, zinc and antimony ore mining; sheep raising and wool; forest products; irrigation raised hay, grains, potatoes, sugar beets, fruits, and high grade garden seeds.

History. The first recorded exploration of Idaho was made by Lewis and Clark in 1805. In 1810, Ft. Henry on the Snake River was established by the Missouri Fur Company. In 1834, Ft. Hall in east Idaho was founded. Missions for the Indians were established by both Catholics and Protestants about the same time. The territory now constituting Idaho was comprised in the territory of Oregon from 1848-53; from 1854-59, the southern portion of the present state was a part of Oregon, and the northern portion, a part of Washington Territory; from 1859-63, the territory was within the bounds of Washington Territory. Idaho was organized as a territory on March 3rd, 1863, but at that time included both Montana and Wyoming. In May, 1864, a part was set aside as Montana and in 1868, Wyoming was organized,

and Idaho assumed its present boundaries. Gold was discovered in 1860, and the population of the territory rapidly increased. From 1857 to 1877 there were many serious Indian outbreaks. Later there were frequent conflicts among the miners. Idaho became a state in 1890.

ILLINOIS

ILLINOIS, an East North-Central State of the Union, lies between latitude 36° 59′ and 42° 30′ N., and longitudes 87° 30′ and 91° 38′ W. It is bounded on the N. by Iowa and Wisconsin; on the E. by Lake Michigan, Indiana, and Kentucky; on the S. by Kentucky and Missouri; and on the W. by Missouri and Iowa. The state has a total area of 56,665 sq. m., of which 622 sq. m. represent water surface. It ranks twenty-third in size among the states.

Illinois' chief industries are machinery, iron and steel, nonferrous metals, food products, printing, apparel, furniture and fixtures, field crops, livestock, petroleum and coal production.

History. The first Europeans to explore the country were French traders and missionaries. In 1675 Father Marquette founded a mission at the Indian town of Kaskaskia near the present Utica. In 1679 La Salle built Creve Coeur, a fort, not far from Lake Peoria. After 1682 the French made a number of permanent settlements which had originated in missions, or in trading posts. By the Treaty of Paris of 1763, France ceded to Great Britain her claims to the country between the Ohio and Mississippi Rivers. Owing to Indian resistance, the English were unable to take possession until 1765. The

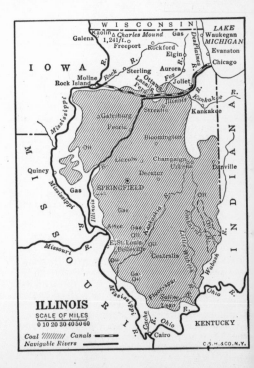

Northwest Territory, of which Illinois was a part, was secured to the United States by the Treaty of Paris of 1783. Illinois was a part of Indiana Territory in 1800; was made a separate territory in 1809; and became a state in 1818. Black Hawk's War occurred in 1832, and the Mormon troubles culminated in 1844. Slavery existed in the state until 1848. Illinois bore a notable part in the Civil War.

Chicago Stockyards, Illinois.

INDIANA

INDIANA, one of the East North-Central States of the Union, lies between latitudes 37° 45' and 41° 46' N., and longitudes 84° 40' and 88° 2' W. It is bounded on the N. by Lake Michigan and Michigan; on the E. by Ohio and Kentucky; on the S. by Kentucky; and on the W. by Illinois. The state has an extreme length from N. to S. of 276 m., and an average width of 140 miles. In area (36,354 sq. m., of which 309 sq. m. are water surface), it ranks thirty-seventh among the states.

Indiana's chief industries are auto equipment, iron and steel, machinery, furniture, glass, soft coal, livestock, dairy products, field crops and canneries.

History. Extensive remains (mounds and fortifications) of the prehistoric inhabitants of Indiana are numerous in Knox and Sullivan Counties. The first Europeans to enter the state found it occupied chiefly by the tribes of the Miami Confederacy, a league of Algonquin Indians formed to oppose the advance of the Iroquois. La Salle undoubtedly passed through Indiana during his journeys of 1669 and succeeding years. Vincennes, founded in 1731, was the first permanent white settlement; no other

was made until after the War of Independence. Indiana was a part of the Northwest Territory which passed under the control of the United States in 1779, and an American settlement was made at Clarksville in 1784. The Northwest Territory was governed under the Ordinance of 1787. Indiana assumed its present limits in 1809 when it was organized as a territory. Indian wars were frequent. In 1810 began the last great Indian war in Indiana, which ended in November, 1811, with the battle of Tippecanoe when Gen. Harrison defeated the confederated Indians under Tecumseh. The territory was admitted to statehood in 1816. Slavery existed until 1830. Indiana took the Union side in the Civil War.

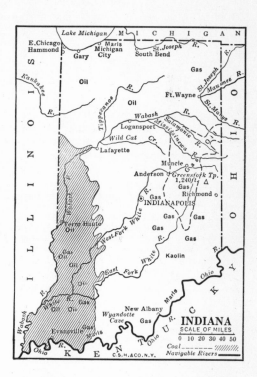

IOWA

IOWA, a West North-Central State of the United States, is situated between latitudes 40° 24' and 43° 30' N., and longitudes 90° 10' and 96° 37' W. The state is bounded on the N. by Minnesota and Wisconsin; on the E. by Wisconsin and Illinois, from which states it is separated by the Mississippi River; on the S. by Missouri; and on the W. by Nebraska and South Dakota. Iowa has a gross area of 56,147 sq. m., of which 561 sq. m. represent water surface. It ranks twenty-fourth in size among the states.

Iowa's chief products are corn and many other crops; livestock and dairy products; cement, coal, stone and clay. Food processing and making farm equipment are important industries.

History. The first white men to visit Iowa were the Frenchmen, Marquette and Joliet, in

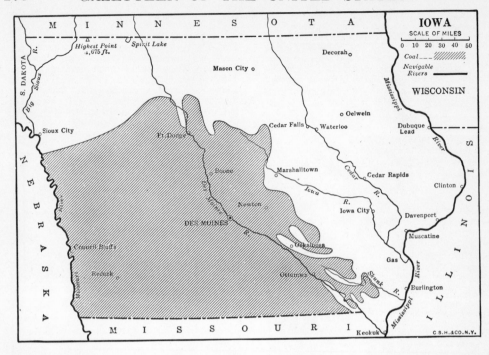

1673, and Hennepin in 1680. They found the country occupied by a tribe of Sioux Indians from which came the name of the state, "Iowa." With the Louisiana Purchase, 1803, the territory became the property of the United States. From 1804-05, as part of the District of Louisiana, it was under the government of Indiana Territory; from 1805-12, it was part of Louisiana Territory; from 1812-21, part of Missouri Territory; from 1821-34, part of the unorganized territory of the United States; from 1834-36, part of Michigan Territory; and from 1836-38, part of Wisconsin Territory. In 1838, the western portion of Wisconsin Territory was named "Iowa" and out of this, the state, with its present boundaries, was carved in 1846.

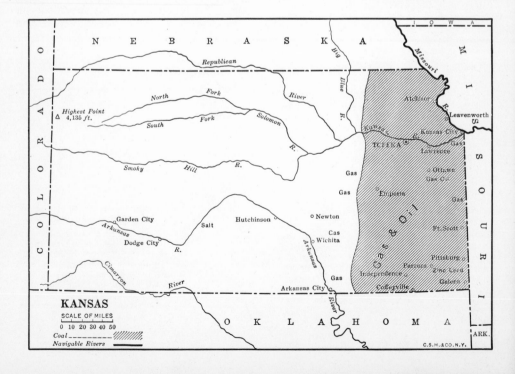

KANSAS

KANSAS, a West North-Central State of the United States, lies between latitudes 37° and 40° N., and longitudes 94° 35′ and 102° 1′ 40″ W. It is bounded on the N. by Nebraska; on the E. by Missouri; on the S. by Oklahoma; and on the W. by Colorado. The state has a breadth from N. to S. of about 200 m., and a length from E. to W. of slightly over 400 m. In gross area, it ranks thirteenth among the states (82,158 sq. m., of which 384 sq. m. represent water surface).

Kansas is a leading state in wheat, cattle, swine raising and flour milling. Other products are corn, oats, potatoes, fruits, dairy products; petroleum, gas, zinc, cement, coal and salt.

History. Kansas was a part of the Louisiana Purchase (1803), and was colonized by both free and slave state settlers. It was made a territory in 1854, and at once became the battleground between the partisans of slavery and freedom. A bloody civil war broke out, in which many almost-battles took place. One of the most ardent of the anti-slavery partisans was John Brown. The Topeka Constitution, prohibiting slavery, was framed in 1855 and the Lecompton Constitution, sanctioning slavery, in 1857. The Wyandotte Constitution, forbidding slavery, was adopted in 1859, and Kansas was admitted as a free state in 1861. It took a prominent part in the Civil War.

KENTUCKY

KENTUCKY, one of the East South-Central States of the Union, lies between latitudes 36° 30′ and 39° 12′ N., and longitudes 81° 55′ and 89° 31′ W. It is bounded on the N., NW., and NE. by Illinois, Indiana, and Ohio; on the E. by West Virginia and Virginia; on the SE. and S. by Virginia and Tennessee; and on the W.

Where "Kentucky Thoroughbreds" are raised.

by Missouri and Illinois. The state has an extreme length from E. to W. of about 400 m., and a width from N. to S. of 175 m. In area, Kentucky ranks thirty-sixth among the states (40,598 sq. m., of which 417 sq. m. are water surface).

Its chief industries are coal mining; agriculture, forest products and furniture; food processing, tobacco, cotton and hemp manufactures; and gas, petroleum, stone and fluorspar extraction. Kentucky's horses are famous.

History. Numerous historic remains indicate that the mound-builders once lived in this territory. The name Kentucky, meaning "dark and bloody ground," commemorates the conflicts

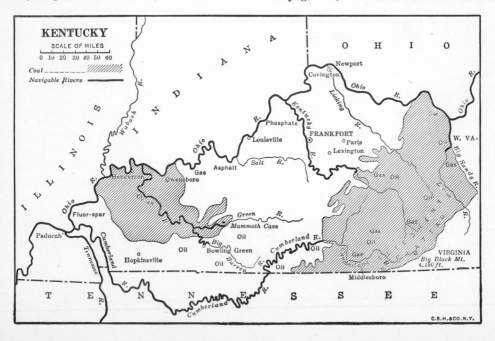

between various tribes of Indians. Kentucky was explored by Dr. Thomas Walker in 1750, by John Finley in 1767, and by Daniel Boone in 1769; was settled at Harrodsburg in 1774; was formed into a county of Virginia in 1776; was admitted to the Union in 1792; was distinguished in the War of 1812 and in the Mexican War; was a slave state, but did not secede; was occupied by Federals and Confederates in 1861; was the scene of campaigns and raids.

LOUISIANA

LOUISIANA, a West South-Central State of the Union, lies between latitudes 29° and 33° N., and longitudes 89° and 94.5° W. It is bounded on the N. by Arkansas and Mississippi; on the E. by Mississippi and the Gulf of Mexico; on the S. by the Gulf of Mexico; and on the W. by Texas. The state extends from north to south about 280 m., and from east to west about 290 m. In gross area (48,506 sq. m., of which 3,097 sq. m. are water surface), it ranks as thirtieth among the states of the Union.

The chief products are furs, shrimps, rice, sugar cane, corn, cotton, vegetables, fruit, pecans, livestock, petroleum, gas, sulfur, salt; forest and sawmill products.

History. Louisiana was explored by De Soto in 1541, and by La Salle in 1682; was settled by the French under Iberville and Bienville about 1700. The latter founded the city of New Orleans on its present site in 1718. In 1717, Louisiana was granted to a company, of which John Law was the head, but in 1731, reverted to the crown; was ceded by France to Spain in 1763, but in 1800 became French territory. It was repurchased by the United States in 1803 and

was created the Territory of Orleans in 1804; had the portion east of the Mississippi annexed in 1810; was admitted to the Union in 1812; seceded in January, 1861; was largely occupied by the Federals 1862–63; and was readmitted in June, 1868.

MAINE

MAINE, the most northeasterly state of the Union, and one of the New England group, lies between latitudes 43° 4' and 47° 27' 34" N., and longitudes 66° 56' 48" and 71° 6' 41" W. It is bounded on the NW. by the province of Quebec; on the N. and E. by New Brunswick, from which it is separated in part by the St. John River, the Grand or Schoodic Lakes, the St. Croix River, and Passamaquoddy Bay; on the S. by the Atlantic Ocean; and on the W. by New Hampshire, the Piscataqua and Salmon Falls Rivers forming the natural boundary lines at the southwest. The state has a total area of 33,040 sq. m., of which 3,145 sq. m. represent water surface. It is thirty-eighth in size among the states.

Maine's chief interests are forest, saw mill, paper, leather, granite, dairy, poultry and fish products, plus Aroostook potatoes. Abundant water power provides electricity for factories.

History. Maine was visited by many of the early explorers, including the Cabots, Verrazano, Gomez, Gosnold, Pring, du Guast, De Monts, and others. The first permanent settlement, at Bristol, dates from 1624. The eastern part of the state was a part of Acadia or Nova Scotia until 1691, at which time the whole region was merged in the "province of Massachusetts Bay." Maine became a separate state in 1820. A dispute with Great Britain over the northern boundary of the state was settled by

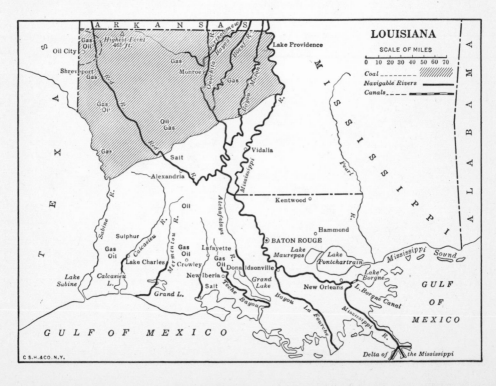

LOUISIANA

SCALE OF MILES

0 10 20 30 40 50 60 70

Coal

Navigable Rivers

Canals

GULF OF MEXICO

C S. H. & CO. N. Y.

Portland Head Light, Portland, Maine.

EWING GALLOWAY, N. Y.

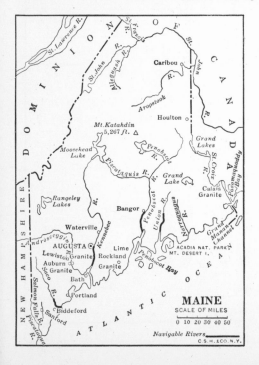

MAINE
SCALE OF MILES
0 10 20 30 40 50

Navigable Rivers

C. S. H. &CO. N. Y.

the Webster-Ashburton Treaty in 1842. The Maine liquor law, the first state law on the subject, was passed in 1851. In World War I, Maine contributed a larger proportion of men (on a population basis) than any other state.

MARYLAND

MARYLAND, one of the South Atlantic States and one of the "original thirteen" of the United States. It lies between latitudes 37° 53' and 39° 43' 36" N., and longitudes 75° 3' 45" and 79° 29' W. It is bounded on the N. by Pennsylvania; on the E. by Delaware and the Atlantic Ocean; and on the S. and SW. by Virginia, the District of Columbia, and West Virginia. It is separated from the two Virginias, except on the extreme west, by the Potomac River and its north branch. Maryland ranks forty-first in area (12,327 sq. m., of which 2,386 sq. m. represents water surface) among the states.

Maryland's chief industries are the building of transportation equipment (except autos); forestry and fishing products (especially oysters); the making of chemicals, apparel and pig iron; coal mining; dairy products, field crops and canning.

History. Maryland, through the grant made by Charles I to George Calvert, first Lord Balti-

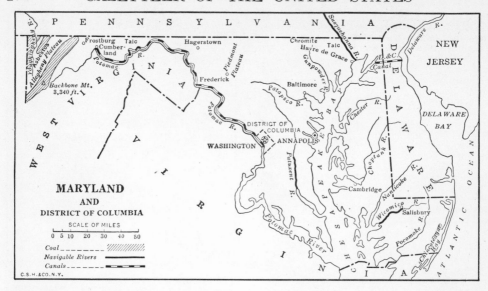

more, became a proprietary colony, and its settlement was begun at St. Mary's, in 1634. During colonial times, it was involved in the Claiborne rebellion and in boundary and other disputes. In 1649, religious toleration was enacted for all sects and churches which acknowledged a belief in the Trinity. For many years, the colony was torn by quarrels between the proprietary party and Puritan settlers. There was a time when Roman Catholics were denied the privileges which Lord Baltimore had granted to Protestants. The city of Baltimore was founded in 1729. The boundary with Pennsylvania was finally settled, 1763-69, by Charles Mason and Jeremiah Dixon, who established

by Vermont and New Hampshire; on the E. by the Atlantic Ocean; on the S. by the Atlantic Ocean, Rhode Island, and Connecticut; and on the W. by New York. It ranks forty-fourth in area (8,266 sq. m., of which 227 sq. m. represent water surface) among the states.

The leading industries of Massachusetts are leather and products, textiles, paper, non-ferrous metal products, machinery, printing and publishing, apparel, furniture and wooden goods, fisheries and products, dairy products, poultry, apples, cranberries and diversified field crops.

History. The coast of Massachusetts is supposed to have been visited by the Norsemen

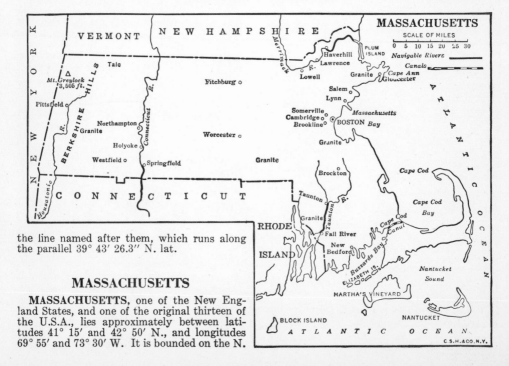

the line named after them, which runs along the parallel 39° 43′ 26.3″ N. lat.

MASSACHUSETTS

MASSACHUSETTS, one of the New England States, and one of the original thirteen of the U.S.A., lies approximately between latitudes 41° 15′ and 42° 50′ N., and longitudes 69° 55′ and 73° 30′ W. It is bounded on the N.

about 1000 A.D.; but the first permanent white settlement was made by the Pilgrim Fathers at Plymouth, on the coast north of Cape Cod, in December, 1620. This was known as the Plymouth Colony. In 1628, a company of Puritans settled at Salem, and from that beginning was formed the Massachusetts Bay Colony which included the settlements of Boston, Lynn, and other towns. In 1692, the two colonies were united.

The early history of Massachusetts is the inspiring heritage of much of America. The state was settled by men seeking liberty for their own form of religious worship and intolerant of all other forms. However, they were far ahead of their European contemporaries; gradually that bigotry diminished and religious tolerance grew; the state became a leader in all that stood for liberty. The War of Independence began in Massachusetts in 1775, with the battles of Lexington and Bunker Hill.

MICHIGAN

MICHIGAN, an East North-Central State of the Union, lies between latitudes 41° 42′ and 47° 32′ N., and longitudes 82° 25′ and 90° 32′ W. The northern peninsula is bounded on the N. by Lake Superior; on the E. by Lakes Superior, George, Huron, and Michigan, and by St. Mary's River which separates it from the Canadian province of Ontario; on the S. by Lakes Huron and Michigan and the Straits of Mackinac which separate it from the lower peninsula; on the S. and W. by Wisconsin. The lower or

Duluth, Minnesota, on Lake Superior.

southern peninsula is bounded on the N. by Lakes Michigan and Huron and the Straits of Mackinac; on the E. by Lakes Huron, St. Clair and Erie, and the St. Clair and Detroit Rivers which separate it from Ontario; on the S. by Ohio and Indiana; and on the W. by Lake Michigan. The upper peninsula is 318 by 164 m., and the lower peninsula, 227 by 177 m.; and the state has a gross area of 57,980 sq. m., of which 500 sq. m. represent water surface. In size, Michigan ranks twenty-second among the states.

Michigan's leading manufacturers are autos and equipment, furniture and store fixtures, copper and other nonferrous metal products, paper, chemicals, salt and dairy products. The chief crops are cereals, clover seed, hay, potatoes, sugar beets and fruits. The fisheries of the upper Great Lakes still yield a sizeable catch.

History. What is now the state of Michigan was probably visited by Jean Nicolet in 1634 at Sault Ste. Marie where the first permanent white settlement was made by Father Marquette in 1668. In 1701 Detroit was founded as a fur trading center by the French. The country was ceded to Great Britain in 1763; later was the scene of Pontiac's War; was surrendered to the United States in 1796; formed part of the Northwest Territory and later of Indiana Territory; and was constituted Michigan Territory in 1805. Detroit was taken by the British during the War of 1812, Michigan was recovered by the United States in 1813, and was admitted to the Union in 1837.

MINNESOTA

MINNESOTA, a West North-Central State of the Union, lies between latitudes 43° 30' and

49° 24' N., and longitudes 89° 39' and 97° 18' W. It is bounded on the N. by the Canadian provinces of Manitoba and Ontario; on the E. by Lake Superior and Wisconsin; on the S. by Iowa; and on the W. by South and North Dakota. Minnesota is about 400 m. in length and 350 m. in width. It ranks eleventh in size among the states, with a gross area of 84,682 sq. m., of which 3,824 sq. m. are water surface.

Minnesota produces over 60 per cent of the iron ore in the U.S. It produces largely of corn and wheat; has the country's biggest flour mills. Hay and oats are important to the livestock, dairy and meat packing interests. Much of the manufacturing is connected with food and kindred products. Forest products are secondary.

History. Before the coming of Europeans, Minnesota was occupied by two powerful Indian tribes, the Ojibways (or Chippewas) in the north and along the Mississippi River, and the Sioux (or Dakotas) in the south and west. The region was first explored by the French near the end of the 17th Century. That part of Minnesota which lies east of the Mississippi River belonged to the Northwest Territory, acquired by the United States in 1783. West of the Mississippi, it was a part of the Louisiana Purchase of 1803. In 1838, the Chippewa Indians surrendered the land east of the Mississippi. Immigration began: Minnesota became a territory in 1849, and a state in 1858. In 1862 occurred a terrible massacre by the Sioux Indians, finally defeated in 1864.

MISSISSIPPI

MISSISSIPPI, one of the East South-Central States of the Union, lies between latitudes 30° 44' and 35° N., and longitudes 88° 7' and 91° 37' W. It is bounded on the N. by Tennessee; on the E. by Alabama; on the S. by the Gulf of Mexico and Louisiana; and on the W. by Louisiana and Arkansas. The state has an extreme

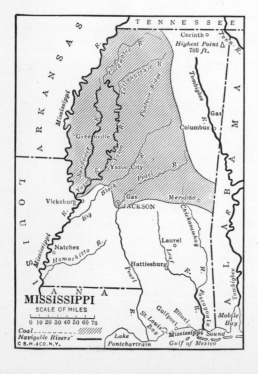

length of about 330 m. from N. to S., and an extreme width of about 180 m., and ranks thirty-first in area (46,865 sq. m., of which 503 sq. m. are water surface) among the states.

This is a great cotton growing state; corn is next in importance, then sugar cane, cane sorghum, sweet potatoes and yams. The shrimp fisheries are outstanding; lumber and timber products, cottonseed oil and cake, and cotton goods are among the valuable manufactures.

History. Mississippi was visited by De Soto in 1540. The Mississippi River was explored by Marquette and La Salle in 1681. An attempt was made at settlement by the French at Iberville in 1699, and a settlement was made on the site of Natchez in 1716. It was ceded by France to Great Britain in 1763; part was ceded to the United States in 1783; the remainder was ac-

quired in 1811. Mississippi was organized as a territory in 1798, and was admitted to the Union as a state in 1817. It seceded in 1861; was the scene of various conflicts during the Civil War; was readmitted to the Union in 1870. In the Mississippi River flood of 1927 more than $45,000,000 worth of property and crops was destroyed.

MISSOURI

MISSOURI, a West North-Central State of the United States, lies mainly between latitudes 36° 30' and 40° 35' N., and longitudes 89° 10' and 95° 48' W. Much of the western boundary is the meridian of 94° 43' W. It is bounded on the N. by Iowa; on the E. by Illinois, Kentucky, and Tennessee; on the S. by Arkansas; and on the W. by Oklahoma, Kan as, and Nebraska. The length of the state from north to south, counting the southeastern projection, is 328 m.; without the southeastern projection, it is 282 m. The width from W. to E. varies from 208 to 308 m. In size, Missouri ranks eighteenth among the states with a gross area of 69,420 sq. m., 693 sq. m. being water surface.

Its chief industries are livestock raising, meat packing; dairy and field crops farming (corn, wheat, tobacco, cotton); lead, cement and coal mining and diversified manufactures.

History. The territory included in the present state of Missouri formed part of the French colony of Louisiana. Ste. Genevieve was settled in 1735, and Ft. Orleans on the Missouri River, had been temporarily established in 1720, but few others were made before the transfer of Louisiana to Spain in 1763. St. Louis was

COURTESY, U. S. D. A.

Missouri Mule "Weanlings."

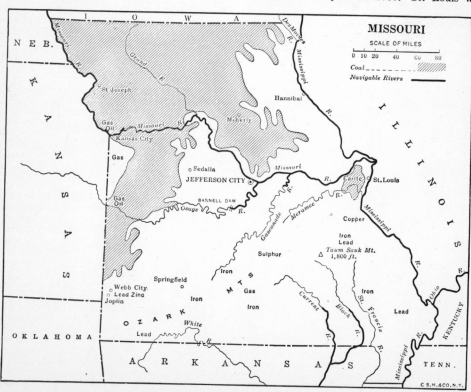

Towing Oil Barges on the Mississippi River.

founded in 1764. It was ceded back to France
in 1800; formed part of the Louisiana Purchase
of 1803; and was included in Louisiana Territory in 1805. Missouri Territory was formed in
1812, and admitted to the Union as a slave state
in 1821. The state did not receive its present limits
until 1835. In the Kansas troubles of 1855, the
citizens of the western border took an active part
against the free state movement. At the outbreak
of the Civil War in 1861, the people of Missouri
were divided with regard to secession, but the
unionists finally prevailed. A world's fair was

held in St. Louis in 1904 to commemorate the
Louisiana Purchase.

MONTANA

MONTANA, a Mountain State of the United
States, lies between latitudes 44° 26' and 49° N.,
and longitudes 104° and 116° 1' W. It is bounded
on the N. by the Canadian provinces of British
Columbia, Alberta, and Saskatchewan; on the
E. by North and South Dakota; on the S. by
Wyoming and Idaho; and on the W. by Idaho.
It has an extreme length from east to west of

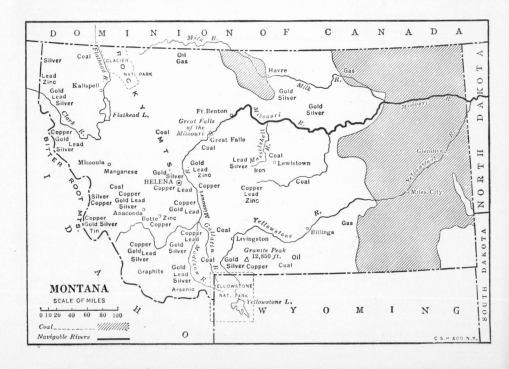

Some of the magnificent mountains, Glacier National Park, Montana.

580 m., and an extreme width from north to south of 315 m. In gross area, it ranks third among the states (146,997 sq. m., of which 866 sq. m. represent water surface).

The chief interests here are copper, gold, silver and coal mining; forest products; livestock; standard fruits, cereals and sugar beets; and "dude" ranching.

History. The portion of Montana east of the Rocky Mountains was part of the Louisiana Purchase (1803); that to the west was part of Oregon and Washington. It was first visited by the French in 1742, and by Lewis and Clark in 1804-06; these explorers were followed by fur traders, trappers and Jesuit missionaries. The part of Montana which was included in the Louisiana Purchase became successively a part of Missouri Territory (1812), of Nebraska Territory (1854), of Dakota Territory (1861), and of Idaho Territory (1863); that which lies west of the mountains became successively a part of Oregon (1848), of Washington Territory (1853),

and of Idaho Territory (1863). Gold was discovered in 1861. In 1864, the territory was organized and in 1889 Montana became a state of the Union.

NEBRASKA

NEBRASKA, one of the West North-Central States of the United States, lies between latitudes 40° and 43° N., and longitudes 95° 10′ and 104° 4′ W. It is bounded on the N. by South Dakota; on the E. by Iowa and Missouri; on the S. by Kansas and Colorado; and on the W. by Colorado and Wyoming. The extreme length of the state from E. to W. is about 425 m., and the extreme breadth from N. to S. 210 m. In gross area (77,520 sq. m., of which 712 sq. m. represent water surface) Nebraska ranks fifteenth among the states.

Nebraska has three great power and irrigation projects. Both livestock and field crops (corn, all grains, hay, sugar beets, soybeans and potatoes) flourish. Oil was discovered in 1939.

History. French explorers followed the Platte

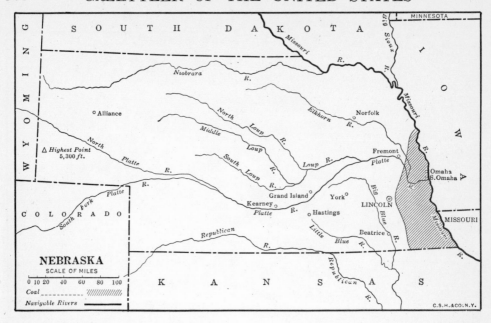

River (or the Nebraska) to the Forks, in 1739. Nebraska passed to the United States in 1803 as part of the Louisiana Purchase, and was explored by several American expeditions. Several trading posts were probably established between 1795 and 1812. In 1823 Bellevue became an Indian agency, and later was the first postoffice in the state. Nebraska was one of the two territories created by the Kansas-Nebraska Bill of 1854. Slaves were within its borders from the beginning, but a territorial law of 1861 excluded slavery. As organized in 1854, Nebraska extended from 40° N. latitude to British America, and from the Missouri and White Earth Rivers to the summit of the Rockies; it was reduced to its present boundaries in 1861 and 1863. The state was torn by bitter factional quarrels over the location of the capital and admission to statehood, and during part of 1866 and 1867, there were two *de facto* governments—the territorial and the state. It was admitted to the Union in 1867.

NEVADA

NEVADA, one of the Mountain States of the United States, lies between latitudes 35° and 42° N., and longitudes 114° 2′ and 120° W. It is bounded on the N. by Oregon and Idaho; on the E. by Utah and Arizona; and on the S. and W. by California. The state has an extreme length from N. to S. of 484 m., and an extreme width from E. to W. of 321 m. In gross area, it ranks sixth among the states (110,690 sq. m., of which 869 sq. m. represent water surface).

Nevada is one of the leading producers of silver, gold, copper and tungsten ore. Livestock, dairy products and field crops are also important.

History. Francisco Garces, a Franciscan monk, passed through the state on his way to California in 1775. Some fifty years later, American and Canadian trappers worked along the Humboldt River. Many overland immigrants, on their way to California, crossed Nevada in the early '40's. In 1843-45, Fremont made a series of explorations in this region. In 1848, by the Treaty of Guadalupe-Hidalgo which concluded the war with Mexico, Nevada became United States territory. It was known as the Washoe Country, California, until September, 1850, when most of the present state was included in the territory of Utah. The first settlement in what is now the state of Nevada was made at Genoa in the valley of the Carson River in 1849. In 1859 the discovery of the fabulous "Comstock Lode" brought thousands of people into the territory. In March, 1861, the territory of Utah was divided at 39° west of Washington, and the western portion called Nevada was admitted as a state in 1864. In 1931, the legislature passed a bill permitting divorces to those establishing a six-weeks' residence, and another bill legalizing gambling. The famous Boulder Dam was built across the Colorado River in 1936.

NEW HAMPSHIRE

NEW HAMPSHIRE, a North Atlantic State of the Union, one of the New England group, and one of the "original thirteen." It lies between latitudes 42° 40' and 45° 18' 20'' N., and longitudes 70° 37' and 72° 37' W. It is bounded on the N. by the Canadian province of Quebec; on the E. by Maine and the Atlantic Ocean; on the SE. and S. by Massachusetts; on the W. and NW. by Vermont. New Hampshire ranks forty-third in area (9,341 sq. m., of which 310 sq. m. are water surface) among the states.

Mountainous terrain and abundant water power have made this a manufacturing state. The leading industries are the making of boots and shoes, lumber and wood products, paper, cotton and woolen goods, and dairy products; granite quarrying; and poultry raising.

History. Among the early explorers who visited New Hampshire were Martin Pring (1603), Samuel de Champlain (1605), and Captain John Smith (1614). The first settlement, of which

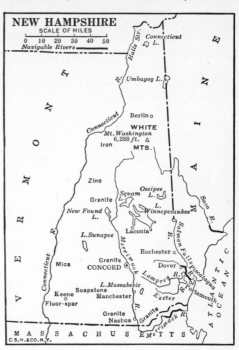

Exterior of a Silver Mine near Pioche, Nevada.

Exterior of a Silver Mine near Pioche, Nevada.

there is positive evidence, was made in 1623 by David Thomson at Little Harbor, now in the town of Rye. In 1641-79, 1689-92, and 1699-1741, New Hampshire was joined to the Massachusetts Colony; but during the intervening dates and until 1775, it was under royal governors of its own. A provisional government was formed in 1776, a state constitution adopted in 1784, and New Hampshire was the ninth state to ratify the National Constitution in 1788.

NEW JERSEY

NEW JERSEY, one of the Middle Atlantic States of the Union, lies between latitudes 38° 46' and 41° 21' N., and longitudes 73° 53' and 75° 35' W. It is bounded on the N. by the state

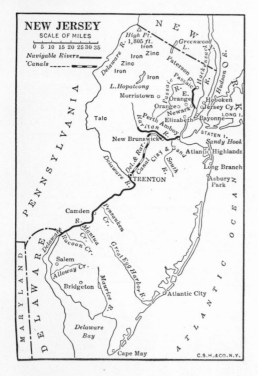

George Washington Bridge looking toward N. J.

PHOTO BY C. P. CUSHING

History. Voyages made with a view to exploration and settlement of the region now called New Jersey may be said to have begun with the voyage of Henry Hudson in 1609. The English claim to the territory was founded on the voyage of Cabot in 1498. The Dutch settled at Bergen in 1617. Soon after, some Swedes settled on the lower Delaware but were expelled by the Dutch in 1655. In 1664, New Netherland passed to the English, and the Duke of York gave the portion included in the present New Jersey to Lord Berkeley and Sir George Carteret. The latter had been administrator of the Island of Jersey, so the American province was named New Jersey. In 1676 the province was divided into West and East New Jersey, the former being under a Quaker proprietorship and the latter under Carteret. West New Jersey soon passed to William Penn who, in 1682, purchased East New Jersey also. In 1702 the government of both colonies passed to the Crown and the two were united. Until 1736, New Jersey was under the governor of New York, but had a separate assembly. New Jersey was one of the original thirteen states and was the scene of stirring events in the struggle for independence. The Morristown National Historical Park, established by Congress in 1933, commemorates some of these events.

of New York; on the E. by New York and the Atlantic Ocean; on the S. by the Atlantic Ocean and Delaware Bay; and on the W. by Delaware and Pennsylvania. It is separated from New York, in part, by the Hudson River, New York Bay, Staten Island Sound, and Raritan Bay; Delaware River and estuary form the entire western boundary. New Jersey has an extreme length, N. and S., of about 167 m.; a breadth E. and W., of about 57m.; and an area of 8,224 sq. m., of which 710 sq. m. represent water surface. It ranks forty-fifth in size among the states.

This is a highly industrial state, with extensive shipping and railway facilities. Among its leading industries are petroleum refining, copper smelting, chemicals, food products, meat packing, making electrical machinery and paints and varnishes, and building and repairing ships. The major farm incomes are from dairy products, poultry, and vegetables.

NEW MEXICO

NEW MEXICO, a Mountain State of the United States, lies between latitudes 31° 20' and 37° N., and longitudes 103° and 109° 4' W. It is bounded on the N. by Colorado; on the E. by Oklahoma and Texas; on the S. by Texas and Mexico; and on the W. by Arizona. New Mexico has an extreme length from north to south of 400 m., and an extreme width from east to west of 358 m. In gross area, it ranks fourth among the states (122,634 sq. m.).

National Forests cover 12 per cent of this big state and provide timber and saw mill products. The chief minerals are petroleum, copper, natural gas and coal. More livestock is raised than field crops which depend upon irrigation.

History. New Mexico was explored by Spaniards from Mexico at various times between 1536 and 1581. Between 1583 and 1595, several attempts at the conquest and occupation of New Mexico were made but were unsuccess-

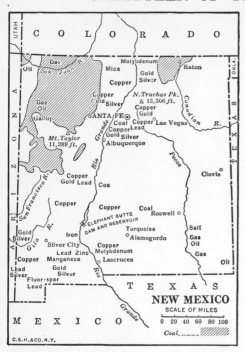

NEW MEXICO
SCALE OF MILES
0 20 40 60 80 100

C.S.H.&CO.N.Y.

ful. Santa Fé, which occupies a site nearly 7,000 ft. in elevation, is, after St. Augustine, Florida, the oldest town in the United States, dating from 1605. An Indian revolt in 1680 resulted in the massacre of over 400 Spanish settlers and the capture of Santa Fé but in 1692 the Spaniards regained their hold on the territory, and European occupation was assured. The history of New Mexico, during the 18th Century, was uneventful. After the achievement of Mexican independence in 1821, New Mexico became successively a province, a territory, and a department of that country. It was ceded to the United States by the Treaty of Guadalupe-Hidalgo in 1848. Previous to that time, American traders had been active in the territory and after that date, the settlement of the region by Americans progressed steadily. The territorial form of government was provided by Congress in 1850 and was inaugurated on the 3rd of March, 1851. Its area was increased by the Gadsden Purchase from Mexico and by the Texan cession of the country lying east of the Rio Grande. New Mexico assumed its present boundaries in 1863. It was admitted to the Union as a state in January, 1912. In 1915 and 1916, frequent raids of New Mexico villages by Mexican bandits caused strained relations between Mexico and the United States.

NEW YORK

NEW YORK, one of the original thirteen states of the Union, belongs in the Middle Atlantic group. It lies between latitudes 40° 30′ and 45° 0′ 2″ N., and longitudes 71° 51′ and 79° 45′ 55″ W. It has a very irregular outline and is bounded on the W., NW., and N. by Canada, from which it is separated for two-thirds of the distance by Lake Erie, Niagara River, Lake Ontario, and the St. Lawrence River; on the E. by Vermont, Massa-

R.C.A. Building and Plaza, Rockefeller Center, New York.

Carlsbad Caverns, New Mexico.

COURTESY, SOUTHERN PACIFIC R. R.

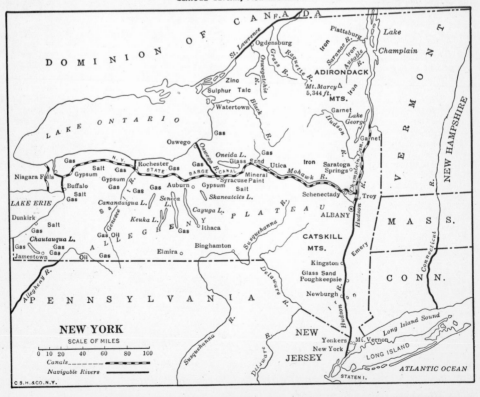

chusetts, and Connecticut; and on the S. by the Atlantic Ocean, New Jersey, and Pennsylvania. The state limits include Long and Staten Islands, and the jurisdiction of the state covers Long Island Sound and the lower waters of the Hudson to low-water mark on the New Jersey shore. The state has a breadth from E. to W. of about 326.5 m., and an extreme length from N. to S. (on the line of the Hudson) of about 300 m. New York ranks twenty-ninth among the states, its area being 47,654 sq. m. of land surface and 1,550 sq. m. of inland water surface.

New York leads all states in the value of its commerce, and in the value of its manufacturing. It ranks high in dairy products, grapes, cabbages, and it's fish catch. Its chief minerals are natural gas, petroleum, stone and cement.

History. Before the coming of Europeans, the territory now known as New York was occupied by the Iroquois Indians (Five Nations). New York Bay was entered by Verrazano in 1524. In 1609, Samuel de Champlain, the French explorer, penetrated the northeastern part of the state, and Henry Hudson, an Englishman in the service of the Netherlands, explored the Hudson River as far as the present site of Albany. A few years later (1613-14) settlements were made by the Dutch on Manhattan Island, and the region was called New Netherlands. Among the early Dutch governors were Minuit, Wouter van Twiller, Kieft, and Stuyvesant. New Amsterdam (New York City) was founded in 1623. The Dutch colony was devastated by an Indian war in 1641. England, basing her demands on the Cabot voyages, claimed New Netherlands, forced its surrender and renamed it New York. New York, New Jersey, and New England were consolidated under Andros in 1686-89. New York was the scene of many events in the French and Indian Wars, and of Burgoyne's surrender (1777) and other events in the Revolutionary War and the War of 1812. The completion of the Erie Canal in 1825 led to a rapid development of western New York and all of the states carved from the old Northwest Territory. New York City was the capital of the United States from 1785-90, and the state capital from 1784-97.

Tobacco picking in North Carolina.

NORTH CAROLINA

NORTH CAROLINA, one of the South Atlantic States and one of the original thirteen states of the Union, lies between latitudes 33° 50' and 36° 33' N., and longitudes 75° 30' and 84° 25' W. It is bounded on the N. by Virginia; on the E. and SE. by the Atlantic Ocean; on the S. by South Carolina and Georgia; and on the W. and NW. by Tennessee. In size, North Carolina ranks twenty-seventh among the states, having a gross area of 52,426 sq. m., of

which 3,686 sq. m. are water surface. Its length from E. to W. (about 503 m.) is greater than that of any other state east of the Mississippi River.

North Carolina ranks high in field crops—cigarette tobacco, cotton and corn leading. The chief minerals are olivine, mica, feldspar, asbestos, stone and clay. The chief industries are textiles, cigarettes, saw mill products, furniture, fixtures and wooden goods.

History. Unsuccessful attempts were made to colonize the Carolina region under the auspices of Sir Walter Raleigh in 1584-87. The first permanent English settlement was made by Virginians at Albemarle on the Chowan River, about 1660. The territory was granted to proprietors in 1663 and 1665. An attempt was made to introduce a constitution framed by Shaftsbury and Locke in 1669 but it ended in failure. A Royal Province was formed in 1728 when North and South Carolina were separated. The "Mecklenburg Declaration of Independence" was passed in 1775; it is claimed that this document formed the model for the Declaration of 1776. North Carolina was the scene of several battles in the Revolution (1780-81); rejected the United States Constitution in 1788, but adopted it in 1789; seceded May 20, 1861. It was the scene of various engagements and military operations in the Civil War. It was readmitted to the Union in July, 1868.

NORTH DAKOTA

NORTH DAKOTA, a West North-Central State of the United States, lies between latitudes 45° 56' and 49° N., and longitudes 96° 32' and 104° 3' W. It is bounded on the N. by the Dominion of Canada; and on the E. by Minnesota: on the S. by South Dakota; and on the W. by Montana. North Dakota has an extreme length from east to west of 360 m., and an extreme width from north to south of 210 m. In gross area, it ranks sixteenth among the states (70,837 sq. m., of which 654 sq. m. represent water surface).

This state is preeminently agricultural despite climate. Its leading crops are spring wheat, rye and flaxseed. It has extensive lignite coal areas; natural gas. Mining, dairy farming and grain-milling are important industries.

History. North Dakota was visited by traders of the Hudson Bay Company late in the 18th Century. It was part of the region ceded by France in the Louisiana Purchase of 1803. It was successively a part of the District of Louisiana, of the Louisiana Territory, the Missouri Territory, the Territory of Michigan, Wisconsin Territory, Iowa Territory, and Minnesota Territory. The first permanent settlement was made by Scottish Highlanders at Pembina in 1812. They had formerly been located at Winnipeg and thought their new settlement was in British territory. The Territory of Dakota was created in 1861 and included the present Dakotas and portions of Wyoming and Montana. In 1863, the boundaries of the Dakotas were fixed at practically their present limits. The settlement of the territory was impeded by the Civil War and by Indian hostilities. Rapid development began in 1872; the territory was divided into North and South Dakota, and both entered the Union as states in 1889. Many advanced social and economic experiments have been made in North Dakota, since the organization in 1915 of the Non-Partisan League. Among these are a state-owned grain elevator and mill, and a state bank at the capital.

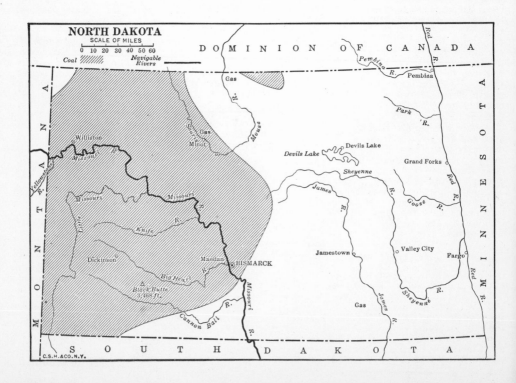

OHIO

OHIO, an East North-Central State of the American Union, lies between latitudes 38° 26′ and 41° 58′ N., and longitudes 80° 31′ and 84° 49′ W. It is bounded on the N. by Michigan and Lake Erie; on the E. by Pennsylvania and West Virginia; on the S. by West Virginia and Kentucky; and on the W. by Indiana. The state has an extreme length from north to south of about 210 m., a width from east to west of 220 m., and a gross area of 41,040 sq. m., of which 300 sq. m. represent water surface; in size, it ranks thirty-fifth among the states of the Union.

It is among the leading agricultural states of the Union. It has extensive coal, petroleum and natural gas resources; also large manufacturing industries, iron and steel leading—machinery next.

History. Ohio was part of the Northwest Territory which, besides Ohio, embraced what are now the states of Michigan, Indiana, Illinois, Wisconsin, and the northeast corner of Minnesota. It was discovered by Europeans late in the first half of the 17th Century, and was claimed by both France and England. France founded her claim on exploration and occupation covering the period between the middle and the close of the 17th Century; England based her claim to the same territory on the discovery of the Atlantic coast by the Cabots, and upon the Virginia, Massachusetts, and Connecticut charters, under which these grants extended westward to the Pacific Ocean. New York also had a claim to the territory. The contest between France and England, known as the Seven Years' War, ended in the cession of the entire Northwest to Great Britain. After winning the Northwest Territory, however, Great Britain no longer recognized those claims of her colonies to this territory, which she had asserted against France, and finally annexed the region to the Province of Quebec. This embittered the colonies and was one of the grievances which brought on the War of Independence and during that war, the Northwest was won for the Americans by George Rogers Clark. Marietta (founded in 1788) at the mouth of the Muskingum, is regarded as the oldest permanent settlement of the state, and the first territorial government was established there. The state was admitted to the Union in 1803. Ohio was the scene of many important actions during the War of 1812, among them Commodore Perry's victory on Lake Erie, in 1813. In no other state have been found so many evidences of man's antiquity as exemplified in implements of stone, copper, bone, and clay, while the most extensive and elaborate systems of earthworks in America have been found at Newark, near Chillicothe, and on the Miami bluffs, near Waynesville.

OKLAHOMA

OKLAHOMA, a West South-Central State of the United States, lies between latitudes 33° 33′ and 37° N., and longitudes 94° 30′ and 103° W. The greater portion of the state is bounded on the west by the 100th meridian; the only part lying west of that is a strip of land about 35 m. wide occupied by Beaver, Texas, and Cimarron Counties. Oklahoma is bounded on the N. by Colorado and Kansas; on the E.

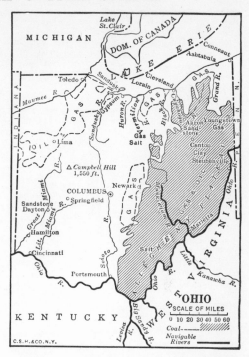

by Missouri and Arkansas; on the S. by Texas and on the W. by Texas and New Mexico. In gross area (70,057 sq. m., of which 643 sq. m. represent water surface), it ranks seventeenth among the states.

It is mainly agricultural and stockraising country. The most valuable crops are cotton, wheat, corn, hay, broomcorn and pecans. It ranks high as a producer of petroleum and natural gas. Manufacturing is increasing.

History. With the exception of the strip comprising the Counties of Beaver, Texas, and Cimarron, the territory included in the present state of Oklahoma was set apart by Congress in 1834 under the name of Indian Territory, for the possession of certain Indian tribes. Oklahoma, the western part of Indian Territory, was ceded by the Indians to the United States in 1866. The treaties under which these lands were transferred stipulated that they were to be used by the government for the settlement of other Indian tribes or freedmen, but not for whites. Many parties of "Boomers" entered the territory, and military forces were required to eject them. In 1889 arrangements were made with certain Indian tribes by which, in consideration of the payment by the government of several million dollars, the clause forbidding settlement by white citizens on this land was cancelled, and it was thrown open for settlement at noon on April 22, 1889. In 1890, this portion of Indian Territory, together with the narrow strip north of Texas, became Oklahoma Territory. In 1893, Congress opened negotiations with the Indians, which led to the passage of the Curtis Act in 1898. That act provided for individual allotment of land to the Indians of Indian Territory, and for a government administered from Washington. When the allotments were nearly all made, Congress, in 1906, authorized Oklahoma and Indian Territories to qualify for admission

Downtown Section of Oklahoma City, Oklahoma.

to the Union as one state, and the state was admitted on the 16th of November, 1907.

OREGON

OREGON, one of the Pacific States of the United States, lies between latitudes 42° and 46° 18′ N., and longitudes 116° 28′ and 124° 30′ W. It is bounded on the N. by Washington; on the E. by Idaho; on the S. by Nevada and Cali-

fornia; and on the W. by the Pacific Ocean. It has an extreme length from east to west of 375 m.; and an extreme width from north to south of 290 m.   In gross area, it ranks ninth among the states of the Union (96,699 sq. m., of which 1,092 sq. m. represent water surface).

Oregon's chief industries are timber, lumber and products, including furniture and wooden goods; agriculture (hops, nuts, fruits, flax, wheat, potatoes, oats and hay); livestock, wool, dairy products, and poultry; extensive salmon

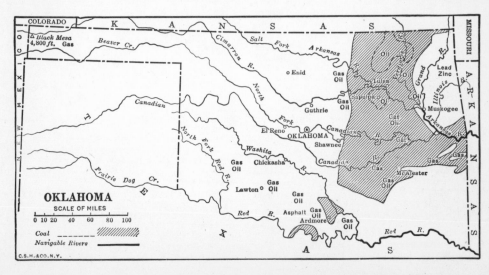

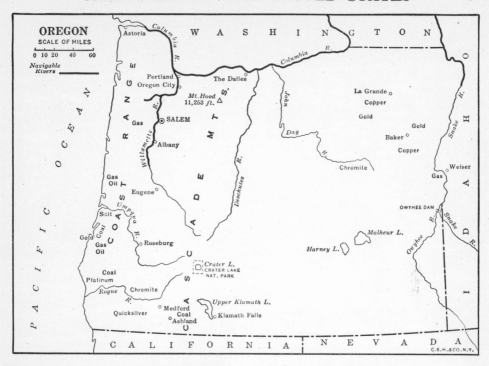

OREGON

SCALE OF MILES

0 10 20 40 60

Navigable Rivers

COURTESY, PITTSBURGH CHAMBER OF COMMERCE

A Pittsburgh Steel Mill.

and other fisheries and canneries; gold mining, and diversified manufacturing.

History. In 1579, Francis Drake sailed along the Pacific coast of the United States as far as 43° N. latitude. He took possession of the country in the name of Queen Elizabeth and called it New Albion. Between the date of Drake's voyage and 1774, the coast was visited by a number of Spanish explorers, the most successful of all being Juan Perez. Among others who sailed along the coast was Bruno Heceta who landed off what is called Point Granville and took formal possession of the country, and later, in latitude 46° 9′, discovered a bay whose swift currents indicated that he was in the mouth of a large river or strait. The Spaniards made no effort to colonize North America or to develop trade with the Indians. In 1778, the English Captain James Cook sighted the coast of Oregon in the latitude 44°, and explored it between 47° and 48°, in the hope of finding the Straits of Juan de Fuca of Spanish accounts. The mouth of the Columbia River was discovered by the American Captain Gray in 1792. It was partly explored by Lewis and Clark in 1804-05. A trading post was founded in Astoria in 1811. The territory between latitudes 42° and 54° 40′ N. was long in dispute between Great Britain and the United States. The claims were finally settled by treaty in 1846. Oregon Territory was organized in 1849, and admitted to statehood in 1859.

PENNSYLVANIA

PENNSYLVANIA, one of the Middle Atlantic States and one of the original thirteen states of the Union, lies between latitudes 39° 43′ and 42° 15′ N., and longitudes 70° 40′ and 80° 34′ W. 'It is bounded on the N. by Lake Erie and New

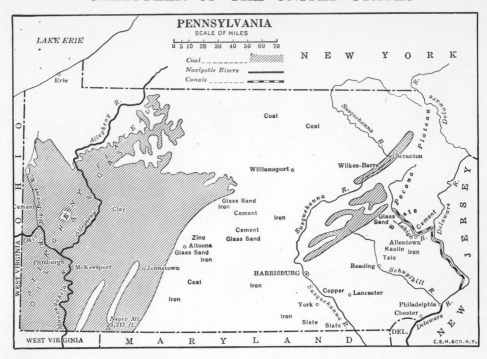

York; on the E. by New Jersey; on the S. by Delaware, Maryland, and West Virginia; and on the W. by Ohio. Pennsylvania is called the Keystone State because it was the seventh or central one in order of the thirteen original states. It is nearly rectangular in shape; is about 303 m. long from east to west and 160 m. wide, and has an area of 45,126 sq. m., of which 294 sq. m. represent water surface. In size, it ranks thirty-second among the states of the Union.

More than half of the land area of Pennsylvania is in farms; the state leads in the production of buckwheat. It also leads in the production of coal and in the total value of all its mineral products. Natural gas is extensively used as fuel and light, and has played an important part in the development of the western part of the state. The greatest industry is the production of iron and steel. Much of the iron ore is brought from Minnesota mines. Pennsylvania ranks next to New York in the total value of its manufactures.

History. The earliest European settlements (1643-81) within the present limits of Pennsylvania were made by Swedish and Dutch traders in the lower valley of the Delaware River. In 1664, the English obtained possession of the territory and in 1681, it was granted by Charles the Second to William Penn, a prominent member of the Society of Friends. In colonial days, Quaker influence was very strong, but religious freedom was given to all. The colony had serious boundary disputes with Maryland, Virginia, and New York, and a dispute with Connecticut over the Wyoming Valley, which was settled in favor of Pennsylvania in 1782. A strong anti-proprietary sentiment grew among the people after the death of William Penn, the great leaders of the movement being Joseph Galloway and Benjamin Franklin. The people of the colony were not united in sentiment over the War of Independence. There were not only many loyalists and many who were opposed to war on religious grounds, but the people generally were satified with the liberal and free government which they already enjoyed. The liberty party, however, became dominant, and Pennsylvania bore a creditable part in the struggle which ended in the establishment of independence. Philadelphia, where the Declaration of Independence was adopted in 1776, became the seat of the Federal Government, except for a brief period in 1789-90, until the removal to Washington in 1800. The state bore a notable part in the Civil War. Many of the miners and ironworkers are of foreign birth, and serious industrial disturbances have occurred at intervals since 1865. A large proportion of the farmers are of German descent, and still speak the patois known as "Pennsylvania Dutch."

RHODE ISLAND

RHODE ISLAND, one of the New England group, and one of the original thirteen states of the Union, lies between latitudes 41° 8' and 42° 3' N., and longitudes 71° 8' and 71° 53' W. It is bounded on the N. and E. by Massachusetts; on the S. by the Atlantic Ocean; and on the W. by Connecticut. Rhode Island is the smallest state in the Union, being a little less than 50m. in length from N. to S., and about 37 m. in width from E. to W., and having an area of 1,248 sq. m., of which 181 sq. m. are water surface.

Textiles are this state's most valuable product, followed by nonferrous metals, iron and steel products. Dairy products and poultry are next in importance.

History. Rhode Island was founded by religious and political exiles from Massachu-

The Pringle House, Charleston, built by Miles Brewton, Colonial Governor of Carolina.

RHODE ISLAND

SCALE OF MILES

0 1 2 3 4 5   10   15

setts. Roger Williams planted the first settlement at Providence in 1636. William Coddington and others settled on Aquidneck or Rhode Island in 1638. Newport was founded in 1639. The Royal Charter for Rhode Island and Providence Plantations was issued in 1663. The government of Rhode Island permitted complete freedom in religious matters. Rhode Island did not ratify the federal constitution until 1790. The first successful cotton mill in the country was established at Pawtucket in 1790. In 1842 occured the Dorr Rebellion, a revolt against conditions which were the outgrowth of the charter of 1663, which served in place of a constitution, gave undue power to country towns, and restricted suffrage. As a result of this revolt, a constitution was adopted. There were two centers of government until 1900.

SOUTH CAROLINA

SOUTH CAROLINA, a South Atlantic State and one of the original thirteen states of the Union, lies between latitudes 32° 2' and 35° 17' N., and longitudes 78° 30' and 83° 20' W. It is bounded on the N. by North Carolina; on the E. by North Carolina and the Atlantic Ocean; on the SE. by the Atlantic Ocean; and on the W. by Georgia, from which it is separated by the Savannah, Tugaloo and Chattooga Rivers. In size, South Carolina ranks thirty-ninth among the states, its gross area being 30,989 sq. m., of which 494 sq. m. are water surface.

Slightly more than half of the land area is in farms, the most valuable crop being cotton. The manufacture of cotton goods, cotton seed oil and cake, and the dyeing and finishing of textiles are important industries, as are also timber, lumber and wooden products, building stone quarrying, clay products, and raw clay.

History. An unsuccessful attempt was made by the French to colonize what is now South Carolina in 1562. The first permanent English settlement was made in 1670. Charleston was founded in 1680. The territory remained under a proprietary government with North Carolina until 1729, when it became a separate colony.

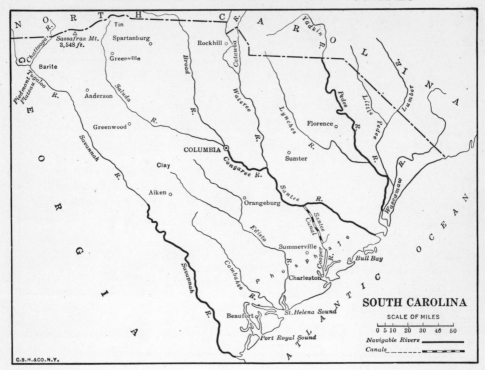

SOUTH CAROLINA

SCALE OF MILES

0 5 10 20 30 40 50

Navigable Rivers ─────
Canals ─ ─ ─ ─

Many of the early colonists were French Huguenots, Scotch, Irish, Swiss, and Germans. South Carolina was the scene of many battles during the Revolution, those of Ft. Moultrie, Charleston, Camden, King's Mountain, Cowpens, and Eutaw Springs being among the most notable. It was held by the British 1780-1781. Its advocacy of nullification nearly led to civil war in 1832-33. It was foremost among the southern states in the advocacy of the states' rights doctrine, and was the first state to secede (Dec. 20, 1860). It opened the Civil War by the bom-

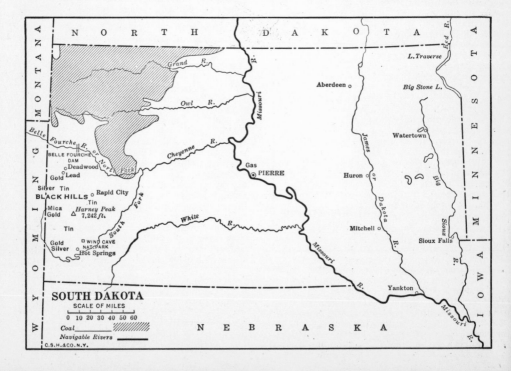

SOUTH DAKOTA

SCALE OF MILES

0 10 20 30 40 50 60

Coal
Navigable Rivers ─────

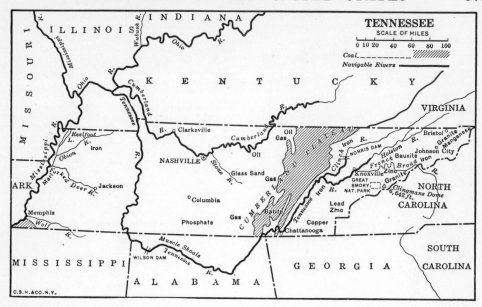

bardment of Fort Sumter (April 12, 1861), suffered severely by the blockade attacks at Charleston Harbor and near the close of the war (in 1865) by the march of Sherman's army. It was readmitted to the Union in 1868. The state was visited by a severe earthquake in 1886.

SOUTH DAKOTA

SOUTH DAKOTA, a West North-Central State of the United States, lies between latitudes 42° 30' and 45° 56' N., and longitudes 96° 26' and 104° 3' W. It is bounded on the N. by North Dakota; on the E. by Minnesota and Iowa; on the S. by Nebraska; and on the W. by Wyoming and Montana. South Dakota has an extreme length from E. to W. of 380 m., and an extreme width from N. to S. of 245 m. In gross area, it ranks fourteenth among the states (77,615 sq. m., of which 747 sq. m. represent water surface).

Agriculture is South Dakota's chief industry, the principal crops being corn, grains, hay, flaxseed, potatoes, and hardy fruits. Livestock raising (cattle, horses, sheep, swine) is even more important than the field crops. Meat packing, dairy products, poultry and flour milling are also valuable. This state stands high in the production of gold and quarries much building stone.

History. The territory included within the present limits of the state was a part of the District of Louisiana from 1803-05; of the Territory of Louisiana from 1805-20, and of the Territory of Missouri from 1812-20. The section east of the Missouri was successively a part of the Territories of Louisiana, Wisconsin, Iowa, and Minnesota; and the western section a part of the Territory of Nebraska. In 1861, the Territory of Dakota was created, including the present Dakotas and portions of Wyoming and Montana. The Dakotas acquired their present territorial limits in 1882. The territory was divided into two states in November, 1887, and both were admitted to the Union on November 2, 1889.

TENNESSEE

TENNESSEE, one of the East South-Central States of the Union, lies between latitudes 35° and 36° 39' N., and longitudes 81° 37' and 90° 28' W. It is bounded on the N. by Kentucky and Virginia; on the E. by North Carolina; on the S. by Georgia, Alabama, and Mississippi; on the W. by Arkansas and Missouri. It has an extreme length from E. to W. of about 400 m., and from N. to S. of 120 m., and in area ranks thirty-fourth among the states (42,022 sq. m., of which 335 sq. m. are water surface).

About 65 per cent of the land area of Tennessee is in farms, the most valuable crops being corn, cotton, hay, tobacco, wheat, oats, and potatoes. Horse and cattle raising are also important. The principal minerals are coal, copper, cement, clay and marble. The growth of manufacturing industries has been aided by TVA development of water power.

History. Tennessee was included in the English grant to Sir Water Raleigh in 1584, and in the later Stuart grants including that of North Carolina in 1663. The region was claimed in early times by North Carolina and by the French and Spanish. The leading settlement was made from Virginia and North Carolina in 1769. North Carolina ceded its claim to the United States, and the territory was formed in 1790. It was admitted to the Union as a state in 1796. It seceded June 8, 1861 and next to Virginia, was the chief battleground during the Civil War. Among the stirring events of that period were the capture of Fort Henry and Fort Donelson and of Island No. 10; the battles of Shiloh, Memphis, Murfreesboro, Lookout Mountain, and Chickamauga; the relief of

Chattanooga and Knoxville; and the battles of Franklin and Nashville. The state was re-admitted to the Union in 1866.

San Jacinto Memorial Shaft, Houston.

TEXAS

TEXAS, a West South-Central State of the United States, lies between latitudes 25° 51′ and 36° 30′ N., and longitudes 93° 40′ and 106° 30′ W. It is bounded on the N. by New Mexico, Oklahoma, and Arkansas; on the E. by Oklahoma, Arkansas, and Louisiana; on the SE. by the Gulf of Mexico; on the SW. by Mexico; and on the W. by New Mexico. Texas is the largest state in the Union, having a gross area of 265,896 sq. m., of which 3,498 sq. m. are water surface.

TEXAS
SCALE OF MILES
0 50 100 150 200

Coal _____ //////////
Navigable Rivers _____

C.S.H. & CO. N.Y.

Almost three quarters of Texas is in farms. Cotton has the highest value, cereals next, the balance being divided among a variety of crops. Vast numbers of beef cattle are raised. Petroleum is the most important mineral. A new use has been found for it in the production of butadiene which goes into the making of synthetic rubber. Manufactures take fourth place.

History. An attempt at settlement was made by Sieur de la Salle about 1685 and several missions were established by the Spaniards in the 18th Century. The region was invaded by various adventurers early in the 19th Century. It formed, with Coahuila, a state of Mexico, and was settled rapidly about 1820-30 by American colonists. Most of these colonists came from the southern states of the Union and brought their slaves with them. A rebellion against Mexico broke out in 1835; the garrisons at Alamo and Goliad were massacred by the Mexicans in 1836; and the Mexicans were finally defeated by Houston at San Jacinto, April 21, 1836. Texas was a republic from 1836-45 when it was annexed to the United States. It was largely the cause of the Mexican War of 1846 and the scene of many of the conflicts in that struggle. By the terms of the treaty which terminated the conflict, the Rio Grande River became the boundary between Texas and Mexico. Texas seceded in 1864, was the scene of many stirring events during the Civil War, and the last battle of that conflict was fought on its soil at Palmito, more than a month after the surrender at Appomatox. A hurricane and high tide in 1900 destroyed 4,000 lives and $10,000,000 worth of property at Galveston.

UTAH

UTAH, one of the Mountain States of the United States, lies between latitudes 37° and

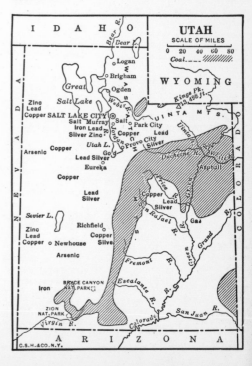

UTAH
SCALE OF MILES
0 20 40 60 80

Coal //////////

C.S.H. & CO. N.Y.

42° N., and longitudes 109° 5' and 114° 2' W. It is bounded on the N. by Idaho and Wyoming; on the E. by Wyoming and Colorado; on the S. by Arizona; and on the W. by Nevada. The state has an extreme length from north to south of 345 m., and an extreme width from east to west of 275 m. In gross area, it ranks tenth among the states (84,990 sq. m., of which 2,806 sq. m. represent water surface).

Utah's chief industries are copper, silver and gold mining; nonferrous metal products; sheep grazing; wool; dairy products and sugar beets.

History. This region formed part of the lands ceded by Mexico in 1848. The Mormons settled here in 1847-48. Utah was organized as a territory in 1850. A massacre of "Gentile" settlers, and other disturbances in 1856 led to the sending of an expedition of U.S. troops the following year. The Mormons submitted to the federal government in 1858. The Edmonds Act of 1882, followed by supplementary legislation, punished and discouraged polygamy in the Mormon Church. Utah was admitted as a state in 1896.

VERMONT

VERMONT (Green Mountain State), the northwesternmost of the New England States and the only one of that group which is wholly inland, lies between latitudes 42° 44' and 45° 0' 45" N., and longitudes 71° 30' and 73° 39' W. It is bounded on the N. by the Canadian province of Quebec; on the E. by New Hampshire, from which it is separated by the Connecticut River; on the S. by Massachusetts; and on the W. by New York from which it is in part separated by Lake Champlain. Vermont has an area of 9,564 sq. m. and of this, 440 sq. m. is water surface. In size, it ranks as the forty-second state of the Union.

History. Samuel de Champlain, the French governor of Quebec, discovered the lake which bears his name in 1609, and thus laid the basis for the French claim to the region. The French built a fort on Isle La Motte in 1665. Part of the country was claimed by Massachusetts which planted the first permanent white settlement (1724) at Fort Dummer in the present

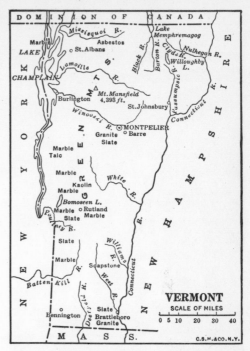

VERMONT
SCALE OF MILES
0 5 10   20   30   40

town of Brattleboro. Soon after 1750, numerous settlements were made under the auspices of New Hampshire which also claimed jurisdiction in the region. New York laid claim to the country as far east as the Connecticut River, by virtue of the charter granted to the Duke of York. George the Third decided in favor of New York in 1764, and discord continued until 1771 when the people declared themselves independent and drew up a state constitution. In 1791, Vermont was admitted into the Union, the first state added to the original thirteen. The "Green Mountain Boys" bore a notable part in the War of the Revolution; and in the War of 1812, and again in the Civil War, the sons of Vermont distinguished themselves by their bravery and devotion to the Union.

"Mount Vernon," home of George Washington, Virginia.

GENDREAU, N. Y.

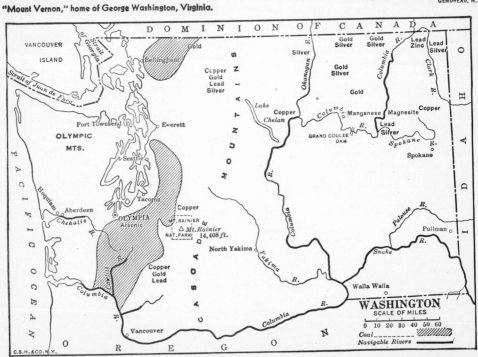

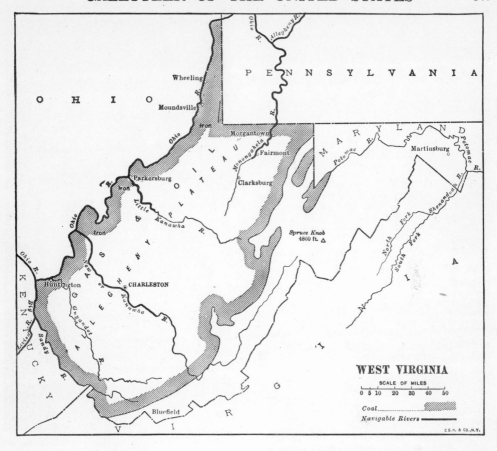

WEST VIRGINIA

SCALE OF MILES
0 5 10   20   30   40   50

Coal..............
Navigable Rivers ———

C.S.H. & CO.,N.Y.

VIRGINIA

VIRGINIA, one of the South Atlantic States, and one of the original thirteen states of the Union, lies between latitudes 36° 30' 28" and 39° 27' N., and longitudes 75° 15' and 83° 40' W. It is bounded on the NW. by Kentucky and West Virginia: on the NE. by Maryland; and on the S. by North Carolina and Tennessee. In size, Virginia ranks thirty-third among the states, its area being 42,627 sq. m., of which 2,365 sq. m. represent water surface.

History. At Jamestown, in Virginia, in 1607, was planted the first permanent English settlement in North America. Capt. John Smith became the head of the government there, established law and order and laid the foundations of industrial life. Slavery in America had its beginnings in the Virginia colony in 1619. At the close of the colonial period, Virginia was the most populous and the wealthiest of the thirteen colonies. In the protest against the Stamp Act and the encroachment of Great Britain, Virginia took the lead, and in the Revolutionary struggle furnished such noted sons as Washington, Jefferson, Patrick Henry, the Lees, and Madison. At Yorktown, Cornwallis's surrender put an end to the contest. In the Civil War, Virginia furnished the great commander, Robert E. Lee. Of the first twenty-one presidents of the United States, seven were Virginians, as was also President Woodrow Wilson. The part played by Virginia in the history of the country has endeared it to all Americans, and the national shrines at Mt. Vernon, Monticello, and the Arlington National Cemetery are visited by hundreds of thousands annually.

WASHINGTON

WASHINGTON, one of the Pacific States of the United States, lies between latitudes 45° 32' and 49° N., and longitudes 116° 58' and 124° 48' W. It is bounded on the N. by British Columbia; on the E. by Idaho; on the S. by Oregon; and on the W. by the Pacific Ocean. It has an extreme length from east to west of 360 m., and an extreme width from north to south of 240 m. In gross area, the state ranks nineteenth among the states (69,127 sq. m., of which 2,291 sq. m. represent water surface).

History. The Strait of Juan de Fuca was discovered in 1592, and explored in 1789. The mouth of the Columbia River was explored by the American Captain Gray in 1792, and further explorations were conducted by Lewis and Clark in 1805. A settlement at the mouth of the Columbia was founded by John Jacob Astor in 1811. The boundary question was settled with Great Britain in 1846. Washington formed part of the territory of Oregon; was organized as a territory in 1853; and was admitted to the Union in 1889.

WEST VIRGINIA

WEST VIRGINIA, the northwesternmost of the South Atlantic group of states of the Union, lies between latitudes 37° 10′ and 40° 40′ N., and longitudes 77° 40′ and 82° 41′ W. It is bounded on the NW. by Ohio; on the N. by Pennsylvania and Maryland; on the E. and SE. by Pennsylvania, Maryland and Virginia; and on the SW. by Virginia and Kentucky. Its greatest length from N. to S. is about 240 m., and its greatest breadth from E. to W. is about 265 m. In size, it ranks fortieth among the states, its gross area being 24,170 sq. m., of which 148 sq. m. represent water surface.

History. West Virginia was a part of Virginia until the beginning of the secession movement in 1861. The separation of these states had, however, been agitated before the adoption of the Federal Constitution. West Virginia was settled largely by immigrants who entered by way of Pennsylvania, and the population included Germans, Protestant Irish, and people from the states farther north. Slavery was rendered unprofitable by the difficulties in agriculture, caused by the rugged nature of the country and the climate. Social conditions were, therefore, entirely unlike those of the eastern part of the state, and little sympathy existed between the two sections. At the outbreak of the Civil War, the inhabitants of the northern and western counties remained loyal to the United States and in 1863 West Virginia was admitted to the Union.

"Old Faithful" Geyser, Yellowstone National Park, Wyoming.

WISCONSIN

WISCONSIN, one of the East North-Central States of the Union, lies between latitudes 42° 30′ and 47° 4′ N., and longitudes 86° 45′ and

92° 54′ W. It is bounded on the N. by Lake Superior and Michigan; on the E. by Michigan and Lake Michigan; on the S. by Illinois; and on the W. by Iowa and Minnesota. Wisconsin is about 300 m. in length from N. to S., and about 250 m. in width, and has an area of 56,066 sq. m., of which 810 sq. m. are water surface. In size, it ranks twenty-fifth among the states.

Wisconsin's chief industries are agriculture, dairy products, lumber production, furniture, paper, leather products and the manufacture of machinery and autos.

History. Wisconsin was opened to wide settlement by French explorers, missionaries, and traders. Among the Frenchmen whose names are associated with its early history are those of Jean Nicollet, Sieur de Radisson, Sieur des Groseilliers, Jacques Marquette, Louis Joliet, René Ménard, Claude Allouez, La Salle, Henri de Tonty, Duluth, and Louis Hennepin. The French claimed, and to a greater or less extent, occupied the territory from 1634 until the close of the Seven Years' War in 1760 when it passed to Great Britain. British occupation was brief and in 1783, it became a part of the United States, and was included in 1787 in the Northwest Territory; afterward in Indiana Territory; in 1809 in Illinois Territory; and in 1818 in Michigan Territory. Wisconsin Territory was organized in 1836 and was admitted as a state in 1848.

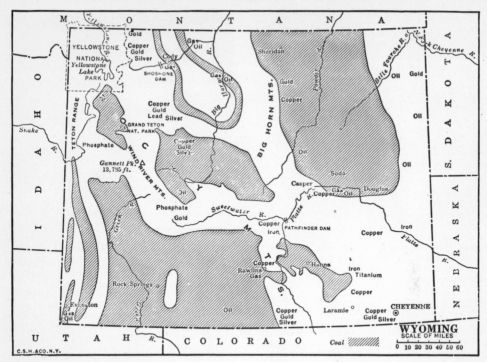

WYOMING

WYOMING, one of the Mountain States of the United States, lies between latitudes 41° and 45° N., and longitudes 104° 3' and 111° 6' W. It is bounded on the N. by Montana; on the E. by South Dakota and Nebraska; on the S. by Colorado and Utah; and on the W. by Utah, Idaho, and Montana. The state has an extreme length from east to west of about 380 m., and an extreme width from north to south of 276 m. In gross area, it ranks eighth among the states (97,914 sq. m., of which 366 sq. m. represent water surface).

History. Fort Laramie, near the mouth of the Laramie River, was established in 1834 to control the fur trade of the Arapahoes, Cheyennes, and Sioux. The United States exploring expedition, commanded by John C. Fremont, explored the Wind River Mountains and the South Pass in 1842. From this time, the favorite route to the Pacific led through Wyoming, but the aridity of the land and the pronounced hostility of the Indians were not conducive to settlement. For the protection of immigrant trains, the United States government built Fort Kearney in 1848, and purchased Fort Laramie in 1849. A Mormon settlement was made on the Green River in 1853. These Mormons afterwards retired to Salt Lake City. Indian hostilities were active from 1851 to 1868. Gold was discovered on the Sweetwater River in 1867, and population increased rapidly. The Territory of Wyoming, with its present boundaries, was organized in 1868. The state was admitted to the Union in 1890.

NON-CONTIGUOUS TERRITORIES OF THE UNITED STATES

ALASKA

ALASKA is a non-contiguous territory of the United States, occupying the northwestern extremity of the North American continent, with neighboring islands. It is bounded on the N. by the Arctic Ocean and Bering Sea; on the E. by Canada; on the S. by the Pacific Ocean; and on the W. by Bering Sea and the Arctic Ocean. The territory is separated from Asia by Bering Strait, about 56 m. wide at its narrowest point. The international boundary between the United States and the Union of Soviet Socialist Republics follows about the 169th meridian to a point opposite Cape Prince of Wales; from there, it bends to the west and southwest and passes finally midway between Copper Island off Kamchatka, and Attu Island of the Aleutian chain. The territorial domain of Alaska, therefore, includes all islands in Bering Sea and those of the Aleutian chain lying east of that line. The mainland portion comprises the large continental mass lying west of 141° W. longitude and a narrow coastal strip, sometimes called the Panhandle which extends southeastward along the Pacific Ocean. The international boundary between Canada and this coastal strip follows a line drawn "east and north from Cape Muzon, in latitude 54° 40' N., to the head of Portland Canal, and thence follows the summit of the mountains situated parallel with the coast to the 141st meridian, but when such line runs more than ten marine

Ribbon Glacier, near Mt. McKinley, Alaska.   OFFICIAL PHOTO U.S. AIR FORCES

leagues from the ocean, the limit is formed by a line parallel with the windings of the coast which must not exceed the distance of ten marine leagues therefrom." Alaska has an area of 586,400 sq. miles.

History. Alaska, formerly called Russian-America, was first visited by Vitus Bering in 1742. In 1799, the whole country passed under the control of the Russian-American Company. In 1867, the United States purchased the entire territory from Russia for $7,200,000 in gold. When Mr. Seward, our Secretary of State, concluded the negotiations for the purchase of Alaska, there were many critics who felt that the country was paying a great price for comparatively valueless territory. It is interesting in this connection to note that as a return for the $7,200,000 purchase money, the United States received untold wealth in mineral resources, farming lands, furs and fisheries.

AMERICAN SAMOA

AMERICAN SAMOA, consisting of the Island of Tutuila and all other islands of the Samoan Group lying east of longitude 171° W., belong to the United States. The total area of the islands, of which Tutuila is the largest and Manua next in size, is 76 sq. m.

Relief. The Island of Tutuila is mountainous, luxuriantly wooded and fertile, and has in Pago Pago the only good harbor in Samoa. It has a United States naval station under a commandant, the government having acquired there a land area of about 40 acres. All the islands are mountainous, with volcanic peaks rising from 2,000 to 3,000 ft. above the sea. The cones are generally quiescent, but volcanic disturbances have occurred in quite recent times. The islands are abundantly watered and the coasts are protected in many places by coral reefs.

History. The islands were visited by Bougainville in 1768 and from him, they received the name of Iles des Navigateurs. After 1889, Great Britain, Germany, and the United States recognized the independence of the Samoan government, making provision for a supreme court and the regulation of taxation and land-claims. In 1900, all the islands east of 171st meridian came into the possession of the United States by a treaty of the same three nations.

CANAL ZONE

CANAL ZONE, a strip of territory, extending across the narrowest part of the Isthmus of Panama from ocean to ocean, of which the United States of America has a perpetual leasehold. The zone begins at a point three marine miles from mean low water mark in each ocean, and extends for five miles on each side of the center line of the route of the Panama Canal. It contains 554 sq. m., of which 170 sq. m. are under the waters of the Canal and Gatun and Miraflores Lakes. The ownership and jurisdiction of the United States extends to the area covered by Gatun Lake and Chagres River, where these waters penetrate beyond the five-mile limit. Included in the Canal Zone are the islands of Perico, Naos, Culebra, and Flamenco, and the United States also owns the Pearl Islands which lie some 60 m. southeast of the city of Panama. The Canal Zone is a military reservation administered by the War Department; it is fortified and occupied by a garrison, in addition to the employees of the Canal and railroad, but no private individuals are permitted to acquire land.

History. The Canal Zone was granted to the United States by Panama by a treaty confirmed by the U. S. Senate on Feb. 26, 1904, the compensation being $10,000,000 and, in addition, annual payments of $250,000, beginning in 1913. The Canal was opened to traffic on August 15, 1914. In 1928, Congress authorized the building of a dam above Alhajuela on the Chagres River, creating a reservoir of sufficient size to maintain the water level of the entire canal at all times.

GUAM

GUAM, an island in the North Pacific Ocean, belonging to the United States. It lies at the southern extremity of the Marianas or Ladrone Archipelago, in latitude 13° 26′ N., and longitude 144° 43′ E., and is the largest island of the group. Guam is about 30 m. long from northeast to southwest, and has an average width of 6½ m. Its area is 206 sq. m.

History. The Marianas Islands were discovered by Magellan in 1521, but it was a century and a half later before any attempt was made to plant a colony and civilize the natives. After the war with Spain, 1898, the Island of Guam became a possession of the United States.

HAWAII

HAWAII, a territory of the United States, occupying a group of islands in the North Pacific Ocean, about 2,000 m. southwest of San Francisco. The islands, twelve in number, form a beautiful chain, which runs from southeast to northwest, and lies in latitude 19° to 22° N., and longitude 155° to 160° W. The archipelago contains 6,406 sq. m. There are eight inhabited islands—Hawaii, Maui, Kahoolawe, Lanai, Molokai, Oahu, Kauai, and Niihau. In addition, there are many uninhabited islands and islets which continue the chain in a north-westerly direction beyond the limits above given. They are valuable only for their guano deposits and shark-fishing grounds. The islands are of volcanic origin, with coral reefs partly encircling most of them, the only well-protected harbor being that of Pearl Harbor on Oahu Island.

Hawaii Island, which gives the name to the group, is roughly triangular in shape, and its coast, unlike that of the other islands of the archipelago, has few coral reefs. Its area is 4,016 sq. m. Its surface is mainly occupied by five volcanic mountains. Of these, Mauna Loa in the southern half of the island is the largest volcano in the world measuring, at its base, about 75 m. from north to south and 50m. from west to east. It rises to a height of 13,675 ft. above sea level. Adjoining it on the southeast is Kilauea (4,040 ft.) whose lava flows have formed the southeastern extension of the island. Northeast of Mauna Loa, joined to it by an intervening plateau, is Mauna Kea (13,825 ft.) or White Mountain, the loftiest summit in the Pacific Ocean. To the northwest, Mauna Loa is merged in Mauna Hualalai (8,273 ft.). The Kohala Mountains (5,489 ft.) rise abruptly from the northwestern shore. Of the above volcanoes, Mauna Loa and Kilauea are still active and, with Haleakala Volcano on Maui Island, are included in the Hawaii National Park.

Maui Island, lying about 25 m. northwest of Hawaii, contains 728 sq. m. The eastern mountain, Haleakala, has the largest crater known in the world. It is from 25 to 30 m. in circumference, from 2,000 to 3,000 ft. deep, and is more than 10,000 ft. above sea level. The mountain mass of western Maui is characterized by sharp ridges and deeply eroded gorges or valleys. Puu Kukui, its highest point, rises nearly 6,000 ft. above the sea. Below this, the Iao Gorge, or valley, five miles long and two miles wide, is cut into the mountain to a depth of 4,000 ft. Many of the valleys of the island are famed for the beauty of their scenery.

Kahoolawe is a small island, 69 sq. m. in area, lying about six miles southwest of Maui. Its bare and rugged mountains nowhere attain an elevation of more than 1,500 ft., and its intervening valleys are used extensively for sheep pastures.

Molokai Island, eight miles northwest of Maui, contains 261 sq. m. It is mountainous, its culminating point being the peak of Kamakou (5,000 ft.). About midway of the northern shore is a peninsula, on which is established the famous Leper Settlement of Molokai.

Oahu Island, twenty-five miles northwest of Molokai, and 598 sq. m. in area, is traversed from northwest to southeast by two nearly parallel ranges of hills which are separated by a wide plain. The highest point on the island is Mauna Kaala (4,000 ft.) in the Waianae or Western Range. This island is nearly surrounded by a coral reef which, in places, is half a mile in width. It is the island most frequently visited because it contains the capital, Honolulu.

Kauai Island, known as the "garden isle" of the group, lies about sixty miles northwest of Oahu. It is roughly circular in form and is 547 sq. m. in area. On the northwest, the island rises for over 2,000 ft. sheer from the sea and above this precipitous wall is a mountain plain; elsewhere the island has a shore plain. Near the center of the island, Waialeale Pk. rises to an elevation of 5,080 ft. The shore plain is broken by ridges and deep valleys. The island is well watered on both sides by large mountain streams.

Niihau Island is the most western of the inhabited islands. It lies nearly twenty miles southwest of Kauai and is 97 sq. m. in area.

History. The islands are said to have been discovered in 1542 by Gaetano, and rediscovered in 1778 by Captain Cook who lost his life in a conflict with natives the following year. In 1790, Kamehameha formed the islands into one kingdom. Missionaries came from America in 1820 and in less than forty years, they gave to the whole Hawaiian people, the rudiments of a common school education and taught them something of domestic science. In 1843, the independence of the kingdom was guaranteed by the French and English governments. Kalakaua, elected king in 1874, died in 1891 and was succeeded by his eldest sister, Liliuokalani who was dethroned in January, 1893, and a provisional republican government set up. The islands were finally annexed by the United States in 1898, and in 1900 were organized as one of the Territories of the United States.

MIDWAY ISLANDS

MIDWAY ISLANDS, two small islands belonging to the United States, lie in the Pacific Ocean in latitude 28° 12′ N., and longitude 177° 22′ W. They are Sand Island and Eastern Island, and are an integral part of Hawaii Territory. They are 1,200 m. northwest of Hawaii, about midway between America and Asia, and are of importance because Sand Island is utilized as a relay station of the Commercial Pacific Cable Company. The islands are low and sandy, almost destitute of vegetation, and are surrounded by a coral reef some 16 m. in circumference, 5 ft. high, about 25 ft. wide, and open on the west side. The sheltering reef renders the island habitable, and Welles Harbor is roomy and safe. In 1936 Pan American Airways established service there.

TERRITORY OF THE PACIFIC ISLANDS

TERRITORY OF THE PACIFIC ISLANDS, —the Marianas, Carolines, and Marshalls— formerly Japanese mandated islands now under American trusteeship, extending in chains over an area of the Pacific Ocean equal to that of the

United States. The total area of the 650-odd volcanic islands and coral atolls in the territory —not including Guam, which has been an American possession since 1898—is only 830 square miles. The islands are economically insignificant—copra, sugar, and phosphates from the larger Marianas are the only export crops—but they have strategic importance. The population of about 50,000 natives is governed by the United States Navy.

History. The islands were discovered by Spanish explorers in the early sixteenth cen-

Included in the administration of Puerto Rico are the island of Vieques, about 21 m. long and 5 or 6 m. wide, and the nearly barren island of Culebra off the east coast; the island of Mona, off the west coast, valuable for its guano deposits; and a number of islets.

History. Puerto Rico was discovered by Columbus in 1493, and Ponce de Leon founded a settlement there in 1510. The island was ceded by Spain to the United States after the war of 1898 and in 1900, civil government was given to the Terri-

Section of Waikiki Beach.   Honolulu, Hawaii.   GENDREAU, N. Y

tury. Contact with Europeans did not become intensive until the nineteenth century, when whalers stopped there for provisions. Spain sold the islands to Germany in 1899. Japan occupied the islands in 1914 and governed them under a League of Nations mandate from 1922 until their liberation by American forces during World War II. On April 2, 1947, the United Nations Security Council approved a trust agreement whereby the United States is designated as the administering authority of the Trust Territory of the Pacific Islands.

PUERTO RICO

PUERTO RICO, an island Territory of the United States, lying in the Atlantic Ocean seventy-five miles east of Haiti, or Dominican Republic. It is the most easterly and the smallest of the Greater Antilles and is intersected near its center by the parallel of 18° 15′ N. and the meridian of 66° 30′ W. It is about 100 m. long from east to west, from 35 to 40 m. from north to south, and has an area of 3,435 sq. m.

tory. Since then, the island has prospered greatly, except in 1928, when a terrific hurricane left 245 people dead and 400,000 homeless, and destroyed property worth $30,000,000 and crops worth $20,000,000.

VIRGIN ISLANDS

THE VIRGIN ISLANDS are a group of over fifty islands in the West Indies, 40 m. east of Puerto Rico. The total area is 133 sq. m., but only three of the islands are important, St. Thomas, St. Croix and St. John. The islands are of volcanic origin, descending steeply to the coast line. The highest point is Crown Hill (1,550 ft.) on St. Thomas I.

History. In January, 1917, the Virgin Islands, formerly known as Danish West Indies, were purchased by the United States from Denmark for $25,000,000. A U. S. Navy base has been established at Charlotte Amalie on St. Thomas I., capitol and largest city in the group.

1. The Alcazar, Segovia, Spain.
2. Bridge and Cathedral, Dinant, Belgium.
3. Plaza del Congress, Buenos Aires, Argentina.
4. Castle of Neuschwanstein, Bavaria, Germany.
5. Lindbergh Theatre from across the lagoon, Mexico City.
6. Looking into the crater of Vesuvius, Naples, Italy.
7. View of the Capitol, Havana, Cuba.

8. The Sphinx at Gizah, Egypt.
9. The famous St. Sophia Mosque, Constantinople, Turkey.
10. Scene in Devonshire, England.
11. A typical canti-lever bridge over a canal in Holland.
12. Camp at Wapta, Canadian Rockies.
13. The Harbor front at Algiers.
14. Morro Castle, Havana, Cuba.

15. A typical farm house in Czechoslovakia.

EXCLUSIVE OF CONTINENTAL UNITED STATES

This alphabetical list of cities and towns gives statistics of population based on the latest official census reports or most recent reliable estimates. Each line begins with the name of a place, followed by the name of the country or state, the population, the index reference and plate number. This index reference gives the location of the city or town name on the accompanying map plates. The name is found within the square formed by the two lines of latitude or longitude which enclose each of the co-ordinates—i.e. the marginal letters and numbers. In the case of maps consisting entirely of insets, the name is found near the intersection point of imaginary lines connecting the co-ordinates.

Where space on the map has not permitted giving the complete form of a name, the extended form is shown in the index. Where a place may be known under different names or by various spellings of the same name, the different forms have been included, to a large extent, in the index. Where an alternative spelling in parentheses is shown on the map itself, the first name gives the local official form, the conventional form following in parentheses.

* Capitals of countries, states and provinces.   † Population figure includes suburbs.

Name	Index Ref.	Plate No.
Aabenraa, Denmark, 12,189	F-9	51
Aachen (Aix-la-Chapelle), Germany, 162,164	B-3	52
Aalborg, Denmark, 60,880	G-8	51
(Aalesund) Ålesund, Norway 18,012	D-5	50
Aalst (Alost), Belgium, †41,778	D-7	55
Aarau, Switzerland, 12,900	F-2	60
Aarhus, Denmark, 107,393	F-8	51
Abadan, Iran, 40,000	F-5	78
Abbeville, France, 16,780	D-2	56
Abéché, French Equatorial Africa, 10,000	L-9	95
Aberdare, Wales, 48,751	D-6	45
Aberdeen, Scotland, 167,259	N-5	46
Abidjan, *Ivory Coast, 33,000	E-10	94
Abomey, Dahomey, 13,000	G-10	94
Acambaro, Mexico, 17,643	J-7	133
Acapulco, Mexico, 9,993	J-8	133
Accra, *Gold Coast, 135,456	G-10	94
Acireale, Sicily, Italy, 36,871	E-6	63
Acton, England, 70,523	B-5	43
Adana (Seyhan), Turkey, 100,367	F-4	76
Addis Ababa, *Ethiopia, 100,000	O-10	95
Adelaide, *South Australia, †382,604	D-7	102
Adelboden, Switzerland, 2,640	E-3	60
Aden, *Aden Prot., 48,338	C-6	81
Adria, Italy, 32,762	D-2	62
Adua (Adowa), Ethiopia, 6,000	O-9	95
Agaña, *Guam, 11,042	E-4	104
Agen, France, 33,397	D-5	57
Agra, India, 284,149	C-3	82
Agrigento (Girgente), Sicily, Italy, 32,951	D-6	63
Agrínio, Greece, 20,981	E-6	67
Aguascalientes, Mexico, 82,234	H-5	132
Ahlen, Germany, 25,697	B-3	52
Ahmadnagar, India, 54,193	B-5	83
Ahmedabad, India, 591,267	B-4	82
Airdrie, Scotland, 25,954	D-2	46
Aix, France, 46,053	F-6	57
Aix-les-Bains, France, 14,556	G-5	57
Ajaccio, Corsica, France, 31,434	F-7	57
Ajmer, India, 147,258	B-3	82
Akashi, Japan, 47,751	G-6	92
Akita, Japan, 61,791	J-4	92
Akola, India, 62,564	C-4	83
Akureyri, Iceland, 6,144	C-1	40
Akyab, Burma, 38,094	B-2	86
Alajuela, Costa Rica, 10,170	E-6	134
Alausí, Ecuador, 12,059	C-4	114
Albacete, Spain, 60,038	F-3	59
Albany, Western Australia, 4,761	B-6	102
Albi, France, 34,342	E-6	57
Alcamo, Sicily, Italy, 38,396	D-6	63
Alcoy, Spain, 44,124	F-3	59
Aldershot, England, 34,281	G-6	45
Alegrete, Brazil, 16,227	B-10	117
Alençon, France, 19,691	D-3	56
(Aleppo) Haleb, Syria, 324,899	G-4	77
Alès, France, 34,731	E-5	57
Alessandria, Italy, 79,327	B-2	62
Ålesund (Aalesund), Norway, 18,012	D-5	50
(Alexandrette), Iskenderun, Turkey, 18,629	G-4	77
Alexandria (El Iskandariya), Egypt, 685,736	A-5	98
Alexandroupolis (Dede Agach), Greece, 17,081	H-5	67
Alger (Algiers), *Algeria, 360,700	G-4	94
Alicante, Spain, 89,198	F-3	59
Alkmaar, Netherlands, †36,550	F-3	54
Al Kuwait (Kuwait), *Kuwait, 25,000	C-3	81
Allahabad, India, 260,630	D-3	82
(Allenstein), Olsztyn, Poland, 29,053	E-2	64
Alleppey, India, 56,333	C-7	83
Alma-Ata, U.S.S.R., 230,528	H-5	70
Almelo, Netherlands, †38,920	K-4	54
Almería, Spain, 73,097	E-4	59
Altagracia, Venezuela, 3,257	C-2	110
Altagracia de Orituco, Ven., 3,395	E-3	111
Altamura, Italy, 31,431	F-4	63
Altenburg, Germany, 51,805	E-3	52
Altona, Germany, 242,006	C-2	52
Alwar, India, 54,143	C-3	82
Amagasaki, Japan, 181,011	G-6	92
Amapala, Honduras, 2,809	D-4	134
Ambala, India, 62,419	C-2	82
Ambato, Ecuador, 21,147	C-3	114
Ambon, Amboina, Indon, 17,078	H-6	89
Ambriz, Angola, 4,717	J-13	96
Amecameca, Mexico, 7,573	L-1	133
Amersfoort, Netherlands, †52,510	G-4	54
Amiens, France, 84,774	E-3	56
Amman, * Jordan, 2,000	D-4	80
Amoy, China, 138,032	J-7	85
Amraoti, India, 61,971	C-4	82
Amritsar, India, 391,010	B-2	82
Amsterdam,* Netherlands, 756,597	B-4	54
Ancona, Italy, 89,198	D-3	62
Anchorage, Alaska, 3,495	J-2	155
Ancud, Chile, 4,078	D-4	120
Anderlecht, Belgium, †86,712	D-9	55
Andermatt, Switzerland, 1,493	G-3	61
Andizhan, U.S.S.R., 83,691	H-5	70
Andorra la Vieja,* Andorra, 700	G-1	59
Andria, Italy, 56,152	F-4	63
Angers, France, 94,408	C-4	56
Angmagsalik, Greenland, 129	P-3	126
Angol, Chile, 12,398	D-1	120
Angoulême, France, 44,244	D-5	57
Ankara (Angora), *Turkey, 227,505	E-3	76
Annecy, France, 26,722	G-5	57
Annonay, France, 15,462	F-5	57
Anshan, China, 165,988	K-3	85
Antakya (Antioch), Turkey, 27,517	G-4	77
Antequera, Spain, 38,530	D-4	58
Antibes, France, 23,574	G-6	57
Antioquia, Colombia, 3,810	B-4	112
Antofagasta, Chile, 49,106	A-4	120
Antsirabe, Madagascar, 22,526	R-16	97
Antung, China, 271,115	K-3	85
Antwerpen (Anvers), Belgium, 256,332	E,6	55
(An Uaimh) Navan, Ireland, 4,123	H-4	48
Anzhero-Sudzhensk, U.S.S.R., 71,079	J-4	70
Anzio, Italy, 7,025	E-7	63
Aomori, Japan, 99,065	K-3	92
Apeldoorn, Netherlands, †79,394	H-4	54
Apia, *Western Samoa, 2,000	J-7	105
Apolda, Germany, 33,439	D-3	52
Aqaba, Jordan	D-5	80
Aracaju, Brazil, 50,306	G-5	116
Araçatuba, Brazil, 16,903	D-8	117
Araraquara, Brazil, 27,724	E-8	117
Arad, Rumania, 87,291	E-2	66
Aragua de Barcelona, Ven., 3,090	F-3	111
Araraquara, Brazil, 27,724	E-8	117
Arbroath, Scotland, 17,637	L-6	47
Arendal, Norway, 11,273	F-7	51
Arequipa, Peru, 91,590	G-11	115
Arezzo, Italy, 60,284	C-3	62
Argao, Philippine Islands, 35,448	D-6	91
Argenta, Italy, 28,032	D-2	62
Argentan, France, 6,711	D-3	56
Argenteuil, France, 53,543	A-1	56
Argos, Greece, 13,440	F-7	67
Arica, Chile, 14,064	A-1	120
Arjona, Colombia, 10,416	C-2	112
Arkhangel'sk (Archangel), U.S.S.R., 281,091	F-2	68
Arles, France, 35,016	F-6	57
Arlon (Aarlon), Belgium, †11,408	H-9	55
Armavir, U.S.S.R., 83,677	F-5	69
Armenia, Colombia, 29,673	B-5	112
Armentières, France, 22,667	E-2	57
Arnhem, Netherlands, †91,924	H-4	54
Arrah, India, 53,122	D-3	82
Arras, France, 33,345	E-2	56
Artemovsk, U.S.S.R., 55,165	E-5	69
Artigas, Uruguay, 16,500	C-1	125
Aš, Czechoslovakia, 24,354	B-1	65
Asahigawa, Japan, 87,514	L-2	92
Asansol, India, 55,797	E-4	82
Aschaffenburg, Germany, 45,379	C-4	52
Aschersleben, Germany, 42,196	D-3	52
Ascoli Piceno, Italy, 38,111	D-3	62
Ashikaga, Japan, 48,310	J-5	92
Ashkhabad, U.S.S.R., 126,580	F-6	70
Ashton-under-Lyne, England, 51,573	G-2	42
Asmara, *Eritrea, 88,900	O-9	95
Asnières, France, 72,273	A-1	56
Asti, Italy, 48,898	B-2	62
Astrakhan', U.S.S.R., 253,655	G-5	69
Asunción, *Paraguay, 109,228	A-6	124
Aswân, Egypt, 22,192	C-3	98
Asyût, Egypt, 60,338	C-2	98
Atbara, Anglo-Egyptian Sudan, 19,800	C-4	98
Athēnai(Athens), *Greece,487,045	F-6	67
Athlone, Ireland, 7,246	F-5	48
Aubervilliers, France, 53,010	B-1	56
Auckland, New Zealand, †263,370	B-1	100
Augsburg, Germany, 185,374	D-4	52
Aurangabad, India, 50,924	C-5	83
Aurillac, France, 22,174	E-5	57
Auxerre, France, 24,052	E-4	56
Avellaneda, Argentina, †279,572	G-7	123
Avellino, Italy, 29,091	E-4	63
Aversa, Italy, 36,960	E-4	63
Avignon, France, 60,053	F-6	57
Avila, Spain, 18,547	D-2	58
Avranches, France, 7,554	C-3	56
Ayacucho, Peru, 21,116	F-9	115

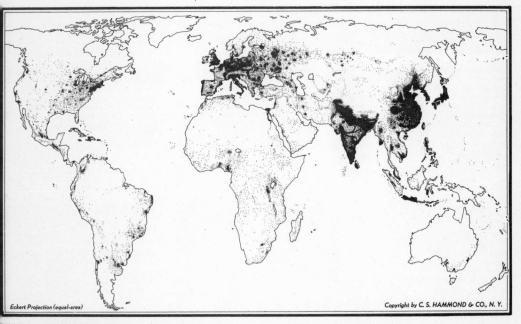

Eckert Projection (equal-area)

Copyright by C. S. HAMMOND & CO., N. Y.

DENSITY OF POPULATION. One of the most outstanding facts of human geography is the extremely uneven distribution of people over the Earth. One-half of the Earth's surface has less than 3 people per square mile, while in the lowlands of India, China, Java and Japan rural density reaches the incredible congestion of 2000-3000 per square mile. Three-fourths of the Earth's population live in four relatively small areas; Northeastern United States, North-Central Europe, India and the Far East.

1. Multnomah Falls, Oregon.
2. Shenandoah River Valley, Virginia.
3. Giant redwoods of Sequoia Nat'l Park, California.
4. Lake Mead, Arizona.
5. Farm scene in Lancaster County, Pennsylvania.
6. Traffic on the Ohio River.
7. Falls in Cumberland Nat'l Forest, Kentucky.
8. Shishold Volcano in the Aleutian Islands, Alaska.
9. Fish ladders at Bonneville Dam, Columbia River, Oregon.
10. Orange groves in the Sacramento Valley, California.
11. Flathead River, Montana.
12. Farming in Wisconsin.
13. Lake Keuka in the Finger Lakes district, New York.
14. Contour plowing in Texas.
15. Palisades along the Hudson River, New York.

INDEX OF CITIES AND TOWNS OF THE UNITED STATES
WITH OFFICIAL CENSUS FIGURES

In this compilation the official population figures of incorporated places are given according to the latest (1950) Federal Census. The symbol □ notes population of townships. For unincorporated places which are not separately enumerated by the Census, recent estimates supplied by local ficials or other reliable authorities are given.

Following the place name is the abbreviated name of the state in which it is located. the population, the map reference and the page number on hich it is to be found. Capitals of states are printed in capital letters.

BETWEEN PRINCIPAL CITIES OF EUROPE

Distances in Statute Miles

FROM/TO	Amsterdam	Athens	Baku	Barcelona	Belgrade	Berlin	Brussels	Bucharest	Budapest	Cologne	Copenhagen	Istanbul	Dresden	Dublin	Frankfort	Hamburg	Leningrad	Lisbon	London	Lyon
Amsterdam	....	1340	2218	770	875	365	105	1100	710	128	381	1360	385	468	228	232	1090	1140	220	458
Athens	1340	....	1395	1160	500	1112	1292	460	698	1200	1320	350	1022	1765	1113	1250	1535	1770	1476	1100
Baku	2218	1395	....	2427	1487	1867	2240	1220	1562	2127	1980	1070	1837	2490	2055	2020	1570	3050	2435	2238
Barcelona	770	1160	2427	....	998	925	658	1210	924	692	1085	1380	860	919	665	910	1740	610	707	327
Belgrade	875	500	1487	998	....	618	850	295	205	750	840	502	530	1327	652	760	1165	1555	1040	752
Berlin	365	1112	1867	925	618	....	401	798	425	300	225	1068	95	815	268	165	815	1410	575	601
Brussels	105	1292	2240	658	850	401	....	1110	700	110	475	1345	407	480	198	301	1175	998	202	352
Bucharest	1100	460	1220	1210	295	798	1110	....	295	982	970	272	725	1560	890	950	1080	1842	1285	1025
Budapest	710	698	1562	924	205	425	700	295	....	590	629	650	345	1176	501	572	965	1515	900	680
Cologne	128	1200	2127	692	750	300	110	982	590	....	400	1240	292	585	93	228	1090	1126	308	370
Copenhagen	381	1320	1960	1085	840	225	475	970	629	400	....	1240	315	768	412	180	708	1520	590	760
Istanbul	1360	350	1070	1380	502	1068	1345	272	650	1240	1240	....	995	1830	1150	1222	1292	2005	1540	1238
Dresden	385	1022	1837	860	530	95	407	725	345	292	315	995	....	852	236	238	885	1380	592	540
Dublin	468	1765	2490	919	1327	815	480	1560	1176	585	768	1830	852	....	671	668	1440	1015	300	720
Frankfort	228	1113	2055	665	652	268	198	890	504	93	412	1150	236	671	....	250	1075	1160	392	350
Hamburg	232	1250	2020	910	760	165	301	950	572	228	180	1222	238	668	250	....	880	1301	448	580
Leningrad	1090	1535	1570	1740	1165	815	1175	1080	965	1090	708	1292	885	1440	1075	880	....	2235	1300	1420
Lisbon	1140	1770	3050	610	1555	1410	998	1842	1515	1126	1520	2005	1380	1015	1160	1301	2235	....	975	850
London	220	1476	2435	707	1040	575	202	1285	900	308	590	1540	592	300	392	418	1300	975	....	455
Lyon	458	1100	2238	327	752	601	352	1025	680	370	760	1238	540	720	350	580	1420	850	455	....
Madrid	912	1463	2742	316	1235	1149	807	1518	1214	875	1272	1690	1100	902	888	1098	1980	313	777	557
Marseilles	627	1025	2238	211	750	730	521	1020	718	528	906	1205	655	875	492	730	1540	810	620	170
Milan	517	900	2028	450	540	570	435	819	476	390	720	1030	435	880	323	570	1315	1350	595	210
Moscow	1325	1388	1175	1852	1160	995	1392	920	965	1285	970	1180	1200	1728	1240	1100	391	430	1540	1560
Munich	415	925	1912	648	475	310	372	725	350	282	520	975	227	855	193	378	1100	1208	526	352
Oslo	568	1610	2118	1330	1112	520	672	1245	920	635	303	1505	620	786	675	445	670	1690	720	1005
Paris	257	1300	2335	518	890	540	170	1152	770	250	634	1390	523	480	295	459	1335	890	210	248
Riga	820	1310	1590	1440	855	520	900	870	685	805	453	1115	585	1210	780	600	300	1940	1035	1122
Rome	808	650	1900	530	440	730	730	700	500	675	948	840	630	1175	698	810	1440	1150	890	462
Sofia	1073	335	1360	1072	231	810	945	194	395	945	1010	315	730	1525	860	954	1218	1685	1235	928
Stockholm	695	1495	1862	1410	1005	503	793	1080	820	722	330	1340	598	1010	730	502	435	1848	885	1080
Toulouse	625	1215	2425	156	930	815	515	1210	883	875	962	1400	762	761	560	780	1635	640	550	228
Warsaw	673	990	1555	1150	510	320	720	580	342	602	415	852	325	1130	550	462	640	1700	890	850
Vienna	580	795	1700	830	300	322	568	520	128	460	538	790	235	1040	370	460	975	1415	762	562
Zurich	375	1000	2050	513	590	410	312	855	498	259	595	1090	342	768	193	432	1225	1058	480	206

FROM/TO	Hamburg	Leningrad	Lisbon	London	Lyon	Madrid	Marseilles	Milan	Moscow	Munich	Oslo	Paris	Riga	Rome	Sofia	Stockholm	Toulouse	Warsaw	Vienna	Zurich
Amsterdam	232	1090	1140	220	458	912	627	517	1325	415	568	257	820	808	1073	695	625	673	580	375
Athens	1250	1535	1770	1476	1100	1463	1025	900	1388	925	1610	1300	1310	650	335	1495	1215	990	795	1000
Baku	2020	1570	3050	2435	2238	2742	2238	2028	1175	1912	2118	2335	1590	1900	1360	1862	2425	1555	1700	2050
Barcelona	910	1740	610	707	327	316	211	450	1852	648	1330	518	1440	530	1072	1410	156	1150	830	513
Belgrade	760	1165	1555	1040	752	1235	750	540	1160	475	1112	890	855	440	231	1005	930	510	300	590
Berlin	165	815	1410	575	601	1149	730	570	995	310	520	540	520	730	810	503	815	320	322	410
Brussels	301	1175	998	202	352	807	521	435	1392	372	672	170	900	730	945	793	515	720	568	312
Bucharest	950	1080	1842	1285	1025	1518	1020	819	920	725	1245	1152	870	700	194	1080	1210	580	520	855
Budapest	572	965	1515	900	680	1214	718	476	965	350	920	770	685	500	395	820	883	342	128	498
Cologne	228	1090	1126	308	370	875	528	390	1285	282	635	250	805	675	945	722	875	602	460	259
Copenhagen	180	708	1520	590	760	1272	906	720	970	520	303	634	453	948	1010	330	962	415	538	595
Istanbul	1222	1292	2005	1540	1238	1690	1205	1030	1180	975	1505	1390	1115	840	315	1340	1400	852	790	1090
Dresden	238	885	1380	592	540	1100	655	435	1200	227	620	523	585	630	730	598	762	325	235	342
Dublin	668	1440	1015	300	720	902	875	880	1728	855	786	480	1210	1175	1525	1010	761	1130	1040	768
Frankfort	250	1075	1160	392	350	888	492	323	1240	193	675	295	780	698	860	730	560	550	370	193
Hamburg	....	880	1301	448	580	1098	730	570	1100	378	445	459	600	810	954	502	780	462	460	432
Leningrad	880	....	2235	1300	1420	1980	1540	1315	391	1100	670	1335	300	1440	1218	435	1635	640	975	1225
Lisbon	1301	2235	....	975	850	313	810	1350	430	1208	1690	890	1940	1150	1685	1848	640	1700	1415	1058
London	418	1300	975	....	455	777	620	595	1540	526	720	210	1035	890	1235	885	550	890	762	480
Lyon	580	1420	850	455	....	557	170	210	1560	352	1005	248	1122	462	928	1080	228	850	562	206
Madrid	1098	1980	313	777	557	....	394	728	2120	910	1474	645	1670	840	1385	1598	344	1410	1110	765
Marseilles	730	1540	810	620	170	394	....	238	1642	445	1165	410	1238	372	895	1225	196	950	620	318
Milan	570	1315	1350	595	210	728	238	....	1408	215	1000	400	1010	295	715	1020	400	705	385	137
Moscow	1100	391	430	1540	1560	2120	1642	1408	....	1220	1030	1538	520	1462	1100	770	1770	710	1028	1350
Munich	378	1100	1208	526	352	910	445	215	1220	....	810	425	800	430	672	811	570	500	222	158
Oslo	445	670	1690	720	1005	1474	1165	1000	1030	810	....	830	531	1242	1295	267	1140	653	835	869
Paris	459	1335	890	210	248	645	410	400	1538	425	830	....	1050	690	1080	950	431	845	770	905
Riga	600	300	1940	1035	1122	1670	1238	1010	520	800	531	1050	....	1155	985	276	1335	350	685	930
Rome	810	1440	1150	890	462	840	372	295	1462	430	1242	690	1155	....	545	1220	569	810	470	421
Sofia	954	1218	1685	1235	928	1385	895	715	1100	672	1295	1080	985	545	....	1170	1080	662	500	780
Stockholm	502	435	1848	885	1080	1598	1225	1020	770	811	267	950	276	1220	1170	....	1281	500	770	908
Toulouse	780	1635	640	550	228	344	196	400	1770	570	1140	431	1335	569	1080	1281	....	1062	725	425
Warsaw	462	640	1700	890	850	1410	950	705	710	500	653	845	350	810	662	500	1062	....	345	640
Vienna	460	975	1415	762	562	1110	620	385	1028	222	835	770	685	470	500	770	725	345	....	365
Zurich	432	1225	1058	480	206	765	318	137	1350	158	869	905	930	421	780	908	425	640	365	....

HIGH SPOTS
of
WORLD WAR II
in
EUROPE & NORTH AFRICA

Copyright by C.S. Hammond & Co., N.Y.

German forces occupy
Denmark and invade Norway
Apr. 9, '40

British army escapes
from Dunkerque
May 31, '40

German Luftwaffe
launches heavy air attacks
over England
Aug. 8, '40

U.S. and Red Ar...
Berlin falls to...

U.S. First Army invades Germa...
at Aachen Sept. 12, '44
Germans launch counter-attac...
in Ardennes Forest Dec. 16, '...

Britain and France
declare war on Germany
Sept. 3, '39

Nazis invade
Netherlands,
Belgium and France
May 10, '40

D-DAY Allies invade France
June 6, '44
Paris liberated Aug. 25, '44

French sign armistice
with Nazis
June 22, '40

Germans o...
Bohemia and...
March 15, ...

Italy declares war
on Britain and France
June 10, '40

Allied forces invade
southern France
Aug. 15, '44

Allies invade Sicily July 9,
Mainland invaded Sept. 3...
Italy signs armistice Sept. 3...
Liberation of Rome June 4...

U.S. forces land at Casablanca, Oran and Algiers
Nov. 8, '42
and, joined by British and French,
drive into Tunisia Dec. '42

Tunisia and Bizerte fall
May 7, '43
Occupation of Tunisia
completed May 15, '43

This *dated events map* of World War II shows the rise and fall of Adolf Hitler's plan of world conquest. Here one sees how the nightmare of Nazi ambition swept across Europe's national borders and built an empire on a cornerstone of blood and terror. Here also one sees how the Nazis lost that empire and brought chaos to their homeland.

Austria and Czechoslovakia were the first to fall under German domination. These were bloodless conquests for they were accomplished by threat rather than war. Then in 1939 Hitler invaded Poland, raising the curtain on World War II. In the following spring Norway and Denmark were overrun. Then came Hitler's greatest victory—the defeat of Germany's ancient enemy, France—and the subjugation of the Netherlands and Belgium.

After his successful invasion of the Balkans, Hitler turned on Russia and drove deep into the interior of that huge land. The Soviets surprised the world by their heroic defense and by their powerful comeback. After 1942 the Germans were gradually driven out of Russia and into their own inner fortress of Germany.

In 1942 the United States and Great Britain joined forces in the invasion of North Africa. This was followed by the invasions of Sicily, Italy, France and Belgium. Then on both fronts Germany was invaded. Hitler's dream of world empire ended at Reims, where the German Army surrendered unconditionally to the Allies.

Russians invade Finland Nov. 30, '39; war ends March 12, '40

Finland signs armistice with U.S.S.R. Sept. 4, '44

Siege of Leningrad lifted Jan. 20, '44

Siege of Moscow lifted December '41

Germans invade U.S.S.R. June 22, '41

Battle of Stalingrad ends in Russian victory Feb. 2, '43

Germans invade Poland Sept. 1, '39; Warsaw falls Sept. 27, '39

Warsaw liberated Jan. 14, '45

Kiev taken by Germans Sept. 19, '41; liberated Nov. 6, '43; Odessa falls to Nazis Oct. 17, '41; liberated Apr. 10, '44

Hungary signs armistice with Allies Jan. 20, '45

Rumania signs armistice with Allies Sept. 9, '44

Germans invade Yugoslavia and Greece Apr. 6, '41

Italian drive to Sidi Barrani Sept. '40
1st British drive to el Agheila Feb. '41
1st Axis drive to Sollum May '41
2nd British drive to el Agheila Jan. '42
2nd Axis drive to El Alamein June '42
3rd British drive to Tunisia Feb. '43

Line of deepest Axis penetration

Line of deepest

Axis penetration

Murmansk

Narvik

Arkhangelsk

FINLAND

Helsinki

Leningrad

G. of Finland

Tallinn

ESTONIA

Riga

LATVIA

LITHUANIA

Kaunas

Kuibyshev

UNION   OF

Smolensk

SOVIET   SOCIALIST   REPUBLICS

Moscow

Orel

Voronezh

Warsaw

POLAND

Lublin

Lwow

Kiev

Kharkov

Stalingrad

Astrakhan

CASPIAN SEA

Budapest

HUNGARY

Odessa

Rostov

Maikop

Grozny

Belgrade

RUMANIA

Bucharest

Sevastopol

Batum

Tiflis

Baku

GOSLAVIA

BULGARIA

Sofia

BLACK   SEA

ALBANIA

Istanbul

Salonika

Ankara

TURKEY

Tehran

Izmir (Smyrna)

IRAN

Athens

Aegean Sea

Crete

Cyprus

SYRIA

Baghdad

Beyrouth

IRAQ

Damascus

Persian Gulf

KUWAIT

Jerusalem

PALESTINE

TRANS-JORDAN

Bengasi

Sidi Barrani

Alexandria

Sollum

El Alamein

Cairo

EGYPT

SAUDI   ARABIA

el Agheila

Y A

8475

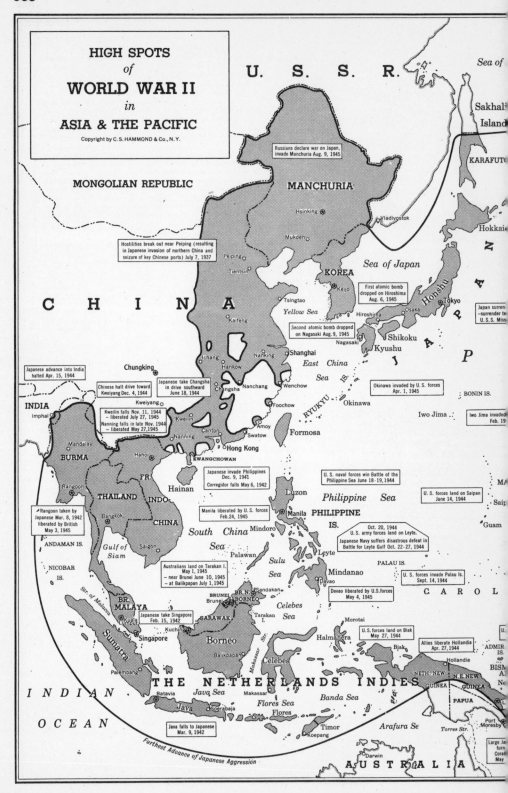

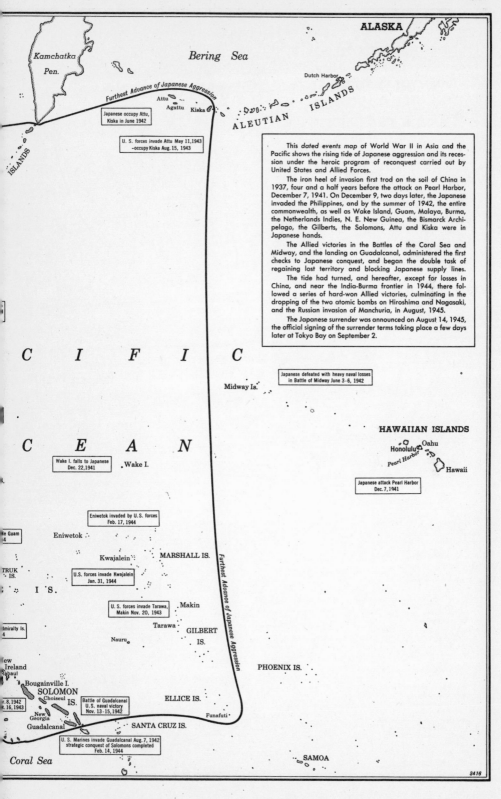

ALASKA

Bering Sea

Kamchatka
Pen.

Dutch Harbor

Furthest Advance of Japanese Aggression

Attu
Agattu
Kiska

ALEUTIAN ISLANDS

Japanese occupy Attu, Kiska in June 1942

U. S. forces invade Attu May 11,1943 —occupy Kiska Aug. 15, 1943

ISLANDS

This *dated events map* of World War II in Asia and the Pacific shows the rising tide of Japanese aggression and its recession under the heroic program of reconquest carried out by United States and Allied Forces.

The iron heel of invasion first trod on the soil of China in 1937, four and a half years before the attack on Pearl Harbor, December 7, 1941. On December 9, two days later, the Japanese invaded the Philippines, and by the summer of 1942, the entire commonwealth, as well as Wake Island, Guam, Malaya, Burma, the Netherlands Indies, N. E. New Guinea, the Bismarck Archipelago, the Gilberts, the Solomons, Attu and Kiska were in Japanese hands.

The Allied victories in the Battles of the Coral Sea and Midway, and the landing on Guadalcanal, administered the first checks to Japanese conquest, and began the double task of regaining lost territory and blocking Japanese supply lines.

The tide had turned, and hereafter, except for losses in China, and near the India-Burma frontier in 1944, there followed a series of hard-won Allied victories, culminating in the dropping of the two atomic bombs on Hiroshima and Nagasaki, and the Russian invasion of Manchuria, in August, 1945.

The Japanese surrender was announced on August 14, 1945, the official signing of the surrender terms taking place a few days later at Tokyo Bay on September 2.

C I F I C

Midway Is.

Japanese defeated with heavy naval losses in Battle of Midway June 3-6, 1942

HAWAIIAN ISLANDS

C E A N

Honolulu Oahu
Pearl Harbor
Hawaii

Wake I. falls to Japanese Dec. 22,1941

Wake I.

Japanese attack Pearl Harbor Dec. 7, 1941

Eniwetok invaded by U. S. forces Feb. 17, 1944

e Guam
4

Eniwetok

Kwajalein   MARSHALL IS.

TRUK
IS.

I S.

U.S. forces invade Kwajalein Jan. 31, 1944

Admiralty Is.
4

U. S. forces invade Tarawa, Makin Nov. 20, 1943

Makin

Tarawa   GILBERT
IS.

Nauru

ew
Ireland
abaul

PHOENIX IS.

Bougainville I.
SOLOMON
Choiseul   IS.
r. 8, 1942
t. 16, 1943
New
Georgia
Guadalcanal

ELLICE IS.

Funafuti

Battle of Guadalcanal U.S. naval victory Nov. 13-15, 1942

SANTA CRUZ IS.

U. S. Marines invade Guadalcanal Aug. 7, 1942 strategic conquest of Solomons completed Feb. 14, 1944

Coral Sea

SAMOA

Furthest Advance of Japanese Aggression

3416

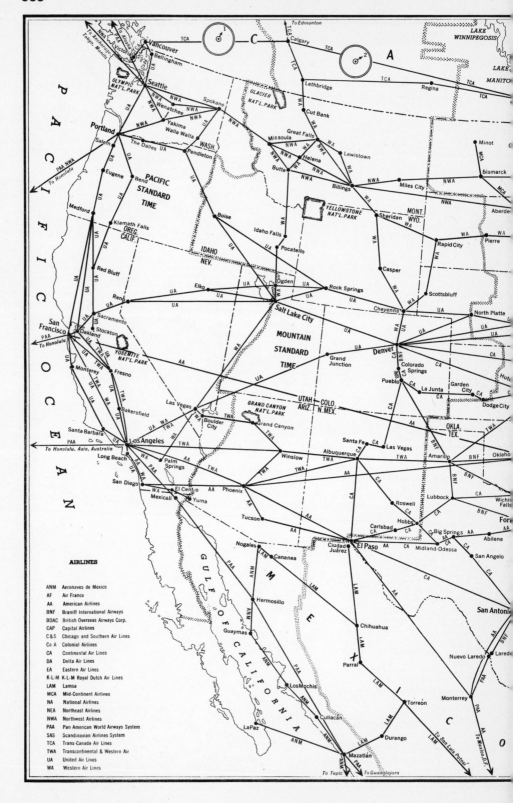

AIRLINES

ANM	Aeronaves de Mexico
AF	Air France
AA	American Airlines
BNF	Braniff International Airways
BOAC	British Overseas Airways Corp.
CAP	Capital Airlines
C&S	Chicago and Southern Air Lines
Co A	Colonial Airlines
CA	Continental Air Lines
DA	Delta Air Lines
EA	Eastern Air Lines
K-L-M	K-L-M Royal Dutch Air Lines
LAM	Lamsa
MCA	Mid-Continent Airlines
NA	National Airlines
NEA	Northeast Airlines
NWA	Northwest Airlines
PAA	Pan American World Airways System
SAS	Scandinavian Airlines System
TCA	Trans-Canada Air Lines
TWA	Transcontinental & Western Air
UA	United Air Lines
WA	Western Air Lines

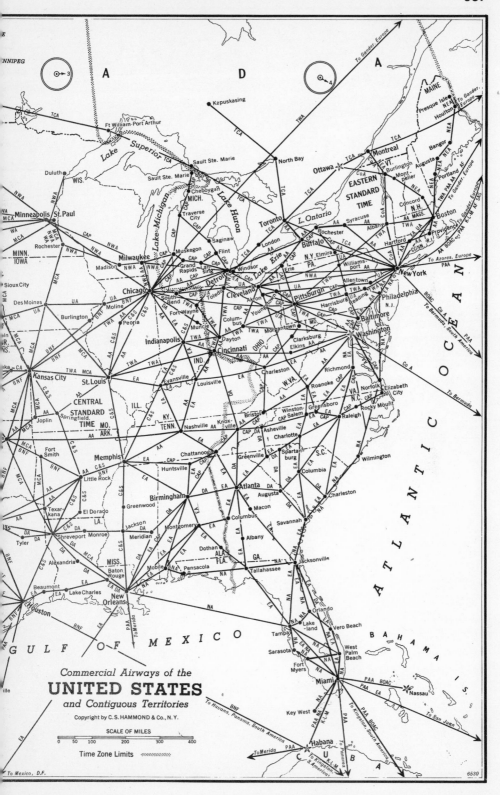

Commercial Airways of the
UNITED STATES
and Contiguous Territories

Copyright by C.S. HAMMOND & Co., N.Y.

SCALE OF MILES

0   50   100   200   300   400

Time Zone Limits

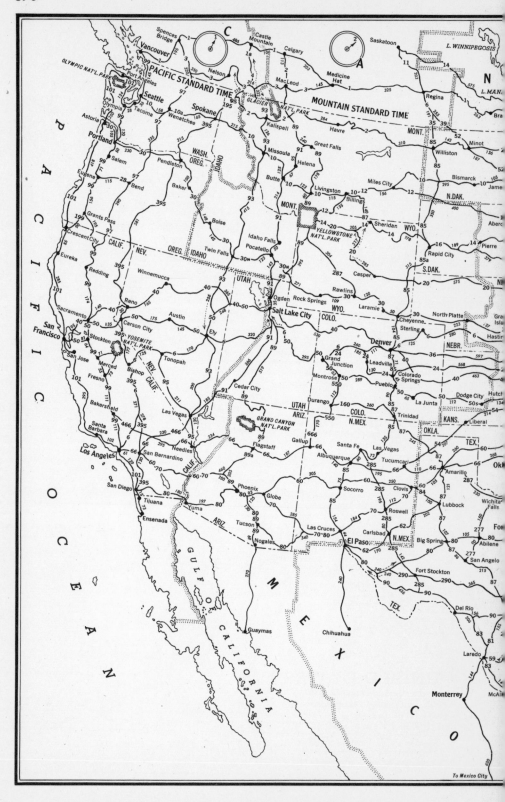

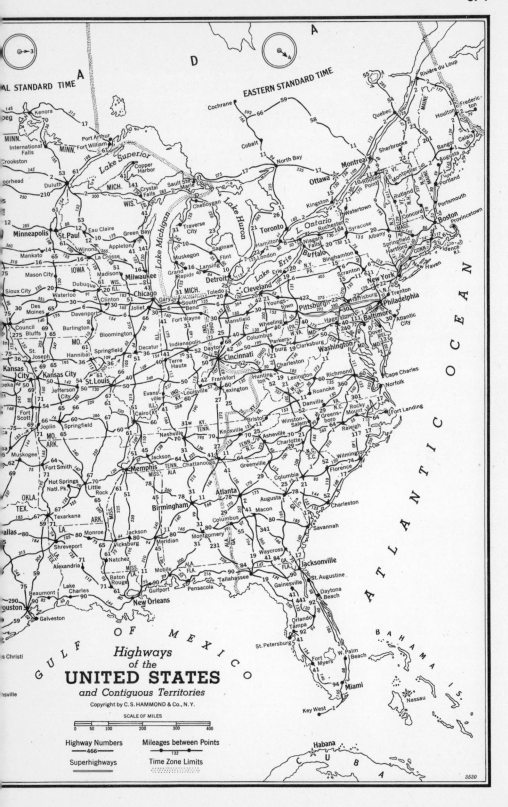

Highways
of the
UNITED STATES
and Contiguous Territories

Copyright by C.S. HAMMOND & Co., N.Y.

SCALE OF MILES

0   50   100   200   300   400

Highway Numbers
—466—

Mileages between Points
●——133——●

Superhighways

Time Zone Limits

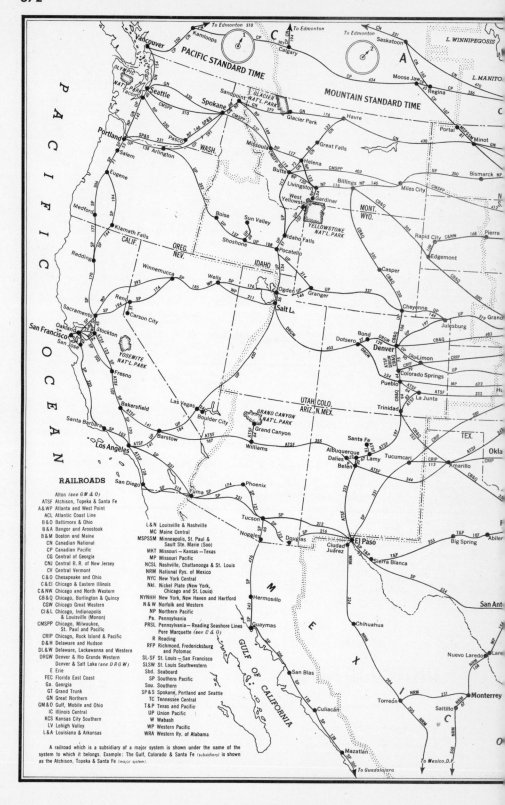

RAILROADS

Alton (see GM & O)
ATSF Atchison, Topeka & Santa Fe
A&WP Atlanta and West Point
ACL Atlantic Coast Line
B&O Baltimore & Ohio
B&A Bangor and Aroostook
B&M Boston and Maine
CN Canadian National
CP Canadian Pacific
CG Central of Georgia
CNJ Central R. R. of New Jersey
CV Central Vermont
C&O Chesapeake and Ohio
C&EI Chicago & Eastern Illinois
C&NW Chicago and North Western
CB&Q Chicago, Burlington & Quincy
CGW Chicago Great Western
CI&L Chicago, Indianapolis
      & Louisville (Monon)
CMSPP Chicago, Milwaukee,
      St. Paul and Pacific
CRIP Chicago, Rock Island & Pacific
D&H Delaware and Hudson
DL&W Delaware, Lackawanna and Western
DRGW Denver & Rio Grande Western
      Denver & Salt Lake (see D R G W)
E Erie
FEC Florida East Coast
Ga. Georgia
GT Grand Trunk
GN Great Northern
GM&O Gulf, Mobile and Ohio
IC Illinois Central
KCS Kansas City Southern
LV Lehigh Valley
L&A Louisiana & Arkansas

L&N Louisville & Nashville
MC Maine Central
MSPSSM Minneapolis, St. Paul &
      Sault Ste. Marie (Soo)
MKT Missouri — Kansas — Texas
MP Missouri Pacific
NCSL Nashville, Chattanooga & St. Louis
NRM National Rys. of Mexico
NYC New York Central
Nkl. Nickel Plate (New York,
      Chicago and St. Louis)
NYNHH New York, New Haven and Hartford
N&W Norfolk and Western
NP Northern Pacific
Pa. Pennsylvania
PRSL Pennsylvania—Reading Seashore Lines
      Pere Marquette (see C & O)
R Reading
RFP Richmond, Fredericksburg
      and Potomac
SL-SF St. Louis — San Francisco
SLSW St. Louis Southwestern
Sbd. Seaboard
SP Southern Pacific
Sou. Southern
SP&S Spokane, Portland and Seattle
TC Tennessee Central
T&P Texas and Pacific
UP Union Pacific
W Wabash
WP Western Pacific
WRA Western Ry. of Alabama

A railroad which is a subsidiary of a major system is shown under the name of the
system to which it belongs. Example: The Gulf, Colorado & Santa Fe (subsidiary) is shown
as the Atchison, Topeka & Santa Fe (major system).

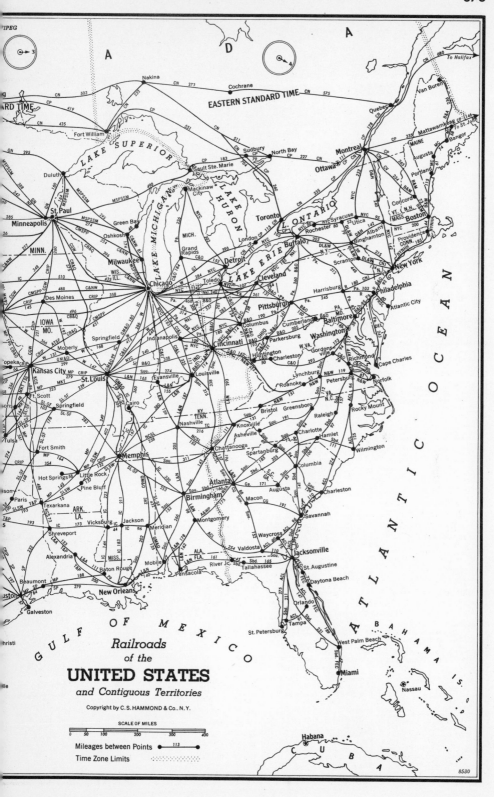

Railroads
of the
UNITED STATES
and Contiguous Territories

Copyright by C. S. HAMMOND & Co., N.Y.

SCALE OF MILES

Mileages between Points ●——113——●

Time Zone Limits ············

TABLE OF AIR-LINE DISTANCES BETWEE

Distances in Statute Miles

Prepared by DEPARTMENT OF COM

FROM/TO	Albuquerque, N. Mex.	Atlanta, Ga.	Baltimore, Md.	Boise, Idaho	Boston, Mass.	Brownsville, Tex.	Buffalo, N. Y.	Chicago, Ill.	Cincinnati, Ohio	Cleveland, Ohio	Denver, Colo.	Des Moines, Iowa	Detroit, Mich.	El Paso, Tex.	Fargo, N. Dak.	Fort Worth, Tex.	Galveston, Tex.	Hastings, Nebr.	Hot Springs, Ark.	Houghton, Mich.	Jacksonville, Fla.	Kansas City, Mo.
Albuquerque, N. Mex.	....	1273	1670	774	1967	838	1577	1126	1248	1417	332	833	1360	228	968	561	803	588	773	1252	1492	717
Atlanta, Ga.	1273	....	575	1830	933	960	695	583	368	550	1208	738	595	1293	1112	750	688	901	498	947	286	675
Baltimore, Md.	1670	575	....	2055	358	1525	273	603	423	305	1505	913	398	1750	1143	1239	1245	1154	964	808	682	962
Boise, Idaho	774	1830	2055	....	2266	1610	1872	1453	1663	1754	637	1155	1671	969	975	1263	1538	934	1384	1367	2098	1158
Boston, Mass.	1967	933	358	2266	....	1881	398	849	737	550	1766	1159	613	2067	1304	1574	1598	1415	1302	922	1015	1250
Brownsville, Tex.	838	960	1525	1610	1881	....	1575	1234	1184	1402	1047	1102	1398	682	1445	471	287	1013	650	1543	1025	923
Buffalo, N. Y.	1577	605	273	1872	398	1575	....	454	392	175	1368	762	218	1690	923	1221	1289	1019	956	560	880	862
Chicago, Ill.	1126	583	603	1453	849	1234	454	....	249	307	918	310	236	1249	571	820	954	566	585	367	861	413
Cincinnati, Ohio	1248	368	423	1663	737	1184	392	249	....	218	1090	509	234	1333	818	839	897	742	569	589	628	541
Cleveland, Ohio	1417	550	305	1754	550	1402	175	307	218	....	1223	617	94	1521	838	1046	1116	871	787	518	768	700
Denver, Colo.	332	1208	1505	637	1766	1047	1368	918	1090	1223	....	607	1153	554	642	643	925	353	749	970	1468	555
Des Moines, Iowa	833	738	913	1155	1159	1102	762	310	509	617	607	....	545	980	397	640	851	256	488	458	1024	180
Detroit, Mich.	1360	595	398	1671	613	1398	218	236	234	94	1153	545	....	1475	745	1018	1111	800	761	427	832	643
El Paso, Tex.	228	1293	1750	969	2067	682	1690	1249	1333	1521	554	980	1475	....	1161	543	723	757	802	1422	1481	836
Fargo, N. Dak.	968	1112	1143	975	1304	1445	923	571	818	838	642	397	745	1161	....	973	1218	440	875	393	1400	548
Fort Worth, Tex.	561	750	1239	1263	1574	471	1221	820	839	1046	643	640	1018	543	973	....	283	544	273	1093	943	460
Galveston, Tex.	803	688	1245	1538	1598	287	1289	954	897	1116	925	851	1111	723	1218	283	....	808	375	1277	799	677
Hastings, Nebr.	588	901	1154	934	1415	1013	1019	566	742	871	353	256	800	757	440	544	808	....	513	666	1178	226
Hot Springs, Ark.	773	498	964	1384	1302	650	956	585	569	787	749	488	761	802	875	273	375	513	....	901	728	326
Houghton, Mich.	1252	947	808	1367	922	1543	560	367	589	518	970	458	427	1422	393	1093	1277	666	901	....	1216	633
Jacksonville, Fla.	1492	286	682	2098	1015	1025	880	861	628	768	1468	1024	832	1481	1400	943	799	1178	728	1216	....	952
Kansas City, Mo.	717	675	962	1158	1250	923	862	413	541	700	555	180	643	836	548	460	677	226	326	633	952	....
Los Angeles, Calif.	663	1935	2313	663	2590	1370	2195	1741	1892	2044	828	1433	1976	702	1426	1212	1423	1177	1437	1787	2153	1356
Louisville, Ky.	1174	317	498	1623	823	1093	483	208	92	309	1035	477	315	1253	818	751	807	693	480	636	595	483
Memphis, Tenn.	938	335	792	1506	1133	777	802	481	410	627	878	485	621	978	882	448	492	591	176	830	591	374
Miami, Fla.	1710	610	958	2368	1258	1100	1184	1190	957	1088	1732	1338	1156	1662	1721	1150	941	1468	983	1545	328	1241
Minneapolis, Minn.	980	905	948	1140	1125	1335	733	356	603	632	609	235	542	1156	219	870	1087	399	722	272	1192	413
Missoula, Mont.	895	1790	1947	252	2124	1706	1740	1348	1578	1640	670	1074	1552	1115	819	1312	1595	891	1385	1208	2070	1167
Nashville, Tenn.	1117	218	597	1631	941	952	626	304	239	456	1018	523	468	1169	900	643	666	697	370	760	502	476
New Orleans, La.	1030	427	1001	1713	1359	536	1087	831	708	922	1079	825	938	986	1221	470	288	870	358	1187	511	678
New York, N. Y.	1810	747	170	2153	188	1695	291	711	568	404	1628	1023	483	1902	1213	1398	1415	1275	1125	849	838	1098
Norfolk, Va.	1696	507	167	2137	467	1465	435	696	474	429	1562	983	522	1755	1258	1226	1195	1216	955	946	548	1004
Oklahoma, Okla.	518	753	1173	1138	1490	659	1117	689	755	946	503	469	905	578	786	188	456	357	260	926	988	296
Omaha, Nebr.	718	815	1026	1044	1280	1061	883	432	620	738	485	122	666	875	390	590	828	135	490	547	1098	166
Philadelphia, Pa.	1748	663	90	2113	268	1614	278	664	501	343	575	972	444	1834	1186	1324	1335	1222	1051	827	758	1039
Phoenix, Ariz.	330	1502	2002	733	2295	1023	1904	1451	1578	1745	585	1154	1685	347	1225	858	1065	901	1094	1550	1800	1042
Pittsburgh, Pa.	1498	520	194	1863	478	1424	178	411	258	115	1320	718	208	1592	952	1097	1140	967	825	530	703	781
Portland, Me.	2015	1022	446	2282	100	1961	438	892	802	603	1803	1197	657	2126	1313	1642	1678	1454	1371	924	1113	1378
Portland, Oreg.	1107	2172	2367	349	2553	1944	2167	1765	1987	2063	985	1479	1975	1286	1248	1612	1885	1271	1733	1638	2442	1398
Richmond, Va.	1628	470	128	2060	471	1428	375	618	399	353	1488	905	445	1695	1180	1170	1154	1142	897	870	953	939
St. Louis, Mo.	928	467	731	1389	1036	975	662	259	308	490	793	270	452	1033	658	568	697	455	325	591	755	238
Salt Lake City, Utah.	483	1580	1858	292	2099	1317	1701	1260	1450	1567	372	952	1490	689	865	977	1249	708	1116	1242	1840	1150
San Francisco, Calif.	863	2133	2451	516	2696	1675	2298	1855	2037	2163	946	1547	2087	993	1447	1445	1487	1297	1648	1833	2375	1506
Schenectady, N. Y.	1823	840	278	2120	150	1770	249	702	605	408	1618	1012	467	1930	1157	1445	1487	1267	1175	776	960	1103
Seattle, Wash.	1178	2180	2341	405	2508	2015	2130	1743	1974	2035	1020	1470	1945	1373	1206	1658	1938	1288	1759	1588	2450	1506
Shreveport, La.	764	548	1064	1433	1410	510	1080	725	688	904	799	624	891	752	1002	209	233	615	142	1043	733	326
Spokane, Wash.	1028	1960	2110	399	2279	1852	1900	1514	1746	1804	827	1243	1715	1238	976	1470	1753	1061	1552	1360	2239	1283
Springfield, Mass.	1889	863	282	2196	79	1805	325	774	659	473	1692	1085	540	1990	1240	1495	1524	1340	1224	860	957	1173
Vermillion, S. Dak.	742	917	1083	973	1314	1161	916	479	694	785	468	187	705	920	284	689	938	167	605	510	1203	284
Washington, D. C.	1648	542	33	2045	392	1493	290	594	403	303	1490	895	397	1726	1141	1210	1214	1139	936	813	647	945

TABLE OF AIR-LINE DISTANCES
Between Representative Cities of the United States and Latin America

Distances in Statute Miles

NEW YORK TO	Miles	SAN FRANCISCO TO	Miles	SEATTLE TO	Miles	WASHINGTON TO	Miles
Buenos Aires	5,295	Buenos Aires	6,487	Buenos Aires	6,956	Buenos Aires	5,205
Bogota	2,474	Bogota	3,863	Bogota	4,166	Bogota	2,344
Caracas	2,100	Caracas	3,900	Caracas	4,100	Caracas	2,040
Guatemala City	2,060	Guatemala City	2,525	Guatemala City	2,930	Guatemala City	1,835
Havana	1,302	Havana	2,600	Havana	2,805	Havana	1,110
La Paz	3,905	La Paz	5,080	La Paz	5,110	La Paz	3,780
Panama	2,211	Panama	3,349	Panama	3,680	Panama	2,020
Para	3,281	Para	5,430	Para	5,550	Para	3,270
Managua	2,100	Managua	2,860	Managua	3,240	Managua	1,920
Rio de Janeiro	4,810	Rio de Janeiro	6,655	Rio de Janeiro	6,945	Rio de Janeiro	4,710
San Jose	2,200	San Jose	3,070	San Jose	3,430	San Jose	2,030
Santiago	5,134	Santiago	5,960	Santiago	6,466	Santiago	4,965
Tampico	1,880	Tampico	1,790	Tampico	2,200	Tampico	1,665

Bureau of Navigation, Radio Division

Memphis, Tenn.	Miami, Fla.	Minneapolis, Minn.	Missoula, Mont.	Nashville, Tenn.	New Orleans, La.	New York, N. Y.	Norfolk, Va.	Oklahoma, Okla.	Omaha, Nebr.	Philadelphia, Pa.	Phoenix, Ariz.	Pittsburgh, Pa.	Portland, Me.	Portland, Oreg.	Richmond, Va.	St. Louis, Mo.	Salt Lake City, Utah	San Francisco, Calif.	Schenectady, N. Y.	Seattle, Wash.	Shreveport, La.	Spokane, Wash.	Springfield, Mass.	Vermillion, S. Dak.	Washington, D.
938	1710	980	895	1117	1030	1810	1696	518	718	1748	330	1498	2015	1107	1628	938	483	893	1823	1178	764	1028	1889	742	1648
335	610	905	1790	218	427	747	507	753	815	663	1592	520	1022	2172	470	467	1580	2133	840	2180	548	1960	863	917	542
792	958	948	1947	597	1001	170	167	1173	1026	90	2002	194	446	2367	128	731	1858	2451	278	2341	1064	2110	282	1083	33
506	2368	1140	252	1631	1713	2153	2137	1138	1044	2113	733	1863	2282	349	2060	1389	292	516	2120	405	1433	290	2196	973	2045
133	1258	1125	2124	941	1359	188	467	1490	1280	268	2295	478	100	2553	471	1036	2099	2696	150	2508	1410	2279	79	1314	392
777	1100	1335	1706	952	536	1695	1465	659	1061	1614	1023	1424	1961	1944	1428	975	1317	1675	1770	2015	510	1852	1805	1161	1493
302	1184	733	1740	626	1087	291	435	1117	883	278	1904	178	438	2167	375	662	1701	2298	249	2130	1080	1900	325	916	290
481	1190	356	1348	394	831	711	696	689	432	664	1451	411	892	1765	618	259	1260	1855	702	1743	725	1514	774	479	594
410	957	603	1578	239	708	568	474	755	620	501	1578	258	802	1987	399	308	1450	2037	605	1974	688	1746	659	694	403
327	1088	632	1640	456	922	404	429	946	738	343	1745	115	603	2063	353	490	1567	2163	408	2035	904	1804	478	785	303
378	1732	699	670	1018	1079	1628	1562	503	485	1575	585	1320	1803	985	1488	793	372	946	1618	1020	799	827	1692	468	1490
485	1338	235	1074	523	825	1023	983	469	122	972	1154	718	1197	1479	905	270	952	1547	1012	1470	624	1243	1085	187	895
321	1156	542	1552	468	938	483	522	905	666	444	1685	208	657	1975	445	452	1490	2087	467	1945	891	1715	540	705	397
078	1662	1156	1115	1169	986	1902	1755	578	875	1834	347	1592	2126	1286	1695	1033	689	903	1930	1373	752	1238	1990	920	1726
382	1721	219	819	900	1221	1213	1258	786	390	1186	1225	952	1313	1248	1180	658	865	1447	1157	1206	1002	976	1240	284	1141
448	1150	870	1312	643	470	1398	1226	188	590	1324	858	1097	1642	1612	1170	568	977	1454	1445	1658	209	1470	1495	689	1210
492	941	1087	1595	666	288	1415	1195	456	828	1335	1065	1140	1678	1885	1154	697	1249	1693	1487	1938	233	1753	1524	938	1214
91	1468	399	891	697	870	1275	1216	357	135	1222	901	967	1454	1271	1142	455	708	1297	1267	1288	615	1061	1340	167	1139
76	983	722	1385	370	358	1125	955	260	490	1051	1094	825	1371	1733	897	325	1116	1648	1175	1759	142	1552	1224	605	936
30	1545	272	1208	760	1187	849	946	926	547	827	1550	630	924	1638	870	591	1242	1833	776	1588	1043	1360	860	510	813
91	328	1192	2070	502	511	838	548	988	1009	758	1800	703	1113	2442	953	755	1840	2375	960	2450	733	2239	957	1203	647
70	1247	413	1117	472	678	1097	1009	293	165	1037	1045	784	1300	1397	937	238	922	1500	1107	1505	326	1286	1173	280	943
402	2355	1522	910	1777	1675	2446	2352	1182	1312	2388	357	2135	2631	825	2283	1585	577	345	2445	956	1420	939	2515	1291	2295
19	923	605	1550	153	623	650	528	675	579	580	1512	345	892	1953	457	242	1400	1983	695	1945	598	1720	745	663	473
..	878	700	1483	195	358	953	778	422	529	878	1264	660	1205	1852	722	242	1250	1800	1010	1867	279	1652	1055	642	763
78	....	1516	2359	821	681	1095	802	1233	1402	1023	1998	1014	1357	2716	831	1067	2098	2603	1229	2740	950	2528	1210	1510	927
00	1516	....	1010	695	1050	1019	1047	692	291	985	1279	745	1145	1435	968	464	988	1585	975	1403	859	1173	1056	238	936
83	2359	1010	....	1582	1733	2030	2045	1162	978	1997	932	1754	2133	430	1967	1331	435	762	1978	395	1457	170	2060	887	1940
95	821	695	1582	....	470	758	586	602	604	683	1445	472	1015	1970	526	253	1390	1958	820	1973	470	1752	863	704	567
58	681	1050	1733	470	....	1173	932	575	845	1090	1318	923	1445	2063	899	599	1433	1923	1259	2098	280	1898	1287	960	968
53	1095	1019	2030	758	1173	....	293	1324	1144	83	2142	313	277	2455	287	873	1972	2568	142	2419	1230	2190	120	1189	204
78	802	1047	2045	586	932	293	....	1186	1095	220	2027	316	565	2458	79	771	1925	2510	426	2440	1037	2211	411	1166	145
22	1233	692	1162	602	575	1324	1186	....	405	1256	843	1013	1550	1488	1122	456	862	1386	1354	1523	297	1324	1412	502	1150
29	1402	291	978	604	845	1144	1095	405	....	1094	1032	837	1318	1373	1020	352	833	1425	1133	1372	617	1149	1205	115	1012
78	1023	985	1997	683	1090	83	220	1256	1094	....	2079	254	360	2419	205	808	1923	2518	205	2388	1153	2159	201	1143	122
64	1998	1279	932	1445	1318	2142	2027	843	1032	2079	....	1829	2345	1007	1960	1270	504	652	2152	1112	1067	1020	2220	1043	1980
60	1014	745	1754	472	923	313	316	1013	837	254	1829	....	545	2174	242	561	1670	2264	350	2172	939	1918	400	891	188
05	1357	1145	2133	1015	1445	277	565	1550	1318	360	2345	545	....	2563	565	1094	2127	2725	197	2513	1484	2285	159	1345	480
52	2716	1435	430	1970	2063	2455	2458	1488	1373	2419	1007	2174	2563	....	2381	1723	636	536	2405	143	1783	295	2488	1293	2360
..	831	968	1967	526	899	287	79	1122	1020	205	1960	242	565	2381	....	699	1850	2436	406	2362	985	2133	407	1089	96
42	1067	464	1331	253	599	873	771	456	352	808	1270	561	1094	1723	699	....	1158	1738	898	1722	466	1500	958	450	710
50	2098	988	435	1390	1433	1972	1925	862	833	1923	504	1670	2127	636	1850	1158	....	592	1950	697	1155	548	2027	785	1845
00	2603	1585	762	1958	1923	2568	2510	1386	1425	2518	652	2264	2725	536	2436	1738	592	....	2548	680	1655	730	2625	1383	2437
10	1229	975	1978	820	1259	142	426	1354	1133	205	2152	350	197	2405	406	898	1950	2548	....	2363	1290	2139	86	1165	313
67	2740	1403	395	1973	2098	2419	2440	1523	1372	2388	1112	2145	2513	143	2362	1722	697	680	2363	....	1820	229	2445	1282	2335
79	950	859	1457	470	280	1230	1037	297	617	1153	1067	939	1484	1783	985	466	1155	1655	1290	1820	....	1621	1333	726	1035
52	2528	1173	170	1752	1898	2190	2211	1324	1149	2159	1920	1918	2285	295	2133	1500	548	730	2139	229	1621	....	2216	1055	2105
55	1210	1056	2060	863	1287	120	411	1412	1205	201	2220	400	159	2488	407	958	2027	2625	86	2445	1333	2216	....	1242	321
42	1510	238	887	704	960	1189	1166	502	115	1143	1043	891	1345	1293	1089	450	785	1383	1165	1282	726	1055	1242	....	1073
63	927	936	1940	567	968	204	145	1150	1012	122	1980	188	480	2360	96	710	1845	2437	313	2335	1035	2105	321	1073	....

TABLE OF AIR-LINE DISTANCES

Between Representative Cities of the United States and Latin America

Distances in Statute Miles

CHICAGO TO	Miles	DENVER TO	Miles	LOS ANGELES TO	Miles	NEW ORLEANS TO	Miles
Buenos Aires	5,598	Buenos Aires	5,935	Buenos Aires	6,148	Buenos Aires	4,902
Bogota	2,691	Bogota	3,100	Bogota	3,515	Bogota	1,996
Caracas	2,480	Caracas	3,105	Caracas	3,610	Caracas	1,990
Guatemala City	1,870	Guatemala City	1,935	Guatemala City	2,190	Guatemala City	1,050
Havana	1,315	Havana	1,760	Havana	2,320	Havana	672
La Paz	4,130	La Paz	4,445	La Paz	4,805	La Paz	3,480
Panama	2,320	Panama	2,620	Panama	3,025	Panama	1,600
Para	3,820	Para	4,580	Para	5,110	Para	3,470
Managua	2,060	Managua	2,230	Managua	2,540	Managua	1,250
Rio de Janeiro	5,320	Rio de Janeiro	5,900	Rio de Janeiro	6,330	Rio de Janeiro	4,798
San Jose	2,100	San Jose	2,420	San Jose	2,725	San Jose	1,425
Santiago	5,320	Santiago	5,495	Santiago	5,595	Santiago	4,553
Tampico	1,460	Tampico	1,240	Tampico	1,470	Tampico	720

BETWEEN PRINCIPAL CITIES OF THE WORLD

Distances in Statute Miles

FROM/TO	Azores	Bagdad	Berlin	Bombay	Buenos Aires	Callao	Cairo	Cape Town	Chicago	Istanbul	Guam	Honolulu	Juneau	London	Los Angeles
Azores	....	3906	2148	5930	5385	4825	3325	5670	3305	2880	8985	7421	4715	1562	5034
Bagdad	3906	....	2040	2022	8215	8618	785	4923	6490	1085	6380	8445	6180	2568	7695
Berlin	2148	2040	....	3947	7411	6937	1823	5949	4458	1068	7158	7384	4638	575	5849
Bombay	5930	2022	3947	....	9380	10530	2698	5133	8144	3043	4831	8172	6992	4526	8810
Buenos Aires	5385	8215	7411	9380	....	1982	7428	4332	5598	7638	10516	7653	7964	6919	6148
Callao	4825	8618	6937	10530	1982	....	7870	6195	3765	7666	9760	5993	5806	6376	4155
Cairo	3325	785	1823	2698	7428	7870	....	4476	6231	780	7175	8925	6352	2218	7675
Cape Town	5670	4923	5949	5133	4332	6195	4476	....	8551	5210	8918	11655	10382	5975	10165
Chicago	3305	6490	4458	8144	5598	3765	6231	8551	....	5530	7510	4315	2310	4015	1741
Istanbul	2880	1085	1068	3043	7638	7666	780	5210	5530	....	7015	8200	5665	1540	6895
Guam	8985	6380	7158	4831	10516	9760	7175	8918	7510	7015	....	3896	5225	7605	6255
Honolulu	7421	8445	7384	8172	7653	5993	8925	11655	4315	8200	3896	....	2825	7320	2620
Juneau	4715	6180	4638	6992	7964	5806	6352	10382	2310	5665	5225	2825	....	4496	1835
London	1562	2568	575	4526	6919	6376	2218	5975	4015	1540	7605	7320	4496	....	5496
Los Angeles	5034	7695	5849	8810	6148	4155	7675	10165	1741	6895	6255	2620	1835	5496	....
Melbourne	12190	8150	9992	6140	7336	8196	8720	6510	9837	9189	3497	5581	8162	10590	8098
Mexico City	4584	8155	6119	9818	4609	2619	7807	8620	1690	7160	5581	3846	3210	5605	1445
Montreal	2548	5814	3776	7582	5619	3954	5502	7975	750	4825	7840	4992	2647	3370	2468
New Orleans	3718	7212	5182	8952	4902	2990	6862	8390	827	6220	7895	4305	2860	4656	1695
New York	2604	6066	4026	7875	5295	3633	5701	7845	727	5060	8115	5051	2874	3500	2466
Panama	3918	7807	5902	9832	3319	1450	7230	7090	2320	6797	9220	5347	4556	5310	3025
Paris	1617	2385	540	4391	6891	6455	2020	5762	4219	1390	7675	7525	4700	210	5711
Rio de Janeiro	4312	7012	6246	8438	1230	2400	6242	3850	5320	6420	11710	8400	7611	5747	6330
San Francisco	5114	7521	5744	8523	6487	4500	7554	10340	1875	6770	5952	2420	1530	5440	345
Santiago	5718	8876	7842	10127	731	1548	8100	5080	5325	8230	9946	6935	7320	7275	5595
Seattle	4720	6848	5121	7830	6956	4964	6915	10305	1753	6124	5785	2707	870	4850	961
Shanghai	7324	4468	5323	3219	12295	10760	5290	8179	7155	5084	1945	5009	4968	5841	6598
Singapore	8338	4443	6226	2425	9940	11700	5152	6025	9475	5440	2990	6874	7375	6818	8955
Tokyo	7370	5242	5623	4247	11601	9740	6005	9234	6410	5649	1596	3940	4117	6050	5600
Wellington	11475	9782	11384	7752	6341	6696	10360	7149	8465	10790	4206	4676	7501	11790	6806

FROM/TO	Melbourne	Mexico City	Montreal	New Orleans	New York	Panama	Paris	Rio de Janeiro	San Francisco	Santiago	Seattle	Shanghai	Singapore	Tokyo	Wellington
Azores	12190	4584	2548	3718	2604	3918	1617	4312	5114	5718	4720	7324	8338	7370	11475
Bagdad	8150	8155	5814	7212	6066	7807	2385	7012	7521	8876	6848	4468	4443	5242	9782
Berlin	9992	6119	3776	5182	4026	5902	540	6246	5744	7842	5121	5323	6226	5623	11384
Bombay	6140	9818	7582	8952	7875	9832	4391	8438	8523	10127	7830	3219	2425	4247	7752
Buenos Aires	7336	4609	5619	4902	5295	3319	6891	1230	6487	731	6956	12295	9940	11601	6341
Callao	8196	2619	3954	2990	3633	1450	6455	2400	4500	1548	4964	10760	11700	9740	6696
Cairo	8720	7807	5502	6862	5701	7230	2020	6242	7554	8100	6915	5290	5152	6005	10360
Cape Town	6510	8620	7975	8390	7845	7090	5732	3850	10340	5080	10305	8179	6025	9234	7149
Chicago	9837	1690	750	827	727	2320	4219	5320	1875	5325	1753	7155	9475	6410	8465
Istanbul	9189	7160	4825	6220	5060	6797	1390	6420	6770	8230	6124	5084	5440	5649	10790
Guam	3497	7690	7840	7895	8115	9220	7675	11710	5952	9946	5785	1945	2990	1596	4206
Honolulu	5581	3846	4992	4305	5051	5347	7525	8400	2407	6935	2707	5009	6874	3940	4676
Juneau	8162	3210	2647	2860	2874	4456	4700	7611	1530	7320	870	4968	7375	4117	7501
London	10590	5605	3370	4656	3500	5310	210	5747	5440	7275	4850	5841	6818	6050	11790
Los Angeles	8098	1445	2468	1695	2466	3025	5711	6330	345	5595	961	6598	8955	5600	6806
Melbourne	....	8599	10553	9455	10541	9211	10500	8340	7970	7130	8330	4967	3768	5172	1655
Mexico City	8599	....	2247	940	2110	1532	5800	4810	1870	4122	2339	8120	10495	7190	7003
Montreal	10553	2247	....	1390	340	2545	3490	5110	2557	5461	2309	7141	9280	6546	9206
New Orleans	9455	940	1390	....	1161	1600	4846	4798	1960	4553	2137	7830	10255	6993	7950
New York	10541	2110	340	1161	....	2211	3600	4810	2606	5134	2440	7460	9067	6846	9067
Panama	9211	1532	2545	1600	2211	....	5440	3311	3349	3000	3680	9430	11800	8560	7580
Paris	10500	5800	3490	4846	3600	5440	....	5710	5680	7300	5080	5855	6730	6132	11865
Rio de Janeiro	8340	4810	5110	4798	4810	3311	5710	....	6655	1852	6945	11510	9875	11600	7510
San Francisco	7970	1870	2557	1960	2606	3349	5680	6655	....	5960	692	6245	8440	5250	6800
Santiago	7130	4122	5461	4553	5134	3000	7300	1852	5960	....	6466	11850	10270	10850	5925
Seattle	8330	2339	2309	2137	2440	3680	5080	6945	692	6466	....	5780	8200	4863	7310
Shanghai	4967	8120	7141	7830	7460	9430	5855	11510	6245	11850	5780	....	2395	1095	6080
Singapore	3768	10495	9280	10255	9617	11800	6730	9875	8440	10270	8200	2395	....	3350	5360
Tokyo	5172	7190	6546	6993	6846	8560	6132	11600	5250	10850	4863	1095	3350	....	5730
Wellington	1655	7003	9206	7950	9067	7580	11865	7510	6800	5925	7310	6080	5360	5730	....

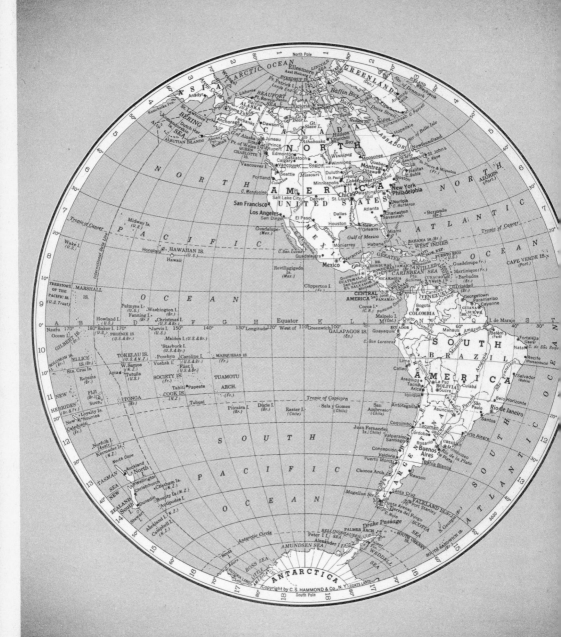

Western Hemisphere